Praise for *TRANSLATED WOMAN*

"Through Behar's work, Esperanza's story of struggle for personal power and dignity against the overwhelming currents of male domination and poverty crosses borders of language, class, culture, and nation. North American readers are presented with a voice seldom found in print. . . . Behar has made her struggle with translation into a sonnet."
—Oakland Tribune

"Part anthropological study, part gripping oral history, part personal confession and part feminist cry of outrage, *Translated Woman* is a brave and unusual work that attempts to bridge multiple disciplines, cultures and literary traditions."
—Boston Globe

"A ground-breaking feminist Latina ethnography. . . . The power of [Esperanza's] story matches any of those recorded by Oscar Lewis and more traditional anthropologists. . . . [A] powerful and brilliant study."
—The Nation

"Remarkably engaging and well written . . . [*Translated Woman*] will be sure to attract a wide readership [including] members of the public who wonder what motivates people to spend time in far off places interacting with cultural Others. . . . An outstanding document of our age."
—Barbara Tedlock, State University of New York, Buffalo

"Not one but two life stories, each reflecting the other, each an act of self-revelation."
—Chronicle of Higher Education

"An achievement, Ruth Behar's volume is a bridge across the abyss we call 'the Rio Grande,' a no-(wo)man's-land where the Hispanic and Anglo idiosyncrasies collide. . . . A crossroad where anthropology and literature meet and a new understanding of translation emerges."
—Ilan Stavans, Tikkun

"Postmodernist writing at its best. . . . Much of *Translated Woman* reads like a novel; but Behar's fine theoretical and analytical skills repeatedly jar us into thinking about real feminist issues, issues that are grounded in the gaps between the U.S. and Mexico, between a privileged female professor and a woman street vendor, between a young mother of a healthy infant son and an older woman who has lost six of her infant children and is estranged from one of her grown sons."

—Women's Review of Books

"A mesmerizing, richly textured overlay of the relationship forged between two women. . . . An important, compelling contribution."

—Booklist

"*Translated Woman* belongs in the same publishing universe as Oscar Lewis's *Children of Sanchez*. . . . Unlike Lewis, however, Behar writes not principally of men but of women to yield for us a sense of another Mexico— a site of strength, integrity, creativity, and *esperanza*. . . . An exciting piece of work that stands superbly alone in the life-history genre as I know it."

—José Limón, University of Texas, Austin

"[Behar's] discussion of her ethnicity and the status of Latinas in general is excellent. Recommended for all libraries."

—Library Journal

"A finely crafted readable cross-cultural encounter between *dos comadres:* feminist anthropologist and informant, *cubanita de este lado* and *mexicana* across the border. . . . *Escribiendo cultura con corazón, compasión y pasión*, Behar moves the serpent to speak, and moves us to read and read again."

—Gloria Anzaldúa, author of Borderlands/La Frontera

Crossing the Border

with Esperanza's Story

RUTH BEHAR

TRANSLATED
WOMAN

Beacon Press   Boston

Beacon Press
25 Beacon Street
Boston, Massachusetts 02108-2892

Beacon Press books are published
under the auspices of the Unitarian
Universalist Association of Congregations.

99   8 7 6

Text design by Copenhaver Cumpston

Library of Congress Cataloging-in-Publication Data

Behar, Ruth, 1956–
    Translated woman : crossing the border with Esperanza's story /
Ruth Behar.
        p.   cm.
    ISBN 0-8070-7052-1 (cloth)
    ISBN 0-8070-7053-x (paper)
    1. Rural women—Mexico—Mexquitic—Social conditions—Case
studies. 2. Ethnology—Mexico—Mexquitic. 3. Mexquitic (Mexico)—
Rural conditions. I. Title.
HQ1465.M63B44   1993
305.42'0972'44—dc20
92-5588
    CIP

Copyright page continues on page 373.

FRONTISPIECE: Esperanza in her garden (1985)
ENDPIECE: Esperanza taking home a bucket of fruit from her garden (1988)

When she hates someone whom she formerly loved, then she seethes with anger and impatience in her whole soul, just as the tides of the sea are always heaving and boiling. Many authorities allude to this cause. Ecclesiasticus XXV: There is no rage above the rage of a woman. And Seneca (Tragedies, VIII): No might of the flames or of the swollen winds, no deadly weapon, is so much to be feared as the lust and hatred of a woman who has been divorced from the marriage bed. . . . Through their defect of inordinate affections and passions they search for, brood over, and inflict various vengeances, either by witchcraft, or by some other means. Wherefore it is no wonder that so great a number of witches exist in this sex.

—Heinrich Kramer and James Sprenger,
The Malleus Maleficarum, or "The Witches' Hammer"
(1486)

Omar Khayyam's position as poet is curious. He was never very popular in his native Persia; and he exists in the West in a translation. . . . I, too, am a translated man. I have been borne across.

—Salman Rushdie, Shame

It is no wonder, in our time of mass migrations and culture collisions and easy jet travel, . . . that we have devised a whole metaphysics for the subjects of difference and otherness. But for all our sophisticated deftness at cross-cultural encounters, fundamental difference, when it's staring at you across the table from within the close-up face of a fellow human being, always contains an element of violation.

—Eva Hoffman, Lost in Translation

GRACIAS

a mi comadre que me dio la palabra

a mis boysitos que me acompañaron

a mi mami y papi y hermano, recordando que hicimos el viaje juntos a este lado, sin saber lo que nos esperaba

Contents

Preface

A translation issues from the original—not so much from its life as from its afterlife.

—Walter Benjamin, "The Task of the Translator"

I expected this to be an easy book to write. To portray the life story of one woman—why should that pose any serious writing problems? I also expected this to be a short book. The life story of one woman— why should that require a very long book?

Of course, I ought to have known. Didn't my comadre keep telling me I was bringing back a big book? *"Se lleva una historia muy grande, comadre,"* she'd say, and she was absolutely right, my comadre. This *is* a big book. Everything seems to have found its way into these pages, even the kitchen sink. I'm afraid there's nothing I can do. You don't choose to write the books you write, any more than you choose your mother, your father, your brother, your children, or your comadre.

So much has been happening in the world while I have been working on this book. The Berlin Wall fell down, the United States invaded Panama and then Iraq in the space of a year, and sexual harassment became a household word. During all this time I have returned, again and again, to that Mexican kitchen with the mint green walls where my comadre and I sat across the table from one another, talking late into the night. At a time when the act of talking across the table with someone quite different from you and listening, really listening, has become so difficult, maybe this book about the encounter of two translated women can be a gesture toward peace.

Yet it is a gesture toward peace situated smack in the middle of the structural inequalities that separate Esperanza and me as women differently located on opposite sides of the border between the United States and Mexico. As I prepare to finally let go of Esperanza's story, I find in the Sunday *New York Times* of February 9, 1992, a front-

page story, "Border Crossings Near Old Record; U.S To Crack Down."
The article describes new enforcement measures that call for building
higher fences, hiring more guards, and "using military vehicles left
over from the Persian Gulf war to patrol border areas." Next to it there
is another article highlighting American fears for the future, entitled
"Shadow of Pessimism Eclipses a Dream." In this time of intense "com-
passion fatigue" in the United States, when stories of homelessness,
violence, and suffering are falling on ears that can no longer bear to
listen, the border separating Mexico and the United States is destined
to become a war zone ever harder to cross from the "wrong" side. I
have borne my comadre's story across to this side, reterritorialized it
here, just when the United States government is gearing up to arrest a
million "illegal aliens" entering from Mexico. I can only hope that her
story will find *un rinconcito*, a little space somewhere on this side of
the border where there are no aliens, only people.

For someone brought up on perfumed mango politeness, there is
a lot more anger in this book than I am used to displaying publicly.
My comadre taught me quite a lot about expressing *coraje*. I grew up
hearing about *roña*, another Spanish term for rage, but I've come to
like *coraje* better. There's plenty of *coraje* here, about being a woman,
about anthropology, about United States policy toward undocumented
Mexicans; some of the *coraje* is my comadre's, some of it is mine, and
some of it belongs to both of us.

Without putting down a word on paper, my comadre has been writing the story of her life since she was five years old, when she began to
impress upon her memory every beating her mother received at the
hands of her father. Yet because it is not in her power to put words to
paper, my comadre left me the task of putting the words down in this
book. I have done as well as I could by my comadre. If nothing else,
I've given her a book almost as big as the life she has lived. May it be
worthy of her. If nothing else, I hope I've made her life in this book too
big for easy consumption.

› › ›

My comadre told me her story and asked me to pass it on here, across
the border. Another comadre, less tormented and *complicada* than I
am, might have carried out this task without too much trouble. But,
alas, for me it proved to be an arduous task, and I need to thank all

the people who inspired me to think of ways to pass on my comadre's story that would not demean, water down, or sensationalize what she had to tell me.

Gracias from the bottom of my heart to Sandra Cisneros, who read the book in its unwieldy early incarnation with a storyteller's ear and gave it a push in the right direction.

I lack the words to thank Deb Chasman, my editor at Beacon, who commented upon every page of this book more times than she probably cares to remember, and who never stopped nurturing this project, even through the difficult moments.

I am grateful to José Limón for the encouragement and sharp reading I so needed at a crucial stage of rewriting.

The women graduate students in my seminar "Women Writing Culture" were among the first readers of this book, before it was truly a book, and their enthusiasm gave me strength. Outside the class, I want to thank my students Charo Montoya and Barbara Walker for many good comments, and Marcia Ochoa, who helped me to see that the central metaphor of this book is my comadre's story about cutting out the tongues of snakes.

Many colleagues at the University of Michigan have responded to different versions of this project over the years, but I especially want to thank Anne Ruggles Gere, Anne Herrmann, Joanne Leonard, Bruce Mannheim, Sherry Ortner, Anton Shammas, and Abby Stewart. And *un millón de gracias* to Laura Pérez, who read the entire book with *cariño* and a sharp critical eye.

Venturing into the history surrounding Pancho Villa, I was glad to have Paul Friedrich, Friedrich Katz, William Taylor, and Paul Vanderwood as my guides, and I wish to thank them for commenting upon my analysis with sensitivity.

My first attempt to talk about my comadre's story on this side of the border took place in the spring of 1986 in a class on life histories taught by Sidney Mintz at Johns Hopkins University, and I want to thank Sid for that early opportunity and for taking the time to comment on the book insightfully. My thanks, also, to Barbara Tedlock for providing intellectual support at both the start and completion of this project, and for her enthusiasm.

I had no idea that I was a feminist ethnographer until Deborah Gordon told me so. I am deeply thankful for Debbie's work and the example she has set for how to think about the history of women's writings within anthropology.

My autobiographical chapter worried me the most, and I would probably have axed it had I not been given courage by Gloria Anzaldúa, Gelya Frank, Janet Hart, and Kamala Visweswaran, each of whom, in different ways, convinced me not to be scared of ending the book by setting things afire. *Gracias*, also, to Gloria for making visible the landscape of the "new *mestiza*," and to Gelya for the idea of the biography in the shadow and that unforgettable letter on pink stationery.

I could not have let this book out of my hands without the blessing of James Fernandez and Renate Lellep Fernandez. *Gracias* to you both for *años y años* of faith in me. And to Jim, my appreciation for keeping the poetry alive in anthropology.

How do I thank my *socio* Teofilo Ruiz? *Gracias, Teo, ahora y siempre.* Finally, to David Frye, *gracias de esta ingrata mujer.*

›››

My border crossings were generously funded by the Harry Frank Guggenheim Foundation and the MacArthur Foundation, whose support of my work over the years freed me to think, doubt, and write. At the University of Michigan, the office of the Vice-President for Research and the Rackham Graduate School, Dean's Office, have generously funded this project. Thank you.

I am glad to have had the opportunity to work through this project in my essays, "Rage and Redemption: Reading the Life Story of a Mexican Marketing Woman," *Feminist Studies* 16 (1990): 223–58, and "A Life Story to Take across the Border: Notes on an Exchange," in George Rosenwald and Richard Ochberg, eds., *Storied Lives: The Cultural Politics of Self-Understanding* (New Haven: Yale University Press, 1992).

My deepest thanks to everyone at Beacon Press, and especially to Carlisle Rex-Waller for her careful copyediting.

›››

A last note: This book is not a work of fiction. My comadre and I chose pseudonyms for every person in her story, including her own name. Esperanza, the name my comadre chose for herself, means hope.

Translated
Woman

INTRODUCTION

The Talking Serpent

"When the Eternal Father threw Eve and Adam out of Paradise, they covered themselves with whatever they could find and built their huts in the countryside. They had a lot of children, and they were embarrassed because they couldn't clothe them all. They covered the ones they could and the others had to remain naked.

"One day the Eternal Father arrived. 'Where are my children?'

"'Here we are,' they called back. And to each other, 'What should we do with all these children? Let's pen these up, the ones who aren't dressed, so he won't see them.' Then Eve and Adam penned up the naked children so they wouldn't make any noise.

"The Eternal Father came. 'How are you?'

"'Fine.'

"'Where are all your children?'

"They couldn't think of how to answer him.

"'What do you have penned up in there?'

"'We have some little pigs penned up in there.'

"'Ah, they're little pigs? Then little pigs they will be for all their lives.' He looked at them and left.

"'Let's get them out, he's gone.'

"As Eve and Adam opened up the pen, they saw that the naked children already had little chubby ears and four paws. They had snouts. They were covered with hair. 'Little pigs you'll be for all your days.' They say that's how pigs came to be. That's why they say that pigs are our brothers.

"Animals used to speak. I've been told that dogs and burros also used to speak. Because, look, when the serpent was about to bite the Holy Virgin, she spoke. We saw that in a movie about Eve and Adam. The Virgin got up on a rock and underneath was the serpent curled up. The serpent said, 'Don't step on me or I'll bite you.' And then the Holy

Virgin turned around and said, 'If you bite me, you'll drag your body around for the rest of your life.' And the serpent got angry and wanted to stand up, but couldn't anymore, and after that it remained on the ground. Didn't you know that, comadre? No, comadre. I'm sure you know it.

"They say you have to cut out the tongues of serpents, because they're in league with the Evil One. The body rots or dissolves into nothing, but the spirit continues to fight. So they say that if in this world you kill a serpent and don't cut out its tongue, in the next world it will turn you in with the Evil One. And your soul, your spirit, will be defenseless. The serpent will say, 'In the other life, you killed me, you took advantage of me.' Serpents talk back to you in the afterlife if you killed any of them and didn't cut out their tongues.

"Comadre, what do you think? Any serpent I find, I kill it, open up its head, and cut out its tongue. So later it won't be telling me I killed it."

›››

This story was told to me in Spanish by Esperanza Hernández, a Mexican woman of about sixty years of age, living in a dusty town on the highway to San Luis Potosí, eight hundred kilometers south of the border with the United States. It was October 1989, the last month of my stay in Mexquitic after years of regular visits beginning in the winter of 1982, and I would soon be returning to Michigan, to my desk and my computer, with another box full of tape-recorded talks with Esperanza.

Before I met Esperanza Hernández, all I knew about her was what other women in Mexquitic had told me: that she had bewitched her former husband, who had abused her and left her for another woman. Cursing him, according to one story, with the words, "So that you will never again see women," she had caused him to go suddenly and completely blind. No one knew exactly how she had done it, but there was some suspicion that she was a *bruja*, a witch, who had thrown special powders at him, or gotten "someone who knows" to do the work for her in San Luis. She had made public the rage she felt for her former husband, and the rumors about her witchcraft powers seemed to reinforce the ancient belief that there is no telling what an enraged woman is capable of doing. I also learned from various people that Esperanza was regarded as a bad-tempered, combative woman that one had to take care not to offend. She was said to have a sharp tongue. Other women thought her a cruel mother, who had gone so far as to throw her eldest son out of the house. As a single mother and a peddler, she was considered to be on the lowest rung of the town social ladder, but she refused to act like a woman of her class: she was neither demure nor defeated.

Hearing the rumors about Esperanza, I was fascinated by the way they echoed the documents I had begun to read from the colonial Mexican Inquisition. Although historians have found them trivial, I could not help but be drawn to the confessions women of every social background made, under duress and often tearfully, about using sexual witchcraft to tame an unfaithful or violent male partner. While these colonial women were desperately seeking relief from abusive male dominance, the cultural assignment of mystic powers to women also made them vulnerable to charges of witchcraft, sometimes by the very men who had hurt or shamed them. I even came across an accusation made in 1740 by a man who lived on an hacienda near Mexico City, claiming that the woman he had jilted made him go blind by using magic she and her Indian mother had concocted. He was sure she was responsible because she had taunted him with the words, "You can still see, blind one? Soon you won't."[1]

To hear about Esperanza, a woman living in the present, within the context of these inquisitorial stories, I felt as though history had come alive. Here was a woman who, unlike the subjects of my readings, I could follow home, talk to, confront, not have to piece together from the fragments of a court transcript. Excited, the anthropologist who had been hiding under the historian's skin boldly stepped forward and stared into the eyes of the living woman, met the challenge of her presence, here now . . .

That's how I would tell the story if I wanted to cast myself in the part of the anthropologist as heroine. But, no, that's not what happened. I continued to sojourn in the safety and comfort of the archives for quite a while longer. A growing discomfort about the close links between the fieldworker and the inquisitor as extractors of confessions was partly what held me back.[2] This discomfort was heightened for me in Mexico by the intense awareness of race and class differences in the countryside and by the way people tended to position me in the role of a rich gringa from the United States. In addition, the rumors about Esperanza had not only fascinated me, they had also proved intimidating, and I found myself unable to seek her out on my own. The truth is I spent an entire year in Mexquitic before I met Esperanza, and it was still another year before I began to get to know her and yet another year before we began to develop a relationship as comadres.

It was in 1983, during the Day of the Dead, that I first came face to face with Esperanza in the town cemetery while I was busy taking photographs. I kept snapping away at the sight of the tombstones people were lavishly decorating with the yellow and orange marigolds known as *zempazúchiles*. The dead are said to cherish the aroma of things. Between frames, I caught sight of Esperanza. She was striking. She held a bulging bouquet of calla lilies and seemed to me like something out of one of Diego Rivera's epic Indian women canvases. As I drew closer, I asked if I might take her picture. She looked at me haughtily and asked me, with a brusqueness I had not encountered before among local women, *why* I wanted to photograph her. I made some weak reply, and she let me photograph her, though I was so nervous that I snapped the last picture on the roll (which, in the end, didn't come out) and moved on, certain that I would have little more to do with her. I think that many of the contradictions of my work with Esperanza were dramatized in that first encounter. I jumped on her as an alluring image of Mexican womanhood, ready to create my own exotic portrait of her, but the image turned around and spoke back to me, questioning my project and daring me to carry it out.

I did not speak to her again until December of the following year, when I saw her in church on the festival day for the Virgin of Guadalupe. I had been away from the town for a few months and, glad to be back, was offering greetings with greater cheer than usual. I found the nerve that day to greet Esperanza and chat with her briefly, and she clearly took this as a sign of my readiness to enter into a relationship. Later that week, as my husband, David Frye, and I were finishing dinner, we heard a buoyant knock at our door. It was Esperanza, coming to ask if we would be godparents of the cake for her daughter Norberta's coming of age party (*quinceañera*). Although I was taken aback by this sudden burst of friendliness, I agreed to bring to the party a big three-tiered cake, with a doll on the top dressed in lavender to match Norberta's outfit. Two months later Esperanza knocked at our door again. She was coming to ask us to become the godparents of her *niño*

Dios, a doll representing baby Jesus that is used in the *acostadas* and *levantadas*, the yearly home Christmas festivities of putting el niño Dios to bed and awakening him amid a rosary, singing, and tamales.

These requests seemed to come out of the blue. It was only years later that I learned that Esperanza had been observing us carefully, noting the way—unlike the town elite and the few American tourists she had encountered—we spoke to everyone, rich and poor alike. And she had learned that we had become the godparents of a little girl born to a poor single mother in the town. Esperanza later told me that she had been moved to see me caress the child as she passed by us on the street. Her observations had led her to think that, although we were from *el otro lado*, "the other side," and probably rich, we would not be so arrogant as to shun her efforts to initiate a relationship.

By agreeing to these requests, David and I became *compadres*, spiritual coparents of Esperanza's daughter and her niño Dios. Esperanza and I would from then on address one another as *comadre* and participate in the intimate but respectful friendship and patronage that goes with being compadres. A *compadrazgo* relation in rural Mexico is typically forged between persons of high and low economic standing, so that as the better-off person in my relation with Esperanza I would be expected to offer financial or other assistance if she requested it. She would be expected, in turn, to offer me small gifts from time to time, say, of produce from her field, and to act with extreme courtesy whenever we encountered one another. But we would also have to improvise a great deal on our expected roles, working them out in the course of our interactions, for I was no ordinary comadre, but a gringa comadre from el otro lado.

Initially, I was not quite sure how to interpret Esperanza's actions. I have to admit I was at a loss about this assertive "informant," who seemed to demand rather than request favors and was much more brash than the other women I knew in Mexquitic. She told us that her niño Dios had fallen off her home altar several times because he was upset at having had to wait too long for his levantada ritual. Her comadre Rosa, who was supposed to have celebrated the levantada, had suddenly left town; and so it was up to us, Esperanza declared in what seemed a scolding tone, to perform the ritual immediately. These requests represented significant outlays of money from David and me, though obviously we could afford it. Yet we were still strangers to her. What other requests would follow? Did she perhaps imagine that we were an easy source from which to tap funds? Was she truly seeking our friendship? When we performed the ritual for her Christ child, we were suspicious enough to bring only what was minimally necessary, the crocheted outfit for the doll and some treats for the guests. We skimped on the oranges and did not bring a piñata. I remember feeling the sense of disappointment among the guests: the gringos, merely students, yet richer than anyone there, had been cheap.

I came to regret this even more afterward. How I wished I could have known how generous Esperanza would later be with me. As I got to know her, I was better able to separate the various myths of Esperanza from the woman herself; but I also found that she had become the incarnation of the myths. And I learned a valuable lesson from my initial reaction to her. I had to admit to myself that the rumors I had heard made it difficult for me to form my own opinion of Esperanza outside of the public script that had already been written about her. I was also forced to realize the extent to which the ethnographic relation is based on power, for indeed, I had felt uncomfortable when an "informant"—particularly another, less-privileged, woman—was assertive and aggressive, rather than complicitous and cooperative as informants "should" be.

As has often been the case in other relationships between the subject of a life history narrative and the anthropologist, I did not seek out Esperanza but was sought out by her.[3] Her manner of persuasion was to feed more words into my tape recorder than the other women, to plunge into levels of complexity and contradiction, and to refuse, simply, to tell her story too quickly. She chose me to hear her story and to take it back across the border to the mysterious and powerful otro lado.

When she first came to my door with the request that I become her comadre, I had not yet gone beyond the twin images I had of her: the romantic image of the intense Indian woman with the calla lilies, on the one hand; the "uncooperative informant" and pushy, witchy woman I had been warned to stay away from, on the other. As I got to know Esperanza, I realized our becoming comadres had allowed us to forge a relationship of mutual caring, reciprocity, and trust. It made it possible for us to transcend, to a certain extent, our positions as gringa and Mexicana. Esperanza's deference to me could be that of a comadre, rather than that of a woman of a rural working-class background; and it meant that I, too, could be, had to be, deferential, offering the kind of formal respect—addressing her as *usted*, the formal "you," shaking hands softly at every encounter—expected from me, in turn, as a comadre. By asking me to become her comadre, Esperanza had opened up a terrain for our exchange. Women ethnographers have often found themselves positioned in the daughter role in relation to the people with whom they work.[4] In giving me the role of comadre, Esperanza also made me "fictive kin," but in a way that both highlighted and formalized the contradictions of the racial and class differences between us.

After our participation in the two ritual events, we began to see more of Esperanza. In the quiet of her small, unlit cinder-block room she told me about her life, folk legends, and her religious worldview. I listened, entranced. Just before we left in 1985, I asked if I could tape her stories. She agreed, and with this we embarked on a series of conversations that continued over the course of many evenings, and many years. In the protective darkness of the night, since she didn't want anyone to know she was coming to talk to me, Esperanza would come to my door just when most townspeople were getting ready for bed. After settling down at the kitchen table, she would ask where we had left off and pick up from there, letting her narrative unfold in episodes like a *fotonovela*. She called what she was telling me her *historias*, referring both to the history and the story of her life. But she did not simply tell her historias, she performed them, telling virtually the entire story in dialogue form, changing voices like a spirit medium or a one-woman theater of voices to impersonate all the characters in her narratives. I did not have to "elicit" her account; rather, it was necessary for me to learn how to listen to her storytelling and performance. Sometimes, I have to admit, her story was exhausting to listen to, especially as it got late into the night. My comadre seemed determined to push her story into my hands and stuff it into my ears, so I could take it back across the border.

Yet Esperanza often found amusing my determined efforts to understand her story; though she wanted to tell me her story and had, in her perception, a sad story to tell, she refused—and still refuses—to succumb to self-pity. Her telling of her history was always full of humor, of a picaresque vitality. The laughter that punctuates all our conversations is, perhaps, also her critique of my academic pretensions: the way I find things "interesting" and cajole her and pounce on her so that she will talk and tell me more; the way I stalk her, photographing her in the city streets where she peddles fruits and vegetables, photographing her in her garden—yes, with her calla lilies.

That I should want to take her life seriously also strikes her as comical in terms of the inversions of social position and hierarchy that it suggests: an educated, obviously middle-class gringa asking an unschooled Mexican street peddler to tell her life story. In a society where privilege and power are the monopoly of the fair-skinned, Esperanza is acutely aware of her dark skin, and of her Indianness. One night in 1987 when we were discussing a folk legend, Esperanza was surprised to discover that David and I were several years older than she had thought; she, in turn, surprised me by attributing our apparent youthfulness to our not being Indian.

"I think we were born the same year as your son Simeón," David said, after Esperanza tried guessing how old we were.

Her teenage son, Mario, who was present, wanted to know: "Then why does Simeón look so much older?"

Esperanza had a ready answer: "It depends on—Simeón is short. Dark. Short. My compadre is a different person. Not like someone from here. Not like—"

"Like the Mexicans?" said Mario.

"Yes," replied Esperanza. "My compadres, on the other hand, they are big, fair-skinned, and here one is dark and short. We're *indiados*. We here are the Indians, compadre and comadre. Imagine, here we are in Mexquitic, where the Indians founded the church, right? . . . So then, who are you going to compare us with, hijo?"

Even as she announces to us that "we here are the Indians," Esperanza claims Spanish as her language and thinks that Indians are people who existed long ago. The "Indianness" she invokes in her conversation with us is that of her social standing and her historical past, but most obviously it is that of her color and physical features. She feels especially Indian next to two gringos like David and me.[5] Yet her Indianness is not based in an ethnic identity, but in race/class distinctions that have developed since the European conquest of Mexico and that continue to assert the power of white-skin privilege. But neither is she *mestiza* in the conventional sense of the word, as often used (incorrectly) by ethnographers, to mean non-Indian. It is more accurate to say that she has been "de-Indianized," her Indian identity (once Tlaxcalan) having been displaced, though not forgotten, in the long process of colonial and postcolonial domination.

Within the distinctions of race and class in Mexico, and from Esperanza's perspective as someone near the bottom of the social hierarchy, our interaction continues to be amusing and amazing. So embedded is her sense of racial and class domination that she has asked me if I am not embarrassed to be seen with her. At the same time, she strives to keep our friendship and work secret, for fear that others will think she is trying to improve her situation by hanging around with the gringos. Thus, although Esperanza and I have developed a close relationship over the years, neither of us would automatically claim "sisterhood." Esperanza represented a model of womanhood that was in many ways foreign to me, and I know that as a woman I, too, seemed "other" to Esperanza. Our relationship as comadres has been a bridge that has linked us in ways neither of us could have foreseen. But no matter how close we may have become as comadres, the fundamental ironies and contradictions of our work together cannot be erased. Finally, our relationship is situated within a long history of mainstream Mexican constructions of Indian womanhood, which mediates all such attempts as ours to cross social borders.

While I was in Mexquitic in the fall of 1989, I was startled to see in a San Luis newspaper a photograph of a woman selling handmade dolls on the street. Taking a closer look, I saw that the woman in the photograph was the same Nahuatl-speaking woman I myself had bought several dolls from on a recent trip to San Luis. The headline above the photograph read, "An Indigenous Entrepreneur Abandoned by the INI" (the INI is the National Indigenous Institute). The caption, in a high moral tone, noted, "This is where *indigenismo*, the essence of our nationality, has gone. To sit in the street and sell crafts because the National Indigenous Institute has spent twenty years 'making plans.'" This statement of concern for the fate of the woman in the picture, and others like her, places the blame on the bureaucratic institution supposedly in charge of Indian matters for not being able to get Indian women off the streets and into more proper work spaces. However,

Nahuatl-speaking women peddle miniature Indian dolls in all the major cities of Mexico, as any tourist knows. These women street peddlers are known as *las Marías*.[6] They are excellent entrepreneurs of the informal economy, who tend to sell in the posh Pink Zone of Mexico City as well as in other large cities like San Luis Potosí.

Esperanza is a woman of the streets, too. Her peddling is part of the tradition of Indian women's marketing, of independent lower-class economic survival extending back in its general features both to prehispanic and colonial times.[7] She calls herself a *marchanta*, and she peddles vegetables, fruit, and flowers from one or two buckets she carries on her head and arm, looking almost as picturesque as the peddler with the sixteen caps on his head from the folk tale "Caps for Sale," as she walks through the city of San Luis Potosí. With her thick brown hair in two long braids, her apron, and a *rebozo*, the fringed shawl draped on her shoulders, she presents herself as a woman of the traditional working class and a woman of a generic Indian heritage.

But Esperanza's "Indianness" is, from the mainstream Mexican perspective, less authentic, more degraded, and therefore outside the realm of the INI. She neither speaks Nahuatl—as did ancestors beyond the reaches of her memory—nor makes crafts to sell. Her "Indianness" does not merit any special attention from bureaucratic agencies; Esperanza is part of the vast marginal Mexican population that has been internally colonized to think of itself as descended from Indians and yet can claim no pride or virtue in that heritage.

Visibly Indian and yet invisibly Indian, Esperanza's vision of self and society is a cross between what anthropologist Guillermo Bonfil Batalla has called *el México profundo*, "the profound Mexico," which is steeped in the legacy of the Mesoamerican world, and *el México imaginario*, "the imaginary Mexico," which is the dream world inhabited by the Mexican elite and those who aspire to form part of it, the world of those who deny the Indian legacy of Mexican culture and embrace the Western civilizing project as their own.[8] Esperanza is a mestiza not because she isn't Indian but because she has a foot in each world, located as she is on the northern frontier of Mesoamerica and the southern frontier of the U.S.-Mexico border. Across the border, as exemplified in the thinking of Gloria Anzaldúa, it has become possible for Chicanas to assert themselves as "new mestizas," to revalorize the notion of mixed identity.[9] But in Mexico a mestiza like Esperanza is Indian for purposes of exclusion and non-Indian for purposes of inclusion.

› › ›

Before my arrival, Esperanza had already thought about her life as a text, telling and retelling her life story to her children and her women clients in San Luis, as well as to the spirit medium Chencha. To her teenage daughters, especially, she was in the habit of telling her story as a lesson to them.[10] In telling her story to me, she undoubtedly wanted me to affirm a particular image of herself, and my listening so attentively to her stories did perhaps add moral weight to them as lessons for her daughters and youngest son; but I was also simply another kind of audience for her storytelling. Her daughter Norberta and son Mario were almost always present for her storytelling sessions in my kitchen in Mexquitic; occasionally her elder daughter, Gabriela, and her mother, Nicolasa, also came. David, too, was frequently there, and beginning in 1987, even my son Gabriel often sat at the table with us, eating cookies until he fell asleep.

Esperanza's story reminds us "that some among our informants are storytellers in their own lives and that the words they provide have not been given to us alone."[11] When I told Esperanza that I thought her life narrative would make a very good book, she agreed, and she took a certain pride in thinking that she alone of all the women in the town had a life of such uncommon suffering to tell; no other woman's story was quite so worthy of being put into a text, or even, she said, emphasizing her life's supreme textuality, into a history, into a film.

Esperanza views her life as worthy of being turned into a story because of her notion of story. Certainly a key model for her is the Christian narrative as a story of suffering, and particularly of bodily suffering as a vehicle for the release of spirit and divinity. A related story form is the Catholic confession narrative; in fact, Esperanza often compared the story she was telling me to a confession that I, her comadre from "the other side," was hearing rather than the priest. Along with these religious sources, her story reveals a strong sense of the melodramatic— a quintessentially female version of the "tragic"—as found in foto-novelas and television, whose soap operas she now watches on a set given to her by me, her gringa comadre. Finally, she draws on cultural myths of women warriors, such as those found in the colonial Mexican Inquisition narratives, that attribute to women supernatural powers to harm the men who wrong them.

Most important for her is the notion of narrative as a progression from suffering to rage to redemption. When I told her that I was also asking other women to tell me their life stories, she was positively shocked when I mentioned among them a younger woman, a respected schoolteacher in the town. "But she, what has she suffered? I never heard that her husband beat her, that she suffered from rages," Esperanza responded. On the other hand, when I let her know that I had talked to the wife of a very respectable townsman who had served as *presidente*, she shook her head with pity after I admitted that the woman had omitted from her life story what Esperanza herself told me: that this woman had come close to leaving her husband after she found him with his mistress, but had ended up staying with him to save face and protect her social position. "How well she covers up for her husband!" Esperanza said, chuckling with pride that she had not swallowed her own rage, had refused to suffer and be still. In her view, the rage brought on by suffering, and redemption through suffering, is what gives a woman the right and the need to author a text. Rage and redemption form the poles of her life as text.

Unlike all the other listeners of Esperanza's story, it was up to me, as the researcher with access to the resources of bookmaking, to transform her "spoken words into a commodity."[12] In my multiple roles as priest, interviewer, collector, transcriber, translator, analyst, academic connoisseur, editor, and peddler of Esperanza's words on this side of the border, I have had to cut, cut, and cut away at our talk to make it fit between the covers of a book, and even more important, to make it recognizable *as a story*, a certain kind of story, a life history. Although Esperanza in her own life is an immensely talented storyteller, the text of her life certainly did not come readymade.

Calling a life history a text is, in one sense, already a colonization of the act of storytelling. Yet the border between the "spoken" and the "written" is a fluid one. So it is not orality versus textuality that I call into question here, with the image it conjures up of the ethnographer salvaging the fleeting native experience in the net of a text.[13] The more relevant distinction for me is Walter Benjamin's contrast between storytelling and information. Information, in Benjamin's analysis, is a mode of communication linked to the development of the printing press and of capitalism; it presents itself as verifiable, it is "shot through with explanation," and it is disposable because it is forgettable. Storytelling, on the other hand, is "always the art of repeating stories," without explanation, combining the extraordinary and the ordinary. Most important, it is grounded in a community of listeners on whom the story makes a claim to be remembered by virtue of its "chaste compactness," which inspires the listener, in turn, to become the teller of the story.[14] It worries me that one does violence to the life history as a story by turning it into the disposable commodity of information. One approach I took to this problem was to focus on the act of life story representation as reading rather than as informing, with its echoes of surveillance and disclosures of truth. I have tried to make clear that what I am reading is a story, or set of stories, that have been told to me, so that I, in turn, can tell them again, transforming myself from a listener into a storyteller.

In my role as storyteller, I had to decide what form to give this book. At first, I was torn between two styles: the seamless style of the testimonial novel, which "invents within a realistic essence" literature from the words of those who usually don't make literature, and the more conversational, stop-and-start style of oral storytelling and performance, which braids pauses, shouts, whispers, interruptions, and digressions into the written account of verbal performances.[15] Finally I realized, as I listened intently to the tapes of my conversations with Esperanza, that I didn't have to choose one style of presentation. Not only could I use the two styles, I *had* to use them both. In my unfolding relationship with Esperanza, the style of our talking to one another had shifted over time, from Esperanza's telling me a kind of novela in 1985 to our talking to one another in a looser conversational style on my return trips to Mexquitic in the years from 1987 to 1990. The later conversations changed in tone as we began to venture outside the kitchen and to ask more daring and honest questions of each other and of our locations on opposite sides of the border. As Esperanza granted me entrance into the world of her selling trips to the city and the world of Pancho Villa spiritism, I came to see how her historias fit into the fuller context of her life.

By using both a novelistic style and a dialogical style in this book, I've tried to keep Esperanza's voice at the center of the text, while also

showing my efforts to hear and understand her, efforts that led me, ultimately, to my own voice. Out of a sense of faithfulness to the process
by which Esperanza and I coproduced the knowledge inscribed in this
book, I've refrained from the temptation to reorder the account; the
chronology of the story is my comadre's, not mine. The book mirrors
our movement through time and space. Every story and conversation
carries a date, for each telling took place on a particular night, not in a
timeless vacuum, and was marked off in the flow of history.

The structure of the book finally fell into shape in a way that I think
neatly reflects the process of how my comadre and I became mediums
for each other's stories. The first two parts of the book focus on my
comadre's historia, as she told it to me in the years from 1985 to 1989.
It seemed important to me that she be the one to speak first in this
book, with as few interruptions from me as possible, because in reality
it was she who had initiated our relationship and told me her story long
before I had begun to think of how I would house what she was telling
me. In the last two parts of the book, my voice becomes more inter-
woven with my comadre's voice, and there is a switch in tone from my
comadre telling me her historia to the forging between us of a *meta-
historia*. The third part of the book focuses on the conversations we had
in 1988 and 1989 concerning the contradictions of the project we were
engaged in—namely, the making of a book out of my comadre's historias. In the final section of the book, I offer a series of reflections—
written from this side of the border and in the context of my location
in the academy—on Esperanza's story and how it might be read from
feminist, historical, and autobiographical perspectives. Each of my reflections can be read as a separate conclusion to the book, but together
I hope they provide a three-dimensional view of Esperanza as well as of
the woman who became her biographer.

›››

Just as Esperanza had her models for what makes a story recognizable as a story, I, too, have drawn from various models in translating
our conversations into a text and becoming, myself, a certain kind of
storyteller. I have looked for models where I might have been expected
to look: in other life histories and in criticism of life histories, as well
as in the recent outpouring of feminist writing on women's autobiographies and oral histories.[16] In those voices I have found examples of how

anthropological and feminist agendas make possible certain kinds of tellings of lives.

In an effort to find a theoretical frame closer to home, I turned to the writings of Chicanos and Chicanas (and other minority voices as well). By the late 1960s, before the issue of ethnography as writing had come to the forefront of anthropological debate, the Chicano critique of anthropology had already posed the question of "who exercises the *right* to write culture in American society," and had sought answers in "the social forces and actors that furnished the enabling conditions for the production of ethnographies."[17] By the end of the 1970s, Chicana creative writers had taken up these questions, not by becoming anthropologists—an identity that had become synonymous with being a sellout to the gringo academic establishment—but by writing their culture in highly innovative forms that combined personal ethnographies with critique, poetry, and storytelling. Poetry, and secondarily the essay, became the key forms of expression for Chicanas striving for an immediacy of language to voice their challenges to the male-dominated Chicano movement, the Anglo-American stereotypes of the acquiescent Mexican woman, and Anglo-American feminist visions.[18]

By questioning the way they have been represented by outsiders and offering, in turn, their own multilayered self-representations, Chicano and Chicana critics have made theoretically salient the issue of what makes ethnographic truths valid discourses.[19] Their criticism and creative explorations are based in a subtle understanding of the uses to which language can be put, as performance, as resistance, as the "carnivalesque."[20] Chicana creative writers have come at the issue of self-representation and verbal art by taking over the English language itself, which they use in fierce, unheard of, subversively feminist ways.[21] From their position straddling selfhood and otherhood, Spanish and English, Mexican identity and *agringado* identity, power and resistance, Chicano and Chicana writers have so radically shifted the terms of cultural analysis that it now seems impossible to imagine doing any kind of ethnography without a concept of the borderlands or of border crossings. The concept of the borderlands, so poetically explored by Gloria Anzaldúa, is rooted in the slippery social landscape created by transnational capitalism and migration, in which rural Mexicans rub shoulders with yuppies in the various border zones that now cut through the entire terrain of Mexico and the United States.[22] I certainly could

not have done without the idea of border crossings in thinking about
what it has meant for me to relocate Esperanza here in her second life
as a translated woman. Nor could I have done without the lessons of
respect for language that define the works of Chicano and Chicana
writers. I have tried here to make this book speak in a voice that has
all the cadences, from rage to redemption, that Esperanza's voice had
when she talked to me in my kitchen in Mexquitic.

› › ›

*Nonfiction enjoys the sort of authority that has not easily
been granted fiction since Walter Benjamin's storytellers
traded their last tales. On the other hand it does give up
something for the privilege, it is dulled by the obligation to be
factual. This is acknowledged by the same people who would
not pick up a novel, but who say of a particularly good biography or history that it reads like one.*

—E. L. Doctorow, "False Documents"

For a long time, when colleagues would ask me what I
was "working on," I found myself alternating between
calling what Esperanza was telling me a "life history" and a "life story."
It finally dawned on me that the most appropriate term was obviously
Esperanza's own, the Spanish word *historia*, which she often used in
the plural, describing her account as her *historias*, making no distinction between history and story. Esperanza certainly understood that
the border between history and story, reality and fiction, is a fluid one.
I, in turn, to make her historias fit into a book, had to edit and reshape
what she told me, turning it into something else, namely, the "false
document" that this book is. Esperanza often noted that her life was
like a film, and preparing her story for publication I felt like a film-
maker with reels of her story before me that I had to assemble using
filmic principles of montage and movement. As I undid necklaces of
words and restrung them, as I dressed up hours of rambling talk in elegant sentences and paragraphs of prose, as I snipped at the flow of talk,
stopping it sometimes for dramatic emphasis long before it had really
stopped, I no longer knew where I stood on the border between fiction
and nonfiction.

The modern academic separation of history and fiction was forged in the nineteenth century with the development of the discipline of history.[23] Before then, as exemplified in a text like *Don Quixote de la Mancha*, the relation between history and fiction was more incestuous. Cervantes, for example, claimed not to be the author of Quixote's *historia* but merely its purveyor; its true author, he announced nine chapters into the novel, was an Arab historian. His task had simply been to have the text translated into Spanish by a bilingual *morisco* in exchange for hefty quantities of raisins and wheat. An *historia* thrice born in translation—what an apposite metaphor Cervantes bequeathed to us for thinking about the hybrid stories that anthropologists produce in collaboration with the people who agree to let their words be borne across borders.

In recent times, as postmodern capitalism has brought the partiality and packaging of truth to the attention of us all, many ethnographers, historians, journalists, and fiction writers have found that, like Cervantes, they, too, are purveyors of a range of "false documents." Whether written as social analysis or autobiography, recent tellings of ethnographic tales, for example, rely on blurred or mixed genres that make it increasingly difficult to give a single label to a work.[24] Our trouble with the fixity of genre is born of quite different circumstances, however, than those which existed in the time of Cervantes. The texts we write today partake of the same crisscrossed genealogy and fluctuating value that characterizes all of our other commodities; they are as polyglot as the automobile parts stamped "Made in Brazil" that are commissioned for a factory in Detroit but produced in a sweatshop in Los Angeles employing Latino and Asian migrants.[25]

Yet even as the truth of whose labor and whose capital produces our commodities becomes ever more elusive, the Anglo-American academy has only slowly come to accept the possibility that history's truth (or ethnography's truth) might be just as elusive. Here is where the border between the two Americas reasserts itself, for in Latin America writers have been confronting head-on the connections between fiction and history since the nineteenth century, when the leaders of newly formed nations were often also novelists intent on writing foundational fictions.[26] Such efforts have continued in contemporary Latin American writings, in which history, journalism, and fiction are seen as converging practices, similarly involved in the process of transforming, as Gabriel García Márquez puts it, "something which

appears fantastic, unbelievable into something plausible, credible . . .
by tell[ing] it straight, [as] is done by reporters and by country folk."[27]

It seems to me that Esperanza's sense of the shifting boundaries between historical and fictional truth is based in just such an understanding of the way the telling shapes the believability of the narrative.
Once, when I told her I liked to listen to her *historias*, she laughed and
asked me if I had ever heard the saying, "*Cuéntame algo, aunque sea
una mentira*" (Tell me a story, even if it's a lie). In a more serious
mood, she would often wonder aloud whether the gringos would believe her *historia*—not because what she had told me wasn't the true
story of her life, but because she feared that an understanding of what
she had told me called for a leap of empathy that she suspected the
gringos might not be able, or willing, to make. No, she finally decided,
the gringos would never believe what she had told me.

›››

From where I now sit, in front of my computer rather than face to
face with Esperanza at the kitchen table in Mexquitic, the story with
which I began this prologue seems redolent with allegorical meanings.
Allegories are like translations; they are stories born again in an alien
tongue. Allegories typically reflect upon a sense of loss, of the past, of
tradition, of authority.[28] Esperanza's allegory, however, looks both to
the past and to the future, to the time before time—the beginning of
male and female sexuality, symbolized in the embarrassingly excessive
procreation of Eve and Adam, and the beginning of language, when animals still spoke—and to the time after time, the afterlife, and the dissolution of the body, when animals will speak again.

In saying that she cuts out the tongues of any serpents she finds in
her garden, Esperanza is speaking, to be sure, of real snakes in real gardens. Yet she is also alluding to a long history of Mesoamerican and
Catholic association of women with snakes that culminates in the image of the Virgin of Guadalupe crushing underfoot the head of Satan in
the form of a serpent. Her words refer as well to a rich serpent lore
widespread among Mexican women that may reflect fears of their own
sexuality and procreative powers, centering on narratives about snakes
that steal breastmilk by fooling babies with their tails, or that lodge
themselves inside the vulva, strangling infants in the womb.[29] While
invoking these well-known meanings, Esperanza still manages to de-

scribe something new—the snake that will tell on you in the next life if you don't cut out its tongue in this life. It is not the milk-stealing serpent or phallus serpent that Esperanza fears, but the talking serpent.

As the one who is no longer just expanding her capacities to listen but sitting here snipping and snipping at the historias Esperanza told me, only to sew them back into this book as a life history, I fear I am somehow cutting out Esperanza's tongue.[30] Yet when I am done cutting out her tongue, I will patch together a new tongue for her, an odd tongue that is neither English nor Spanish, but the language of a translated woman. Esperanza will talk in this book in a way she never talked before.[31]

Across the border, in a new language, my comadre told me I could do as I pleased with the historias she had related to me as her true confessions. Let the gringos read them. Her only fear was what the other women in town would think if they ever read what she had confessed to me. They'd laugh like hell, and they would certainly talk. After all, wasn't it the wagging tongues of the serpent women in town that told me about Esperanza, that scared me away from her, before I even set eyes on her?

From the time of the Spanish conquest of Mexico, the translator and the traitor, figured in the shape of a woman, Malintzín, translator and lover to Cortés, have been seen as synonymous in the Mexican male historical imagination.[32] Malintzín, the speaking subject, became La Malinche, who betrayed her people to the Spaniards by giving her tongue and her body to Cortés and, like Eve, was to blame for being the mother of a "fallen" people. Chicana feminists have sought, in their recent writings, to reclaim Malintzín—who was known as *la lengua*, literally, "the tongue," by Cortés and the chroniclers of the conquest—as a subject speaking for herself rather than being spoken for. Ironically, Malintzín left no record of her own voice, for she could not write the languages she translated so fluently. The Chicana writer likewise finds herself trying to give voice both to herself and her community in a literary language that is alien to the tradition from which she stems. Feminist awareness is always complicated by the numerous contradictions that emerge for women in attempting any kind of speaking or self-representation. For Chicanas, like other women coming into the world of letters without a sense of entitlement, it is further complicated by the recognition that the "invitation" to cross racial and ethnic boundaries by translating themselves does not ensure them (or any women of color) that their reality will be believed and respected en el otro lado.

In different ways, both Esperanza and I partake of the double-edged identity of a Malinche. By being willing to reveal more of herself to me than any other woman in Mexquitic, more than the official version of a woman's life, more than was proper to reveal to a gringa, it can be said that Esperanza has been a traitor, translating for me in ways that transgress the norms of Mexican rural society, where people keep their personal and familial identities as tightly walled as they do their houses. That she knows she's a traitor, even if a vulnerable traitor, is clear from her fear of other women in town getting a hold of her historias. I, in turn, have compounded this act of betrayal by translating Esperanza's historias, her "lies," for gringos to read. Now I've gone and put these lies in a book, and who can say whether this book will do Esperanza any good?

In telling me her historias so I would put them into a book that would talk in the tongue of the gringos, Esperanza definitely placed both herself and me in a paradoxical position. In the masked tongue of translation, she hopes she'll be invulnerable to the snakes; only in her original tongue would her confessions be dangerous. But with the border between the United States and Mexico, like the border between life and death, being so permeable, can I, no matter how hard I will try, keep guard over this book? How can I be sure it won't return to talk where it shouldn't?

No doubt about it, this book is a talking serpent. Too late to cut its tongue now.

PART ONE

Coraje / Rage

call me witch
call me hag
call me sorceress
call me mad
call me woman. do not
call me goddess
I do not want the position.

—Alma Villanueva,
"witches' blood,"
from **Bloodroot**

Angelito, who died without closing her eyes (1985)

Some nights in 1985, 1987, 1988, 1989

In the kitchen with the mint green walls and the dark pink cracked cement floor tiles, two women sit across from one another talking, a tape recorder between them. Our chairs creak and are not very comfortable; they are cheap wicker chairs that have become worm-eaten over the years. The wobbly kitchen table, one of David's first efforts at woodworking, is covered with a plastic tablecloth imitating an embroidered design of green and purple. On the table are soda bottles, a plate of cookies, and several plastic containers of boiled water, as well as a container of spring water brought from Texas for my son Gabriel, alone, to drink. Against one wall is a shelf, also David's work, that holds a few enamel plates, some boxes of cereal and rice, a couple of amber-rimmed drinking glasses, and a set of knives, forks, and spoons—the kind of flatware with the wood bottoms you used to get as a bonus at gasoline stations—that have been with us since college days in Connecticut and New Jersey and have now found their way to this little house in Mexico. On a small shelf next to the facing wall there is an old toaster-oven, boxed and put away each year and taken out again, a beige hot pot, also put away and taken out each year, and two enamel basins, hand towels drying on their edges. A dorm-size refrigerator, dented, scratched, starting to rust around the sides, bought on the street in Austin one year as we headed for the border, makes its burbling sounds, periodically startling us. A gas stove with three burners, only one of which works well, rests against a side wall, near an old rusted sink that is beyond cleaning. Altogether, a very luxurious home by town standards. Many things that have traveled with us for years are here: the white teapot that lost its lid; the little French expresso cups with the thumb-print designs bought in Greenwich Village the summer I lived there with David and was disowned by my parents; a cracked ceramic plate, rejected by my sister-in-law as a beginning potter; and in the bedroom adjoining the kitchen, on the mattress bought secondhand from a tourist agent in San Luis, the sheets with the huge orange and yellow marigolds that I remember on my parents' sofabed in the first one-bedroom apartment we had in the United States, sheets washed to aged softness and fragility, but not yet worn through. Outside, in the open courtyard, are the bougainvil-

25

lea, quietly unfastening its fuchsia leaves, and the big black butterflies, a disguise of witches, that flutter noisily like awkward birds. All the lamps are out, except in this kitchen. The stillness is interrupted only by the sound of trucks roaring down the highway every now and then. In this place, in this stillness, in the night, one storyteller speaks to another.

ONE

The Mother in the Daughter

Her eyes reflected the corn sheaves as her busy hands crushed the golden spikes and made clusters that would become tortillas, dampened with tears.

—Nellie Campobello, My Mother's Hands

It is July 1, 1985, the first time I will try taping my conversations with Esperanza. After talking informally for a while, I say, "Comadre, I'd like you to tell me about your life. From your first memory."

I have barely finished making my request when Esperanza breaks out in torrents of laughter. Her children, Norberta and Mario, laugh with her, amused by the hilarity I have provoked. David has just turned on the tape recorder and the tiny red battery light flickers like a firefly.

As the laughter dies down, Esperanza says, "Comadre, what a life, what a life I've had. My life is a very long story. My life has been very sad. Sad. Black, black. Like my mother's life. Look, do you want me to tell you from the time I was born?"

"Yes," I respond, unaware that this is a joke.

There is more laughter. "I'm very scandalous about laughing and talking. My sister says to me, 'Ay, woman, what are you saying? Laugh calmly. Be serious. You get too excited.'

"'That's the way I am. I'm not bitter like you,' I say to her. 'Even though I've had some black times in my life, I haven't been defeated.' As my mama says, 'Maybe when I'm lying there dead. But not as long as I'm still here.'"

The swallows that have built nests in the rafters of the courtyard suddenly fly around noisily. Esperanza tells me she has also seen bats in our house, and to be careful, because bats are not auspicious creatures. We stop to listen, and in the meantime I pass around sodas and cookies, as I will do at all our later talks.

Sitting forward and looking me in the eye, Esperanza now says, "Look, comadre, why would you like me to tell you about my life since childhood?"

"It seems very interesting," I reply earnestly.

"Well, look. Since I was born, God only knows."

Esperanza is laughing again, as are her children. I try to keep a smile on my face, but I am beginning to feel like a fool.

"My mama says that I was born at three in the afternoon, behind the *metate*, the grinding stone. My mama went with my papa to a rancho, there in La Campana. Mama tells stories. She tells stories about when I was born, about the life we went through. The life she suffered with my papa. He's still alive, my papa, but it's just like mouthing the words, 'I have a papa,' because he doesn't get together with us and we don't get together with him, either. He never spoke to us as his children. He treated us as though we were dogs. That's how he treated us.

"He's very rough, my papa. And I am, too. When I get angry, when the children make me get angry, I grab them, and are they in trouble! Just then, I have a black soul, I surely do. We're marked by the way we live, aren't we? We're marked by our parents, aren't we?

"I remember when I was growing up, when I was five or six. Ay, my papa gave my mama a life eternal. He beat her a lot. Because one of the babies died. Because my mama had the baby in her arms. Because she didn't serve my papa quickly enough. Because she didn't have tortillas for him. My papa would beat her for anything, that's what I remember.

"Back then it was my sister, who was the eldest, I, and my brother, and another one who died, still a baby. You know how one is as a small child. We'd start to scuffle, get into mischief, like kittens or puppies do. And my papa would arrive and say, 'What's that racket you're making, you goddam children!' My papa always spoke to us in curses. 'What's with all that racket of yours? You goddam children. And you, you daughter of who knows what, why don't you quiet down the racket that those children of yours are making?'

"Everything offended him. 'Why are you laughing? Are you making fun of me because I'm drunk?'

"We would stand there trembling. And when he beat us, he used a machete. But a big one! My papa used it to chop the maguey and to

chop firewood, to chop *quiotes*, to chop logs. There were some big ma-
chetes, *cuchillotas*, in those days. That was the kind my papa used.

"Oh, when he'd beat us! When my mama would get serious, she
wouldn't utter a word, nothing, and my papa would say, 'I'm speaking
to you! Answer me! What a racket! You kids are nothing but pimps for
your mama!'

"And we'd remain there, trembling. My sister and I. My brother.
Mama had thick braids, and he'd grab a braid and drag her in front of
us. And then he'd say, 'Just dare go. Just dare yell, you goddam
children.'

"So I remember the black life my mama suffered with him. Once he
struck her with a machete. My mama tells that story. When he struck
her with the machete, I wasn't aware of things yet. I started to become
aware when he smashed the cup. It was one of those cups of the old
sort, because there aren't any of them anymore. They were like lightbulbs, little lightbulbs. Half a lightbulb, right? Those were the cups
they had then. Who knows what they were called, but those were the
sort my mama used.

"My Papa would grab at her with whatever he found, and once he
hurled one of those cups at her head and broke her head open. So much
blood came spilling out of my mama. And she did nothing. The blood
was streaming down, but my mama didn't cry. Nor did we.

"On one occasion my mama and papa were in the middle of cursing
and kicking each other, and it occurred to my sister to go and tell my
godfather, who was the *juez*. And then my godfather goes and stands in
the doorway of the room. He says, 'Compadre! Don't do that! Leave my
comadre alone. Don't hit her anymore.'

"Oh, no, my papa didn't want to listen. He looks at him and says,
'And you, who in the name of what asked you to come? This is my
family and I'll devour them however I please. It's no one else's
concern.'

"My godfather says, 'That's fine, compadre. As you say, in your
house it's fine. But don't do that. You don't want to kill my comadre. If
you see that my comadre is misbehaving, you should let the authorities know. Don't you be doing wrong and then end up responsible.'

"'They can punish me however they like. But in my house I rule.
And I'll know what I do. So get out of here immediately! Even if you're
my compadre, what did you come to do?'

"'Well, compadre, don't be beating my comadre anymore. Leave your family alone. Don't hit them anymore.'

"'No, no. No more.'

"After my godfather left, my papa looked at my sister with eyes full of rage. Another beating for my mama and a beating for my sister, for having gone to tell."

›››

"My papa, because he drank, didn't work. The day he took *aguamiel* to sell in San Luis, right away he'd drink up his earnings, halfway home. Or he'd buy two or three little kilos of corn or five little kilos of corn, whatever a large jug could hold. We were lucky if he brought back five kilos of corn before the night fell, and all of us so hungry. Mama says, 'What could I give you? You'd cry to me. And what did I have to give you?'

"The neighbors knew my mama suffered a lot. 'Hey, Nicolasa,' they'd say. 'While you're waiting for your husband, come grind up my *nixtamal*. *Andale*, come on. You're so good at making *gordas*.'

"That's what my mama did. She says she'd take on two, three, what they used to call *cuarterones*. Now they're called kilos. She'd grind up two, three, four cuarterones, just with the metate. My mama was one of those women who knew how to grind corn. She'd break up the nixtamal, and my mama says that in a little while she'd be done with two, three cuarterones of nixtamal. Mama would make tortillas just with her hands. My mama says, 'I laugh at the daughters-in-law of today. Now they're in heaven. And they still say they suffer. If they suffered as I did! Right away I'd fill up the basket with tortillas. They'd give me a large plate full of nixtamal and right away I'd get it ready and make three, four, thick fat gordas, and give them to you children to eat. By the time your papa got back, I had already fed you.'

"When Papa returned, he would say, 'What's up? By now you must have something for me to put in my mouth. What have you done all day?'

"He wouldn't let her respond to what he said. He would hit her with a switch or kick her or take off his belt and beat her. And then it was our turn. Then he'd say to my sister, 'Listen, you. Where was your mama all day?'

"In a whisper my sister would say, 'She went for water.'

"'What, you children couldn't go for water? So she went for water, is that right?'

"My mama wouldn't tell him where she had gone, because then he would go and mistreat the people she had worked for. 'Why do you pay any heed to this *vieja*, this old woman?' he'd go say. And to my mama, 'What are you going about to other houses for? Are you going around crying that you're hungry?'

"Everything struck him the wrong way."

›››

"When I was eight years old, I remember, my mama had a child who died. Then she had another and he died. There were three of us left, two girls and a boy. And that was when my papa took my sister and me to La Laguna. That's why I know those parts, the Lagunera fields.

"My father went there with another family—another man, his wife and his family. 'Hey, Fulano, it's the time for the cotton. Let's head for the Lagunera fields.' 'Sure, why not, let's go.' 'Right, to hunt up something out there, cause here we're real short. Let's go for the cotton harvest.' So he left my mama here to break open the *magueyes*, to take out the *miel*, to *raspar*. 'We'll be back within two or three months, God willing.' He left my mama here all those months.

"We toasted tortillas on the *comal* and left them out to dry, to make *tostadas*. Two big sackfuls of tostadas, because they had to last us two or three weeks, maybe a month. All the way to La Laguna, walking. From dawn to nightfall. At night we would stop by the side of the road, and then for us women—well, little girls—it would be nothing but shouting: '*¡Orale!* Start making the fire!' We'd eat beans and the tostadas, some coffee, and then lie down to sleep in the countryside. The next day at five in the morning, '*¡Orale!* Time to get up!' And walk and walk all day.

"And finally we got to the Lagunera fields, the cotton fields. Long rows, all you could see were the fields turning white with cotton, ready to be picked. So they went off to find out who the owner was, to ask for work. 'We're from San Luis Potosí. We came to look for work.' 'Yes, sir, that's what we like. There's plenty here.'

"And we set to work. He brought three bags, big canvas bags, one for him, one for me, and one for my sister. The three of us. '*Orale*, get to work. As much as you can manage.' You tied the bag to your waist and dragged it along behind you, down the row, and filled it with both hands with the cotton balls. We'd fill them up because we were good workers. And if not, he'd hurl curses and kick us.

"We'd fill the bags, then they'd weigh them and pay us. So much a kilo. Oh, over there it's 'Long live God!' We'd eat. And buy this and buy that. You worked in the sun over there, but people didn't lack for anything. Between the cotton fields there were watermelon patches. And they sold what they called French bread, which is like our *bolillos* here, but more delicious. They bake the most delicious bread there. 'Long live God!'

"After the cotton was picked, there was still work. The beans were ready for harvest. We stayed three months, then another and another— nearly half a year. When we got back, my father was loaded with pesos. But did he ever clothe us from head to foot? Never! All the money he brought back went to drink. He brought us home practically naked, wearing skirts made of canvas. The cheap guaraches he bought us there wore out along the way, and when we got back here we were barefoot."

› › ›

"And then when we arrived, people started to tell my papa that my mama was taking to the road. Of course—she was walking from La Campana to San Luis to sell the miel. As soon as my papa got back from La Laguna, he was ready to kill my mama.

" 'So you've been getting around, right?'

" 'Me? With who?'

" 'You've been going out with the whole gang of viejas who like plea-sure, and with *pelados*.'

"Mama held back, held back. Until one day she spoke up. He had beaten her and then ordered her to go get the aguamiel. Then he left for San Luis, saying he'd be back by midday with the corn.

"Back then we had a burro that my papa would ride on his way back from San Luis. My papa would come back and drink at those houses where they sold *pulque*, and the burro would be braying. And we'd hear him. We recognized our burro's bray.

"Mama said, 'Your papa is on the way. I think I hear the burro bray-ing. At what hour is he going to bring the corn? And then he gets here saying he wants to eat, and why don't I have something for him to eat.'

"That's when my mama had it. I remember Mama saying, softly, 'I'll be back in a little while. I'm going to see your papa. Let's see if he doesn't beat me for going over there. I'm going to tell him to let the burro go.'

"Lord of my soul, she went to see him!

"My papa was having some pulque when she got there. And he fixes his eyes on her. 'And you, what in hell? Who in hell, you daughter of who knows what.'

"She says, 'I came for the burro. I want to unload the corn so I can get the nixtamal ready. What will I give you to eat? And the children, what am I going to give them to eat?'

"He says, 'Do you want to eat *me*? Get outside! Don't come in here, because if you do, you're going to pay for it!'

"Then my mama says that she started slinking back to where the burro was. To let the burro go.

"'Don't let go of my burro!' In that instant my papa got closer, and he almost hit my mama with the machete. Luckily the machete hit the burro instead. Then my mama says she ran. She left the burro behind.

"And he's yelling, 'You'll pay for this at home! Who told you to come here? I don't want viejas following me around wherever I go. I'm no child. You'll *pay* for this at home!'

"No, my mama has an ugly *cuento* to tell.

"She returned, my mama. He stayed there with his friends. His friends said to him, 'Come, Tomás. Have another pulquito. Come, man. Don't get mad. Come have another pulque. Come!'

"What the men were doing was giving my mama a chance to go, to let her escape. Then my mama says she came home. It was the hour of the evening prayers.

"'*Hijos*. Your sister hasn't come back?'

"'No. She stayed with her *abuela*,' I replied.

"'Look, get into bed,' she says to me and my brother. 'Go to sleep now. You can lie down in the kitchen.'

"'Why, Mama?'

"'Lie down,' she says. 'I'll be back right away. I'm going with Doña Pancha. Go on and lie down. I'll be back soon. He won't take long in getting back, your papa.'

"'And if he gets back and doesn't find you?'

"Then she said to me, 'Hija, I'm going to tell you the truth. Your brother is small, he doesn't know. Tomorrow your sister will be back.

Tell her that I'm leaving. I'm going to my mama's. I can't put up with your papa anymore. Just now, for going to see him, he hurled a machete at me, only I escaped because I squatted down behind the burro. But he said he'd punish me. He said he'd kill me when he got home. No law can help me, nothing. If the law punishes me for my actions, let it do so. But I want you to stay here. I won't take you. Children I didn't bring with me! Children I won't take with me! So lie down now. I'll be back very soon. Lie down.'

" 'You're leaving? Are you really going to come back?'

" 'Yes, yes. In a while I'll come back for you. Now I'm going to go see Doña Pancha, and I'll be right back. I'll be right back for you.'

"So she fooled us. And we stayed there. The night fell. It must have been eight in the evening, or nine, when he got back. Cursing. Shouting. And we were trembling. My brother fell asleep. He was the smallest. I was the one listening. No! Lord of my soul. He arrives, enters the house. And he calls out and calls out, 'Nicolasa!' Like that. 'Where are you, daughter of who knows what mother.' And the kitchen door opens. 'Where are you?' He went to the room and didn't find her. And then behind the house, 'Nicolasa! Nicolasa, where are you? Where did you go? Where are you?' She had left the light on for us, an oil-burning light. And he turns to us, 'Where's your mother?'

"Silence.

" 'I'm talking to you, daughter of —. You're pretending to be asleep. Where's your sister?'

" 'She's with my abuela.'

" 'And where's your mama?'

" 'I don't know. We don't know.'

" 'How come you don't know? You pimps!'

"My mama says that the señora she went to see lived close by, and they could hear the noise. The woman of the house told her, 'Ay, Doña Nicolasa, don't go back to that horrible viejo. Leave him!' But they didn't want to be responsible for my mama. The woman said to her, 'Go, Doña Nicolasa. What if that Don Tomás comes now and decides to hurt us or kill us because he finds you here? Go now!'

"They convinced her not to stay there. My mama went to another house. And there they said to her, 'No, really, don't try to leave now. Wait until tomorrow. Wake up early and then go. Leave that viejo.

Leave him already! You've already left the little ones. Leave them there. Let's see if he'll kill them. Maybe he'll devour them.'

"That night he says to me, 'Where's your mother?'

"'I don't know. I don't know.' He pulls me out from under the covers. And he whips me with his belt three times. I was starting to cry when he says, 'Just dare cry.'

"And out he goes again, like a dog with rabies! Out he went, laughing and shouting. He went to get more to drink. And he didn't come back until dawn. He was really hungover. Not drunk anymore, but very hungover, right? He says to us, 'You better tell me where your mother is, or I'll kill you!'

"'We just went to bed. She didn't come back. I don't know where she is.'

"Then he went to see my abuela. And then it was my sister's turn. 'Come on, where's your mother? She's left with her young man, your mother. She's gone with her young man.' And he says, 'Are you going to make me something to put in my mouth, or what? You're all the same. Whores, just like your mother.'

"*Diosito santo.*"

›››

"Believe me, we put up with him for eight days after my mama left, eight whole days. Yes, I think it was eight days later that my papa filed a charge, accusing my mama of having left him. He plopped the three of us on top of the burro and took us to court. And they went and called my mama. She was with my Uncle Miguel.

"The presidente then was Alejos Hernández, Don Alejos. I remember very well how he said, 'Let's see, Don Tomás, what's up? Let's see, here is the señora.'

"'Yes, señor presidente. I accuse this señora because she left my house. She abandoned her children. She left them there in the house, and she came here to be with someone else.'

"'Ah, really? Who is that other person?'

"He says, 'Well, she came to be with another person. She's not alone. She came to be with someone else.'

"'Let's see, Doña Nicolasa. Why did you leave?'

"'Yes, yes, señor, I left. All the years I've been with him have been a life eternal! I had so many, so many children with him. But he's never treated me well. I've suffered so much—he's beaten me so much. He's beat me on the head and everything. And I've never brought a charge against him. Until now, I've never accused him. And I don't accuse him. He accuses me. One day he threatened me with a machete and I escaped. There's no law to help me, but I can't bear him anymore.'

"Her voice fell to a whisper. 'Why have I left? Because I'm hungry and naked, as they say. If I don't raise a goat, if I don't raise a chicken, I haven't got a rag to wear. He tells me I have someone else. Well, let him bring that man here that he speaks of!'

"'Tomás?'

"'And even with that, so what? There was no motive.'

"'Didn't you throw the machete at me? You said you were going to kill me when you got home. Why should I be putting up with it? So many *long* years that I've put up with you! And the life you've given me. It's impossible to put up with so much.'

"'Well,' he says. 'Well, I don't know—I like to have a few drinks.'

"The presidente says, 'No, Don Tomás, that's not what it is.' And he pauses. 'Well, what do you think?'

"'Me? I want to take her back! Because she has her family.'

"She says, 'My family?'

"'Why did you leave without your family?'

"'When I came to live with you, I didn't bring children. So they're yours, too. Support them, or *devour them*! Better that you should devour them! In any case, you don't regard them as family. You regard them as enemies. The way you beat them.'

"'So you won't stay with me?'

"'No, I won't. Even if the law punishes me, I won't stay. Not now, not ever.'

"'There it is, Don Tomás. The señora has stated her reasons.'

"My mama stuck out her chest. She said she wouldn't stay with him. And she didn't.

"'By civil law, you're married,' said Don Alejo, 'but the señora doesn't want to be with you any longer. We're the authorities, but we have no right to keep you together by force. After the way you have behaved, there's nothing else for you to do, Don Tomás, but to support your family. The señora says she won't follow you. So leave her then!

Support your children, take them home. And here on this paper we'll note that you came to a peaceful settlement.'"

› › ›

"Upon arriving back in La Campana, he was in a rage, swearing. Curses and beatings were what we got from him. He ordered us, my sister and me, to cook. The next day he woke up and went back to his drinking. He'd get really drunk. And it was curses!

"Well, Monday passed, Tuesday passed, Wednesday passed, Thursday passed, Friday passed. My mama left pigs behind, the ones she raised. She left pigs, she left chickens, she left goats. And he, in those eight days we were there, sold the best animals. Sold the pigs, sold the chickens, left only the worst ones. And what did he do with all the money? Drinking parties for himself. We didn't have anything to eat in the house, nothing, until he took the mielita to sell.

"On Saturday he went off to sell the miel. And we sat waiting and waiting and waiting. Even my sister, who was the oldest, didn't have the sense to sweep the kitchen or the courtyard or clean out the ashes. We'd wake up and play. There was a wall left from the room he had cut down when it came out too large. We had driven a stick into the wall, and there we'd be, hanging from it, jumping up and down, the three of us, my brother, my sister, and me.

"Well, on Saturday—I still remember that day—Papa went to San Luis. The church bells rang at ten o'clock, then at eleven. It was late. The livestock were bleating with thirst and hunger in their pens. There we were playing and playing. We hadn't eaten anything. And then my sister decided to let out the goats, the few goats left.

"It was during the *nopalito* season. It must have been March, April, around then. My mama left behind three gardens, three gardens my mama left him. By the kitchen and courtyard, there was a nopal, a huge nopal that gave lots of *tunas*, lots of prickly pears.

"Goats will devour the nopales if you let them. They'll just gulp down the little nopalitos in the bud. And he'd say, 'Take out the animals right away to the woods, away from the house.' The house was walled with nopalitos all around.

"So that day we let out the cattle. And the goats got into the nopales. And we're just playing, up and down. It was almost twelve. The goats were just thrilled to be let loose in the nopales. The lambs were pulling up the weeds around there, but the goats could reach the no-pales, and they ate nopales. No! He must have seen them as he got closer to the house.

"'She-goats! You daughters of a goddam mother!'

"*¡Santo entierro!* My sister ran out in a rush, pulling my brother along with her, 'Come on, here comes my Papa.' And I stayed behind like a dumb little monkey.

"He says, 'Daughter of a goddam mother, I'm going to kill you right now!'

"He threw down the jug with the corn, and he grabbed a lasso and came over to me. And he knocked me down! And I fell! He knocked me down from the chimney, and then he grabbed the lasso and tied me up by my neck and took me outside. And my bottom was exposed, though it wasn't the first time he'd seen it. He was always hurling us around. There we were without underwear, without anything. That time he hurled me around until he was exhausted.

"'I'll be back soon, daughter of a goddam mother. And if I return and you don't have anything for me to put in my mouth, I'll kill you once and for all!'

"Ay, Holy Mother. And he went off, talking aloud to himself. He left the jug of corn. So I took out the ashes and lit the fire. My mama had a large pail, and I put the corn in there. I put in the water, put in the lime. I knew how to make nixtamal. Young girl that I was, I knew how.

"So I put the nixtamal on the fire and went to find my sister. She was hiding out in one of the hills in the woods, far away.

"'Hipólita. Hipólita. Hipólita.'

"Then I say, 'Look what he did.' And there I am with the lasso marks etched on me.

"She says, 'Ay, why didn't you run?'

"'How was I going to run? He'd beat me worse.'

"'You deserved it. Why did you stay?'

"'Because you ran away. You think I want to put up with him?'

"Then she says to me, 'Listen, what did he say?'

"'He said that we should make him something to eat, and that he'll be back in a while, and that if in that while we don't have his food ready, he'll kill us.'

"Then she said, 'Listen, you know what? I've been thinking that I want to leave. I'm going with my mama, back to the pueblo,' she says, in a whisper. 'If you want to come with me, let's go. And if you want to stay, then stay! I'm going with my mama. And I'm taking my brother. I'm not going to leave him behind.'

" 'But how will we leave?'

"She says, 'Look, now at about three in the afternoon, we'll put the animals in the pen and we'll leave. If you want to come, let's go. If you want to stay, then stay.'

" 'No, I'm not staying.'

"Then she says, 'Go on, go grind. Make some gordas.'

"I say to her, 'But don't leave me behind, eh? Don't leave me.'

"Scared as I was, I don't know how I did the grinding nor how I made him the gordas. Uneven maybe, but I made some gordas.

"So my sister arrived. We penned up the goats. No sign of anything. It was already four. We left the house—but with what fear! If we saw anybody coming, we'd hide behind a fence of magueyes. It was already late. And my sister was carrying my brother.

"We went along following the brook. We climbed to the clearing, crossed it, and stopped there. Suddenly we saw my father. He was already close to what they call Los Cuatro Vientos. There everything was *milpas*. Now the highway is there. But all of that was milpas! Nopales. Maguey. And he was in the milpas with an uncle of his who's now dead. Buying a maguey.

"And we were going up toward the clearing. And the sun was already setting. The clearing is still like that—you pass by a brook, and you walk a little more and pass another brook, and one comes out to Mexquitic. It seemed to us that he was coming right behind us, to take us back. 'No,' my sister says. 'If he sees us, he'll kill us!' We didn't even know how we made it. As we got past the hill, we said, 'Now we're in Mexquitic. We're free of him at last.' "

›››

"We arrived just as the night was falling. We went with a comadre to find out where my mama was. And Mama starts saying, 'What's happened? Has your father had enough of you? That's why I left without bringing children with me. What did he do to you?'

"We started to cry. And Mama said nothing else. She just said, 'Ah, all right.'

"Then the next day, they called for us at the local court. A message was sent to my mama: present yourself, with your family, at the court.

"'Let's see, Doña Nicolasa. Here the Señor Don Tomás has come to accuse your family of having robbed him. He also wants to know why the children left. He says there was no reason for them to leave.'

"My mama says, 'What was he robbed of? The children didn't rob him, what was robbed was my work that stayed behind. Why did he make the children want to leave? It's his family, and he can't stand them. There's the proof. You didn't want to believe it, Don Alejos.'

"'Let's see, Don Tomás, why?'

"'No, look, I come to accuse these young girls who don't want to be with me. Because I tried to educate them to do the housework, to teach them, they left. They robbed me of some blankets and left me with nothing.'

"'They robbed you? Let's go to the house to bring back what they robbed.' My mama took him on. 'Let's see. You've got all the livestock, right? Who worked for it? I wasn't of any use to you, was I? There are all the chickens, there are all the pigs, right? Isn't that so?'

"'Well,' says the presidente. 'Let's see, how did all this come about?'

"Well, I didn't say a word. Not me. The one who spoke was my sister.

"'This is what happened. The goats ate the nopales. And then he got back from San Luis and we were playing, and he started mistreating us. I ran off, but my sister didn't. He beat her. Look, there are all the bruises on her.'

"Then he says, 'Let me see. Ah, there they are indeed. No, Don Tomás, that's not good. Here we are the authorities,' said Don Alejos, 'but we don't authorize children to be with their parents if they're going to be mistreated. You don't treat your family well.'

"Then my sister spoke up again. 'All he ever does is curse us and mistreat us, calling us whores of our mother.'

"'Look,' my mama says. 'They don't have to suffer because of me. After all, they're his children and he is their father, why should he treat them badly? The fact is that he's no man. He's no man because he's not responsible for his family. He never treats his family well. He treats them worse than animals! An animal you at least show some consideration for. But he shows no consideration for his family. Just the same, I'm not trying to take his children away from him. His daughters came seeking me, and here they are. I tell them to stay with their father, but they don't want to. They've come to me because they know who will take care of them and who will mistreat them. That's not the love of a father for his children.'

"My mama said so many things to him there.

"'Well, well,' the presidente said. 'Here the family will decide. You, little girl, is this man your father?'

"'No, he's not my father!' That's how my sister responded.

"'Is this señora your mother?'

"'Yes, she's my mother.'

"'Then the señor is not your father?'

"'No, he's not my father. And I don't love him now nor ever.' She put it very clearly to them.

"Then the presidente said, 'All right, there it is, there it is, Don Tomás. They don't recognize you as their father. That's it. You lost, Don Tomás. *Ni modo*, eh? So you, Doña Nicolasa, take them home with you.'

"'Well, he will have to give me half of the animals that were left in the house, pigs, chickens, cattle, that I left there,' my mama said. 'The lambs are his. But the goats are mine, because my mama gave them to me and I raised them. And since my daughters took care of them, he has to give me half of the lambs. And I have to get my other things which were left there.'

"The presidente said, 'Yes, very well. Very well.' He says, 'Yes, you may go get your things.'

"And Mama says, 'Yes, señor, I'm going to get them. But I want the comandante to go with me to this man's house so that he'll be sure to give me my things.'

"Well, that's how it was. That's what was agreed.

"We went, my mama and I went with the comandante. My sister no longer wanted to go back. We found him in the house, and he had to give us half the cattle, but he had already sold the best of it. Animals, pigs, nothing was left of them. Just two burros. He gave us a burro. And he had to return all of my mama's things which had stayed there, kitchen things of hers, her metate, her molcajete, because my abuela had given them to her, the mama of my mama.

"So we came back with half a dozen little goats, some lambs, the burro, and the metate and the molcajete. As for the burro, my compadre Diego Hernández, now deceased, asked to borrow it, so it wasn't in our house very long. My mama loaned out the burro so it would eat, right? It was the burro that used to warn us when my papa was getting home from San Luis."

› › ›

"After my mama returned to Mexquitic, my papa took up with someone else, a woman who had been widowed twice. Now he had to have been going around with that vieja already. How is a man going to hook up with another woman in eight days, from one day to the next, if he doesn't already have her? We left with my mama, and the vieja ended up in his house.

"Around that time my mama said to me, 'I want you to take the goats out to pasture, *ándale*. And the lambs. Teach yourself how. Don't fall asleep.'

"So I'd go out with the goats, the lambs. I'd join up with the other goatherds. I wasn't alone. I'd take the old path—that was years before the highway was there, but already there were cars passing by. That's how I spent my time.

"One day I was out there with the cattle when my abuela, the mama of my papa, came. She found me there at the edge of the path.

"She says, 'Silly ones, why did you leave? Your mama cleared a path, and you two followed. Your mama left. Your mama likes pleasure— she didn't want to be with your papa. And you two followed along.'

"'He treated us badly.'

"'Well, you know how he is. You should know how to be patient with your papa. Let's go to the house, *ándale*.'

"Even crazy I wouldn't have gone. I listened with one ear.

"She says, '*Andale*. Let's go home, child.' She says, 'Bring the cattle. Your papa is away. He took the woman to La Laguna. I'm alone, just with your Uncle Celestino. Let's go, so you'll keep me company.'

"She had cattle of her own. 'We'll both go out with the cattle, the two of us,' she says. 'You'll keep your goats there, you'll become a *macha* there. You'll keep the cattle that they gave your mama. It will all be yours. You'll be at home. Look, with me you won't lack for anything. With me you'll have enough to eat, just me and you, just me and you. However you look at it, you'll do well. Come on, hija. What do you say, yes or no? I'm going to mass. And on my way back, you wait for me here, and I'll take you.'

"I wanted to go because my mama, how could she support us? There was hardly enough for her, my brother, and me. I could see very well that she didn't even have enough to hold herself together.

" 'If you want to go with your abuela, go. But take the goats,' my mama said. 'Go, let her support you, so you'll eat something of your papa's at least, something of what I worked for. There will be nopales left. At least go eat them, *ándale*. When you're ready to come back, bring the cattle.'

"The following Sunday my abuela came to mass. She had sweets for me, and *gordas de horno*, and everything I could want to eat. 'Here, hija. Let's go.'

"Well, let's go! And there I went."

› › ›

"*¡Híjole!* Now what's to come. Mine is a very long life, a very long historia, comadre!

"So, she took me with her, leading my cattle through the path with her cattle. And then I suffered a black life with her.

"She gave me food to eat, but then it was, 'Come on, hija, to the hills. Bring me firewood. Now bring me water. *Andale*, wash the dish. *Andale*. Grind the nixtamal. *Andale*.'

"She taught me where to go with the cattle. 'You'll come back through the hills. This field is mine. Look, hija, I have a lot of fields for you to inherit. If you lean on me, when your papa returns you can get together with him, and you will become the owner of all these fields. Look, I've got land, your papa's got land. Now that your sister and your mama don't want to be here—well, help yourself. Stay put here.'

"Yes, she egged me on, however she could. Those months passed. More and more and more, more drudgery from her. I don't know if it was laziness on my part or what. She said a lot of things to me. She'd also speak to me just like my papa did. She'd say such words to me, as though I were already a grown-up woman, such ugly things she'd say. She gave me food to eat, but mistreating me the whole time. When she wanted to, she also had her drinks.

"I had been with her for about half a year when the day arrived that my papa returned with his mistress.

"'Good evening.'

"'Good evening.'

"'Were you asleep, Mama?'

"He didn't know I was there.

"Then she says, 'Ah, hijo. So you're back?'

"'Yes, we're back. Just now,' he says.

"'I'm very pleased, hijo,' and who knows what else. 'I bet you don't know who I've got here? Your daughter.'

"'My daughter? Didn't they say that I'm not their papa? So what do they want? What are they looking for?'

"She says, 'But it's not the one who said you weren't her papa.'

"'Then who?'

"'Well, Esperanza.'

"'Didn't she also say no? What does she goddam want with me here?'

"'Quiet! The poor thing has been here for a few months already,' she says. 'I found her, poor thing, with her mouth dry. I told her to come with me.'

"'Ah, they're having such a good time with their mother that they're coming back here.'

"No, he hurled curses, insults. I just listened, as though I were a little rat lying there.

"They went to sleep at the woman's house. Then another day dawned. No, lord of my soul. The next day he came to my abuela's house. With him back, I really needed to make the sign of the cross over myself.

"'I'm going to take her, Mama.'

"'Yes, take her, she's your daughter. Take her.' She says, 'Let her go do something for you, sweep for you there. She should come back to take the cattle out. She's here with cattle and all.'

"He sent me ahead to sweep up the house. Then they went to the woman's house. They went to get the burros and their suitcases and returned. Then my papa says, 'Obey what this woman tells you. In place of your mother, you have to do what she says you ought to do.' And to the woman he said, 'Give her orders. Tell her to bring you fire-

44

wood. Tell her to bring you water. And hit her so she'll wash the dishes. Tell her to grind the nixtamal and put the nixtamal on to cook.'

"Well, I put up with it that day and the next. Since I was back, they lived in my papa's house. They would lock themselves up in their room. When I'd wake up, he'd scream, 'Esperanza!'

"'¡Mande!'

"'Did you light the fire? Did you light the stove?'

"Then one day I was lolling about, who knows for how long, with the metate. It was the metate that the vieja had brought from her house. I had to grind in the metate, grind up the nixtamal. And if I wasn't grinding the nixtamal, I had to be bringing water or firewood. That day, she said to me, '*Andale*, you know what your papa ordered you to do. Why don't you do as you're told? Go bring me water. Let's see what your mother taught you.'

"And I talked back to her. 'Ay, how you order me around, as though you were my mama.' No, I answered her badly. No, lord of my soul, he came back, my papa. And she told him. And he turned me into a dancing dog. And off they went to the vieja's house. They left and I stayed behind, crumpled up in a corner, because he beat the hell out of me.

"I said to myself, 'I'm leaving because I'm leaving.'

"What did I bring back with me? A sackcloth. A huge sackcloth, which is what they gave me to cover myself with, a sackcloth we had brought back from La Laguna. I left secretly, all by myself. At midday. They didn't even see me. They expected to find me, expected me to have brought them water. And I came back to my mama again!

"Ay, but my mama gave me such a good scolding. But not even crazy I would go back with my abuela. And then she said, 'Did you like it? *Andale*, just you and your stepmother? Wasn't your abuela going to leave you the inheritance? You see?'

"Ay, ay, ay.

"'And the goats?'

"'They're with my abuela,' I whispered.

"Before eight days had passed, we went to get the cattle back from my abuela. When we got there, my mama was feeling courageous. She intended to grab the vieja there in the house and beat her, but the vieja ran away. In the house, Mama found a stick and she beat at the walls

45

with it, scraping up the adobe. That was the house where we had lived. Then we went to my abuela's house and got our cattle back. There were already little goats that the she-goats had borne.

"My mama said, 'Now they're going to accuse me of having gone there and torn the room apart, and of having made the vieja run away.' But my papa didn't even accuse my mama. Nothing. It was all over between them."

›››

"So we stayed with my mama. My mama worked for my comadre Mariana, and from that she supported us.

"One of our lambs was eaten by the coyote, several others died, and the three goats that remained my mama gave to a man who guarded cattle every day.

"The years passed. My mama didn't have the means to send us to school. Neither me nor my sister. I finished the first grade of elementary school and that was it. My sister got to the third grade. My younger brother did even less.

"That's when the *finadita* Mariana spoke to my mama about how I was just sitting around. My sister was working for Doña Tomasa as a *pilmama*. So the finadita Mariana got me to watch over the turkey with the little turkeys.

"My mama used to send me to the river. I'd sit there with the turkey. They would give me my food, and I would return at four, with the turkey and her little turkeys. Day after day, day after day with the little turkeys, until the little turkeys grew big. Turkeys grow eating in places where there are watercresses. Chickens are wily. Not little turkeys.

"Well, they were already getting big. And then, yes, everything came together in me. Was it living through those bad times, all the sun I got, the months I spent with my abuela? All that came together in me. My head hurt—the pain would go away and then come back. There was a day when I was sitting on a rock and, out of the blue, it came. Drip and drip and drip. The rock was being bathed with blood. I couldn't move. If I stood up, it all came dripping down. So I just sat there with my head burning, trying to take care of the turkey with her little turkeys. They had gone into the thicket, there by the dam. There used to be quite a thicket there; now there's nothing. I felt dizzy, but I grabbed the turkey and started walking. I used to put the turkeys in a bag, and the big turkey I'd carry in my arms. I struggled going up the path, trying to snatch up the little turkeys. And there I was swallowing blood. I was covered with it. At last I got home.

"I knocked on the door. My mama opened the door and down I fell, on top of the turkeys!

"'What's happened, woman?' My mama saw me like that, covered with blood. 'Muchacha, you're going to kill those turkeys.' My mama got scared. 'Who hit you? Did you fall? What happened to you?'

"I couldn't talk. I kept swallowing it all.

"'Blood came out of my nose.'

"'When?' she said.

"'A while ago.'

"'*Ave María Purísima*. What am I going to do?' Mama sat me down. Then my mama went to my comadre Mariana's to ask for alcohol. And she said, 'Oh, dear God, did she fall?'

"'No, she says that blood came out of her nose. She says she left a trail of blood.'

"'For heaven sakes, little one, why didn't you come back? Were you going to keep waiting there, dying, fainting?' That's what my comadre Mariana said to me. 'What was it, muchacha? Did you sit in the sun or what?'

"'No, my head hurts.'

"'Rub her with alcohol. Rub her with alcohol—there's the bottle.'

"Mama rubbed me with alcohol. And then the very blood that was dripping and dripping, my mama would spread that very blood on me.

"'Rub her down with the blood so that she'll feel revolted by it and it'll stop.'

"They rubbed me down with my very own blood, they piled it on. Ay, dear God. At least that calmed it.

"The next day, they sent me out again with the animals. 'But don't sit in the sun,' they said, 'because it's bad for you.'

"The next day, again the same thing happened. That time I just barely made it home. Then my comadre said, 'Put her to bed.'

"At that time Don Juan González was very ill. And a doctor came from San Luis to cure Don Juan. That was lucky for me. My comadre Mariana said, 'Ay, Nicolasa, don't let the girl die.'

"'Well, it must be from the bad times she's been through. She was with her abuela for a while—God knows what her abuela did to her. I don't know why she's ended up with this. Or might it be from the time her papa beat her? She must have gotten hit in the lungs—I don't know. Their papa beat them a lot. This one he hung,' she says.

"'Well, maybe that's what she has.' Mariana says, 'No, Nicolasa. Go on, look, the doctor is there with Juan. Tell him to please do you the favor of coming to see the child.'

"My mama went. And the doctor came to see me at home. He started to examine me. And he says, 'Ay.' He says, 'Listen, this girl is very ill. This girl must have fallen. She's got a hemorrhage in her brain. What did you do to her? Did you hit her? Or did she fall? She's got a bad head wound. She could go at any moment.'

"Then my mama said to him, 'Well, doctor, the very truth is that when she was so many years old, her father, the man I used to have, her father, hung her.'

"'Hung her? This child?'

"She says, 'Yes, he hung her.'

"'And what was the reason?'

"'Well, there wasn't one. He hung her feet up, head down, and just left her hanging for a while.'

"He says, '¡Qué bárbaro! So you're no longer with this man?'

"'No.'

"'Well, that's what she has. All her blood went up to her head and now she's weak. It's a hemorrhage, what she has. If she recovers from this, it will be a miracle. She'll either get better or die.' He says, 'How old is she?'

"'She's nine,' my mama whispered.

"'She's been badly abused, badly tended. You should take better care of this child.' Then he says, 'But here's this medicine.'

"They gave me the medicine. I don't know what it could have been, but they went and filled the prescription. Holy cure! Blessed be God.

"'I won't send you out with the turkeys anymore,' my mama said. 'They're already big and anyway there are no more watercresses left for them.'"

› › ›

"And then it happened that the daughter-in-law of my sister's *patrona* needed a *muchacha*, a girl to help her. My mama said, 'Hija, you're going to go to San Luis. You're fine now. Nothing hurts you. It's clear that you're better. I don't want you to be around the house. And I can't send you out into the sun. You're going to go work as a pilmama. You'll live close to where your sister lives. If you want to go see her, she'll be right there.'

"I was so afraid.

"'Come on, hija. Look, there you're going to eat well. Here you know how it is.'

"I was almost ten years old when she took me to be a pilmama. They told me that all I had to do was carry the child in my arms. But when my mama left, how I cried! The only consolation I had was that my sister was there and the houses were near one another.

"To eat they'd give me a little centavo bun, a little bun that used to cost a centavo. And three little tortillas. And a teaspoon of whatever the meal was. And they put me to bed in a room where there were lots of rats! During the day I took care of the child, carried the child around, but at night they put me in a room that was horrible.

"The patrona would say to me, 'Look, you want to go out for a while? There's your sister, go with your sister. Just take the boy—but care for him, don't drop him. Anyway, my mother-in-law is there. You can come back later.'

"I told my sister everything about the way I was being treated. So she told her patrona, 'Look, señora, my sister says this and that about the señora. She says she doesn't want to stay because they make her sleep where there are lots of rats.'

"'Yes, Maria Luisa is very dirty. She's very rough. Why don't you come here? If you don't want to be there, then come here.'

"'I've only been there eight days, but I don't want to stay. Today I'm going to tell my mama that I don't want to be there, because they put me to sleep where there are lots of rats. And to top it off, the child eats a lot.'

"How much he ate! And then, for me, a little bun, and three little tortillas. So my sister told her patrona that I would work for her, too.

"There were just two people where my sister was, the señora and the señor, and what a huge house they had! My sister swept, washed floors, cleaned dishes, cooked, for the two people. Outside they had a long, long space that was pure lawn. My sister couldn't keep it weeded. So the señora asked me to water the lawn. Every other day I'd water it and weed it, pulling out all the dry leaves from the grass. That's what I did. We earned three pesos a month. Three pesos. But do you know that with three pesos we bought shoes, we bought a dress, everything. Cheap. Three pesos, eh?

"But we were hungry. They'd give us a spoonful of this and a spoonful of that. 'That's for you.' And the coffee that we boiled for them, we made in a special little pot for them, with their milk especially for them, too. And to the coffee grounds that were left, we had to add water. 'Pour water in, kids, because this coffee still has a lot of strength. Don't throw that coffee away. Put water in it and that will be for you.' And they'd give us a quarter container of milk. A quarter of a liter for each one of us. That was the milk. The viejita, the señora, would say, 'Here's your milk. One for you, one for you.' A little one-centavo roll. That was it. Day after day. At dinner, the leftovers of the food they had eaten, the little bit that was left, was for us. 'Save that for your supper, or have frijoles and the milk and the roll.' *Híjole*, we were hungry.

"The señora would say, 'Here, bring me three centavos, five centavos worth of bone for the dog.' At the butcher shops they used to sell these huge portions of bones. Maybe meat was cheaper, or there were more animals, more cows—I don't know. They'd almost give away those portions of bones for the dogs. And there was some meat on those bones. Skin here, nerves there, some meat—but for the dog. 'Boil it. Serve those bones to the dog. After they've cooled, give them to the dog.' That was the dog's supper. In the morning, the dog would get some milk with coffee, whatever they left in their cups with a piece of bread or bits of sweet rolls. The dog got that. Big dog, a big huge dog. And my sister and I would eat the bones meant for the dog!

"I lasted a year there. I got used to it. At least my sister and I were together. Then I don't know how it was that I got out of there, but I went to another house. Alone. I was a pilmama, for a lawyer. I was older by then. With the lawyer I lasted a year and a half. Then I left. But my sister and I saw each other every eight days. More or less, we managed. Then a señora, who's now dead, ran into my sister and me in the street, and she said, 'How much do you earn there?'

"'Ten pesos.'

"So again my sister and I got together, and that time we both worked in a luncheonette near the Hidalgo Market. The owners were from Guadalajara. And they had a luncheonette. There we worked nights, because they made *pozole, tostadas, tortas*, everything. That was night work. During the day we cut up onions, tomatoes, lettuce, put the pozole on to cook, put pigfeet on to cook, cow feet on to cook, the tender calf pieces. That was the pozole. Then we cut up lemon, radishes. No, we had work to do. But we did eat well. We cooked, and in the evening we waitressed until midnight. People went to the movies and came out at midnight and the luncheonette would fill up.

"We lasted for a while in that luncheonette. There we had our first photograph taken of ourselves. We were earning fifteen pesos. We had a good time, though it was tough in the evenings. We'd go to bed at one o'clock, one-thirty, two in the morning, and then get up early the next day. It was tough. And then we got bored.

"Somehow we heard that somewhere else they paid more. So the two of us took off again. I went to another house. My sister, with a different señora. By then we were each earning eighteen pesos.

"I ended up with two viejitos. I was already fifteen by that time. At that house it was a sister-in-law living with a brother-in-law. The sister had died, the wife of the señor, and the sister-in-law, who had never married, remained in the house. The señor paid me, and I'd help the señorita. What I had to do was sweep the front steps and the front room, care for the lawn, sweep the señorita's room, the dining room, and the kitchen. And I had to cook. The señor's room I hardly touched at all. I did very little for him because he always said, 'Don't do my room every day. Just once a week.' He was one of those retired viejitos.

"I was happy there. I spent over a year and a half there, almost two years. Then the viejita said, 'Look, I'm going back to my *tierra*, to León. Miguel will stay by himself. The house is his, and he's about to sell it. Miguel says that if I leave, you can't stay here. If he's alone he can go eat at a hotel. Don't say we're throwing you out, but you can start looking for something else.'

"After the viejitos I found another job, near Reforma. There I lasted less than half a year. I was already sixteen, seventeen. I went to work with a daughter and her father. I lasted a short time, because the daughter had a boyfriend and sometimes she would leave me alone with her father, and I didn't like that. I was always suspicious. So I left.

"My sister was living nearby. We were always close to one another. I told my sister I was leaving my job. And she told her patrona, who

said, 'You know what, María is sick, and now she's got a daughter.
Who knows if she'll come back to work in the kitchen.' She had a
beauty parlor, the patrona. 'Why don't you come here?'

"I lasted there for close to a year working as a cook. No, it was a
happy life. The señora's name was Lola. She's still alive. We had a good
time working for her."

› › ›

"At that time we were at our peak, already nineteen, twenty years
old. And then it was my turn to lose.

"We'd come back to Mexquitic every year, my sister and I, for the
fiesta for San Miguel. They gave us some vacation time. They gave us
eight days, I think. And during those eight days, the hawk swept me
up!"

Esperanza laughs heartily. She has been talking continuously for almost three hours.

"When I got married, my sister scolded me. She said, 'So you've gotten tired of supporting my mama? You've gotten tired of giving her
money? There where you're going, you won't suffer, you won't have to
work.'

"No! She threw salt on me!" Esperanza's giddy laughter fills the
nighttime stillness. "Well, comadre, I told you my life was very long.
And I'm not even up to the middle yet."

"It's very interesting," I reply unwittingly.

Still laughing, Esperanza exclaims, "My comadre! Everything is interesting, isn't it?"

It's already after midnight and her younger son, Mario, rubbing the
sleep from his eyes, says, "The cock is going to crow soon!"

"Comadre, and I've still got to tell you about what happened when I
returned to Mexquitic. That's the really good part, what's still to come,
that life eternal. Maybe I'll even start crying. The life I lived."

Again she laughs, but more cautiously now. "As I say, my life is an
historia, a great big historia. It's a movie. To suffer just like my mama.
Here"—pointing to the space between her brows—"he kicked me
twice. Here"—pointing to the side of her head—"he threw a machete
at me. And I suffered the same life as my mama."

The Cross of the White Wedding Dress

*Sometimes Pedro and I have quarrels and he hits me and I get
angry. When I am very angry, I become ill. Then I don't know
what to do. I want to shout as though I were drunk and soon
my stomach hurts me. . . . Then I feel something like a bird
flying in my breast. I feel the wings beating and hitting me
inside my breast.*

—*"Esperanza," speaking to Oscar Lewis,* **Pedro Martínez**

If I can never own nothing, he told her, I will have women.

—**Alice Walker,** **The Third Life of Grange Copeland**

*The first time she had been so surprised she didn't cry out or
try to defend herself. She had always said she would fight
back if a man, any man, were to strike her. But when the moment came, and he slapped her once, and then again, and
again, until the lip split and bled an orchid of blood, she
didn't fight back, she didn't break into tears, she didn't run
away as she imagined she might when she saw such things in
the telenovelas. . . . Instead, when it happened the first time,
when they were barely man and wife, she had been so
stunned it left her speechless, motionless, numb. She had done
nothing but reach up to the heat on her mouth and stare at
the blood on her hand as if even then she didn't understand.*

—**Sandra Cisneros, "Woman Hollering Creek"**

*July 2, 1985. After hearing about her childhood in the nearby rancho
of La Campana, I was curious to go there with my comadre and see
what it was like. "Pues vamos, comadre," Esperanza immediately
said. "Mañana vamos." She was excited, it seemed to me, that her*

story had so sparked my interest. We set off, late morning, as a light drizzle fell with the sun still half-shining. We could have taken the bus or our car, but Esperanza insisted we walk. Soon it began to really rain and then it began pouring. There was no place to go for cover without getting pinched or stabbed by prickly magueyes and nopales, so we just kept on walking. By the time we got to La Campana, a clearing of a few scattered houses, it had stopped raining. "This is where I was born," Esperanza announced, unfolding her damp rebozo, from which she had improvised a rain hat. "In this little rancho, comadre. Now you've seen it with your own eyes." That evening, Esperanza returned with Norberta and Mario. "Maybe you're going to get tired of seeing so much of us," she exclaimed as they came in, single file, through the narrow wooden door and shook my hand. "Oh, no, of course not," I said, leading the way through the courtyard and into the kitchen. We took exactly the same seats as the night before, and Esperanza got right into her story.

"Have I told you that when I got married they registered me as being eighteen years old? They couldn't find me in the records, so they put me down as being eighteen.

"As for the man, well, he was from Mexquitic. And I was working in San Luis. And every time I came back, he'd see me. I'd go down the street, and he'd dart out at me. I didn't pay any attention. And then he'd say to me, 'Ohhhhh! So proud, aren't you?'

"I'd pass by, as though nothing had happened. And I'd tell my mama. And she would say, 'No, no, no. Go to your job. Go to your job.'

"And the father of the other boyfriend I had would tell me to believe in his son, that he was going to leave his other girlfriend, but I decided I didn't want him. And so I said, 'Noooo. No, no.' And his father would say, 'Stay with my son and things will go well for you.' And I said, 'No, that's fine, but he has someone else.' And he would say, 'Ah, but she has someone else, too. She's got someone else and they've got a child. You'd be better.' And I, 'Well, yes, but no.' The father and the son nagged me a lot, but I was the one who refused.

"Every time I came back, he'd see me. He'd wander around, he'd go to the hills, and sometimes he'd whistle and whistle. And my mama would say, 'Ohhhh, what goldfinches are those that just see the flowers and start to sing?' Goldfinches singing? It was him hanging around.

54

"'Esperanza, *qué hubo?*' he'd say. And he'd say things about my other boyfriend.

"Just as he'd be talking to me, my mama would call, '*Andale*, girl, what are you doing?'

"'Oh, nothing. I'm coming.'

"And I'd go inside again. That was as much as I talked with him. And that's how it went on. No, I had nothing to do with him. Nothing. Just, '*¿Qué hubo?*' and '*¿Qué hubo?*'

"I don't know. I didn't plan on going off with him. But he'd talk to my younger sister, the one who's married in San Luis; she was eight years old at the time.

"'Juana!' he'd yell as he'd come up this way. 'Juana! Call Esperanza. I want her to come out and talk to me.'

"He'd come secretly, without my mama knowing, when she was out selling pulque. The next day he was back again. There he was knocking.

"'Ah, Esperanza,' my sister would whisper. 'It's Julio. He says, "Juana, Juana, tell your sister to give me a little water."'

"And I said, 'Ask him if he doesn't see the dam?'

"Well, everything I said then, he sang back to me afterward when I lived with him.

"My sister repeated what I had said to him, 'She says that don't you see there's a dam?'

"And he said, 'No, I want the water to come from her. Tell her to give me a little water, to come here.' He knew my mama was out selling on the street.

"So I finally came out. And he said, 'Come on, Esperanza, bring me a little water.'

"'You want me to give you water? Don't you see the dam there?'

"'Ohhhh, why so angry? You, so angry. What are you thinking?'

"'What do you care about what I think?'

"He says, 'Ohhhh, how proud.'

"And there he was at the door of the house. There he was at the very entrance. There he was.

"'Well, yes, *ándale*. Don't be mean. Give me a little water.'

"'Get him some water! Juana!' My sister brought him the water. There he was with my sister. Who knows what he said to her. I put on my rebozo and snuck out through the back of the house. I left him there with the girl and went to find my mama. But all she said to me was, 'Why did you come? Go on, go home. I don't want people saying that I have my daughter here so the men will come over and buy pulque from me. No, go home.'

"'All right, I'm going.'

"It was the thirtieth of December. And the next day was the New Year. My mama got back at about five and said, 'Go get the miel, *ándale*. It's time for the raspa of the magueyes.' We had three magueyes in the garden of that Don Tacho Martínez. And my younger brother says, 'I'm not going.'

"And my mama, 'Yes, go with Esperanza.'

"'No, I'm not going.'

"I said to my mama, 'He doesn't have to go with me. I don't need him to follow me.'

"'Well, *ándale*. Go get the miel. But don't take too long.'"

›››

"So off I went down the street, and he saw me going alone. Well, what do you expect? I'm there working on the magueyes when, *zas!* He grabs me from behind. I was leaning forward, getting the miel out of the magueyes. I didn't even see how he got into the garden. *¡Zas!* And he comes around and pinches me in the ribs.

"'And you, why do you grab me?' I could see he was drunk. 'Let go of me!'

"'How can I let go of you? I won't let you go.'

"'What do you mean you won't let go?' I said. 'Do you rule over me, or what?'

"Then he says, 'Oh, *chi*. Why so delicate?'

"I said to him, 'Look, get away, move back, or I'll hit you with this scraper, eh?' I was cleaning out the maguey with the scraper. When I was done, I grabbed the pail and the scraper and got ready to leave.

"As I started walking away, he grabbed me by the braids. I said to him, 'Listen, those are not proper manners. Why are you doing that?'

"'So you won't go.'

"'So I won't go? I've got nothing to do with you.'

"He says, 'Since you've had nothing to do with me before, now you will.'

" 'Not if you force me.' I picked up a rock. 'Are you going to let go of my braids or not? If you don't let go, I'll throw this rock at you.'

"So there we were, I saying no, no, and no, and no, that no and no, and he, look, that this, and yes—who knows what. Well, it got late. The sun set and it got dark, and I said to him, 'Now let me go.'

"That was when he grabbed my rebozo. But I pulled myself away and unwound myself and left him clinging to my rebozo. Then I bent down to pick up the pail and he tried to grab me again. 'Listen,' I said. 'You know, not that way. That's not how you treat a woman.'

"The night had fallen. There he was, holding onto the rebozo. I was without my rebozo, just with my pail of miel.

" 'Come on,' he says. 'Let's go to my house.'

" 'No, not me. I've got nothing to do at your house.'

"We came out near where the Pachecos have their house. His mama had another house there. And he says to me, 'Come here. Now go inside.'

" 'I'm not.' And then I said to him, 'Let go of me. My mama must be looking for me.'

" 'Well, now it's impossible for your mama to find you.'

"It was 1949. The big New Year's dance was going on in the presidencia. We battled it out all night, he wanting to do his things with me and I not letting him. We spent the whole night like that. He didn't get me to step inside his house, nor did we go to the dance. It was a battle in the night. And then it was almost dawn. Before people could see us, we went to find his mama.

"Sometimes, I think now, I could have run off. Nothing had happened. I could have gone to my mama, or returned to San Luis. But I thought, if I go home to my mama, what a beating she'll give me. And I said to myself, well, regardless of what my mama may think, I know that nothing happened to me. But the talk of everyone would be that I spent the night with him. People were not going to think that I passed the time so decently; people were going to speak badly of me, and all that was going to hurt my reputation. Now that I'm in this, I thought, I may as well go on with it.

" 'Well,' he says. 'Let's go. Come in. Come inside.'

" 'No, I'm not going inside.'

" 'All right,' he says. 'I'm going to tell my mama.'

" 'Tell your mama. If she's in agreement, yes. If not, I'll leave. After all, I didn't lose anything, as they say.'

"So he went in to see his mama. She and her man were asleep inside when he went to speak to them. He told them everything, who he was bringing over and who not.

" 'Well, bring her in, bring her in. Why don't you invite her in? Why do you have her waiting outside? Bring her in.'

" 'She doesn't want to come in.'

"He was in there for a while, maybe fifteen minutes. At last, he came out. He says, 'Come inside. My mama says for you to come in.' Then I went in. And that was it.

" 'Come in, young woman,' she says. 'Come inside. What happened? Sit here. Let's see, sit here.' And she makes the sign of the cross over me. She makes the sign of the cross and then says, 'Listen, what's your reason for going with my young man?'

" 'I came because he promised to marry me. He's going to do his duty by me.' Then I said, 'That's why I came, and if not, nothing's lost. If you're not in agreement, I'll go away. After all, I didn't do anything.'

" 'Is that so, son? Is it true that you're prepared to do your duty by her?'

" 'Well, yes. That's what I said to her, that I'd marry her.'

" 'Ah, very good.' And she says, 'Will your mama be in agreement?'

" 'Who knows?' I said.

"We were settled. 'Now in a little while, when it dawns, you should go see your mama.' "

› › ›

"No! Lord of my soul. Just at the break of dawn, I got ready to step outside. My mama had been looking for me during the night. Then she asked my sister to tell her with whom she had seen me hanging around. The next day, as soon as the dawn had broken, she left for their house. I was on the doorstep when I saw her glaring at me.

" 'Get away! Shameless!' she said.

"What could I say? Such embarrassment, such shame.

" 'Very soon you'll pay for this.'

"She had come to accuse me. She filed a charge against us. But soon after, my mother-in-law patched things up. She got Blas, now deceased, who had been presidente, to serve as her spokesman. 'No, don't worry.

We'll triumph over the señora. She's going to have to give in. You'll see. Don't you worry.'

"'And now that she's filed a charge?'

"'She will only sue you if your son doesn't do his duty by her daughter. But, after all, your son is going to marry her, right?'

"'Yes, the young man is prepared to marry her.'

"'So she can't do anything. Out of rage, maybe, she had to do what she did—but you'll see, in a little while we'll convince her.'

"My mama brought us to court. She was furious when she arrived. Then Blas arrived. Then came my mother-in-law and Don Simeón, the man who lived with her. He wasn't my man's father. He had been born under his authority, that's all.

"'Doña Nicolasa, they're going to do their duty by your daughter. How terrible it would have been if she had just been kept busy, day or night, if she had been kept busy and then not had her duty done by her. But the young man is going to marry your daughter. Give thanks that your daughter won't be going around falling, that she won't be *fracasando* somewhere else. At least now there's someone who's going to take her in,' Don Blas says.

"That's how my mama was won over. But my mama also spoke up. 'Well, if he's such a man and can keep his word, then I want them to go to church once and for all.'

"They took us to the church right away, found witnesses for me, witnesses for him. My mama gave her permission. 'I want him to marry her. If he just wanted a good laugh at her expense, then today he's going to do his duty by her.'

"No, it would have been better for me if she had just let me be as I was!

"It was January of 1949. My mama got tough. Right away she had them put the yoke on me. 'In fifteen days, she'll be married in a civil ceremony. And before the month ends, they've got to get married in church.'

"As for the priest, he said, 'The señorita, after all, was abducted, *robada*. She was not *pedida*, he did not ask for her hand. But that's all right. She's not going to be with the young man now until they get married by the church.'

"So my mama took me back home, and did she give me some good scoldings! I was so sorry. How had I allowed myself to be so deceived?

How was I convinced from one moment to the next, I who had nothing to do with him? Afterward, when I was with him, he repeated everything I had said to him. No! Afterward he treated me very badly."

› › ›

"Fifteen days later, we were married in a civil ceremony. 'In so many days she will be married by the church. She will have to learn the *doctrina*, and he too.' But Julio was a good friend of Padre Herminio, who let him get married without learning the doctrina. He couldn't recite any of it. But I could. I learned the doctrina and I confessed.

"Since I had gone off with my *novio*, I didn't have the right to wear a *corona*, a crown. Only a veil. My godmother curled it up in the form of a crown and put it on my head. The priest had said, 'All those brides who have been abducted, who go off with their grooms, cannot wear crowns. To church they cannot wear a crown. The ones who may wear a crown to church are the ones who've been pedidas.'

"Even if the godparents said, 'Padre, we'll pay. What will you charge us so that the bride will be able to wear a crown?' he'd say, 'No, I won't allow it.'

"Well, I thought to myself, I'm not the only one. Many, many girls didn't wear crowns. One time I saw a girl, who I guess had gone off with her novio. The godmother must have put the crown on her anyway. And then the priest said, 'Let's see, who is the godmother? Where are the godparents of the bridal couple?'

"The godmother said, 'Padre, here I am.'

"'Let's see, was her hand asked for? Was she pedida?'

"'Well, no. No, Padre, no.'

"'Haven't they told you that here the brides who run off can't wear a crown when they get married?'

"And the padre reached over and pulled the crown off! Poor young man, poor bride! The bride was put to shame, she and her godmother.

"So when it was my turn—well, I, too, had just run off. Nothing to be done about that. I didn't wear a crown, so? It wasn't just me. But afterward priests like Padre Samuel would say, 'For my part, put horns on if you want. Wear horns! Put on whatever you want. All I care about is that you come closer to the grace of God, that you get married, that you not be living together just like that.' Since Padre Samuel, they all wear crowns, whether they've been asked for or not, they go *corona-das*. But when I got married, that other padre was much stricter."

› › ›

"Back then, they used to hold a vigil for the bride and groom the night before the wedding. He had his vigil in the *jacal*, and I had my vigil in the room where my mother-in-law sold her pulque. They lit a candle for each of us.

"My mama stopped by for a while and then left. And there I was with my godmother. They sat me down on a chair and my godmother next to me and the big candle there burning.

"And my godmother says, 'Ah, what a girl.' She says, 'How old are you? What work do you do, and where did you live, and who's your mama?' She was trying to get me to talk. Then it was midnight, then it was one o'clock.

"My mother-in-law and her people were outside slaughtering the pigs and making the *mole* for the next day when we would be married. No, they made a good *molazo*. They slaughtered a pig, a lamb.

"'You're getting sleepy, comadre,' my mother-in-law says, coming into the room. 'Lie down here, comadre.' And to me, 'You, girl, there's a lambskin, lie down there, so you'll get some sleep.'

"The candle kept burning. The next day, we woke up around six. And then it was, 'Get ready, get up,' and then it was eight, and then it was nine. I got married on a Thursday, during the week, in a private wedding. The mass was between nine and ten, I think.

"As the bells began to toll for the first time, they took out the wedding dress. The dress was made by Doña Clara Vásquez. His family had the dress made for me, and they bought me shoes.

"When I went to be measured for the dress, Doña Clara said to me, 'So, you're getting married, young woman?'

"'Yes.'

"She says, 'Good, but be careful.' She says, 'A white wedding dress is very beautiful but also very punishing.'

"Why did she say that to me? It made me giggle.

"Then she says, 'Well, young woman, let's see how it goes for you. Sit for a while, little thing. What a girl. How did you believe Julio?'

"So she said that to me. And Doña Chela, now deceased, who was teaching me the doctrina, she told me the same thing. She says, 'Girl, weren't you doing all right at your job? Now you're going to be so-and-so's daughter-in-law?'

"'Well, yes.'

"'You're going to marry?' she says. '*Tonta*. You're a tonta.'

"That's what the deceased Chela said. She was very close to the padre. All the brides ended up with Doña Chela. And Doña Chela would teach them the doctrina. There was a great big book, a thick, thick, thick, thick book that belonged to Padre Herminio, and he'd lend it to the deceased Doña Chela, so that from there she could teach the brides about what they had to do and what marriage was about.

"Then Doña Chela said to me, 'You tonta, why did you go end up with those women? Those women go in and out. They're *mujeres del gusto*. And that's where you decided to end up. Now you'll see what will happen to you, the life you're going to have.'

"'Why?' I said.

"'Don't you see what the daughter is like? And then your mother-in-law—who is she? That Julio isn't even a son of Don Simeón. That Julio is a son of Don Teodomiro. It's just that Don Simeón took him in. That Timotea brought him along when she joined up with Simeón. He's just a son of his because he was born under his authority. But he's not really a son of Simeón. So, you see? How did you let yourself be deceived? Well, now you're ruined.'

"'Well, yes,' I said, and went and told my mama. And my mama says, 'You see? They told you. They're telling you. I already told you. But you didn't want to understand. Why didn't you tell me that pelado was going around wooing you?'

"'I don't know.' And now sometimes I say to her, 'But you, Mama, too, why did you give permission for me to get married right away?'

"'And why would I have wanted you the way you were?' She says, 'You weren't so innocent there all night. So look, go ahead and take her.'

"'You think wrong of me.'

"'And I bet that pelado was going to just let you sit around?'

"'No, it's not true. Why did you go and marry me off? I was without a care,' I told her. 'Of course, he had left me a little tattered, but nothing else.'

"'Well, I doubt it. I believe it, and I don't believe it.'

"'No, Mama. Why did you go and give permission for me to get married at once? And, if he had done something, so what? We wouldn't have married; we'd be as we were. And if I had a child, or had two, or however many, but if I saw that I was having a bad life, I'd leave him. But I wouldn't be weighed down by books. Church books!'"

›››

"And that was it. We got married that day.

"In the morning, my mama brought me a bouquet of flowers my sister had gotten for me. In the past the brides had natural flowers in their bouquets, not artificial ones like they do today. All the brides carried a bouquet of calla lilies.

"My godmother dressed me, got me ready. 'There goes the bride!' They had two big candles in church. Now they don't have them anymore. They had two huge candleholders, each with a candle. And they made you kneel before them. One candle for each.

"My sister, my mama, and the godmother who had baptized me went to the mass. And straight away they went home. They didn't wait to be taken to my mother-in-law's. They left after mass and went home.

"Everyone threw confetti and candies at us. The candy balls bounced off our heads. There used to be some big candy balls. I guess you didn't get to see them. No photographs were taken; there was nothing of that. Whoever wanted photographs in those days had to go to San Luis.

"That day passed. I spent it alone with his people, because none of my people, none of them, came. My mama had been angry with my mother-in-law for years. They had a quarrel of many years' standing. My mama said, 'Didn't you know that I can't stand that vieja? Why did you go end up with her? What, didn't you know?' That's why my mama warned me, 'When you get married, don't expect me to visit you. And she didn't come see me. I spent the day alone."

›››

Eight days after we married, I stepped out as far as the front door to peek at the street. I took it as a joke that it was the same thing to be single as to be married. I went to the door, leaned out. I'm leaning out the door, and my mother-in-law is in the other room selling pulque, with the men there. And a man passes by. He's walking past, going up the street. And he looks at me. Well, that seemed funny to me. I just stood there, and I didn't go inside.

"Suddenly, she grabs me by the hair, by my braids, and pushes me inside. She says, 'What the hell? What did you go out for? What are you looking for?'

"It was the first scolding I got from her! After that I was really sorry I had gotten married. But what could I do? So she finished pushing, shoving, and hitting me. 'So that you'll know that from now on things are not the same as when you were single.'

"Then she said, 'This is where you ended up. Here, you're done with Mama. Here, you're done with girlfriends. Here, you're done with compadres, with boyfriends. Here, you're done with comadritas. Here, you came to know your obligation toward your husband, nothing else, to carry out the obligation you've taken on.'

"Right away she sentenced me. And that was my life eternal. I tell you, it's a very black life! During sixteen years. I held out for sixteen years."

› › ›

"By the year 1950, I was going to be a mother. The first little girl I had with him, she lasted nine months. I became sick with *coraje*, with rage, because I found him with someone else, a girlfriend he had. After the first time he beat me, he didn't stop—every eight days, every fifteen days, for anything, for anything that happened and made him angry. He'd arrive and get angry with me. And if I talked back to him and said, 'Well, why do you beat me? What am I doing?' he'd say, 'Shut up!' He'd give it to me, and leave me dripping blood.

"Then I had the child. The child was going on nine months, she was almost nine months. What could I do? How could I leave? How, now that I had a family and all? At that time, my sister-in-law lived in the house because she had left her husband. There she was going around having fun. It was my sister-in-law who told me, 'He's going around with someone else, and who is it going to be but that vieja Docinda. She's a maid who's with Doña Felicidad.'

"And I said, 'Ah, who knows.'

"He'd come home, and for anything at all he'd mistreat me. He'd give me a punch, he'd kick me, even if I was holding the child. Always with the child stuck to me, so she could suckle. And my sister-in-law would say, 'Has he come back, that Julio? Now why are you crying? Did that Julio hit you already?'

"'Yes.'

"'Shameless man, taking advantage. He's going around with his tail out, and you're bothering him!' My sister-in-law would say that. She was the only one who was a little nicer. She was what she was, but she was a nicer person than her mother.

"It happened that a lot of people were around town during those days because the bishop had come for confirmations. One afternoon there was no firewood. So my mother-in-law says, 'Where's the boy?'

"'Who knows? He hasn't come back.'

"Then she says, 'Listen, Antonia, the two of you, go and get firewood. There's no sign of the boy. Who knows where he is. Go bring me some bits of wood to burn.'

"My sister-in-law had a little girl, and I had mine. The father of her girl was a man called Inés, but she left him for Don Adalberto Gutiérrez.

"So my mother-in-law says, 'Put the children to bed. Give them the breast and put them in their cribs. Go get some wood from around the dam so you won't have to go very far. Don't take long coming back, so you'll return before the children wake up.' And to my sister-in-law she says, 'Take the woman with you, so you'll get some firewood. If the man gets angry, let him get angry. He doesn't want the woman to go out into the street. But he doesn't even bring her any firewood nor water nor anything. Meanwhile, he's strolling about. Let's see if he feels ashamed with so many people around and his wife going to fetch firewood herself.'

"Fine. So she takes me along. We walked to the hill of El Calvario, stopping at the edge of the dam. Then she says, 'Eh, Esperanza.'

"'What?'

"She says, 'Look who's there.'

"I could see, in profile, that woman washing. And he was behind a rock—hidden behind a rock. He had taken off his hat, so people wouldn't recognize him by his hat.

"She says, 'Look at him—look who's there! Look, there's that Julio! Ay, he doesn't even see himself. He's with that vieja. Didn't I tell you that she's the mistress he's got? That's her. I heard that she used to be his girlfriend. And he's still got her! Married and everything, he's still chasing that vieja!'

"So we walked on and went to get the firewood. We quickly gathered up some firewood. We're coming back, each with a measure of firewood, and he's still there!

"She says, 'Look at him. Shameless man. There he is.' She says, 'Don't pay any attention. Just leave him alone. Don't you be getting sick with coraje. Just let him be. Let him be for the sake of the little girl. For the sake of the little girl you have, do it for her.' She says, 'Let him be, that shameless man, but I'm still going to give it to him.'

"And there we come, there we come, there we come. We climbed up El Calvario. There was a path up there. That's where we took a rest. There were a lot of people around.

"They were down below. And the woman was washing. And he was hiding nearby, talking with her. Then my sister-in-law says, 'Let's go see him.'

"'Yes, I'll go see him. But I'll take on the vieja because I'll take her on. It doesn't matter if we end up in the dam, but I'm going to take her on right now. I don't care if they kill me!' And we start approaching, going down El Calvario. He didn't see us, or pretended not to, so excited was he at being with the vieja. I picked up three or four rocks. Then my sister-in-law says, 'Don't lower yourself. I know what I say. Do it for the child.'

"I thought to myself, she's right. And I didn't break the coraje, the rage inside me. I felt such coraje. I let the rocks fall from my hands. *Pon, pon, pon*, down they went in their direction. If I hit them or didn't hit them, down they went.

"'Let's go,' she says. 'Because he's going to come up and find us here. He's going to say it's us.'

"I said to her, 'But he saw us and everything. You think he's not going to know it was us? Well, let's see how things go for me.'"

› › ›

"When we got home, the children were crying and crying and crying and crying. My mother-in-law says, '*Andale*, women. The girls are crying and crying.'

"I threw down the firewood and took the child in my arms. And soon after, my sister-in-law whispers to me, 'Eh, Esperanza, don't give the child the breast to suckle right now. Don't let her suckle. It's better if you boil a little chamomile and give it to the child. Don't give her the breast now. You, too, have some herbs. Don't you see that your milk will hurt the child? The coraje you felt. You don't think so? I even felt coraje, and he's not my husband, just my brother. So imagine you.'

"'I already gave her the breast.'

"The child was crying and crying and crying. I picked up the child and, yes, I gave her the breast to suckle, that's the truth. Well, I got sick with rage, and the child sucked it in. She only sucked a little bit. Hardly anything at all. But it made her ill. She felt it right away. Soon after she seemed to be fainting. You don't have to believe me, but that night the child became blocked, couldn't go at all. And there was nothing I could do for her. She was so distressed and grimaced so much. What could she have and what could she have? I'd put a diaper on her and she'd be dry. She couldn't urinate. Nothing.

"She got blocked, lasted for eight days like that. At the end of the eight days, she was gone. Just as she was dying, she started to come out of it. And then she died. That was the illness she had. She died, my first one.

"If only his mother had said, 'Take the child to a doctor.' Back then you had to go to San Luis, because there weren't any doctors here. Now we're in heaven, as they say, because we have the medical center.

"It was the señora who helped me through my births, the midwife, who said, 'But man, Doña Timotea, didn't you know? You should have boiled some anise herbs and spread her with an ointment made of sow bugs. You should have crushed them and spread them on the child. You should have boiled some anise herbs right away when the child became obstructed. How long has it been?'

"'Eight days already.'

"'¡Qué bárbaros! The child waited a long time for you to do something for her.' And then when we were alone, the woman said to me, 'The child became blocked because of your anger. You got sick with coraje and the child drank it in. And with that, she had it. *Pero qué bárbaros, de veras* . . . And your mother-in-law? That Julio, the man?'

"'No, well—'

"'*¡Híjole!* Poor child. Well, what are we to do now? She's already dead.'"

›››

"So there you have it. The child died. And it was *la mala vida* for me. He'd say terrible things to me, and I'd talk back to him. I had started to talk back. I didn't need more rages. It was one continual raging. I didn't eat. I just had my rage from his beating me, pulling me, grabbing me by the braids and dragging me. I was alone with my rage. He did what he wanted to with me.

"I gave birth to my second child. That one died in a year. He came down with attacks of vomiting and diarrhea. And I couldn't do anything for him. The illness would go away, and the next day it would start again. I was breastfeeding him, giving him the poison itself. As that señora who got me through my births used to say, 'How are your children going to get better? If your mother-in-law mistreats you, the pelado beats you, makes you suffer corajes, you're badly fed, and you with the child stuck to you. Well, what do you expect? How are they going to grow? No, they can't grow that way.'

"She'd say that to me when I was feeling ill, and she'd come give me a massage, right? That's when she said those things to me, but secretly, so that my mother-in-law wouldn't hear, because she was always trying to catch the midwife in the act of saying something to me, giving me advice. That's why she'd tell me secretly.

"With the second child, his eye burst. That viejita, the midwife, was one of the ancient ones, and she'd say, 'Look, this child's eye burst, but it's because of the *ojo*. And this eye is someone's from this very house. Because when children are given the eye by outsiders, they cry, they get a fever, they vomit. But this child isn't crying. He's just got a fever, so it's someone in the same house. It could be his grandmother, his aunt, someone. Ay, those *ingratos*. How this poor innocent is being eaten.' And she says, 'Poor innocent thing. Tell them to clean him.'

"'They've already cleaned him.'

"'Too bad you didn't tell me right away. Not now that the child's eye has burst.'

"He could only see with the one eye, and it started drying up until all that was left was the bone. Then came the vomiting fits and diarrhea. And the señora said to me, 'No, the child won't live. This child won't live. How long has he been ill?'

"'Almost three months.'

"'In three more months, he'll be dead.'

"Said and done. He died also. The first one died, the second one died, and the third one died. The third one was another little girl. And she got the same thing, vomiting and diarrhea. Just before her second birthday, she died and she died. And it was my martyrdom—to see all my children die. Sometimes I'd say, 'It's not worth it to me to have a family, just to have them and me getting worn out for nothing, having them and then they die, and your family won't do anything for them, and me—what can I do?'

"Then he'd say to me, angry, 'Well, you swallow them.'

"'Well, yes. I don't have anything to eat, so I swallow them.' I'd answer him like that and get another beating for it.

"'Shut up!'

"'Then why do you say I swallow them?'"

› › ›

"So what could I do? I'd just pass the time crying. Then I had that other boy, the oldest. He was the fourth. Then the other son followed, and that was it. And with the fourth child I had—that's the son who lives with his father and doesn't speak to me—when he was nine months old, the man hit me on the head with a machete.

"He came back drunk, cursing me, cursing my mother, and who knows what. What could I do? We slept on the floor. There was no bed. I say that I'm in heaven now, comadre. I'm in heaven, I say, because I have my bed. I don't sleep on the floor anymore on a sack. We slept on the floor, a sack for a pillow, any old thing that you could spread out. No, we were really poor.

"I spread out a sack and put down a pillow for him to sleep. I sat down with him, because when he was drunk he didn't want me to leave his side. I had to be there with the child, be there holding the child in my arms. So I made his bed for him and he lay down. And there he was swearing, swearing, swearing—pure curses and curses. I just listened, I with the child there. Then I saw that he was asleep.

"On the fire I had the nixtamal, eh? I had the nixtamal. I had put on the pail of nixtamal, the nixtamal that my mother-in-law would give me, right? Because we lived together. And I said to myself, The nixta-mal is on the fire, it's cooking. I didn't make a sound. I said to myself, He's asleep. He's asleep—Pretending to be asleep!

"I went to the kitchen to check on the nixtamal. And there I am stir-ring the pot. And I think to myself, No, the nixtamal isn't ready yet. It's not ready yet. I stirred up the fire. It occurred to me to sit there, resting against the chimney, with the child on my lap.

"It didn't take ten minutes for him to appear at the door of the kitchen. 'Daughter of who knows what mother,' he says. 'You left your man asleep, right? What did you think, that you'd go out with the other one while you left me asleep?'

"I was resting against the chimney, with the child on my lap. Just as I looked up, he said, 'And don't you raise your eyes to look at me!' Whenever he wanted to talk to me, he had gotten into the habit of hit-ting me. He treated me like a dog, and I ask for your pardon in say-ing that.

"I used to wear a hair clip, a small one, on the side of my head. The only thing that protected me was the hair clip. Just as he was speaking to me, the machete was already coming over my head. And *zas!* He says to me, 'You daughter of who knows what mother, you went out, didn't you?' *¡Sopas!* 'Isn't it true? Daughter of who knows who. You left me asleep and you went to see your young man.' And then he says, 'And don't you raise your eyes to look at me!' and whacks me again.

"When I saw that it had been the machete, it was coming down hot, hot. The blood was coming down. Dripping. Blood. And I started crying.

"He saw that the blood was streaming down, but he turned and left. He just gave it to me and left, cursing. And then maybe he got scared. So he went to tell his mama. In those days, his mama did her selling at the house of Don Berna—but outside. She had a stall made of wood where she sold soft drinks, pulque, liquor, crackers, sweets. So he ran to tell his mother what he had done to me, right? And then his mother, not to leave the stall unattended, left her son there and came home.

"Seeing that he had left, I went outside. The blood just kept stream-ing down, and there I was with the child in my arms. I was crying in the courtyard when she came. 'And now what?' she began saying.

'Why do you cry? Now what did you do to yourself? Why do you have blood there? What happened? Did you fall, or what?'

"I didn't answer her. And then she says, 'It was coming to you. You deserve it.' With your pardon, comadre, she said to me, 'You're all a bunch of wild mules.'

"I still didn't say anything. I stood there, crying and crying and crying. And again she said, 'You deserve it. You're all wild mules.'

"It still burns where he hit me. I feel it burning whenever I get sick with coraje. My mama says that the wound healed treacherously, by the will of God alone. They didn't cure me or anything."

› › ›

"A month passed, and the wound on my head healed. I'd lay awake at night thinking, with my child asleep at my side. He didn't sleep with me. He slept in the better room, where his mother slept.

"It was during the month of August and there were prickly pears. He wasn't speaking to me. He was angry because I had talked back to him again. And my mother-in-law says, '*Andale*, hijo. Get the burros ready, and we'll go to the woods. I bought some prickly pears in the woods. I'm going to take another man to help us cut the prickly pears and peel them.' They'd bring back pails of them to make *colonche* to sell. 'Let's go! The señora can stay and do the cooking.' She threw some money at me. Other times she'd toss me the corn so I would grind it. I had to have their food ready when they returned.

"As soon as they left, I grabbed the child in my arms and took off! I went to my mama! How terrified I was that people might see me up there. I said to myself, I'm going to find my mama and see what she tells me. I remembered how my mama had said to me, 'I told you and you didn't understand.' So I thought, *Híjole*, if I go and cry with my mama, she's going to say that she warned me. But I'm going to go see her anyway, and see what she tells me! So I went and told her the whole story.

"And she says, 'Tonta, now that you've left, leave! Go work! You just have the one sad child and look how he mistreats you.' She says, 'Leave him already! Go work! You know how to support yourself in San Luis. But just don't get me into it, you don't have to get me into it.'"

› › ›

"So what do you think? That's what I did. I took off! With my kid and all. When they returned they didn't find me.

"I went to my godmother's, and my godmother took me to San Luis. My mama didn't get involved. My godmother was the one who took me to San Luis and found work for me.

"I went to work with that blessed son of mine. He was nine months old, almost ten months. Oh, what a crybaby he was! Crying and crying and refusing to eat. He just wanted the breast, only the breast, and all that time I had to keep working. Oh how that boy cried. He really cried, that kid. And me working. I knew how to work—sweeping, washing floors. So I put myself to work.

"My mama would see that Julio hanging around. But Mama didn't speak to him. She'd see him around, strolling in the fields. But he never thought to ask, 'Listen, where's your daughter?'

"I finished up a month of work in that house and started another month. And the kid, how he wore my patience thin, because he only wanted to be with me. I'd lock him up in his room, 'There, cry all you want.' And I'd work. The child turned a year old and started his second year. At two and a half, the boy still wouldn't give up breastfeeding. He didn't want to eat, he just wanted the breast. So the patrona said, 'Listen, Esperanza, send the boy to your mama, so that he'll forget the breast. After eight days, your mama can bring him back or you can go get him. Maybe this way he'll start eating and having his milk in a little cup. The boy's already big. He shouldn't be breastfeeding anymore.'

"My mama came for the boy and took him with her to Mexquitic. And during those eight days, Julio must have heard the kid crying. He'd be strolling by, but he wouldn't say, 'Oh, is your daughter here?' He didn't say anything; he'd just stroll past. Well, after eight days, my patrona sent me home. She says, 'Your mama hasn't come back. If you're worried about your child, go get him. And let's see if he eats now.'

"No, lord of my soul. I went to get the child. I took the bus and got off in front of the school. Right away he saw me. He saw me going up the path. That night he hung around listening. He heard me saying, 'Tomorrow I'll go back to San Luis.' No! As I was about to leave, the comandante arrives at my mama's. 'Doña Esperanza,' he says. 'Here's an order that you appear before the juez.'

72

"And my mama says, 'You see? Don't let yourself be had. Tell him what your reasons were for going to San Luis. I'm not going to get into it. I'll say that you came for the child. After all, you're my daughter; I've got to let you in. If the law punishes us, then let it.'

"So I went to see the juez with my child in my arms. Julio, very smug, very smug, with his mother, telling the juez how long I had been gone from the house. I felt such coraje that I wanted to grab him and kill him. It was May tenth and what a rainstorm was coming down! They used to have beautiful fiestas on the tenth of May, for Mother's Day, but with the rainstorm, they didn't do anything that day.

"They had me waiting for a while, and then the juez said, 'Here is the señora, your wife, who you say left the house.'

"'She's been gone for a long time. We went on an errand and left her in the house. When we returned she was gone.'

"'Señora,' the juez says to me. 'If you were having a mala vida, then you should have gone to the authorities, not just taken off on your own like you did.'

"And that Julio says, 'Well, look, señor, since she's my señora, I'm trying to get her to come home with her child. I'm doing it for the child's sake. It's true that she left. But now that she's back and has her child, I want her to return home.'

"Then the juez says, 'Let's see, señora, here's your husband who wants you back. He's ready to pardon you and take you back.'

"'I'll never go back to him. Even if the law punishes me, I won't go back to him.'

"'But he's your husband.'

"'He's my husband—there's no doubt about it. But what a life I've had with him. If we eat, it's because his mother supports us. If not, he doesn't worry about me.'

"Then my mother-in-law spoke. 'Listen, woman, what's gotten into you? He's your husband! Why don't you want to be with him? Do you want to be falling? It's not you who suffers, it's your child.'

"'And you, how do you know if my child suffers? I think that's what he came into the world for. And I'm suffering to support him.'

"Again she says, 'Do it for the child. Tomorrow you'll find another pelado.'

"'So I'm going to find another pelado, right?'

"'You see how she is? Insolent!' my mother-in-law screams.

"'You're married. The law says so,' the juez says.

"'Let the law say so, let the law punish me. But I won't stay with him. I married young, and I've had nothing but suffering from him! He's always telling me that I have lovers. But he never admits why it is that almost all of our children have died.'

"The juez says, 'Ay, señora, you really mean it.'

"'I won't follow him! Punish me however you want to, but I won't follow him.'

"'Didn't you say it was her fault, Don Julio?' the juez says. 'Well, I think you're both at fault!' So they ended up locking both of us up, I in one cell and he in another.

"This really upset my mother-in-law. 'Why did you lock up my son? She's the one who likes pleasure! No one threw her out! She left because she felt like it.'

"The juez says, 'No, señora, according to their statements, they are both at fault. Let them decide if they'll stay together.' And then the juez says to us, 'I'm going to give you another hour to decide. Both of you, go to the courtyard. Don Julio, let's see if you can convince your wife.'

"Listen, I don't know what they gave me. He was in one corner and I in another. And the child was roaming around. He says to the boy, 'Come here.' The child saw him and laughed. I was fuming. Then he says, 'Eh, Esperanza, forget it already. Why do you feel so much anger? Forget it already. Look, the child likes me.'

"'I suppose that's because you're so good at supporting him.'

"'Look, it's going to be a different life. When you come back to me, it will be another life. It won't be the same as before. If you want, we'll move to our own house.'

"They had given us an hour to think, so he had to hurry. He says, 'Look, woman, I know where you were working. I know who you were with. That's why I'm taking you in. Do it for the child's sake.' And he says, 'Let's go home. It will be different from now on.'

"Well, as fast as you can say Jesus, he convinced me. The papers written up and everything. He won me over! As fast as you can say Jesus, they spread the magic powders over me and I was persuaded!"

› › ›

"Noooo, comadre, wait! He deceived me. It was my martyrdom. Noooo! And then it was a worse martyrdom. And he never moved out. Never left his mother's house. He said he would look for work, but he never did. And our arguments continued. And then I had Simeón. I had him and it was martyrdom. When he'd get drunk, he'd say, 'This one is not mine. You brought this one back with you.'

"That Simeón, they say he looks just like me. They named him after the fake grandfather, the man who had been Julio's stepfather. So I'd say to him, 'Well, if you didn't think he was yours, then why did you take me back? Was I offering myself to you?' And because I spoke these truths, he'd beat me. Fifteen days after the boy was born, he was beating me again. He was very drunk and when his mother and sister came back from doing their selling, he announced, 'You tell this daughter of who knows who that her young man has just left.'

"*Ave María Purísima*! And then I said to him, 'But what young man do you see?'

"'Don't talk back to me!'

"And as fast as you can say Jesus, he gave me one. He gave me the first kick and just as I looked up, another one. That was when my brow split open. Noooo! As fast as you can say Jesus, it was a stream of blood. And I had the little kid in my arms—born just fifteen days before. Everything full of blood. And no one took care of me! I was healed by the will of God. Yes, he kicked me twice, and my brow split open. And my child, covered with my blood!

"Well, that day passed, another day dawned, and me with my face torn apart. He knew what he was doing. Afterward he'd go off and leave me there with his mother. He was a treacherous dog: he'd attack and then run away."

› › ›

"He had seven women while he was with me. And they were all young girls. I don't know what he gave them. It must have been pure love, because he didn't have any money since he never worked.

"That Doña Eufemia, the one who sells by the school, was his mistress. We don't speak to one another, that woman and I. She was his mistress and I knew it. I myself found them. They say that Eufemia and her sisters came here all the way from Cenicera because she had a child with her very own father! Every time her mother would get drunk she'd say to her, 'Because of you, we're here. Because you were shameless enough to go around with your own father.'

"That Julio would return home drunk as a pig after being with that Eufemia, and it was beatings for me. At least Simeón was a stronger kid. He wasn't so prone to colic. He'd get corajes from my breastmilk, but he wouldn't get sick. Not like the others, who died and died and died. And the other boy, he revived during those months I was away.

"Ready to pick a fight, that Julio would come home, wanting to eat, and if the plate wasn't clean, or if there was a hair in the food, or if I didn't serve him right away, he'd get so angry.

"My comadre Mariana lived near that Florencia and her daughters. She was my comadre because she and her husband were godparents to Simeón and the other boy. And she said to me in mass, 'Listen, co-madre, he's with that Eufemia! I can say so because we see them in the mornings, at midday, and at night; we see that he's with her. I can see them from my courtyard. And her mother doesn't mind at all. Knowing that my compadre has a wife, why does she let her daughters be with him? If you want to see him, just wait there one day and you'll see him.'

"One, two, three months later, the comandante came to the house.

"'Where's Don Julio?'

"'He's not here. He must be in the milpa.'

"'I bring an order to imprison him.'

"Finally he came.

"'Hijo, what did you do?'

"'Why?'

"'What have you done to make the police come looking for you? You're to go to court right away.'

"'I haven't done anything.'

"'What do you mean, you haven't done anything? They've come asking for you, and they told me to tell you right away that they're waiting to put you in jail.'

"'But I haven't done anything.'

"He came into the kitchen and looked at me with eyes full of anger. He went to court that day and didn't return. And his mother said, 'You know, he's in jail. What could the boy have done?'

"But my sister-in-law snapped back, 'Of course, the bridegroom is in jail! Why not, if he's going around being a bridegroom? What a shame-less man! Having his wife, what does he want, what's he looking for?'

"His mother would take his food to him while he was in jail, and he ate there in his own dirt, that's where he ate.

"He was let out, and then a few months later—once again! He had played around with someone else. 'Hijo,' his mother calls out, 'the offi-cer says that there's a woman who wants you to return her hairpins and her rings. Whose hairpins are those that you have over there?'

" 'Oh, I just found them.'

" 'No, hijo. Don't be like that. You have your wife. What are you looking for? Why do you have all those hairpins? The officer says that a woman complained that she wants her hairpins back. You're a mar-ried man. Why are you hanging around with a young girl?'

"Every time he would chase after a young girl, her parents would file charges in court. They'd come to an agreement, charge him twenty, thirty pesos. And then three, four, five months later, he'd be at it again.

"As I say, it's a long story. One day beaten, pushed around, and an-other day, fine, because he didn't beat me, because he was too busy playing around with young women. And then it was that Eufemia. And then it was that Silveria. And then there was another one from Picacho also. Because of that one, they were going to take him to the peniten-tiary. He had done it too many times. He had a record already. Be-cause of that one, he had to go into hiding. And because of her, we had to leave for San Luis. We left with the two older sons and two of the babies who had not yet died."

› › ›

"No, comadre, it's a great big historia. I can keep going. I never fin-ish. I've still got a lot to tell. There's no one here who has a story like mine. And I've forgotten many things. But some things are etched in my mind. I'd have to tell you about when we left Mexquitic after he escaped from jail, and about when he was hiding from the law in San Luis, and about when he got involved with the last woman, and about when I had my last child by him, who was a boy named Juan.

"It was while I was waiting for the last boy to be born that he found the woman in San Luis. For her, he left me. He left me just as I was about to give birth. I was eight months pregnant, within days of giving birth. I found them in San Luis—and did I grab them! I grabbed her nice and pretty, comadre!

"He was selling ice cream pops on the outskirts of San Luis, hiding from the authorities because he had escaped from jail. He was supposed to have been sent to the penitentiary. And his mother was shelling out money so he could stay in hiding.

"No, I tell you, it was a black life. And there I was within days of giving birth. His mother would send me to San Luis after him, saying, 'Go find the boy and tell him to give you money. I don't have any. Sometimes I sell pulque; sometimes I don't. What do I support you with? Go, he's had all week.'

"'What do you come for?' he'd say when he saw me.

"'Well, your mother sends me. I've brought you your clothes. Your mother said you should give me some money from what you've earned this week.' But he didn't want to know anything about me.

"My mother-in-law made me collect *mejorana* and *hierbabuena* from the garden. 'Go on, tell him to give you money for your trip—and take these herbs, sell them around there.' People bought those handfuls of mejorana and hierbabuena for five centavos. What was I to do with the centavos that I'd earn from selling fifteen or twenty handfuls?

"You may not believe this, comadre, but I even begged. I'd take the older boy with me, and sometimes I took the younger one. I was within days of having a child. And I couldn't find anything to eat.

"I'd go to his aunt's house, where he was supposed to be staying, and she'd say, 'No, he hasn't come here. I know he sells ice cream pops, but I don't know where he stays. One day I think he brought a woman with him to sleep here. He comes back late at night, and he sleeps next to the courtyard in a little room I lent him. I saw him through a slit in the door, saw him go out and saw a woman with him who wore a scarf on her head. I think he's bringing women to my house.'

"So I would return despairing of not having found him. Another week passed, and he still wasn't back. I'd sell the herbs at five centavos for a handful. I'd go selling from one house to another. The truth is I was hungry. His aunt didn't give me anything to eat. So I went begging. And I'd trade with people. If they didn't want to buy my herbs, I'd give them away just so they'd give me a tortilla for the child. So I wouldn't find him anywhere, and I'd go back home.

"I'd say, 'I'm back.'

"'Ah, you're back. Well, *ándale*, did you find the man?'

"'No.'

"'Is that the truth? If you're lying, if he gave you money—Here, go buy corn, so you can soak it and give the kids something to eat.'

"'Your niece told me that he's got someone else. They've seen him at the ice cream place with her. She's a maid. Chila told me she's seen him with her and that she's his mistress.'

"Chila was my mother-in-law's niece. She addressed me as *tú*, even though that Chila was only four years old when we got married. She'd speak to me as *tú*. 'Eh, Esperanza, and that Julio? What did he tell you?'

"'He didn't give me any money.'

"'Ah, he didn't give you money.' Then she says, 'Aahh, Esperanza don't be a tonta. That Julio's got another vieja. I saw him. He was coming along with his ice cream cart and stopped on the corner where she lives—she's a cat.' A cat meant she was a maid. 'She works in that house. She's bigger than you. Taller than you. I'm telling you, but don't tell anyone I told you. He's shameless. So get smart. Spy on him!'

"I would go see him, and he still wouldn't give me anything. I'd come back, and my mother-in-law would argue with me, about why didn't I give her the money so she could buy corn. My patience was wearing thin.

"'Go on, the kids are out of school. Go on. Don't let yourself be had. You go and demand that he give you money. He's worked all week. Doesn't he know he's got a family to support? Let him give you something to get through the week, because I don't have enough to support you with my pulque. Sometimes I sell and sometimes I don't. Don't let yourself be had. Tell him to give you money.'

"When I went back to look for him at his aunt's, she says, 'He hasn't been back here for a week. I don't know if he's out selling ice cream pops or what. It's been a week, and he hasn't come by here. So that you'll know if he's really selling ice cream pops, go spy on him! You know where he gets the pops. Go by there at about five o'clock. Spy on him! I know he's got a vieja.'"

› › ›

"So I took off. I was eight months pregnant! Within days of giving birth! I got up my courage. How I don't know. I was so asleep. Afraid. Humiliated. Lord of my soul! I took off down Calle Arista, offering my herbs and asking for charity. I took Simeón with me. Simeón was about eight years old. Another two died after him, two girls, and then I had the last boy, Juan. Just my fourth and fifth survived. All my other children died.

"It must have been about four o'clock. Someone had given me a taco, and I had given it to the boy and he had eaten.

"'Let's go. Come on. We're going to wait for your papa. Let's see if we find him.'

"Said and done. We were on Calle Reforma, and as we approached the corner the boy stopped in his tracks and so did I. Then he says, 'Look, Mama, look Mama! There's my papa. Look at him there! There he is! There he is!'

"'Ah, yes, it's him.' I had brought him clean clothes, so he had changed. Then I said, 'Aahh, man, yes, it's him. It's him.'

"'Look, and he's got a vieja with him! He's got a vieja!'

"'Ah, yes, so that's her. That's the one your Aunt Blanca was talking about. That's her.'

"'Look, she's a young girl.'

"'Run ahead, son, run ahead!' I couldn't go very fast, so I said to him, 'Run ahead. Get to the corner, and when they turn, you stand at the corner and watch which way they go. While I get to the corner, you watch and see which way they go.'

"Whatever it took, I was going to catch up to them. Afraid as I was, humiliated as I was, but at that moment when I saw him with the vieja—no, lord of my soul, I think I even lost my fear. I said to myself, Now it's win or lose, whatever my fate. Alive or dead!

"So the kid ran ahead, and I after him. How fast I moved! Eight months pregnant, but I couldn't feel the weight. I was carrying a canvas bag filled with the tortillas people had given me, tortillas I had to beg for.

"There they go, there they go. Very few people were out on the street. One person going one way, another going another way. And there were the two of them.

"No, at that moment I wasn't afraid of anything! Lord of my soul, they were just getting to the end of the block, and I was almost to the middle of the block. They stepped down from the sidewalk to cross the street to get to the next block, but ever so slowly. They had to stop because the cars kept passing and passing. On Calle Arista some cars

go one way, some go another way. So they had to stop. At the very moment they stood waiting, as he held her by the arm, as they stood waiting while the cars kept passing, at that moment I got closer to them.
But they didn't even see me coming.

"As they stood there, she turned just a little, a liiiiittle, since he was
holding her by the arm. She turned, a little, a liiiiittle. But because she
didn't know me, when she turned like that I got closer and grabbed her
hair! With both hands, I'm pulling at her hair. And then I'm letting go
with one hand and giving it to her.

"'This is how I wanted to find you,' I said. 'What's new? What do
you say to your girl? Do you say you're a bachelor? A young man, a
boy? Well, you're wrong. If before you had yours, now I have mine.'

"I changed in that moment and I don't even know how.

"'And who's this? Daughter of heaven and earth,' I said to her. 'You
believed him, didn't you? Did he tell you he was single? Well, here is
his family, and here am I. And we have another son. And how many in
the grave? And you, why are you here? For how many women haven't
you gone to jail?'

"And bang! I bring her down to her knees just slapping her! But
the woman didn't even know how to use her hands. He let go of her,
and I pulled her along and threw her down like a dog. And she didn't
bend. I pulled her up to the sidewalk and pushed her against a window
and grabbed her by the hair and made her kneel against the window. I
brought her to her knees just by slapping her. The blood dripped down.
And he, seeing how I had her, grabbed me by the hands. He said, 'Leave
her alone. What's she doing to you?'

"'So you can still say what's she doing to me? You should have
thought of that before. You're shameless!' And I said to him, 'How are
you, runaway convict? You've escaped from jail in Mexquitic. Here
you're going around like a child. Well, you're wrong.'

"He tried to grab hold of my hand, because I was holding her by the
hair with one hand and with the other hand I was forcing her to kneel
against the window. Just as he's squeezing one of my hands, I release
the other and give him a good punch! His hat goes flying! And then he
lets me go, to run after his hat. And I yell after him, 'Defend her! Defend her once again! If before it was your turn, now it's mine.' The
woman cried like a child.

"I said to him, 'Today you walk to court.' I had the courage to say

81

those words. But who was going to take him? How was I going to cart them both to court?

"'Who? Me? Go to court? You're crazy.'

"'Yes, I'm crazy. And you've taken nice and pretty advantage of me,' I said to him. 'But you can keep her. It's all over for us.' At that moment I lost my respect for him. I no longer respected him as my husband. I called him *tú*.

"'You're shameless. I respected you as if you were more than a father. And now look how I find you,' I said. 'Come on, defend her. And you can kill me right here, if you want to. You've got me in a good spot.'

"But he didn't intervene again. I kept slapping her, tugging at her, and wondering whether the police would see us. The vieja was dripping blood. It must have been from the punches I was giving her, because the vieja was dripping blood. She was wearing a plaid dress, an apron, and a string of pearls. She had on a string of pearls and her hair was permed. And nooo! I pulled. I tore her dress. That blessed string of pearls went flying all over the ground. I shook her and gave her a shove. After that I couldn't do more. I let go of her and she ran off.

"She took off in the direction we had come from, and he took off in the other direction. And I stayed right behind him. There I went, like a weed behind him, talking to him and talking to him, and he talking back, and me talking, and he talking, but he didn't lay a hand on me again."

› › ›

"The sun set and the streetlights came on. I went to tell his aunt. And his aunt says to me, 'You wretch! You did that and the police didn't see you? Why did you go and do that? Why did you go and punch the girl, or the woman, or whatever she was. I bet it's not even true.'

"'Well, if I did wrong, it's too late now. But he won't laugh at me anymore,' I said.

"'You did wrong, you know. You were lucky the police didn't see you. If they had, you would have been punished, not her or him. You would have been the one punished.'

"'Well, all right. That was my luck, that the police didn't see me.'

"I went to bed with my coraje. Of course, the baby would be born sick. With so much coraje, what could you expect?

"The next day, I returned to Mexquitic and told my mother-in-law. And she didn't believe it.

"'Go on, liar. You're a liar. You're a gossiper. How can you think that the boy's got someone else?'

"'Well, don't believe it.'

"That week passed. The following Friday she says, 'Go on and see the man. See if you can find him.'

"And I said, 'Why should I go? He's got someone else—what am I going for?'

"She says, 'Go, so we can know for sure if he's with her. Take his clothes to him, go on.'

"So she sent me back. That time I went prepared with a knife he had given me. He had spent time at home hiding from the law, and he would tell me to take the burro and bring back the juice from the magueyes. He'd send me all the way to Milpillas to get the juice from the magueyes. 'Look, woman,' he had said to me, 'I'm going to give you this knife. If some son of whatever attacks you or tries to grab you, stab him with this knife.'

"That time I didn't take Simeón. I took my other son, Macario. I said to him, 'Hijo, let's go see your papa.' So off we went again. I said to myself, This time I'm prepared. I've got the knife.

"I got to his aunt's house and she says, 'He hasn't been here. Spy on him out there.' On the street a señora I knew saw me and said, 'You're going to see Julio? He goes by here every afternoon. In that stall he buys pastries for the vieja. They have a soda, he gives her the pastries, and they sit there eating. Every night they go by here.'

"So we went there to spy on him. I said to the boy, 'Your papa will pass by soon.' We were so hungry. And I had fifteen or twenty centavos. At that time one dealt in centavos. One peso, two pesos, that was what I had. 'I'm going to buy some tortillas,' I said, 'and we'll spy on him from the tortillería.' Just as I'm about to enter the tortillería, I see the ice cream cart coming around the bend.

"We rushed into the tortillería and hid behind the door. The lady at the tortillería says to us, 'What happened, señora? Is someone bothering you?'

"'I'm so sorry I rushed in. But that man you see there with the ice cream, that's my man, and I'm spying on him because they've told me he's got someone else.'

"She said, 'Aahh. What a shameless man. Hide, hide! Is that him, the ice cream man? I want to get a good look at him.' She was in front, handing out tortillas.

"He passed the tortillería and went around the corner and up all of Calle Coronel Espinosa. Then we stepped out of the tortillería and watched from the corner. There he goes. As the ice cream cart approached, out came the woman to the door.

"'Look, there she is,' I said. 'That's where he has her. Don't let them see you, hijo.'

"From the corner we could see them. How much fun we had seeing the woman come out to meet him and how he stood there hugging her. And there we were watching them!

"It was the same woman I had grabbed. Ay, I thought, if he turns around he'll see us, but he didn't. From his cart he pulled out an ice cream pop and gave it to her—in her mouth! He was very jolly, very jolly with her.

"'Come on, hijo.'

"We walk and walk. We crossed the street, got to the curb. There I go, there I go walking, there I go, there I go. And he didn't even turn around. Not for anything. He didn't budge.

"And I get to the lamppost. Well, what isn't God's will, you know . . . Because it's true, I had bad intentions. I said to myself, 'If I don't hit him, I'll hit her. One or the other.'

"He was leaning against the door. And there was the lamppost. I get to the lamppost, just two steps away from the door, when someone says to him, 'Look out!' And he turned around. And he saw me! And the woman remembered me! She flew back inside and closed the door on him!

"'Don't try hiding her. I already saw you.' And I with my hand in my bag. And I say, 'So, what's new? You go on doing the same thing, right? Well, I don't care anymore. You've made fun of me right and left. The only thing I want is the daily sustenance for your family. That's all. If you want to be with her, be with her, but you're going to give me the daily sustenance for the family. If not, right now I'll go to the police here in Tlaxcala and tell the police to take you away with your mistress and all.'

"'What, what, what? What's wrong with you? What's your problem?'

"'You see what my problem is. Hunger is my problem!'

"He says, 'What are you hiding?'

" 'I'm not hiding anything.'

" 'You're not hiding anything, right?' He was laughing.

" 'Look here,' I said. And I went to the door and pulled the string and the door opened. I put my foot in the door. And he lunged at me so I wouldn't get in. And the woman was in the middle of the courtyard gasping for breath. Then he grabs me and says, 'And what are you going to do?'

"I reached with my hand and pulled out the knife. 'Look at what I brought with me.'

" 'Ay, woman! What are you going to do?'

" 'Right? What do you think, that these are the same times as before? Everything changes!' And I was within days of giving birth.

" 'What's happening to you? You're crazy.'

" 'Yes, I'm crazy. Because I'm being driven crazy.'

"There we were, yelling like town criers. At that moment a Coca Cola cart arrived. We moved away from the door and waited while the neighbors bought their Cokes.

" 'All right now, give me my daily support,' I said. 'If you don't give it to me right now, I'll have you locked up. It's no trouble for me to walk one or two blocks to the station and bring the police. How far can you run, anyway, with your ice cream cart?'

" 'Ay, woman, what's your problem, woman? Stop it. Go home,' he says. 'Go home already. I'm not doing anything to you. You're the one who comes here making a scandal. Why do you want to do that? Why do you want to bring the police?'

" 'Why? You know why. Look, you're not going to trick me. Come on, we're going to the station, with your mistress and all.'

"So off I went, walking, walking. Somehow I got up the courage. I went walking down the block. And he followed me, saying, 'Where are you going? I haven't done anything to make you go to the police.'

"And I said, 'Well, give me my daily support, that's all I'm asking you for.'

" 'I left you at home with my mama.'

" 'Oh really? And what am I to eat there? Air? And the children? Your mother sends me to see you. Just tell me once and for all that you don't want me.'

"I got him as far as the police station. And then we got tired of arguing. He gave his son an ice cream and wanted to give me one, too, but I said, '¡*Andale!* Despite the shape I'm in, I don't want one.' But he won the boy over with the ice cream he gave him.

"He says, 'Go to my aunt's house. I'll be there in a while. I'm going to go drop off my cart and the ice cream, and I'll meet you there. Go on now, I'll meet you there.'

"Well, he tricked me. Tricked me like a dog! He never came. I returned the next day and, again, nothing. At his aunt's house, I found a blanket. I said to myself, I'm going to take this blanket just to take it. But, unfortunately, he arrived. And he says, 'So, you're going?' I didn't answer him. 'I'm talking to you. Are you going? Look, I'm not doing anything to you.'

"'What happened with the vieja yesterday?'

"'What vieja? You've been dreaming.' He was being impertinent as usual. 'If you're leaving, then go already. I have you with my mama. What are you coming to do here?'

"'What am I coming to do here? *Híjole,* even the question is stupid.'

"'And now you're going to take the blanket? Then I won't have one here.'

"'But your sons need a blanket.'

"'My mama will find one for them. Go with my mama and she'll give you one. This is my blanket. I need it.'

"'And what am I to give the boys to eat?'

"'But I don't have anything to give you.'

"And he wasn't capable of giving me a centavo. Since then, since that day that he kept the blanket, we've not spoken another word to one another."

THREE

The Rage of a Woman

"All these things
make a woman,"
he said
while beating my stirrings
and bruising my hopes.
I listened for a long time,
but raged my rage
through inner ears that echoed
  I dream
  I dream . . .

—Lolita Hernandez, title poem of Quiet Battles

Structures of domination are best understood if we can grasp
how we remain subjects even in the moments in which we are
being intimately and viciously oppressed.

  —Lata Mani, "Multiple Mediations"

July 13, 1985. Two days after my talk with my comadre, David and I
made a quick three-day visit to Mexico City to meet with David's
younger brother and our sister-in-law, who had come down by train
from Texas. We ran around like tourists with them, going to the
Museum of Anthropology, the house of Frida Kahlo and Diego
Rivera, and the ruins of Teotihuacán, where the cap to our gas tank
was stolen. Upon our return, Esperanza appeared at our door one
morning ready to take us on a walk to her milpa and her flower gar-
den, where for the first time in my life I saw how calla lilies grow in
water. On that occasion, fresh from my trip to Mexico City, I photo-
graphed my comadre with her calla lilies. Only later would I learn
the story of how she had acquired her field and garden. When Esper-
anza came to my kitchen that July night, there were still other things

she wanted to tell me about her last days as a wife in the house of her husband.

"The truth is, the story is this: he was in San Luis all those months because he had escaped from jail in Mexquitic. That last time he had been in jail for eight days. When the eight days were almost up, my mother-in-law said to me, 'I'm tired of working the magueyes. Has the boy come back yet from jail?'

"'No, I don't think so.'

"She says, 'Go on, *ándale*. He's touchy about you being out on the street. He doesn't want you to go out, so let's see if he'll feel ashamed if you bring him his food. Take him the jug.' There was a jug with food and tortillas. 'Go on, let's see if it makes him feel ashamed.'

"So she sent me out to bring his food to him. There he was in jail. And he says to me, 'Who sent you?'

"'Your mama.'

"'Ah, *pues*. So, who did you talk to out there?'

"I just answered, 'Here's your food.' There in jail I served him. So we ate, and then he said, 'Now go. I'll be watching you.'

"He had to be there maybe two more days. And after that he had told his mother that they were going to move him to the penitentiary in San Luis. The next day he came home.

"'Hijo, you're home?'

"'Yes, I'm back.'

"'So are you free, or what?'

"'No, I just got permission from Chebo'—that was the name of the guard—'to come home. I said to him, "Go on, Chebo. Let me go home. I've got to shave. See how I look after eight days here?" And he gave me permission to come home.'

"'What are you going to do, hijo?'

"He was so serene. The two of them were in the room talking. And I was in the jacal with the baby. I had just given birth four, five days before; that baby died, too. All I saw was that the two of them stepped out of the room, he in front, and his mother behind him. And his mother gave him something. Just as I stepped out into the courtyard, I heard her say, 'Here, hijo.' And then she said, 'With this, when you're questioned tomorrow, just wriggle it like this. Put it in your pants pocket and wriggle it.'

"And I saw how he put out his hand and his mother gave it to him. He took it and put it in his pocket. I saw that and then ran inside. I didn't want them to say I was watching them. 'Do that. With this they won't send you anywhere. Hijo, with what I gave you, they won't lock you up. You'll see.'

"What did she give him? I don't know. Because my mother-in-law knew how to do evil. Then she gave him three garlic cloves, but really large cloves. That I did see. As he left she said to him, 'They won't do anything to you, hijo. They'll roar a little, but it's got to stop.'

"It got dark and we went to sleep. My mother-in-law lay down with me in the jacal. Me with the two boys and the girl who had just been born. Because the girl was still little, my mother-in-law slept with me in the jacal to keep me company. So we went to bed and fell asleep, and soon the dogs started barking. Then they quieted down. 'There's a knock at the door!'

"She got up as though she had been expecting it. 'Who? Who is it?'

"'Me.'

"Then she says, '¡*Ave María!*' and gets up. 'Well, hijo, what happened?'

"'Quiet, man. Quiet, maybe they're following me.'

"'How did you get out, hijo?'

"'I jumped the wall.'

"The walls used to be very low. Now they've fixed it up.

"'Mama, I'm leaving,' he whispered. 'Give me money for the fare— and to manage tomorrow. I'll be back the day after tomorrow. I'll find work. I'm leaving the family with you. When I start working, I'll send money.'

"Pelado! Good for nothing!

"So he left. 'Careful, hijo. Don't let them see you.'

"'No, I'll do what I can so they won't see me. Tomorrow, at dawn, you go and act as though you're taking food to me so they won't blame you and think you've been in on it. You go bring my food as though you don't know anything.'

"The next day she says, '*Andale*, woman. Get up and grind. Grind the nixtamal. Make some tortillas. And put some food in the jug.' She told me what to do. So there I go. What was I to do? I had to obey her. So I made the tortillas and put some beans in the jug.

"She says, 'Go on. Go to the jail and pretend he's still there. You pretend you're going to see him. And when you see he's not there, ask for him. Ask for him and that's all. If they say anything, tell them you don't know.'

"So I go and there's Eusebio, the guard. He says, 'Who are you looking for?'

"I say, 'I'm bringing food for my man.'

"'What man? Isn't he in your house?'

"I felt so humiliated. 'No, there's no one there. Isn't he here?'

"'How you pretend.'

"I kept silent.

"'Isn't he at home with his mother? He escaped last night. How could you not know? You just better turn him in!'

"That's how it happened. The next day passed, and the next, and soon everyone knew he had escaped from jail. People would go for pulque with my mother-in-law and say, 'Doña Timotea, I thought your son was in jail—.'

"'Yes, because of some woman. They say she was a señorita, but who knows? As they say, it's not the men who are to blame. It's us women who have to take the blame. Knowing the man is married, why do they go around talking to him and doing things with him?'

"'I agree. The woman should have been punished, too. She deserved to be punished.'

"'Yes, but she had help. So what's to be done for my son?'

"'Where is he? Is he in jail?'

"'We don't know. They say he's lost. As I told them, they're going to have to return my son to me. He'll have to appear, unless they swallowed him whole!'

"That's what she said to people, so that people would repeat what she said and think it was the truth. The days passed like that. And then a month later, he came back—in the middle of the night.

"'¡Ave María Purísima!'

"'Woman, open the door.'

"'Who could it be?'

"The dogs barked. Then she says, 'Ah, it's the boy.' At one in the morning he was back from San Luis. He had walked all the way.

"'What happened, hijo?'

"'No, Mama. I didn't go far. I've eaten up all the money. That's what I supported myself with. It's all gone, and I've come to ask you for more.'

"Then she says, 'Ay, no, hijo, I told you already. I gave you one hundred and fifty. That was all I had. I gave it to you so you'd go far away. We were waiting for a letter. Fifteen days, another fifteen days, and now a month. And nothing. I was worried. Why didn't you write?'

"He says, 'No, Mama. I've been in San Luis with my aunt. I'm with my aunt. Now my money's all gone. I've come to ask you for more if you have it.'

"'No, hijo. I don't have it. I thought you had gone far away.' His mother was angry that he hadn't gone some place far away!

"So the next day dawned. And the next day. And there he was hiding in the house. And he went on like that—another day, two days, eight days, fifteen days passed, and then the months passed. He stayed on for a year, shut up inside the house, moving between the jacal, the room, and the kitchen. And they'd send me out to work the magueyes. And they'd send me out to the milpa. Meanwhile his mother was busy selling. And they'd send me out. I had a little baby girl. I'd leave her in her crib.

"She'd say, 'Leave that child there. Go to Milpillas. Go bring aguamiel. Will you let her go, Julio?'

"'She can go.' He was shut up in the room. 'Let her go. But go do the raspa and don't take too long.'

"I'd go on a burro. A jug on one side, a jug on the other. And I'd take the *acocote* to suck out the juice. They'd send me out to do the raspa and the little child would stay at home. Simeón was still young. He'd spend the day sleeping. The baby would wake up crying and crying. And once they sent Simeón to rock the baby. Well, he hurt her. It was one of those cribs made out of sackcloth, and he got into it to rock himself and jabbed his elbow into the baby's chest. I was coming back from the raspa. All the way from Milpillas. With the burro, I'd circle around the dam.

"When I got back, it was, '*Andale*, woman, the baby's crying and crying.' And there he was bursting with rage. He said, 'Now you finally get back? You daughter of a goddam mother. How come you couldn't get the raspa done faster?'

"'You think it's so nearby?'

"'But, man, such a long time. No matter how much I tell you not to be late, look how long you take.'

"Day after day it was like that. They'd send me out to do the raspa in the morning. Day after day. And when I'd get back, we'd get into an argument. He'd say to me, 'You went with your men. Or is it your mother you went to see? Now you're free to roam around. That's what you like, isn't it? And I'm here and can't go out.'

"I'd lose my patience and say, 'And why is it that you can't go out?' I'd answer him like that."

› › ›

Esperanza pauses, and it occurs to me to ask, "So you really didn't have any lovers while you were married?"

Esperanza is taken aback. "Me?" She laughs. "Ay, how was I going to have lovers? I wasn't even master enough of anything to go anywhere."

"So all those accusations were groundless?"

"Of course. I was innocent. That's why I felt so much coraje. And afterward they left me in the street. I could have found another man to be my husband, but I didn't want one. I was better off alone. That way I could go wherever I pleased, and no one could say anything to me. That other man I had was much younger than me. I was thirty-six when Julio left me. And this other man was twenty-five. I might have been with him, but . . ."

"He was the guard who—" I begin.

"*¡Andale!* So you knew him? When he first spoke to me, he was twenty-five. Afterward he got married in El Saucito. Then he started seeing the wife of the man who killed him . . ."

She pauses. I can feel that we've hit upon a rough edge of her story. I'm not sure whether to ask any further about her relationship with this man, who was murdered in 1983 in a bloody fight in the central plaza of Mexquitic. He was the father of her two daughters and youngest son, and yet she refused to live with him in any steady arrangement. She has little to say about him. . . . Or maybe she's embarrassed because her children by this man are always present when she's telling her story? To speak about her relationship with this man, she would have to speak about her desire and her sexuality, the things "down there" that she will not speak about except elusively.

"Why don't you tell us about the time when your mother-in-law threw you out?" I say to get the conversation going once more.

Her son Mario, excited by my interest, says, "Tell her, tell her!"

Chuckling, Esperanza says, "So you're enjoying my story?" And again she picks up the thread of her tale.

› › ›

"It was sixteen years of martyrdom. And I'm not even up to the middle of it yet. I haven't told you about when my girl died. That happened while he was hiding in the house after he escaped from jail the second time. That's how I ended up pregnant with the girl. But my mother-in-law would tell people that her son was lost.

"She'd say, 'I have no idea where my son is. He got lost in jail.'

"'So your daughter-in-law, why is she—'

"'Hush, don't you remember when she went off, when the children were on vacation?'

"'Ah, so your daughter-in-law went to San Luis and came back with that baggage?'

"'Yes.'

"'And aren't you angry?'

"'Even if I am, what can I do? I'm putting up with it for the sake of the children.'

"He was in hiding in the house for almost a year. That was when the girl died. We had a wake for the girl in the main room.

"'Comadre, comadrita. And my compadre?'

"'I don't know,' I had to reply. 'It's been a year since we've heard from him.'

"'Dear God! Poor child. My compadre gone and the child dead.'

"'Yes, what are we going to do?'

"And there he was, hiding in the jacal! The next day the girl was buried, and he was still there. And November came. I remember because that was when the boys got out of school. And November came and mother and son started to fight, she shouting, 'You kept man! ¡Atenido, mantenido!' and he whispering, 'Quiet, Mama. You're taking advantage because you see how helpless I am.'

"'Leave! I'm sick of you and your family.'

"I had twenty pesos saved up. Twenty pesos I had saved from the peaches we had sold. Twenty pesos I hid away so they wouldn't see them. And he didn't have a thing, his arms folded.

"'Go on, pack your things,' he said. I packed the few *tiliches* I had, the few cooking things, a few clothes of mine and the children's— hardly anything, because I really didn't have anything.

"We slept for an hour, two hours. Then he said, 'Get up! Let's go!' It was three in the morning. We had to leave before the cock crowed, when it would be too late.

"'Boys, boys, wake up! Let's go.' The boys were bigger by then. They were nine and eight years old. They got up right away.

"'Go on, tell my mama we're leaving,' he said to me.

"'Me?' I said.

"'All right, wait for me. I'm going to see my mama.'

"He knocked on the door and spoke to her. Even though they had argued, we didn't leave without saying adiós."

› › ›

"There we were in the hills, on the edge of the highway. He in front, the children following, and me behind. Every time a car passed, he'd cover his face with the blanket. We took the old path. You don't have to believe me, but we saw the dawn in El Saucito. Then we crossed the Avenida de la Paz and got to Veinte de Noviembre, where his aunt lived.

"'Will you give us permission, Aunt?'

"'Yes, it's fine. But what sort of work are you going to do?'

"'I'm going to work selling ice cream pops. I'll pick them up in the morning and go sell them on the outskirts.'

"That's what he did. He put me to work selling prickly pears. And we lived with his aunt, his mother's sister. We stayed with her all of November and December and up until the beginning of January. Those three months passed more or less well.

"And then there comes the vieja. He with his cart and the old Nana with him. I was selling prickly pears when she sees me and says, 'Good morning!' I didn't answer her.

"'Oh, how angry you are!'

"And the boys, 'Abuelita, Abuelita, Mamita!'

"'Hijos, I came to see you. I came to tell you to come home. Because they're asking for you boys in school. There was an *ejido* meeting and they called out your name, hijo. About the field. I've come to advise you to send your wife home and the children back to school. That way they'll see that the woman is there. Otherwise, they'll take the field away. You can stay here, hijo, and sell ice cream pops, keep working, and send them money. The woman can come on Fridays when the kids get out of school and stay until Sunday. She can take your clothes home to wash them. You stay here and work and give the woman money so the children can eat, because sometimes I sell and sometimes I don't.'

" 'That's fine, Mama. It's fine. What you say is right.'

" 'All right, hijo. Take care of yourself, hijo, don't let them see you.'

"For about a month we were fine. He'd give me money, and I'd cook for him. And the next week I'd come back. He gave me money— twenty, thirty pesos when he gave me a lot. But I had to give the money to his mother. 'Here, give this to my mama. Let her buy the corn.' I had to give her the money.

"But after a month, he started looking down at me. That was when he found the other woman. That was when his cousin told me that the woman was a cat, a maid. And that was when his aunt told me, 'I saw him with a woman who wore a scarf on her head. I think he's bringing her here to sleep. I don't know if he's selling ice cream pops or not. I think you better spy on him.' That was when I found him with the vieja.

"You know, my mama has often said to me, 'You covered up for that pelado, that Don Juan. And you see the kick in the pants he gave you? When you found him with the other woman, why didn't you turn him in? You were considerate toward him. Surely you didn't think he'd take you and your children in again?'

"Well, I guess I did think he'd leave that vieja and come back to me. I thought he'd come back."

› › ›

"And then I myself fell, *fracasé*, having these other children. And now my children are grown. So now, what? I pass by. There he is, just lying there. You've seen him, haven't you?" Esperanza asks, pausing to sip her soda.

"Yes," I reply, "we've seen him." He's a lean, dreary-looking man

who sits at his doorway in the afternoons. "He's blind, isn't he?"
I say.

"He pretends to be blind!" She starts laughing. "People say he's told them that I've bewitched him! He's told his own sons. No, this story is too long, comadre. And we're only halfway through."

› › ›

"So in June I gave birth to the child my mother-in-law had told everyone I picked up in San Luis. Julio was in Tampico with his mistress. I caught them in May. And in June I gave birth. My mother-in-law found someone to baptize the child. We called him Juan because he was born on San Juan, the twenty-fourth of June. And a year later, exactly a year later, was when that man came back. Not to the house, but to Paso Blanco, where his sister lived.

"I was with my mother-in-law. The child had been baptized, but he was sickly. He had diarrhea, fevers, vomiting spells. What could you expect with my coraje?

"And then, at the end of May, the beginning of June, his sister came. I was at home. And the boy Macario came running to tell me, 'Mama, Mama. My Aunt Merce is here. What do you think I heard her say?' He came running to the house to tell me. Mother and daughter were at the pulque stand.

"'My Aunt Merce was at the stand, and she didn't see me. I scrunched myself up against the wall. And I heard her say, "My brother doesn't want her anymore. He's at my house and he says he doesn't want her, so what do you have her there for? Why don't you throw her out?" And then she said that the vieja is very nice, a very nice girl; she's very nice and she loves him a lot. She even puts the food in his mouth, in my papa's mouth.' He had been listening to them talk. And the boy says, 'I heard everything, Mama. But then I moved and made a sound on the boards. And my abuela looked up and scolded me for listening to what was none of my business. So I ran and came back here.'

"The boy told me that at about four o'clock. Then it was five, six, seven, eight. I didn't go anywhere. The children were out playing. I had the baby, who was still little. He was going on his first year, yes, in June. He was going to be a year old in June. I think his birthday was just eight days away. But he died before his first birthday.

"My mother-in-law closed her stand at about eight and came home to eat. I had to serve her dinner. We couldn't eat until she ate. If she got back at nine or ten in the evening, we had to wait until then to eat. She had to serve herself first. So we're waiting for her. And she comes and says, 'What do you think, woman?' But I already knew.

"She says, 'Well, Merce came. And what do you think she came to tell me?'

"'Who knows?'

"'Who knows if it's true, but she tells me that the boy is at her house. He's there in Paso Blanco. And he's got a woman. She tells me she's very good looking, very pretty. I won't believe it until I see it.'

"'Ah.'

"There she was eating and eating. 'Well, Merce told me. Merce came to tell me to throw you out. That's what the boy says to do. He doesn't want you anymore. I said, "Well, she hasn't given me any cause for throwing her out. He's been away for a year from the house. Or two years already." And Merce said, "My brother doesn't want her anymore. He doesn't want her because she was very disrespectful to him when she saw him in San Luis."'

"Then I answered her back. 'Look, you as the owner of your house and me as just a sad lodger, you can throw me out at any hour of the day you please.' And I said, 'The woman that's with my husband is his wife, isn't she? And I'm just a sad mistress. So if you tell me right now that it's feet first, I'll be on my way.'

"'That's what my girl says my boy said to her, but who knows? So, it's up to you. I'm not asking you to stay nor to leave. You know what you do.' There she was, eating and eating. Finally she finished what was on her plate.

"'Well, go to bed. I'm going to bed, too.'

"She went to bed in her room, and I was in the jacal with the children. The baby had been sick for days. He wouldn't eat anything, so I had to give him the breast. And I felt such coraje, of course I did. But what could I do?

"The next day she was angry and I was, too. I thought to myself, we'll go on for that day, and another day, and another; we'll go on for another week. And the baby was limp with fever. Now what was I to do? I thought, If I go to my mama with this baby, this baby that's not going to live . . . I thought, I'll hold back until I see the end of this child. If I leave now with the child all sick, I'll be bothering my mama when he dies at her house. Why should I make my mama bury him? I thought to myself, I won't go. I'll wait and see what becomes of the child."

›››

"So I sent one of the boys. 'Go tell your abuela and ask her what I should do.' And my mama didn't wait. She went and told my sister. And my sister told a señorita, who is a lawyer. My sister and I had taken care of her when she was five years old. She and her brother were lawyers. My sister and I became women working at their house. I worked in the kitchen. The señora's name was Dora, and her daughter was Rosita. And my sister went and told Rosita. She's a lady lawyer. She was still working then, because she hadn't gotten married. My sister told her about the mess I was in. And my sister told my mama and my mama came to tell me.

"'Guess what your sister told me? She went and talked to Rosita. She asked her what you should do. And Rosita says for you to wait for her, that she's coming to see you. Let's see how it goes for you. You'll have to come to an agreement with your mother-in-law. Let's see what sort of feud there will be. And you're going to turn the pelado in!'

"The day arrived when Mama said Rosita would come. The child was more and more and more limp. I said to myself, Now I'm going in fiercely, I'm getting into this fiercely. I was washing the baby's rags. The boys were in school or out in the street.

"Suddenly there's a knock on the door. I was there alone, and my mother-in-law was across the street at her stand selling. There's a knock and Rosita says, 'Hola!' And then she says, 'Come, Esperanza, come here.' I was afraid. I didn't know what was going to happen. 'Come with me,' she says. 'Don't be afraid.' She pushed open the door so I stood facing her. 'How are you? What are you doing? Where's your mother-in-law?'

"'She's there at her stand.'

"'Good, that's good. Let's go. Please do me a favor. Show me where the office of the presidente is located.'

"'But my mother-in-law will see us.'

"'It doesn't matter if she sees us. Let's go, you can talk to me afterward.'

"'Wait for me. Let me get my baby.'

"'Go on, *ándale*. Bring him.'

"I put on a little rebozo and got the baby. Rosita had already stepped down from the curb and was standing next to her car. She had come with her father and her brother. When I stepped down, she said, 'Get in. Accompany us over there.'

"Everyone in the street could hear what she said. And there we go. I was shaking. I felt something horrible. I thought to myself, What am I going to do? Maybe my mother-in-law won't let me back in. She'll say it's my fault. I felt the world closing in on me. Rosita says to me, 'How have you been, Esperanza? Your sister Hipólita told me your story. Don't be afraid, Esperanza. Nothing is going to happen to you. You're going to win, not him, even though you shouldn't have covered up for that viejo.'

"'Is this it?'

"'Yes, there in front.'

"'*Andale*, let's get out.'

"'Good morning! Excuse me, where is the public ministry?' I didn't even know where it was myself.

"He says, 'I'm the secretario. What can I do for you, señorita?'

"She says, 'Look, sir, I come with this señora. I come on her behalf. I want you to attend to her.'

"'Yes, we're here to serve you, señorita.' He was very attentive, that man who's now deceased. He knew very well how to judge who was guilty and who wasn't. And now it's not like that. Now you're guilty unless you can pay.

"'I come with this señora, on her behalf. I'd like to take care of things now, but she's not ready yet.' Then she says, 'So I'm just coming to recommend her to you. When she's ready, I want you to do me the favor of attending to her.'

"'Of course, señorita.' He knew what my life had been like, and he knew that the man had been in hiding. 'Yes, señorita. If you like, we'll take care of it right now. We'll bring in all the people we need to.'

"'You see what I tell you, Esperanza? ¡*Orale!* Once and for all!'

"'No,' I said. 'I can't now. She's not angry with me now. Let's wait until she really throws me out. It won't be much longer. In a while, maybe even tomorrow, I'll be here.' Somehow I found the courage to speak up.

"'Good, Esperanza,' she says. 'When this señora comes with her complaint tomorrow, or the day after tomorrow, please do me the favor of attending to her.'

"'Yes, señorita, of course. We're at your service.'

"And Rosita says, 'You see, I'm telling you, Esperanza, don't be afraid. You've got all the rights, not him. How many years has he been gone?'

"'Two.'

"'There you have it. He's lost all his rights over you. And you don't belong to your mother-in-law.' After that, Rosita went with her father and her brother to buy some gordas de horno and they said adiós.

"I went home and got on with my chores. My mother-in-law was at her stand. A little later she came inside and said, 'So, you're back? You've gone on your stroll?' And then, 'Did that skinny she-dog come to take you out? There's one for her and one for you.' She said that because Rosita's father and brother were with her. And with that she turned and went back to her stand.

"I was really angry, but I said to myself, I won't leave until I see what becomes of the child. I spent my bitter hours in that house. She was constantly saying to me, 'They're coming to take you out. Get ready, they're coming to take you out for your stroll.' That was all she could say those last days I was with her."

›››

"And then the child was worse, worse, worse, worse, worse—until at last he died. The child died in just a few hours.

"There was nothing to be done. She didn't try to get him cured. She didn't call the doctor. Nothing. I gave him a little chamomile tea, but I didn't have any medicines to give him. So the child died. I don't remember if the child died during the day or at night. I can't remember. But I know he was laid out during the day, and at night we had the wake. A few children brought flowers.

"And then a señora who's since died came from Milpillas. I'm inside the jacal, and she comes over and says to me, 'Good afternoon, young woman, good afternoon.'

"'Good afternoon.'

"And she takes two steps and comes to the door and says, 'Listen, woman, get smart, because your mother-in-law says that you swallowed the child. Your mother-in-law says that you swallowed the child and you're going to have to pay for it.'

"I just stayed there thinking. And the woman stepped down. She told me not to say anything about what she had told me. Then she went back with my mother-in-law and said 'I'm back, comadrita,' but without letting on that she had said anything to me."

› › ›

"The next day, the child was buried. It was a Thursday, during the week, I think, but it doesn't matter—that day passed. One day passed and another day and another day. Almost eight days had passed since the child had been in the ground and I, as always, was stuck inside the house. There I was when it occurred to me to stand in the doorway. I said to myself, Who knows where the boys are? And me, why am I stuck in here? I went to the doorway and stood there. I saw the children playing in front of Dorotea's house, at the intersection, and I stood watching them. I'm there when I see Dorotea coming down the street. She had her stand near the house.

"'Good afternoon, Esperanza.'

"'Good afternoon, Dorotea.'

"'What are you doing there so sad?'

"'Oh, I'm just standing here.'

"'Ah, Esperanza. Did your child die?'

"'Yes.'

"'*Híjole*, so many of yours have died.'

"'Yes.'

"'Was he ill?'

"'Yes, and the diarrhea finished him off.'

"'Oh, how awful! What martyrdom you've got to put up with, really.'

"I didn't say anything.

"'And the pelado?'

"'He's in San Luis.' That came out of me. 'He's in San Luis.'

"'Ah, he's in San Luis. So how come your mother-in-law tells people that you just picked up your baby, that she doesn't know where her son is. But she does know where he is, doesn't she?'

"'He's got a mistress.'

"'Ay, then why does your mother-in-law wash herself with purity soap, saying she doesn't know anything about her son and that you had the child on your own and that she let you stay because she's so good, that because of your children she didn't want to throw you out, and that she doesn't know anything about her son and that you just picked up your baby just like that?'

"'Yes, that's what she says. Of course she knows about the man. He's been in San Luis. He has another mistress, another woman.'

"'¡*Andale!*'

"We were talking like that when we turned and saw her coming.

"'There comes your mother-in-law. *Andale,* she's going to flatten you out.'

"'Yes, I know.'

"'She mistreats you, doesn't she? I've heard that she mistreats you.'

"'Yes,' I said. 'It's martyrdom.'

"Then she says, 'All right, I'm leaving. No, maybe I better stay. Otherwise, she'll say that we saw her and that's why I'm running off. I'll just stay here.'

"There she comes and comes and comes, passes Don Berna's house, and there she comes. And Dorotea didn't leave. She changed the topic of conversation. 'The children are playing, isn't that good?'

"Finally she arrives, and Dorotea is in the street and she steps up to the sidewalk and says, 'Good afternoon.'

"'Good afternoon.'

"And just as my mother-in-law entered the house, Dorotea said, 'All right, Esperanza, I'll be seeing you.'

"'Yes, *ándale.*'

"Then my mother-in-law says, 'So, that's what you wanted, right? That's why you swallowed the child. To be in the street! Who are you looking for? What do they ask you? What do they say? What do they want to know about your life here? Do they look at your belly, to see whether or not it is full?' And then, 'Did you go get condolences from your mother? You're nice and calm here at the door. You must have gone to see your mother.'

"As she said that, I didn't move away from the door. From the moment she said that to me, I lost my fear. I wasn't afraid of her anymore. I think someone even wound me up after that.

"And she went on, 'What does that vieja ask you? What does she want to know? Does she want to know how your mother-in-law treats you? Do you eat, or not eat? What does she tell you? Does she bring you messages from your mother? I go to do my errands and I leave you here, thinking you're in the kitchen like a señora, like a decent señora. A respectable señora is not out in the street. Only those women who have nothing else to do are out in the street. Loose women.'

"She stepped forward to go inside, but I didn't move away from the door. I just moved over a bit so she could pass. And she went inside, muttering to herself, and opened the door to her room. She always kept it closed with a lock.

"When I heard her repeating that I had taken my mama's advice and that I had gone to see my mama and who knows what else, I got angry and went to the door to her room and said, 'How it infuriates me to hear you talk about my mama. My mama hasn't offended you in anything. So why do you keep mentioning my mama?'

"'Why are you arguing with me?'

"'Look, if before you had your way with me, now I'll have my way with you. So now, tell me everything you want to tell me.' I said, 'You've worn out my patience. You and your son. Especially your son. The way he's treated me. Why did the child die? Why did all our other children die?' I said, 'If before you had yours, now I'll have mine. Now go ahead and tell me everything you want to tell me and let's see how things go. And if you want bruises, then there will be bruises. These are not the old days anymore when you could grab me by the neck and try to strangle me, or beat me with the mesquite log.' I stood in the courtyard saying all that to her.

"She said, '¡*Chíngate! Chíngate tú sola.* If you want to *chingar, chíngate!*'

"'You can really say them, can't you?'

"'You're crazy. ¡*Chíngate tú sola!*'

"And she was inside her room and I was outside. And I yelled out to her, 'I'm not the master. Your son, yes, he can come and go as he pleases, but I have to be here like a slave!'

"She put the aguamiel into her pulque and took off for her lover's place. It was in the afternoon. God knows at what time she got back. Neither she nor I ate dinner. I just fed the children. I deliberately went to the pot myself and served the children their dinner.

"There was no corn to eat the next day. The next day, it must have been seven or seven-thirty when I got up. She was up, too. She was leaving to do the raspa. She pulled out a peso and fifty centavos and threw it at me. 'There's the money. Go buy corn and make a tortilla for the boys.'

"I didn't answer her. And she left. I went to Doña Paula's, and with that peso and fifty centavos, I bought a kilo of corn, or a kilo and a half of corn. All those years I had been grinding the corn with a metate since he wouldn't let me go to the mill. I set out my nixtamal, and when it cooled I went to Doña Paula's. I said, 'Doña Paula, will you grind this nixtamal for me and I'll owe it to you?' Doña Paula is a good person. 'Yes, of course.' I don't remember what she charged, but it was very little.

"I had her grind up the nixtamal and took the ball of dough home. And I was lighting the fire to start making tortillas when my mother-in-law came back. And there she was getting angry with the chickens. I think she was peeling corn when she said, 'Boys! What are you doing in the street? You—' Well, treating them badly.

"She was already drunk. And she was also fasting. She kept going on, 'My house will be for whoever helps me, for whoever looks after me; that's who my house will be for.' She just kept chattering away. 'My house will be for whoever knows how to look after me and my harvest, not for those who don't do anything.' And so on.

"But I couldn't take it anymore. I was about to take out the comal to make the tortillas and the words came out of me, what with her saying that her house would be for whoever helped her harvest, whoever took care of her. That got me angry. And I put down the dough.

"'Listen, if you go on with your sermons—Once and for all, throw me out into the street. Why are you talking so much?' And then I struck at her heart when I said, 'Let's see, you. What do you say? That you don't know where your son is, right? That I had that child with some pelado I found in San Luis? That he's not your son's child? And you cover up for your son, don't you?' Then I raised my voice and said, 'Isn't it true that you cover up for your son? You say you don't know where your son is. Well, I'm going to go accuse you before the presidente.'

"'Ha!' she says. 'You think I'm afraid of you?'

"'No, you're not one to be afraid. I'm the one who's afraid. But we'll see. I'll see you in court.'

"She says, 'In court?'

" 'Yes,' I say.

" 'Well, you go if you've got something to settle in court.'

"I said, 'No, not me. You!'

" 'Ha! You're crazy.' "

› › ›

"I put the dough away and ran to see the juez. I went right away. It was about eleven, twelve o'clock. I told my boys, 'I've reached my limit. There's no reason for me to be putting up with my mother-in-law. Well, let's see what advice they give me.'

"When I got to the juez he said, 'Good morning. What do you say, señora?'

" 'Now I'm coming to put in a complaint.'

" 'So did you get kicked out?'

" 'Yes, feet first.'

" 'And your husband?'

" 'He's in San Luis.'

" 'Ah! So why does your mother-in-law say she doesn't know where he is? How do you like that?'

" 'Now that my child is dead, I've had it.'

" 'Ah, you had an *angelito*?'

" 'Yes, the child died.'

" 'Well, there's a rumor that your mother-in-law says the child was not your husband's, that it was another man's.'

" 'I'm up to my ears. Look, it's like this.' And I told the juez every-thing, the whole story.

" 'It all makes sense now. But that vieja was so good at dissimulat-ing. Well, you're the one who's in the right, so don't be afraid. Noth-ing's going to happen to you. But what a pelado! And we weren't even able to snare him,' he says.

" 'He's been in Tampico. And a year ago I caught him with his mis-tress in San Luis!'

" 'You should have turned him in, there in San Luis!'

" 'But how? What was I to do, a woman alone? I wanted to—I was near the station in Tlaxcala, but I don't know . . .'

" 'You endured a lot. But if you had turned him in during those days, he wouldn't have gotten out in twenty years! Because his major crime is to have escaped from the law. That's his biggest crime. But that's over with. Now let's see what your mother-in-law says.'

"'What should I do?'

"'You don't have to be there anymore. You have to put up with a husband, but not with a mother-in-law. Take your things and leave. Don't say anything else to her. But if she lays her hands on you—we'll really do her in. That vieja, we'll do her in.'

"'Look, she's not there now. But if, as you're telling me, I get my few things together and pack them up and start to leave, what should I do when she comes back and shoves me back inside? Then what?'

"'¡Híjole! She's really got you under her control, doesn't she?'

"I was with the juez when she entered the room. And the guard said to her, 'Señora Timotea, the juez wants to talk to you.'

"'Me? I don't have any business with the juez. I've come to settle another matter here.'

"'Señora, the juez wants to speak to you. He's waiting for you.'

"Whether she wanted to or not, she had to see him.

"'Señora, we're calling you because you've filed a charge, and here the señora has also filed a charge against you.'

"'Oh really? Good.'

"'Yes, the señora has filed a charge against you. She says that you've thrown her out.'

"'I threw her out?'

"'Let's see, señora, go on.'

"'I'm accusing her for the following reasons. I've already told you the whole story. It's my man, her son, who's told me to leave. I found him with his mistress in San Luis. And while I was living with my mother-in-law, she spread the rumor that my child was not her son's child. And she claimed not to know where her son was. Well, her son escaped from jail, and she's been covering up for him. She knew where her son was then, just as she knows where he is now. And that's all of it.'

"Then he said, 'Ah, that's fine. Now you, señora, what do you have to say to your daughter-in-law?'

"'She says that I threw her out, but that's not true.'

"'Yes,' I say, 'it's true. You've beat me worse than if I had been married to you. So I've had enough.'

"We said so many things to each other that day.

"'Yes, señoras. A mother can't pay for her son and a son can't pay for his mother. So the two of you have to reach an agreement. You, Señora Timotea, say you won't receive her. Your daughter-in-law says that she won't enter your house again. So that's simple enough. Now the only question is her husband. But given how many years her husband has been away, he's lost all rights over her. So the señora has no other choice but to find her way as best she can and to support herself and her sons.' And then he says, 'Señora, you say you don't want her at your side. Then do it for her sons. Take in your grandsons!'

"My mother-in-law said, 'Me, grandsons? I don't have grandsons. She already left with her sons. I don't want family responsibilities.'

"'So you don't want your grandsons?'

"'No,' she says. 'She left with her sons, and now I don't want them to enter my house again.'

"'She doesn't want her grandsons, señora. You will have to take charge of your family,' the juez says to me. 'From now on, you will only have your sons to make you suffer.'"

FOUR

The Daughter in the Mother

It is our tradition to conceive of the bond between mother and daughter as paramount and essential in our lives. It is the daughters that can be relied upon. Las hijas who remain faithful a la madre, a la madre de la madre.

—Cherríe Moraga, Loving in the War Years

July 29, 1985. Two weeks passed before Esperanza could come back to talk to me in the kitchen. During that time, David and I returned to Mexico City to work in the archives for several days. I continued to collect women's confessions to the Inquisition even as I listened to Esperanza's confession. The day after we returned, on July 28, Esperanza stopped by early in the morning to invite us to a birthday party for Mario that same afternoon. I cheerfully said we'd be there and bring the camera. Yet I actually dreaded the thought of having to go up to her house on a Sunday, when everyone would be around watching and wondering what business the gringos had to take care of at the top of the hill where all the witches were said to live. Before I knew Esperanza, I had frequently climbed up that hill overlooking the church to visit with Doña Primitiva, a petite, wily woman who still lives in the old-style jacal thatched with maguey leaves. Doña Primitiva has a reputation in Mexquitic as a "curandera" who also knows how to work evil, and I had sought her out because I was trying to learn what the stories about sexual witchcraft that I was finding in the Inquisition documents had in common with contemporary beliefs and practices.

One afternoon I sat watching as Doña Primitiva performed a "ventosa," cupping a woman's lower back four times with a large glass lined with rubbing alcohol, which she lit to suck out the cold. Lying on her stomach in Primitiva's jacal, the woman who was being cupped said that her husband drank too much and she just wanted to get him under control. She reported in veiled terms to Primitiva that the jar with the potion was "half-finished," that it seemed to help, and that, "no, he hadn't noticed." As I sat listening, David suddenly whispered to me to come out for a minute. He had been talking to Primitiva's current male partner in another jacal, and I imagined he would tell me he was ready to go home. I excused myself, and when I came out David said, "Nestor has gone to do an errand. Quick, look at this. You won't believe it." I followed him to the dense forest of nopales behind Primitiva's house. On one of the nopales, an old doll with cracked glass eyes was hanging from a rope elaborately wrapped around its neck. The doll looked as if it had been streaked with blood. Several weeks later, I saw another doll hanging out in front of Primitiva's jacal, and that time I asked her about it. She told me nonchalantly that it was for a "trabajo," a job she was doing for a woman who wanted to leave her husband so she could join up with another man she liked better.

I continued to seek out Primitiva for some time after, but soon she began to grow suspicious and seemed less willing to answer my questions about her involvement in witchcraft. For a year she kept promising to take me to a centro, where the spirit medium talks to the devil at midnight in a house full of books of black magic as well as unsavory things like skulls and infants' joints. One day, when I was tired of her stalling and she was tired of my questioning, she pointed in the direction of Esperanza's house, which is a stone's throw away from her jacal, and said, "Go there, that mother and daughter who live there are witches. We can't stand each other. They don't talk to me and I don't talk to them. Maybe they can tell you something." Little did I know that eventually I would get to know that mother and daughter. But as I became friendly with Esperanza, it became almost impossible for me to visit Primitiva without making my comadre suspicious of my motives. In climbing that hill just beyond the respectable center of town, I had landed in a nest of old hatreds. When I was up there, I feared that Primitiva would see me with Esperanza or that Esperanza would see me with Primitiva. I couldn't yet know that my comadre, with her stories, was slowly but consistently winning me over to her side.

∞ "So they wrote up a piece of paper. I still have that paper with everything written on it, everything she said to me, everything I said to her. And then the juez says to me, 'Now you'll have to support yourself as best you can.'

"And I said to him, 'Well, I'm going to have to get what's planted in their field.'

"And my mother-in-law says, 'You're not going to take anything in my son's field.'

" 'We're not the proper authorities to handle those affairs,' the juez says. 'Those affairs have to do with agrarian laws, so that will have to be taken care of in the Department of Agrarian Affairs. That's where they handle land questions. If the papers come to us, then the señora will be given the field. But first go and take care of it there.' And then he says, 'Here, Doña Timotea, here's your copy.'

"She walked on ahead, and I stayed behind. The juez says to me, 'Well, señora, here's your copy. Now support yourself as best you can. Don't let your sons starve to death. Go live some place where you'll be happy.'

" 'I have my mama.'

" 'Señora, you have an ounce of gold if you have your mama.' Then he says, 'Let your mama take you in.'

"I had left a box of the boys' clothes at Eugenia's stand when I went to see the juez. Those clothes had been given to me by my sister, some clothes for my boys and some for me. I really had nothing. I almost had to use one hand to cover my front and another hand to cover my back. And I went back to my mama."

› › ›

"Fifteen days after I left my mother-in-law's house, I took a walk to the field. With my own two feet, I went to the field and brought back corn and beans! I gave that to my boys to eat. Another eight days passed, another fifteen days passed. People I knew would say to me, 'Don't give in, Esperanza. Don't leave them the field. Look how much you worked! It can be for your sons! If you don't have anything now, tomorrow you'll have something. Ask your mama for help, even if it's just a loan. You work and plant the field and it will be yours!'

"Yes, I said to myself, I'm not going to let it go. So I went to see the comisario, who at that time was Don Emilio. My mama went with me.

'Listen, Don Emilio, I've come to ask you for advice about what I should do.'

"He says, 'No, you have the very best right.' He talks kind of funny, you know. 'You have the very best right.'

" 'You mean, you think they would give it to me?'

" 'One, two, three, they'll give it to you! Don't you see that an ejidatario can't have two fields? If you don't get smart and put in a request for it, the field will end up in someone else's hands.' And he says, 'Don't be afraid, Doña Esperanza. Look, I'll go with you, if you like.'

"So Don Emilio took us. 'Let's see, señores, what can I do for you?' the man there said. His name is Zúñiga. They say he's the one who divides the cheese in the Department of Agrarian Affairs.

" 'Well, you know, sir, I come because I want the field that belongs to my husband, who has left me. He's been away from Mexquitic for two years, without attending to the ejido. He's not looked after me nor his family. I was with his mother, but we had an argument and I'm no longer living with her. So I'm fighting for the land.'

" 'Very well. How many years do you say he's been away?'

" 'It's been two years since he's worked the field.'

" 'And what is your mother-in-law's name?'

" 'Doña Timotea.'

" 'Let's see,' he says. There were so many secretaries there. 'Let's see, please draw up some papers for me. One for the comisario, one for her, one for the mother-in-law, one for the judge, four, five copies.' Right away. *Sshhhh*—you could hear the typewriters.

" 'Very well. Yes, señora, you have rights to that field.' Then he said, 'Take these papers. This one is yours. You, as the comisario, will take one, give one to the juez and another to that señora Timotea. And you are to return on so-and-so day.' About three days later. 'And the señora is to come, too. Tell the señora that I'll be waiting for her in the Department of Agrarian Affairs. Tell that to the señora Timotea. And you, come back, too, señor comisario. So we can come to an agreement.'

"The comisario took the copy to my mother-in-law. Then another day, there we go again.

" 'Are you the señora who was here yesterday?'

" 'Yes, the day before yesterday.'

" 'Good. Did your mother-in-law come?'

" 'Yes, she's outside.'

" 'Call her.'

" 'No, not me.'

" 'Call her, would you, comisario?'

" 'Doña Timotea, they're calling you inside. Go inside.'

"She looked at me with eyeballs full of anger! Looked at me and Don Emilio. Afterward she had the nerve to tell people that Don Emilio, with your pardon, was my lover. She said he was my lover because he helped me to get the field.

" 'This señora has come to make a claim on her husband's field. She says her husband has been away from the ejido for a long time and he's not looked after her nor her family and that you have been supporting them.'

" 'Yes, señor, my son left his family with me. Señor, the truth is my son was put in jail and then he got lost!' That's what she said, and I felt like throwing her out head first!

"Then he says to her, 'So you don't know what's become of your son?'

" 'No, señor.'

" 'Very well. How many years has it been since your son last exercised his rights over the field?'

" 'Oh, just a short time,' she tells him. 'A short time, just two years.'

" 'Ah. Well, look, señora, this señora has come to fight for the field, and I think you should give it to her. The field belongs to this señora.' He told her that!

" 'But why should I give it to her? Ever since my son has been lost, I've been the one responsible for that field. So why should I give the field to her?'

" 'Understand me, señora. If you're saying you won't give it to her because you've put a lot of money into it, then you're wrong. Since the moment your son left, you should have given the rights to the land to the señora. When your son returns, charge him all the money you've put into the field. But you're going to give the field to the señora.' Then he says, 'What do you have planted there?'

" 'I have corn and beans!'

" 'Very well,' he says. 'You, señor comisario, you're going to be in charge of distributing what's in this field to these señoras. When the harvest is ready, you're going to say, all right, señoras, let's distribute the harvest. If there are five, six furrows, or ten, twenty furrows, then divide it half and half. Eh? And you, señora, you will collect everything allotted to you and you'll leave the field to the señora. After that you don't need to return to the field anymore.' "

›››

"And then the following year was when my mama began to be sick. From the year that we planted, the next year was when my mama began to be sick with that pain in her stomach. It started with her saying she felt a pain all along her waist, as though she were in labor.

"One day my sister says, 'What happened to you, Mama?'

" 'I don't know. I don't know what it could be.'

" 'No, Mama, did you feel coraje, some kind of coraje?'

" 'Yes, I do feel coraje with that woman, with everything she's going around saying about me.' Because people would tell my mama what my mother-in-law was saying. 'She's telling everyone I'm rich now because I have a nice field.'

"My sister took Mama to San Luis to get prescription medicine two or three times. But even with the medicines, my mama got worse and worse and worse. That pain and that pain, and she unable to eat or get out of bed. And then her head was throbbing, hurting. What could it be? They gave her injections and spoonfuls and pills. And my mama was worse and worse. After she got sick, she couldn't get the juice from the magueyes anymore; she couldn't make pulque anymore.

"And that Primitiva, she went to a centro every time there was a *bajada de espíritu*, every time a spirit came down. She hadn't come in a while to visit my mama. Because that Doña Primitiva is a sister-in-law of my mama, or rather was a sister-in-law. She had lived with a brother of my mama. And that Primitiva also went around with that Julio of mine. She was his lover! I saw them hiding behind an adobe wall. My mother-in-law told me about them. 'That pig! ¡Vergonzona! Don't you get corajes. Just don't pay attention.' That was when she was being a little bit nice to me. And after I left my mother-in-law's house, that Primitiva became more friendly with my mother-in-law. And Primitiva would also talk with my mama. Whatever we told her, she would go and tell Timotea. Who could have known? Primitiva would come and say, 'Nicolasa, how are you? Give me some pulquito. Ah, your girl is here now. You see what men are like. So she's here with you?' And my mama would say, 'Yes, she's here with me now, my girl. They threw her out because they caught her doing it, you know. But not her husband. He's pure, he's clean.' She'd say that and Primitiva wouldn't keep quiet. She'd go and tell my mother-in-law.

"So one day she came. 'Sister-in-law, sister-in-law! What are you doing? What's up Nicolasa?'

" 'Here I am.'

" 'What does your mama have?' she asked my sister.

" 'I don't know. She's sick. We don't know what she has.'

" 'Give her the medicine, she'll get better. Poor Nicolasa.' And she left. Two, three days later she came back to see my mama.

" 'How are you, Nicolasa? How are you doing?'

" 'Not well.'

" 'You're still ill, Nicolasa? You're not any better?'

" 'No, I feel worse and worse. And this pain I have, as though I were in childbirth, but it's getting worse and worse. And my head's throbbing.'

" 'What can it be, Nicolasa?'

" 'Who knows what it could be.' My mama was really weak by then.

"The one who cried was my sister, Hipólita. And Primitiva said to her, 'Listen, Hipólita. I'm going to tell you something. I don't think your mama has a good illness.'

" 'Why, Doña Primitiva? Why do you say that?'

" 'Just by looking at her. You've already gotten prescriptions for her.'

" 'Yes, we've gotten prescriptions twice. She's finished the medicine, and there she is worse than before.'

" 'Well, if you want and if you like, I'll take your mama to a centro. If you have faith, of course. I'll take you, but you'll have to pay my fare.'

" 'Ah.' Then my sister says, 'Mama, Mama, we're going to take you. Doña Primitiva says—'

" 'Yes, Nicolasa, I'm telling the girls that you don't have a good illness. You've been bewitched, you've got a bad illness.'

"Mama got up and my sister and I changed her clothes.

" 'Doña Primitiva, please do us the favor. Don't worry about the fare. We'll take you, we'll pay your fare, just so you'll do us the favor. Let's see if my mama gets better.'

"We pulled Mama up by the arms and led her all the way from the house to the highway."

› › ›

"Just past the water tank in San Luis was the spiritist centro.

" 'Here it is. Come here,' that Primitiva says. She spoke first. 'Angelita, Angelita. Good morning, good morning, Angelita.'

" 'What do you say, Primitiva? What do you say?'

" 'Angelita, I've brought you this señora. The girls are her daughters. This señora is very sick. She's my sister-in-law. Well, we used to be sisters-in-law. Her brother already died. But we're sisters-in-law just the same. My sister-in-law, poor thing, she's sick. Her family says that they've tried to cure her, but she's not feeling any better.'

"Angelita says, 'We're going to see right now. Please come in. Take them in.' She had a little room with an altar. 'Let's see, señora. In the name of God, let's see. Let's see what's going on.' She had a big crystal ball full of water next to the altar. Then she says, 'Well, how did it start?'

"My mama could barely speak, so my sister and I told her. And she just kept looking at the crystal ball. Whatever we said, she'd look into the big crystal ball. 'Ummm. *Híjole*, woman. You come really sick. You've come so close. They've got you bewitched, woman. *Qué bárbaros.* Look how they have you.'

"Primitiva says, 'Isn't it so, Angelita? I told her right away. I told her daughters right away.'

" 'Yes, it's true. You'll get better, but you're going to have to fight. It's going to take a while for you to get better. But you will get better. In the name of God, I'm going to put my hands on you.' Then she had my mama stand up, and she swept her with some brooms and who knows what lotions she put on her. Then she prayed over her, she swept her and prayed over her. 'This was done to you'—she was looking into the crystal ball—'this was done to you. *Qué bárbaros*, what wretched sorts. This was done out of vengeance. It's vengeance that they did to you because of your family.'

"Right away I thought to myself, *Híjole*, I think it's that vieja Timotea who's done this. Because of my mama's family? Well, who else but me? Because I took the field away from them. But, you see, my mother-in-law did it with that Primitiva. We thought Doña Primitiva was a good señora. She was what she was, but we didn't think she would have done my mama any harm. But why did she do the evil to my mama? Because she got together with that vieja Timotea. The very woman that Primitiva took my mama to see, that very woman told my mama. Angelita said to my mama, 'Be careful. Don't confide in her. She's a—' And she uttered a curse. 'Well, you've also got her part in this. This is a team that they've formed, three or four people who together did this evil to you, out of pure envy, coraje, and vengeance. That Primitiva, you also have a share of her . . . You say she's your sister-in-law?'

" 'Yes, she was with my brother for a while.'

" 'So you see? That's why she had a guilty conscience. They had you in a corner moaning, but then her conscience started to bother her! What happened was that your mother-in-law invited her to do the work, and together they said, "Let's do her in!" '

" 'But the very one who did it is a light-skinned fat woman,' Angelita told us.

"Yes, she was light-skinned, fat, white, mottled. Fat with deep-set eyes. My mother-in-law.

"To cure the sick and to learn what they have, they work at night. The centro that cured my mama had images. The white centro and the red centro, that's where the images are. And at the black centro, that's where you find the Evil One. Those black centros are for ruining a person, killing another person. But if you work with the Evil One, do you think God will pardon you? No, in these white centros they have images of the Lord our God, the Virgin of Guadalupe, the Virgin of Perpetual Aid, the Virgin of the Sacred Heart. Those are the ones they work with. They entreat them so that everything will come out all right. They're like souls, souls to serve another soul.

" 'Look, here what I see is a light-skinned fat woman with deep-set eyes, a dark, short woman, and a man, a dark man.'

"That man was a man my mama had lived with. She had two sons with him. But, you see, this man was also my mother-in-law's lover. That vieja mother-in-law of mine took up with my mama's man. It's true my mama wasn't married to him, but my mama had two sons with that man.

"That viejo beat my mama. He would go over to my mama's house drunk and give her some good beatings. People would tell my mama that they had seen him fooling around with my mother-in-law. And then everyone knew that her own daughter went to bed with him. And that man, whose name was Román, used to be called 'the Blackman,' because he was dark-skinned, very dark.

"My mama and that viejo used to fight a lot, until my mama said to him, 'Leave right now. After all, I'm not in your house. I'm in my own house. Go to your lover down there. I don't want to see you here ever again.'

"He beat my mama. I've said to her, 'You see, you left my papa because he beat you, and you came here and found another one just like him who also beat you.'

"At the centro my mama said, 'Yes, I think it's that viejo, Román. You see, I threw him out. I said something to him about that vieja Timotea. And I threw him out, told him I didn't want him back in my house. After all, he was not supporting me nor my children. I was the one who was selling pulque to support myself.' And then my mama says, 'You know what he once said to me? "Daughter of who knows what mother, you're going to remember me. Soon you'll see. I'm black and I look like I'm nobody, but you're going to remember me. Just me and my black cat, that's who will save me! That's who will help me!"'

"That's what he yelled at my mama when she threw him out. 'And you'll know who I am! And you won't make fun of me again!' So it was clear that it had been him.

"'Here I see a woman, and another person, and then a dark man.' That's what Angelita said. 'Look, I'm going to tell you the truth. Don't say anything to that Primitiva, since you say she's your sister-in-law. But she's also ruined you. I'm telling you. Keep your mouth shut. Don't tell her I told you. But she knows. She knows, because she's learned it here. Then she says to you, "Are you very ill, poor thing?" But she also put her grain of salt into the pot.'

"Later we learned that it was Primitiva who had made the doll. But to finish telling you the story, Angelita said, 'I'm going to make that Primitiva cure you. And I'll fight it out with the other two. All night I'll work for you. All night I'll fight with them until they let go of you. But I'll have to make that Primitiva cure you. I'm going to give you the remedies and the brooms so she can cure you herself. But don't tell her I told you. Let her cure you, so you'll get better.'

"They were brooms made of bunches of pirul, parsley, rosemary, and other herbs which are used to sweep out illnesses. She said to us, 'Take these brooms and tomorrow go see her. Go at about noon, just as it's about to strike noon.'

"The next day, 'How are you, Nicolasa? What did Angelita say to you?'

" 'You know what, she sent you a message. She said that you should do her the favor of curing me.'

" 'That I should cure you? How can I cure you? It's in her hands. I can't cure you.'

" 'That's what she said. She said that you should cure me.'

" 'Dear God, no.'

"Angelita had warned my mama, 'And she's not going to want to do it. But she has to. I'll make her cure you.'

"Then Primitiva says, 'No, not me. You're in her hands. That's why I took you to her. How am I going to cure you if only she knows how she's curing you? If you get sick, then it's going to be her fault.' That's the story she made up, but she did cure my mama, even though she didn't want to. She swept and swept and swept Mama. And prayed I don't know how long over her.

"The next day when my mama went to the centro, Angelita says, 'She didn't want to do it, right? But she had to. At least she's now removed the part that she had in it.' Then she gave my mama five or six sweepings.

"Mama could walk again, and she was eating more. That pain in her belly was starting to subside. But she still had those throbbings in her head.

"And then one day Primitiva came to the house and said, 'Nicolasa, when did you agree to go back to the centro?'

" 'Angelita told me that I didn't have to go back for a while.'

" '*Andale*, Angelita is dead.'

" 'She died?'

" 'She died in just one moment.'

" 'But she's a big woman, full of life.'

" 'Well, she's dead. I went to look for her the other day, and they told me she had died. She's in the ground already. I went to see her and didn't find her.'

"Suddenly Angelita was dead. She was curing someone, fighting
with whoever had done the evil to the person she was curing. She
fought the entire night, but her opponent won the battle. The other
one won, and she died."

> > >

"Shortly after Angelita died the throbbings became concentrated in
Mama's eye, in that eye that's sunken now. A little pimple appeared on
her lid, and that pimple gave her pain and more pain and more pain
and more pain as it grew bigger. The pimple was a big ball she had
there. And my mama was sick, sick, sick.

"That Primitiva stopped coming by. And people would visit from the
rancho of La Campana and say, 'Ay, comadre, what's wrong?'

"And my mama, 'I don't know.'

"'But what an ugly pimple you've got.'

"'Yes, I don't know. It must be full of water, or who knows . . . God
only knows what it is.'

"That vieja Timotea, she even gave herself away. When my mama
was being cured by Angelita, she ran into the vieja Timotea one day at
Doña Clara's store. And my mama felt a lot of coraje, knowing who
had done the evil, right? When my mama went to Doña Clara's store,
the vieja Timotea was there buying something. And my mama says,
'Ay, Doña Clara, give me a little bread. I'm hungry. I'm just hungry
thinking about how I can't see anymore. I can see with one eye, but
with the other one I can't. I'm practically dying. Please give me a little
bread.' My mama talks like that. 'Here they just want to finish me off.
I can see with one eye, but not with the other one. I think it's failing
me. Give me a little bread, will you?'

"And then Doña Clara gave my mother-in-law her change. My mama
was standing at the door saying all of that when the vieja goes to the
door and says, 'And wait till the other one goes, you daughter of—'

"Imagine, she gave herself away! Don't you understand it that way,
comadre? When she said, 'And wait till the other one goes,' she let it
be known that she was the one doing the work.

"And then after Angelita died, my mama's eye had a big ball on it
that turned black, a reddish black. I'm not lying to you. The very tip of
the pimple had turned black and red. When the ball on her eye burst,

the swelling went down. But the wound wouldn't close up and form a
scab. My mama would be talking with someone, and then she'd start
dripping pus and blood. Pus and blood, pus and blood. She went on like
that for seven years, my mama. Don't you see how her eye ended up
sunken?

"One of Mama's comadres said to her, 'Look, comadre, if you like,
I'll take you to a very good señora there in Morales who knows how to
cure.' But, no, that señora wasn't able to make her better. And then
we took my mama to another señora who my sister knew. And no,
she was just throwing her money away. They would say, 'Yes, señora,
you're ill. But you're going to get better.' But they couldn't do anything
about her eye. They'd put things on it, and it wouldn't form a scab.
They couldn't get that eye to heal. With each day my mama's eye was
festering. With each day. Her eye was consumed, sucked dry. Nothing,
nothing, nothing could heal that eye. Then finally, thanks to my sister,
she found that señora from Ojuelos.

"Where my sister worked, there were three other maids besides her.
And my mama would go visit my sister, and they would see her eye.
My sister told them that my mama had been like that for a long time,
but that she couldn't find anyone to cure her. 'That might be a bad illness, Hipólita,' one of her companions told her. 'That's so strange, poor
señora. Look, my mama knows a good señora from Ojuelos. She's very
good at curing. The señora is from Ojuelos, and she comes to cure in
San Luis. And she's a good friend of my mama's. My mama gives her
permission to stay at our house. She stays for two nights and then goes
back to Ojuelos. But she comes here to cure sick people. And my
mama says she's very good.'

"So that señora from Ojuelos looked Mama over and said, '*Qué bárbaros*, señora! You've got very little time left. How long have you been
like this?'

"'I'm going on seven years.'

"Then she says, 'You're bewitched. You're reaching the end of your
line. And you're buried in your own house. I know what I'm telling
you. If you want to, I'll go pull you out of your house. I'll pull you out
because you're buried. They've got you in your own house.'

"When the señora cured my mama she put some cream on her eye,
and Mama said it felt as though ants were crawling all over her eye.

My mama had such an urge to scratch it, and she'd tell the señora, 'I feel this desperation, it's awful.'

"'No, don't move. Let them come out. Don't be afraid. Hold back. Let them come out.'

"And she'd remove bugs, white ones with dark heads. One came out and then another one popped out and then another one. They were chubby things, really ugly little animals. And then she'd take those worms and drop them on a rag and burn them. That's what the woman did, there in the house where she'd go to cure.

"'As I say, you're bewitched and you're buried. If you like and want me to finish curing you, I'll pull you out. I promise you I'll get you out. But you have to buy me a new pot and get a pirul branch and a bottle of holy water.' She said she would come at noon.

"When the señora arrived, my mama said, 'I've got the pot, the holy water, and a branch.'

"The woman rested a little bit. Then she says, '*Andale*, now. It's almost time.' And outside, below the front window, just below the window, that's where Mama was, right there at the entrance to the house.

"First the señora prayed, prayed, prayed. Then she says, 'Here! Here you are. Bring the pot, the bottle of holy water, and give me the branch.' And she took the branch and made the sign of the cross on the ground. Then she stuck the branch in the ground and poked. She stuck her hand into the loosened earth. And then she said, 'Here you are. Yes, here you are. Here you come. Now I've got you.' She pulled, pulled, pulled, pulled out her hand and said, 'Cover it for me. Cover it for me!' And she grabbed the pot and scooped the thing into it and covered it with her hand. 'Now pour holy water here in this hole and cover it with earth. And put a rock or a nopal stem here so there won't be any signs that we've been digging.'

"She went into the room. We brought out a chair for her, and she sat down. 'Let's see how you are, woman,' she says. 'Let's see, let's see how you are.' There was a big mass wrapped in paper and cloth. And in the middle of it there was a bottle, one of those wide ones, with its own cap. She loosened the threads. It was all tied up, all knotted. She loosened another thread and another thread. And my mama was sweating. She was sweating and sweating and sweating, and it was sweat and sweat. Then the señora says, 'Of course, because you're inside the bottle and it is discharging all the rain water and all the heat from the warmth of the earth—the bottle is discharging all of that. That's why you're feeling that.' And done. Then she says, 'Now I've got it.' Then she says, 'Look, there's even a piece of paper here.' A piece of paper was stuck inside the bottle. And there, too, was the wax doll.

"That wax doll was just like my mama. With one eye just the way hers was. They gave her eyes, a mouth, and hair, and the hair was my mama's very own hair. Well, ever since that happened to Mama, we're a little more careful. But, you see, sometimes I can't break the habit of combing my hair and letting the hair fall where it will. I try to put it in the potted plants, but some of the hairs fall in the courtyard and then when it rains the water edges them down. Well, the hair on the wax doll had been stuck on. The hair was slightly curly, because my mama has curly hair. When she lets it out, it's a little bit curly. So they put hair on my mama. But from side to side, there were pins. From side to side, there were pins! And her hair was all knotted up. And the part that was the head was rotting. It was half-melted. Haven't you ever seen a piece of candy that's been sucked and tossed to the ground, and then the ants get into it and a little sunken spot gets formed where it's dissolved? Well, that's how she had her head. The wax was sunken. They dressed her in black. The doll was dressed in black. They made a very good copy of my mama. With her long full skirt, because she used that kind of skirt, and with her blouse, the kind of blouse she uses. And with a sunken eye.

"The señora says, 'There you are. Just look at how you are. You were almost gone. Now, God willing, you'll be saved. You see, you just had a little bit to go.'

"She took out the piece of paper that was inside the bottle and unfolded it. I haven't forgotten those words. It said, 'Hipólita, if you don't cure her, you'll sing for her. And if you cure her, it will cost you a thousand pesos.' And the señora did charge a thousand pesos. Everything was cheaper then, but we thought that was a fortune.

"'I'll see you another day,' the señora says. 'I've still got to finish curing you. I've removed the last of the worms, but I haven't healed your eye yet.' My sister paid the señora and took her back to San Luis.

"Never again did my mama see that woman! At the house where the señora used to cure, they told Mama that she didn't come anymore.

And she didn't come anymore and she didn't come anymore. She didn't want to cure my mama anymore."

› › ›

"My mama felt better because the woman had removed the worms and pulled her out of where she had been buried. That was the only consolation she had. But her eye was the same. Pus with blood, pus with blood. Until finally, because when God wills it or permits it . . . I don't know how to tell you. Until I took her to a very good woman.

"We've known her now for sixteen years. She's from Mexico City, near Mexico City. She's told us she started studying when she was ten years old. That's when she started that kind of work. She was the one who finally cured my mama. She was really young then.

"While Mama was ill, I had found my path and started selling in San Luis. One day a señora in San Luis who used to buy my things said to me, 'What do you think? An angel has landed in my house. It's been fifteen days since she came to my house. I gave her permission to stay. She wanted me to rent her a room. An angel from heaven. And she's very young. A young woman who knows how to cure has landed in my house.'

" 'Really?'

" 'Yes. I've already told her I won't charge her rent. I took her upstairs to the room I have up there. And she told me where she was from and what she does. And I told her my problems. And she says, "Don't worry, señora. I'll take care of it." I told her about how that viejo of mine is trying to take away my daughter and my son and how I'm working and he keeps getting in my way, even though he already has a mistress. And she told me she would help me.' Then the señora says, 'Tell your mama. Bring your mama here so she can be cured. She's very good at curing, even though she's so young. She must be fourteen years old.'

"That señora had a room up a flight of stairs, next to the door to the roof. There in a corner the girl had her little altar. 'Look, I want to introduce you to a friend,' she says. 'She tells me her mama has been sick for many years. They did evil to her; she's been through a lot of hands, a lot of centros, and they haven't been able to cure her. Please cure her. She's my friend. Poor thing, her mama is ill.'

"And Cresencia, the girl, says, 'Yes, of course, of course.'

"'But we live in a rancho far away,' I tell her.

"'That doesn't matter. Bring her here to me. When will you bring her?'

"'I need to see if Mama still wants to be cured and whether my sister wants to pay for it, because I don't have any money. My sister works and since she's not married, she's the one who pays for the cures.'

"'Yes, tell her. Bring your mama here.'

"'Let's see if I can.'

"And then suddenly, the boy, that boy Macario, got sick. He had an illness in his feet. Suddenly he had tremendous pain and burning when he wore his sneakers. He'd take off his shoes, and then the pain and burning would go away. Just like that. And that started because one night as he crossed the river during the evening prayers he saw a woman named Leona curing someone else.

"It was getting dark, but he could see it was Doña Leona. He said, 'I saw her and I hid. Doña Leona was praying and praying and praying and talking and talking and healing and healing that person there by the edge of the river. I saw how she was curing. She was making such noise and murmuring and sweeping the woman and talking to the river, and then she did something with a knife. I just stood there watching. Then she threw the branch into the water. Then they finished and brushed off their clothes. And after they walked off, I went down to the river. Some brooms were there in the water and I crossed. I even passed by where they had been. And as I'm coming back, I feel something squeezing, itching my feet, burning inside my shoes, as though I had thorns inside. And since then, Mama, I've had this sickness in my feet. But it's only when I put my shoes on that it hurts and burns.'

"'Who knows? Maybe you picked up some of the evil?'

"During those days I saw the señora, the one who had introduced me to the girl. So I told her about this and she says, 'Bring your boy, too. And bring your mama.'

"That very day I came and went and returned with the boy. I said to him, 'Wash your feet, because she's going to cure your feet.' So he washed his feet, put on fresh socks, and we left.

"As we arrived she says, 'So you're the young man? Let's see. Now we'll see what you have. We'll see it now.' And she put a towel on her lap. Then she says, 'Now, I give showers, eh? I give showers.' She made us laugh.

"I told her about my mother-in-law, but she said, 'No, don't suspect anything. The evil wasn't meant for him. He picked up the evil, but it wasn't meant for him. He must have stepped on it, and that's how he got it. When people do a curing, the evil, the sickness, stays there. The smoke from it just stays there. But if there's a breeze, the air makes it dissolve. When they finished curing that person, he passed by and picked up the evil, because he stepped right where they had been doing the curing.'

"She prayed over him and washed his feet and dried them well with a towel. And she prayed again and put some cream on him. 'Let them rest for a moment. Don't put your sneakers on anymore. Put on some guaraches. Don't you have some guaraches?'

"So she healed his feet. I don't remember how much she charged me. But he got better. Then she says, 'Bring your mama.' We did take a while in taking her until my sister got the money. We had to convince my mama, because she was already bored with the whole thing. 'No, hija, don't go wasting any more money. You've seen how much they charge.'

"'But, Mama, they pulled you out of where you were buried. No, Mama, let's go.'

"'Well, hija, if you think you can do it, let's go.'

"The next day I took her. And Chencha, who we knew as Cresencia back then, was just a young girl, but she was the one who finally cured my mama. In three months, Mama was herself again."

FIVE

*Con el perdón suyo, comadre,
no vaya a ser que el diablo
tenga cuernos**

Within patriarchal society, women who are victimized by
male violence have had to pay a price for breaking the silence
and naming the problem. They have had to be seen as fallen
women, who have failed in their "feminine" role to sensitize
and civilize the beast in man.

— bell hooks, **Talking Back**

Our sons will not grow into women.

— Audre Lorde, "Man Child," from **Sister Outsider**

I've learned two things.
To let go
clean as kite string.
And to never wash a man's clothes.
These are my rules.

— Sandra Cisneros, "For a Southern Man,"
from **My Wicked Wicked Ways**

August 5, 1985. We were putting the dinner dishes away when we
heard a rapping sound at the door. I quickly wiped up the plastic
tablecloth and went to see who was there. "Comadre," Esperanza
whispered, "I hope we're not too early." She pulled down her rebozo,
which had been covering her head and half her face. "No, not at all.
Please come in," I replied and opened the door wide. Esperanza tip-

---

* "With Your Pardon, Comadre, Doesn't the Devil Have
Horns?"

toed in and shook my hand warmly but respectfully, then Norberta, giggly and embarrassed as always, clambered up the last step, almost tripping, and gave my hand an affectionate tug. "Now let your brother in! Quick!" Esperanza said to Norberta, who was dawdling at the front door. Norberta moved aside and Mario hopped in, also giggling but not embarrassed like his sister. "Now close the door!" Esperanza said nervously. Mario closed the door behind him, and I led the three of them through the courtyard and into the kitchen. I never knew exactly when Esperanza would visit, and I always wondered what would happen if she came when we had other guests over, or if people arrived while she was at our house. She was always anxious about keeping our talks secret; and when she told me something revealing about herself or other townswomen, she would lower her voice dramatically and look around, as though the walls were listening.

I had to admit that I appreciated my comadre's desire for privacy. I was still hesitating about getting into a relationship with Esperanza and wasn't yet sure if I wanted people to know we had become so friendly. During the day, I would still visit the respectable married women who live in the town center and rarely leave their houses. Or I would spend time with my poor and good-hearted comadre Pancha, who was caught in the kind of destructive marriage that Esperanza had fled, trying to raise her young children by selling prickly pears and pulque. I still thought that I would one day write about all the women I knew in town, not just Esperanza. And when that project looked too daunting, I'd tell myself just to write about the women who spoke to me from the dead pages of the Inquisition courts; they wouldn't embarrass me or talk back, I thought. But Esperanza, I could see already, was making me change my course. I had spent close to three years developing relationships with other townswomen and listening to what colonial women had said to their inquisitors. Now, at the last minute, after all that work, here I was, still a little scared of what my relationship with Esperanza might mean, still unsure of how I had let her take over my research, and yet strangely glad for another night together at the kitchen table.

∞ "Three years after I left his mother's house, the viejo came back with the vieja. I waited three years for him. What do you think? I was thirty-five then. And after that, it became known that I was going to *fracasar* with Gabriela. That was when his mistress began to be seen in the street. My mother-in-law would take her along to fetch firewood or to work on the raspa of the magueyes. By then it was all right for her to be seen on the street because I was pregnant with my daughter. My mother-in-law would say to her, 'She can't do anything to you now. She's pregnant. *Fracasó.*' My mother-in-law would go out with her son's mistress, and she would tell people that the woman was her goddaughter! People would say, 'Well, Doña Timotea, where's your son?'

" 'I don't know where he is, señora. His woman left. She's hanging around with the men. You see how she's already pregnant. As for my son, I just don't know. This poor girl, this woman, is my goddaughter. Her husband left her, and she came to stay with me since she's my goddaughter and I'm alone in the house. Neither his woman nor my grandsons wanted to be with me. And this woman was abandoned with her little boy and another one who's at home. So she's with me now, my goddaughter.'

"I knew who the woman was, and I knew she was no goddaughter of hers! That vieja, I'd say to myself, with your pardon, that vieja is a pimp. And there he was hiding out in the house.

"And to me people would say, 'Why don't you turn him in?'

" 'Oh, he's going to think I'm crying for him. He's going to think I'm crying for him to take me in again.' "

›››

"I was pregnant with my daughter. And then the mistress had another one and another one, and then my mother-in-law died.

" 'They're holding the wake for your mother-in-law. Your mother-in-law died of hunger. She was very ill. Now she's dead.'

" 'Well, the way she treated me. She never treated me as though I were family or as though I were her son's wife. She threw me out into the street to indulge her son and his mistress. Is she going to render accounts to God?' Going to confession all the time!

"They held the wake for her. Then she was buried. And her son there hiding out. When she was put in the ground, only the woman went and the children she had.

"And soon, soon afterward people started to tell us. Soon, soon afterward Doña Elvira said to my mama, 'Listen, come here. I didn't want to believe it. I saw her all the time, going to mass with that woman and a bunch of children. Man, I just couldn't believe it. They told me that Julio's there. I couldn't believe it. She went around saying that it was your daughter who liked to go pleasure-seeking, and that she didn't know if her son was dead or alive. But now when she died, I went to see her. And there he was! He's very fat, full of life. And I went to speak to him. Julito, how are you? But he's blind. He's blind, but not with his eyes closed. His eyes are just all white.'"

› › ›

"So it was just the two of them. And I would run into the woman on my path. When I would go to sell in San Luis, I'd see her. The viejo would stay at home with the children, and she would go to San Luis to do washing. I still felt a lot of coraje. One day I provoked her. I passed by her side and threw a bag of salt at her and hit her in the face. And she plopped her baby on the ground and rolled up the sleeves of her sweater.

"I said to her, '*Andale*, however you like.' I had a basket of vegetables, or maybe it was prickly pears, to take to San Luis. '*Andale*, now you feel very strong, now you feel like you're the queen, right? Yes, I'm the mistress and you're the wife, right? You daughter of — Well, greet me already! Come on, don't chicken out!'

"She just stood there.

"'You've laughed at me, you know. Remember what happened in San Luis? You've laughed at me. Don't chicken out, come on!'

"If she had hit me, I would have thrown the basket at her or at the baby. But no, she didn't dare touch me. She just stood there cursing me out. I said to her, 'You've laughed at me, but you're not going to do that anymore!'

"I lifted up my basket and got on the bus. And I heard someone say, 'That woman should be on her knees to Esperanza!' Everyone knew about my life with the viejo. 'Instead of Esperanza mistreating her, she's mistreating Esperanza. Now that's really turning things upside down!'"

› › ›

"What nerve that woman had. When I became pregnant with my daughter, what nerve she had to be stepping in my path. But we never spoke again. And then three months later, she left.

"The woman used to talk to her neighbor, Roberta, the wife of Severino. She would tell Roberta, 'If I go to San Luis, he tells me at what time I can go and at what time I'm to come back. No, I'm going to leave. Why should I have to put up with this pelado?'

"And when Roberta told me what the woman told her, I said to Roberta, 'Now she's realizing it?'

"She used to go do washing at a house in San Luis. She had five children—two boys and three girls or three boys and two girls, who knows? She'd take the oldest one and leave the others with the Tata there. It was the older daughter who told on her.

"Julio said to her, 'Hija, when your mama goes to San Luis, what do you do there?'

"And the girl said, 'My mama? My mama goes to a señora's house. The señora has a store, and my mama stays in the house doing the washing and the señora goes to her store. My mama and I stay in the house. And there's a señor in the house who just lies around in bed.'

"'Ah, really?'

"'Yes.'

"'And your mama?'

"'My mama does the washing. When she finishes the wash, she hangs up the clothes and then that señor gets up and goes to where my mama is doing the wash. And then my mama hangs up the clothes and that man puts his arms around her and they get into bed.'

"'Ah, really? And you?'

"'They give me some toys and I stay playing outside.'

"That day when the woman got back, he was furious. They say he grabbed her with his cane! A blind, blind man, but he grabbed her with his cane and jabbed her. He was jealous. And she, 'Those are lies. It's not true. If you don't want me to go, then why do you send me? Why don't you support me?'

"The woman was getting bigger, and he would say, 'If you have a *fracasó* tomorrow or whenever, I'll know it's not mine. I'm telling you.' Every time he looked at her, he'd say that. And finally she left.

"She said she was going to San Luis. But it was a lie. She went to her town and soon after her brother came. He had a pickup truck. The vieja told the children to wait with the Tata. Then she went up to the top floor, and from above she threw down everything she had—clothes, cooking things, she threw it all into the pickup truck. And then all she said was, 'Children, come here, come here.'

"They left. They closed the door, and they didn't even say adiós."

›››

"She swept his house clean! All she left him was the last pair of pants he was wearing. That's what Roberta told me. That he didn't eat for eight days, that there wasn't anyone to give him even a sip of water during eight days.

"You pay for everything. Sooner or later, you pay for everything. Nothing is forgotten. Did he think he wasn't going to have to pay for what he did to me? I told him, 'You've got a lot more to go through.'

"Roberta said, 'Poor man. I'm telling you because I sent him a taco.'

"'Ah, you did?'

"'It's that we saw how the vieja left, and it was Severino who said, "Listen, send that man a taco. Send him a taco with the girls, so they'll see how he's doing. Even his sons don't come to see him. That poor man, what does he have to eat there?" Anaís took the taco to him. She knocked on the door. He said, "Who are you?" "We have a taco for you from my mama, Roberta." "Ah." He opened the door. "Here, my mama sent this. My papa, Severino, sent you this taco." "That's fine, thank you. Thank you. It's been eight days since I've eaten anything."'

"'Ha!' I said. 'He should have come to his senses before then, don't you think? How come he didn't see what he did to me? Knowing that he had a wife, why was he so violent, acting like he was the best cock around?'

"Then Roberta said, 'Well, I sent it to him, and now I've sent him another taco today because Severino told me to.' And she says, 'I went and talked with him. He's all alone. And he says that even his sons don't stop by.'

"I said, 'Is that right? He really gave his sons a good example, didn't he? He raised them so that they would take care of him in his turn, didn't he? How old were they when he abandoned them? And now because he's in misery, he wants to have sons.'

"She said, 'No, really. Poor man. How silly, he could be doing very well with you.'

" 'I wasn't worth anything. With your pardon, I was the most beggarly woman here in Mexquitic,' I said to her. 'But she was rich, a señorita and everything. So why did she leave? Because he's such a good
man? A provider? He was used to having his mother support him. Now
that his mother is dead, the woman's gone, too.' "

› › ›

"I knew San Luis very well. Don't you see that I grew up working
there? The year after my mama planted the plot, when she started to
be ill, that was when I found my path as a peddler. Seeing how ill she
was, how was I going to hope that she would support me and the boys?
So I found my path. I said, 'I'm going to San Luis.' Because I had land, I
had herbs. And I would collect the herbs and go sell them. I'd offer
them for sale along with all the other women selling vegetables. And,
if not, I'd go and sell house to house. They paid me five centavos for
the herbs. Everything was cheap then.

"And I decided I would do all my selling house to house rather than
just standing in the street. I knew my way around. I wasn't going to get
lost. I'd knock. It seemed a little strange to me, right? But I'd knock
and offer what I had. I lost my shame. And I found I have luck. God has
helped me. It's a blessing from God that I'm lucky. Several women
envy me because I'm lucky. And the women who buy from me in San
Luis say, 'Ay, marchanta. There are other women who come selling,
but they're not like you. The others are ugly, bad-mannered. But you
have luck for selling. First of all, luck. Second, you're friendly. You
know how to sell.'

"During the week the boys were in school, so I'd go sell by myself.
I'd knock at a house and offer what I had. 'I have this today. Would you
like some?'

" 'Yes, of course.'

"I would give them the herbs. And then, 'Wait a moment.' They'd go
inside and bring out big bags of bread, or plates with two, three, four
tortillas with food. And I'd go to the next house, and it was the same.
Blessed be God. Even now I thank God. Everything is more expensive
now—it's not like before—but still, 'Here, marchanta, I have your
bread ready. Look, here I have this plate of food for you to take with
you. I'm going to give you a bag so you can take it.' Eh? Blessed be

God. Blessed be God that I haven't lacked, that I haven't died of hunger.

"One day I was selling and a woman says to me, 'Here, this is for you. Take this bag of clothes. And your husband?'

" 'Well let me tell you about my husband.'

" '¡Qué ingrato! How can he be so bad? Well, you just take care of your sons. And maybe you'll find another man.'

" 'No, what do I want a man for now? I just beg God to help me, because what am I going to do alone with two sons? They'll grow up. Sons grow up. And we all sleep in the same room. I distrust my sons because men are men. It's fine when they're little, but they grow up. What will I do alone with them?' " Esperanza pauses and says to me, "With your pardon, comadre, doesn't the devil have horns?"

"What doesn't—? Please say it again," I reply, in earnest confusion.

"Doesn't the devil have horns?" she repeats, laughing.

"The devil?"

"Yes, of course!"

I try to laugh, too, but I really don't get it.

"Well, comadre, haven't you read the Holy Scriptures? What does it say? When the Evil One stuck his tail and his feet in the way of our Lord, what did he say to our Lord? He told our Lord that if he was so holy and so wise and such a miracle-maker, why couldn't he make a loaf of bread venerate him? You see, wherever God went, the Evil One followed him. There is always something to perturb us.

"And so I would say when they asked me, 'What am I going to do when my sons grow up? I just beg God to give me a daughter!' That wish came true. And, ay, what corajes they've given me!

"And they'd say to me, 'Ay, get married, marchanta.'

" 'No, why would I want to do that now? Why do I want to be bothered by some viejo? After the life I had with that wretched man. I feel so happy now.'

"So I tell you, that's how things went along. That's how I found my path. The breeze blew. And my boys, I brought them food to eat. We'd eat three times a day. We had frijoles, rice, bagfuls of bread, pails of bread that I would come home with. I didn't lack for anything.

"I'd tire and take another route, knock at other houses, not knowing a soul. I'd knock and say, 'Do you need this?'

" 'Yes, sell me that. But how would you like a taco? I'm going to give you a taco, señora.' Like that. 'Don't you want these clothes?' The boys were growing up. 'Look, I have these pants here, these shirts here for your señor.'

"I'd say, 'No señora, I don't have a señor. Well, yes, I have one, but he's not with me. So that's why I sell alone and this is what happened to me.'

" 'Ah, but you have sons?'

" 'Yes, I do.'

"That's how I dressed them, got shoes for them, got clothes for them. I supported them. I got them through elementary school. I couldn't give them more than that because back then there wasn't a secondary school here. A year or two after they finished elementary school, the secondary school was being built. But the truth is I didn't have money. I said to them, 'Look, I can't, hijos. But if you want to study, then work and study. They say the books for secondary school are more expensive.' I could give them food to eat and a pair of pants and a shirt. People gave me good shirts, good jackets, good shoes. They even gave me shoes."

› › ›

"The years passed. I became pregnant, *fracasé*, with the older girl, Gabriela. Then I had the next girl. And that's how I went on with that other man. And then I had the boy. And finally I said to myself, Now it's time to put away the basket. Yes, I've put the basket away. You know, I'm getting old, comadre. People say, 'Go on, have another one.' And I say, 'Man, what a pity I can't anymore.'

"You know, they say here, 'A large family is no bother. The more children there are, the more jobs there are to do.' That's what a man from here, who's since died, used to say. His daughter Felicidad never married, but she had a relationship with a married man. She had about a dozen children with that Adalberto Gutiérrez. And people would say to her papa, 'Well Don Miguel, how many grandchildren do you have? You've got so many, and your daughter is in the house and always pregnant.' You know how people are. But he'd say, 'Yes, my daughter is surrounding me with my grandchildren. One takes care of my goat. Another takes care of my pig. Another takes care of my chicken. Another takes care of my lamb. Another takes care of my burro. Another takes

care of my horse. Another brings me firewood. Another brings me water. Another one goes to the milpa. So they don't disturb me at all. So
if my daughter has twenty children, then there are twenty tasks that
can be done. Isn't there a saying, "Twenty children, twenty tasks?"
They don't disturb me. I am glad to support my grandchildren. I'll support all the children my daughter brings me.'

"My children don't disturb me either. One daughter supports me.
The other daughter, Norberta, does the household chores. She knows
how to do everything. We don't cook anything special—beans, rice,
and sometimes we make chayotes. '*Andale*, make them like this.
Learn how.' She fetches firewood, she washes the plates, she feeds the
animals. Sometimes I scold her, because she's not totally well. You
know that she fell out of her crib once when she was with my mama?
She's a little slow because of the way she bumped her head that time.
But if I ask her to do something, she does it. She knits. I don't know
how to knit, and my older daughter doesn't know how to knit, but
Norberta knits very well. So she helps me. I go work my field and I say,
'*Andale*, heat up the tortillas. Bring me something to eat.' And she
brings my food to me.

"If I send them to the milpa, they go to the milpa. We go to the milpa
and I take the girl and the boy, and I send them home loaded down like
burritos. And *órale*. My youngest boy is still growing and I tell him,
'You're the one who's going to support me. Tomorrow, whenever,
you're going to be the only one responsible. Let's see how you do it.'

"So as I say, children don't disturb. It's true they're hard to raise.
When they're little they run out of pants or a shirt or shoes. And they
have to eat. And when they get sick, one has to cure them. All those
children of mine who died, it was because they weren't taken care of.
What means did I have? How could I take them to be cured? But afterward when I had my daughters, if they got sick I'd run to the doctor.
With God's help and with medicine when they needed it, they
survived."

› › ›

"And did your other man help you at all to raise the children?" I ask,
tentatively trying to open the subject again of her second relationship.

"Well, he just helped me to get them baptized. And then he got
married."

"Did he want to marry you?"

"Yes, but I didn't want to. He even said he'd give me my own house. But I didn't believe him. I said to him, 'No, I don't want the obligation.' He was twenty-five, and I was thirty-five. And then my older boys didn't want him either. They'd say, 'We're not going to respect him. We have our papa. So we don't want him. If he just dares to hit us, we'll kill him.' So that was why I didn't try living with him."

"And would you have wanted to marry him?"

"Well, if I had wanted to marry him, I would have had to pay for my divorce."

"So you weren't legally divorced?"

"Don't you see that we never spoke to one another again? So we just left it at that. And then that Jorge got married to someone else. And then afterward he took up with a daughter of Josefina Rodríguez and they put him in jail. Afterward he got sent to the penitentiary, because he had raped the girl. No, he was like that. That's why he got killed. Don't you see that he was the lover of Camila's daughter-in-law, the wife of that Eutiquio?"

"Who killed him, right?"

"Yes, he killed him." She lowers her voice to a whisper. "But he was also courting death. They say that he was with me and then he was with someone named Rosario, with whom he had twins. That's why I said to myself, Why should I bother with this man? Then he got married, and after he got married he became a guard here in the municipal government. Then he hung around with that Efigenia. He even took up with that Justina, the widow Justina Flores. He also brought her into it! Her, too!"

"So you knew he had a lot of women when you were with him?"

"Yes."

"And it didn't bother you that he had other women besides you?"

"I said to myself, Let him take whatever path he likes. After all, I wasn't washing his clothes. I didn't have any obligations toward him at all. When he'd see the girls in the street, he'd give them a hundred pesos, or fifty pesos. And that was it."

"But did you feel love for him, affection?"

"And what would I have gained from feeling anything if he wasn't at my side?" she responds, laughing at a question she clearly finds absurd. "Then when I learned he was going around with Eutiquio's woman, when my boy told me, 'Don't be talking to that Jorge. That Jorge is going around with that vieja Ignacia. I saw him with her,' I thought to myself, Forget it. So I started cutting him off. Then we heard he had been killed."

"And didn't you feel sad to hear he had been killed?"

She laughs again. "What was there to gain from being sad? Justina felt it more than I did. She said to me, 'Listen, Esperanza, put on mourning clothes.'

"'Me, put on mourning clothes? Why? My mama hasn't died. Who knows if I'll even wear mourning clothes when my mama dies? I don't like to wear black.'

"'Ay,' she says. 'You're not going to mourn for him? The poor man died.'

"I said, 'Well, that's what he was looking for and that's what he found. If a man lives in peace, then you can ask why. But he looked for it and found it.'

"She says, 'Ay, you're heartless. I do feel sad. Poor man. He was very nice.'

"'Yes, he was a nice person. It's true that he was a nice person, but he was looking for death. He went after death. Why did he go and offend that woman?'

"I didn't see what happened, but my boy Simeón told me about it. And my younger children saw it. What people say is that the two men were drunk and that Eutiquio got into an argument with Don Nacho— because Don Nacho said that Eutiquio owed him money. And then Don Nacho sent a boy to fetch the guard Jorge. And Jorge came out, and he saw that Eutiquio was there with his wife. And Jorge said, 'What's your problem, Don Nacho?'

"'Look, Jorge,' says Don Nacho. 'I called for you because I want you to lock up that man. He's treating me disrespectfully and he owes me money.'"

Mario, who has been listening attentively, intervenes here. "I think it was because of twenty pesos." This discussion, after all, is about the death of his own father, though he and Norberta have not said a word until now.

"Who knows?" Esperanza continues. "Then Jorge says, 'Pay him, Eutiquio. Pay him already. Pay Don Nacho and go to sleep.'

"And then they say that as he spoke, he was eyeing the woman and that maybe Eutiquio saw him and he said, 'You son of who knows what—' And he turned and gave his wife a slap! He kept putting his hands on the woman. And Jorge was saying, 'Go on, Eutiquio. Go on, woman, take him home. Put him to bed.'

"But that Eutiquio started to get more and more out of line. And Jorge was saying, 'Come on, let's go. I'll take you,' and pulling him away. He was pulling him away when Eutiquio started to curse out Jorge.

"They were halfway up the street and that Eutiquio was saying, 'Son of who knows how many mothers!'—and going on and on."

"And hitting the woman," Mario adds.

"Yes. They were already near the church door, and he kept right on hitting the woman. And the woman was walking along crying. And Jorge, for some reason, kept following them."

"And she was pregnant," Mario adds again.

"So he kept hitting the woman and cursing out Jorge. So there they go and there they go and there they go, and the man keeps right on cursing and saying things to the woman and hitting her and threatening her while Jorge—who knows why—keeps on following them. They went up the street and passed Anita's house and then . . ."

Mario, who wants so much to tell the story of his father's death, chimes in, "Then Eutiquio took out a big knife. A little child was there and says to him, 'What are you going to do?' And the child ran to tell Eutiquio's woman, yelling, 'Grab the knife!' But she didn't have time to stop him."

"All of you were out there watching, and I was at home lying down," says Esperanza. "And then I thought, Why isn't this boy back yet? Maybe I should go look for him. Because this boy was out in the street and I sent this girl out after him. 'Go on, bring the boy home. It's getting dark and he's not back yet.' And she went and ended up watching the fight. It was getting dark; it was already seven, eight o'clock. They came back and didn't say a word. Nothing. They didn't say, 'Mama, you know what happened, what we saw.' Neither of them, not even the girl. They were straight-faced. They didn't say anything. The next day Simeón told me.

"He says that when he killed him . . . This is what they say. I don't know, I didn't see it. They say that Eutiquio was hitting the woman and that Jorge went in to try to defend her. They say that when the guard went in to defend the woman in her house, the other one already had his knife ready. And then they say that the guard shot at Eutiquio and the woman stuck out her hand to try to pull the gun away from the guard, so he wouldn't shoot her viejo. He burned her fingers and the bullet hit Eutiquio's feet. Then Eutiquio took out his knife and stabbed him in the back."

"Six times. About six times," says Mario.

"And they say that he was just able to get out, to leave the room. He ended up sprawled over a fence.

"The next day I sent Gabriela out for water. 'Go and bring some water from the garden. Go see if there's water.' But she took a long time coming back. So I went to the door to look out and Simeón came over. 'Who are you looking for?'

"'The girl. I sent her out for water, and she hasn't come back yet.'

"'Where did she go?'

"'To the river or the garden.'

"'She must be standing around watching.'

"'Why?'

"'Don't you know that they killed the guard last night?'

"'Really?'

"'Yes, Jorge. They killed him. Eutiquio killed him. He killed him there at Meregildo's house. He tried to bury the knife, but the police came and took him away.'

"Finally there comes the girl, walking up the street, distracted, with the bucket of water on her head and looking and looking. As I say, it was an ugly affair, but after all, that's what he was looking for. As they say, whoever lives by the sword dies by the sword. He had killed. How many deaths did he owe? Two deaths, I think."

"He had killed, too?" I ask in a timid voice.

"Yes, he owed two deaths already," Esperanza says flatly.

"Jorge?" asks Mario, who seems taken aback, too.

"Who else? Yes, he owed two deaths. He had already served time in the penitentiary."

› › ›

There is a silence and that makes me nervous, so I decide to change the subject and ask Esperanza about the problems she's had with her older son, Macario. As soon as I mention his name, she jumps up from her chair and laughing says, "Comadre, I'm leaving. It's late already!"

"It's just ten o'clock," I say.

"Yes, exactly. No, that will take another two, three days."

"Just for that?"

"You're going to take back quite a long *historia* with you, comadre. Well, comadre, what are you going to do with this *historia*?"

"I don't know. Study it, I guess."

Esperanza bursts out in giddy laughter. "Study it!" Soon she settles back into her chair and says, "Look, the story about the boy goes like this. When the boy was twenty-five, my older girl was twelve years old. I would go to San Luis and leave them alone at home. The girls were in school. I would say to them, 'Look, girls, when you get out of school, you make tortillas. There's the dough. Put beans on to cook. Make tortillas. When the boy comes home from work for lunch, have some tortillas ready for him.'

"I got that girl Gabriela used to working early. I showed her how to make tortillas when she was twelve going on thirteen. '*Andale*, learn how.' And I would say, 'I'm going now, hijo. The girl is there. When you get back at midday, if the tortillas are cold, tell her to light the stove and warm up the tortillas for you, so you can eat.'

"I trusted him until the girl said, 'Mama, when I get out of school I'm not going to make any tortillas.'

" 'Why? Tell me.' She didn't want to say anything to me. 'Tell me what's wrong. Is the boy doing something to you?'

" 'When Macario comes, I'm going to run. I'm not going to be in the house.'

" 'Why? But tell me why.' And to the younger children I'd say, 'Let's see, you tell me.' They were little then. 'What is it? Come on.'

" 'That Macario hits us, Mama. He hits us and then he tells us to get out of the way.'

" 'Ah, I didn't know that.'

"The next day, I said, 'Tomorrow I'm going to San Luis.' But I didn't say anything to him. I just said, 'I'm going to San Luis, so please behave.'

" 'Why do you say that to me? To behave?'

" 'Because the girls say that you're going around scaring them and pushing them out of the way. What do they do to you? Why do you scare them?'

"'Mama,' he says, 'I came at midday to eat, and there was nothing. The girls weren't back from school. They were in the street. They're lazy girls. They were probably out there with their boyfriends. Why don't they get back earlier? I had to eat cold tortillas. There was no fire, nothing. I was hungry, and they didn't want to do anything.'

"So I said to the girls, 'Let's see, what do you do?' The girls wore serious faces and didn't say anything. And finally they said, 'No, Mama, he hits us and makes us run and tries to grab us.'

"Well, it went on like that. Before I'd leave to go sell, I'd say, 'Look, hijas. Go to school and come back here and make tortillas. Tell him that I say that he shouldn't hit you. I'm going to San Luis now.' The boy wasn't around. He was in the field. 'Tell him not to be bothering you.'

"When I got home, the younger girl was coming out of the kitchen and he was sitting there. He stuck out his foot, making her trip. And I heard her say to the boy, 'Why do you stick out your foot? So I'll fall, right? You burro!'

"And I said, 'What's going on here? Why do you speak to each other this way?'

"'Who knows?' Macario says. 'She's a spoiled girl. Your little girl is very spoiled; she says a lot of things to me.'

"'Make them want to respect you, then,' I said. 'You're the oldest, and you should act in a way that they can respect you. Don't you see they're growing up? If you behave well toward them, they won't misbehave with you. And, look, there's something else I have to tell you.'

"'What? What? What else?'

"'Look, the girl told me that they don't want to stay with you because when you come back at midday, you run after them and you try to grab them. Why?'

"'Me? Me? When? They're liars, gossipers. When have I done that to them?'

"Then the younger girl says, 'You run after us and you try to hit us, and you run after Gabriela the most!' Norberta was little then. She was seven years old.

"And Gabriela said, 'Sometimes he comes and I'm in the kitchen making tortillas. I'm just starting, and he comes and sits down and pinches me in the ribs. And I tell him to stop fooling around. Then he says, "*Andale*, give me my food. I'm hungry." Then he curses me.'

"'And what else does he do to you?'

"'That's all. He just pinches my ribs. There he is pinching and pinching my ribs, and then he grabs my hair and tells me to go get inside the jacal.'

"'Ah, very nice!' I said. And I said to him, 'Why are you doing such evil things?'

"'What am I doing to them? Do you think your little girls have been offended? Take them to be checked, so you can see if I've offended them.'

"'That's not good. You shouldn't talk that way about the girls. They're your sisters. They may not be real sisters, but they're sisters of your own mother. Why do you pinch their ribs? Why do you put your foot out so they'll fall? Why, why do you try to lift their skirts?' That's when I started having the girls wear pants under their skirts.

"I was angry and said to him, 'Look, listen to me. Be grateful at least that I supported you, that I got you through school. I didn't get you very far, but at least you can write your name. And who has supported you? Has your father supported you? And who supports you now, clothes you? It's true I had my *fracasó*. I'll know how I pay for that. But I didn't take you to a stranger's house. So why don't you behave properly?'

"'But what do I do to them? Your daughters just—'

"I said, 'Look, maybe the girls bother you, but they don't bother me. Go ask a dog, see if a dog can cook you a meal. You're a grown man now. If you find it so easy, grab some vieja on the street. If you want to get married, get married. I'm not stopping you. But I don't want you *fracasando* with my girls and getting them pregnant. I leave you in the house, trusting you, not so that you'll go around doing evil things to the girls.'

"'Ah! What do I do to them?'

"'But you have your intentions. You're grown up, and I'm a woman alone. How do I know you won't even try to force yourself on me when I'm asleep? That's why I don't want to sleep in the same room as you now that you're grown up.' And I said, 'As long you behave properly and you're a good son, you can stay at my side. But if you behave badly, then it's the street for you. You have your father, right? Let's see if he supports you; let's see if he tolerates you the way I'm tolerating your bad behavior toward my family. We're not animals,' I said to him. And I threw him out."

›››

"He returned two weeks later, and then things calmed down for a while. I'd say, 'Look, children, I'm going to San Luis now, but be careful.' And to Mario, the youngest son, I'd say, 'You stay here like a man and tell the girls to do things. You tell them what to do.'

"And then, when the girl was thirteen going on fourteen, she says, 'No, Mama, I won't anymore—'

" 'Why? What happened?'

" 'No, Mama, look—'

"And the girl clammed up and wouldn't tell me. Then I said to the other girl, 'Let's see. You tell me, Norberta.'

" 'Mama, yesterday when you went to San Luis that Macario arrived while Gabriela was making tortillas. We went out to play, and he was in the kitchen with her. And Gabriela was crying. And he told us to get out of there, to go and play, and he cursed us. And Gabriela was there in the kitchen . . . then Gabriela screamed . . . Gabriela screamed!

" 'Be quiet, be quiet,' he was saying.

" 'And she was saying, "You're going to get it when my mama comes back."

" 'We were playing when we looked and saw that he had his arms around her. He put his arms around her and took her into the jacal. And then he closed the door. We were very scared because he had told us to stay away. We were afraid to get close to the room. Macario was saying, "Be quiet already." And she was crying and crying. So we got closer and saw that Gabriela was crying, and he was covering her mouth. And he was doing something to her . . .

" 'We got closer and looked in through the little holes in the siding, and Gabriela was crying and choking and crying. We went to the door. He hadn't locked it. We went to the door, and Gabriela had her pants pulled down. He was already naked. And we saw them. He was naked and he was holding both her hands with one hand, and he was covering her mouth and trying to unbutton her dress.

" '*Híjole*, when we opened the door! And I said, "You're going to get it when my mama gets back." And he said, "And you children of who knows what, why did you open the door?" We said, "We're going to tell my mama." And then that Macario tried to push the girl down from the bed to the floor. Her pants were pulled down and he was naked. We saw him.'

" 'And the girl?'

" 'The girl ran out and pulled up her pants. And I said, "I'm going to tell my mama!" And the girl was crying and crying. And then he cursed us and said that if we told you he'd kill us!'

"So it was the younger children who told me. When that Macario got back at midday, I said to him, 'Listen, what did you do to the girl yesterday?'

" 'Me? Nothing.'

" 'What do you mean, nothing? You did something to her. Tell me what you were doing to her.'

"And I grabbed a stick and said to him, 'You're going to tell me what you did to the girl. Why did you take the girl to your bed? What were you doing to her?'

"Yes, I was rough with him, I was rough with the boy. I hit him that time. I managed to strike him twice.

" '¡Arrastrado! ¡Sinvergüenza! You'll see, arrastrado. You're going to see what's going to happen to you. You have no shame,' I told him. 'I thought you were a good son. What are you trying to do to the girl?'

" 'What did I do to her? Take her to be checked and find out if it's me or someone else.' "

››>

"And the girl was crying, too. I had also hit her."

"You hit the girl, too?" I ask, frankly shocked.

"I hit the girl, too."

"Why?"

"Because she wouldn't tell me. It was the younger girl who told me everything. I was a little suspicious of the girl because she seemed to be making eyes at the boy. And I said, 'You're going to tell me everything,' and I gave the girl two beatings. To the boy I said, 'Don't come back here ever again. Get out of here! Go and support yourself.'

"I told the other boy, Simeón, 'I'm going to file a charge against that sinvergüenza, so he'll be in jail for a while.'

"'No, Mama,' the boy says. 'What are you going to do? Look, the one who's going to damage her reputation is your daughter. Not the boy.'

"'Ah, so you defend him. You defend him, right?'

"'No, Mama, it's not that I'm defending him. What I'm saying is that it's your daughter who's going to lose face.'

"'So you want me to just let him go on with his wicked ways? Pretty soon he'll be putting his hands on me when I'm sleeping.'

"'Ay, Mama. I know what I'm saying. Don't go, Mama. You're going to discredit the girl. It's going to discredit her as much as him, but it's going to be more of a discredit for her.'

"So I didn't do anything. I held back."

› › ›

"Macario left and didn't come back that night. The next day, there he was again. And I said, 'There's no one like a mother, right? You still have the nerve to return. You have no shame at all. You make a life for yourself however you like. I no longer want you as a son. Why don't you go live with your father? You're old enough now to support yourself and your father.' He was lying in bed with the covers up to his head. And I reached for a broom handle and hit him with it twice. 'Go on, leave already. You have no shame.' He didn't say anything. I think he was crying.

"The next morning, I left for San Luis. 'Well, Mama,' I said. 'Please keep an eye on the children. I'll be back in the afternoon.' And when I returned my mama told me, 'You should have seen your son cry.'

"'I believe it, and I don't believe it.'

"'He cried like a child. I even felt sorry for him. He's certain that you're throwing him out because the girls are gossips. He just stood there spitting up and spitting up and standing there crying and saying, "My mama is throwing me out and I don't know where to go. But it's not true that I did that."'

"It occurred to him to go stay at my comadre's house, since he's her godson. On Sundays, they told me, he'd get very drunk. Fifteen days passed. Then Simeón said to me, 'Macario spoke to me. He asked me about you.'

"'He doesn't need his mother, right? But he does, doesn't he?'

"'Ay, Mama. He says he's sick.'

"'Ah, he's sick now? Tell him to go confess to the priest what he did to the girl, and to ask for forgiveness. Then he can come home again. But how can I trust him? What embarrassment, what shame, if tomorrow the girl ends up pregnant. Wouldn't it be embarrassing if it were her own brother's child? *Santa María Purísima*, I'd prefer that it be anyone else's than her own brother's.'

"Another fifteen days passed, and I said to Simeón, 'Go see who you can find to come on Saturday and sow the beans and corn.' It was April, time to sow.

"He must have talked to his brother, because Macario came to see me.

" 'Mama, Simeón told me you need someone to sow the corn and beans. If you let me, I'll find someone, Mama.'

" 'Well, do it, and pay for it.'

" 'I'll go this afternoon. And . . . can I come home?'

" 'All right.'

"And that was how he found his way back into the house. He returned, and I washed all his clothes for him. But I would say to the girls, 'If he tries anything again, tell me right away. And don't let him do it. Run away!' "

›››

"So he finally calmed down for a time. The girl was fourteen already. And then suddenly, there he was seeing a niece of that Primitiva. The woman had already had a son with my brother. And she had even had a daughter with her own brother-in-law!

"It was around that time that he said to me, 'Mama, I'm going to ask for some land where my godmother Tere lives. We can't keep on living here with my abuela. Let's ask for some land, and we'll make a house there. There's room to make a house for me and another one for you. If Simeón wants to live with us, that's fine. If not he can find a woman and live somewhere else.'

"Simeón had just gotten back from working in the United States and had brought back some money. And Macario said, 'We'll have enough to make a house.' And Simeón said, 'Yes, of course.'

"They put in the request and it was granted. 'Look, look, here. Here's a good place to make a house. I'm going to make it like this and like this,' says Macario. 'I want Simeón to help me. *Orale*, Simeón, help me.' And Simeón, 'Yes, of course.'

"Simeón had nearly finished the house and was getting ready to put a second floor on it when Macario refused to help his brother any longer. That was when he started with the vice of seeing that vieja. I'd get back from San Luis and say, 'Listen, what have you done?'

"'I went to work, Mama,' Simeón would say.

"'And Macario?'

"'Macario hasn't come by here.'

"'So what does he do all day?'

"Then the younger children whispered to me, 'Mama, Macario is with that Rita.'

"'Teodoro's daughter Rita?'

"'Yes. He was with her, talking and talking. We passed by, and the two of them were sitting together.' A few days later again they said, 'Mama, Macario hasn't come by here. Macario was with that vieja Rita. They were standing by Doña Petra's magueyes.'

"Then I saw them myself, the two of them sitting under a tree. 'Ah,' I said to myself. 'Look at them there.' I saw them and didn't say anything.

"That night I said to him, 'Macario, so you're not going to work anymore? You're not going to help Simeón build the house? Are you just going to hang around with that vieja? What does she say to you? You know the children told me they had seen you talking. I didn't believe it, but now I believe it. Why are you getting involved with her? Aren't you ashamed?'

"'Ashamed of what? She's a girl and I'm a boy. She's young and I'm young. So why should I be ashamed?'

"'Look, I'm not interested in whether she's a girl or a vieja. If you want to get into a relationship with her and *engañarte*, you're doing wrong.'

"Then I said, 'On the one hand, it's worth it just not to have you *fracasando* with my girls, but I also want you to think about what you're doing. What's going to be the point of all the years you've spent waiting and holding back? Now, look, that's not the worst of it. The worst of it is that the vieja was already had by your own uncle! If the vieja hadn't been with your uncle, and if she hadn't had a child by your uncle, it wouldn't have mattered to me if she had twenty or thirty children. After all, I wasn't going to be the one to support them. But she was your uncle's woman. What are people going to say, that we're a pack of animals? You couldn't find any other woman except her?'

147

"'I don't care. I'm not going to try to please you.'

"'So you're determined to get involved with her *a la brava*.'

"'Yes, I am. After all, she's a girl.'

"'Fine. I was telling you for your own good, but you don't want to understand, so *ándale*. But so long as you're involved with her, I don't want you stepping foot in my house, here in my mama's house. If you leave that woman, you can come back. Search for the poorest woman in the world, the most loathsome one you can find, or the lamest one, but not that woman!'"

› › ›

"The next day I went to San Luis and came back in the afternoon. Simeón was getting ready to put the beams up. And just as he was putting up the beams, Macario said to him angrily, 'Listen, Simeón, why don't you stop? Stop working on my house now. I'll pay you back for the material. Just leave me the house.'

"'Look, I don't want to argue. I'm making this house for my mama because you gave me permission to do it. I'm making it for my mama, eh? I'm not planning to live here. The house is for my mama. You said it would be for her.'

"So I got back from San Luis, and Simeón said to me, 'What do you think, Mama? Macario got angry with me and told me to stop working. And there he is with the vieja. When I saw him in the morning, he was with the vieja over there by Doña Petra's magueyes. I think the vieja is telling him what to do.'

"'*Híjole*, and now what?'

"'No, Mama. I'm not going to work anymore.'

"'So you're just going to leave him the house?'

"'Yes, I'm going to leave it to him.'

"Later that night Macario came to the house. He had such nerve coming over to eat dinner! As soon as he arrived I said, 'Listen, so you threw your brother out. Why?'

"'Look, leave me the house. I'll pay for the materials.'

"I said, 'Well, you'll pay him for the materials and you'll pay us for our work, for the work the girls did and the work I did.'

"'Look, I'm not going to pay for anyone's work. I'm just going to pay for the materials.'

"It turned into a big feud. But Macario kept coming to my house to eat, *descaradamente*, to have lunch and dinner. I went and told my mama, and I told my brothers and sisters. And then Mama says, 'Look, hija, I'm going to give you a piece of land.'

"'Ay, Mama, I already feel bad about being here. When my brothers and sisters visit, I feel like I'm just hanging on like a chick, but one whose children are grown up. I guess I'll go build a house there on the milpa. Or I'll request a piece of land somewhere. Otherwise, I'll go to San Luis, with my kids and all.'

"But my mama didn't want her house to be empty, and so she gave me some land near hers. She gave it to me in writing. My mama signed the paper. It was written up as though the land had been sold to me. And from that time, the sister who's married in San Luis and the brother who's in Monterrey began to be angry with me, because Mama gave me some of her land without their permission."

› › ›

"For a while things seemed a little more peaceful. I thought maybe he had stopped seeing the vieja. He acted happy, as though nothing were happening. He put the roof on the room, and about eight or fifteen days later he said, 'Mama, my room is ready. It's dry. Now the poles can be taken down. I'm going to bring my bed over now, because the room is empty.'

"'Fine.'

"So he took the bed. Then he says to me, 'Mama, I bought a stove.' He bought a stove with the money he had earned from working in the factory. He didn't give any of it to me. 'I bought my little stove,' he says. 'What if you throw me out suddenly? At least I'll be able to go to my room and heat up my tortilla.'

"'Fine.'

"'Mama, give me that little mat to put by the side of my bed.'

"'Yes, take it.'

"'It would be nice if you'd give me that chair and that little bench.' He had bought a dining set. 'I'm going to take my table.'

"'Ah, yes. Take it.'

"'When you need it, Mama, I'll bring it back.'

"'Fine.'

"'It would be nice if you could give me those sheets for my bed.'

"'Take them.'

"And he took a bedspread. He found some blankets. 'Bring them here to wash them,' I told him.

"He was already sleeping there at the new house and coming to my house to eat. Sleeping, that is, with the vieja! Who knows for how long the vieja had been going there to sleep with him.

"And that was around the time when Simeón brought his woman here. I said to Macario, 'Tomorrow I'll be going to Rioverde, somewhere around there. We're going to settle things with the girl Simeón brought home.'

"'And I'm not invited?'

"'Ah, if you want to go, then you can pay for your fare. No one is taking me.'

"'Maybe Simeón doesn't want me to go.'

"So I called out, 'Simeón, they're speaking to you. Are you inviting your brother?'

"'He can come.'

"'All right, then I'll go.'

"He went with us and took along his radio and a big tape recorder he had bought. Simeón took some photographs of us on the way there. So we went and arranged things, and when we came home they had a civil ceremony right away because her family had demanded that they get married. I told them they should live together first. Why spend money until they know if they can stand each other? So the matter of the girl was settled and she came back with us to live.

"Simeón would go to work in San Luis, and the woman would stay home with my kids. I'd go to sell. Macario was still coming home to eat. And he would say to me, 'Mama, I think Simeón is looking at me funny. He must be thinking I want to win over his woman.'

"I said, 'But why are you going to take away his woman? He's your brother.'

"'That's what I think, because when I come over he looks at me with angry eyes. But for as long as you live and look well upon me, I'll come to visit you. But if you tell me not to come back, I won't bother you anymore. I have my house now.'

"He was giving me the soft treatment, very lightly, very gently."

›››

"Weeks passed, or maybe a month—I don't know how long—but a day came when Macario said to me, 'Ay, Mama. I have a toothache. Give me a pill, won't you?'

"I gave him a pill. And I said, 'I'm going to San Luis. If you want to come at midday, fine. You can go to the kitchen and get your food.' Simeón's woman stayed shut up in her room.

"When I returned from San Luis, I said to Norberta, 'And Macario?'

"'He hasn't come, Mama.'

"'Not even to eat?'

"'No.'

"I said, 'Ah, that boy must still be sick. Let's eat, and we'll go see him at his house. He must be sick and in bed. Maybe he can't get up because of his toothache.'

"So we finished eating dinner and we left. I took Norberta with me. The night was clear and there was no moon. We climbed up around the hill and got to the courtyard of his house. A candle was lit inside. The water doesn't reach as far as his house. He has to go down with his buckets to bring up water for his plants. He already had plants around his house.

"My girl and I got closer. The door was only half shut.

"I could see him coming up the hill. I could see the tip of his hat. He was bringing water from down below. As I get closer to the house, who do I see but the vieja lying in bed with her stomach up in the air! I saw her and felt such coraje! And I went inside, lord of my soul. But I made a mistake. I should have locked the door behind me.

"I went into the room and got on top of her! I said, 'And you, who gave you permission to be here? Did you help us work on the house? You were the one who got my boy to take the house away from us. You were the one. You descarada, you vieja!'

"And I grabbed her by the hair and slapped her. But the vieja didn't lay a hand on me. She cried like a child. And she screamed. Macario was coming up the hill, and he heard the screaming and came running over with his buckets. And he says, 'Out of here! I don't want arguments in my house.'

"He squeezed my hands together so I couldn't hit the woman anymore. I was only able to slap her three times. When I grabbed hold of the vieja's hair, he yelled, 'I'll take you out of here if you don't let go of her hair!' and pushed me against the door. The door frame was made of bricks, and I cut my hand on the bricks so badly it went numb. He kept me there, crucified against the wall. And I tried to bite his hand and kick him so he'd let go of me. He finally rammed his knee against my legs and kept me pinned down like that until I let go of the vieja's hair. When he released me, God made it possible for me to find the stick he had used to carry the water buckets, and I gave him two thrashings with it.

"He said such insolent things to me. And I said, 'Tonight I'm not leaving until you get that bum of a dog out of here. We didn't work so you'd bring this vieja here to sleep with you. You could have made your own house. You traitor, you liar!' I said to him. 'Look, you could have taken up with the most beggarly woman in the world, but not with this bum of a vieja. What do you think we are, dogs? You may be a dog, but I'm not going to allow this vieja who was my brother's woman and my sister-in-law to also be my daughter-in-law. So I'm not leaving. I'll stay here until dawn if I have to.'

"And, no, the vieja jumped out the window! I saw her flabby stomach as she waddled away. Later Doña Roberta said to me, '*Híjole*, you really got that Rita moving to a good rhythm. She came running back to her house so fast she was trotting!'

"So the vieja left, and I stayed there with that Macario. I said to him, 'You were giving me the smooth treatment, weren't you? You're a traitor, a liar. What sort of a son are you? What did you do to me? You crucified me.'

"But he gave me back all of my things. He threw them outside. I myself took down the curtains and reclaimed the little rug and the desk and the blanket and the bedspread. And I said, '*Orale*, so you'll know. I was your mother. Now I'm not your mother. You were my son. Well now you're not anything of mine!' He turned up the volume on his tape recorder so he wouldn't hear me.

"When I got home with Norberta, everyone was asleep. I got back and I fixed myself a strong drink with a few limes so I wouldn't get sick. With that coraje, I could have really gotten sick, but I nipped it with the limes and the liquor. And he and I have never spoken again."

› › ›

"Sooner or later, you pay for everything. That's the only consolation left to me. Sooner or later, you pay for everything. What I say, especially, is that the worst thing is to be disrespectful to your parents. I've heard it said that it's dangerous to be cursed by your own parents.

"And now the boy, when he sees me, whether in San Luis or here—he turns away and walks in the other direction. So he's with his father now. Once his vieja and I got going, and she said things to me and I said things to her and that pelado Julio got into it too and said, 'Vieja, you daughter of—'

"We got started up, and he said things to me and I said things to him. When I pass by and see him sitting there, how my intestines burn! I feel a lot of coraje. Of course, I do. The life I had with him left me scarred, beaten. How he took advantage of me. And now he's so big with his son there.

"I do feel coraje, that's true, toward both of them, father and son. After the way I sacrificed myself. But you pay for everything, sooner or later you pay for everything. If you don't pay, you owe it, comadre, in this life.

"For my part, I just wanted to defend my family. He wanted to abuse my girl. How was I to say, 'Yes, son, have your sister. Do that.' She might not have been his real sister—but, listen, you have to have some respect. As for the vieja, if he had been thinking, he would have said, 'Listen, it's my mama, the only one I have, and I'm going to do as she says. I'll obey her and find someone else, whoever it is.' But no, it was easier for him not to.

"But I know that the vieja used evil ways to get him. The vieja had that vieja Primitiva do the work for her. I know because Lourdes told me. And Lourdes is the wife of Guillermo, and that Guillermo is a son of Silvestre, a brother of Teodoro, who is Rita's father. Look, that viejo Teodoro knows his witchcraft. That Primitiva knows her bit. That Primitiva once even said to me, 'If you want to get back at Julio, I'll do it for you.'

"Lourdes told me everything. She used to talk a lot with me. Now she just says, 'Good morning, good afternoon.' But that time she said to me, 'Listen, Doña Esperanza, it was like this. That Rita took your son away using evil ways. That Primitiva did the work.'

"'Ah, yes?' I said.

Love potions bought at the market at San Luis Potosí

" 'Yes.'

"And she said, 'I used to go to the hills with my goats, and that Rita would go, too, with her goats. And that Macario would come by to see her. And she once said to me, "Lourdes, let's whistle at that Macario." I said, "Why? What do you have going with him? Is he talking to you?" She says, "Yes, he's been talking to me for a while. I have another guy in Jaralillo, but this one's talking to me now. What do you think?" '

"And then Lourdes told me she said, 'Look, Rita, if you get involved with that Macario, you know it's not going to go well for you. Doña Esperanza isn't going to want you. She's not going to like it if you get involved with her son. Because she's going to say that you were already with her brother, isn't she? But that Rita said, "So what? Who cares if she doesn't want me? Macario loves me very much. Even if his mother gets angry, I'm going to snare him. And if I can't snare him by good means, I'll snare him by some other means." So you see, Doña Esperanza,' Lourdes said to me, 'get smart. Your son is with Rita but not by good means. She's got him because Doña Primitiva did the work for her.'

"That Lourdes can't stand that Doña Primitiva. That's why she told me everything."

› › ›

"So you didn't try to get help from a centro?"

"No, I didn't want to waste my money on that. I thought to myself, I'll have to spend money. And what do I want him for? So he can come to my house and force himself upon my girls? I don't trust him anymore. I yelled at him once, 'You abuser, wanting to rape my girl. Be thankful I fell asleep and felt sorry for you. If not, you'd be locked up, you descarado.'

"'Ha, ha.' He just laughed."

Esperanza pauses. "So you see, it's an ugly story." Rising from her chair, she says, "Now we'll be going."

"No, tell another one," says Mario distractedly, half-asleep.

"Tell another one," Esperanza mimics. "He sounds like he's drunk. It's midnight. Now we're finally done."

"No, comadre, not yet," I say, not wanting our storytelling sessions to end so quickly.

"Ay, comadre," Esperanza says, laughing. "Let's see if the imps don't come out when we cross the bridge. But I'll be ready for them. If one of those little bundles pops out, I'll grab a rock. I've got good aim, comadre."

SIX

*Mi hija, amárrate las faldas**

Do not seek him who will be your companion as if in a market place; do not call to him as if you were aflame in the springtime, do not go about desiring him. But also, take care not to disdain the one who may be your companion, the one chosen by the Lord. For if you look down on him, it might be that Our Lord would scoff at you, and finally you might become as a public woman.

With these words from my mouth do I give all this to you. Thus before Our Lord, I fulfill my duty. And if perchance you cast this away, still you know it. I have fulfilled my duty, my little woman, my little daughter. May you be happy, may Our Lord bring you success.

—A Nahuatl father's counsel to his young daughter, in
    Miguel León-Portilla, Pre-Columbian Literatures of
    Mexico

August 10, 1985, my last taped conversation with Esperanza that year before our return home to the United States. Not knowing that my conversations with Esperanza will continue in later years, I feel compelled to create a sense of closure, no matter how artificial, and I find myself that night asking some rather crude questions. How odd that I was seeking to round things out after having imagined for years that I would become an expatriate in Mexico. I had few illusions of becoming a professor in the United States because I had botched up a job interview soon after finishing my dissertation and been told to get a speech coach.

In the course of my efforts to learn about witchcraft, I was told about a woman in the rancho of Corte who is a clairvoyant; she is

---

"My Daughter, Tie Up Your Skirts"

especially good at finding lost things and getting undocumented Mex-
icans safely across the border. The friend who arranged for my meet-
ing with this woman said that I had to go see her with a problem, not
simply to ask questions about what she did. So I decided to ask her if
she could help me with my career. She prayed over me and blessed a
white flower I had brought, telling me to keep the flower under my
mattress and to have faith. Sure enough, a few weeks later two tele-
grams arrived in Mexquitic offering me postdoctoral fellowships in
Baltimore and Ann Arbor. I was able to string them together, so I now
knew I'd be taken care of for the next four years—thanks to the
clairvoyant in Corte who got me across the border. But what would
become of my kitchen talks with my comadre? Was this as far as we
would go? Everything was still possible . . .

∞ "Could you tell me a little more about your life now? How
do you see your future? For yourself and your children?"
Esperanza looks puzzled. "I don't understand you. What do you
mean?"

"What is your life like now?"

"Well, I'd have to say that, in part, it's fine. And, in part, it's tiring,
because I'm a man and I'm a woman. I'm tired and I have to go on
working, so that I can see my youngest son grow up, right? Simeón
says to me, 'Mama, don't go sell anymore.' And I say to him, 'Look, if I
work, I eat. And if I don't, what will I have? I've got to move ahead
however I can.'

"So I go on with life. I feel tired, but on the other hand, I'm happy,
thank God. I'm happy because wherever I want to go, I go. No one can
tell me where to go. But I'm tired because since I turned thirty-five,
I've had to go out and find my way in life, support myself like a man. I
had to raise my children, right? One was eight and the other was ten
when Julio left me in the street, and the first son didn't marry until he
was twenty-seven and the other son didn't marry until he was twenty-
five. And then I've had to raise the other children, too.

"All those years, I have been both man and woman to them, supporting them, helping them grow up. I go to work in the fields. I'm thankful to be able to harvest something, not much, but at least five or ten
kilos. I go to San Luis, I come back, and I eat and I go to sleep late. And
the next day, there I go to the field. How many women are there in

Mexquitic who use the hoe, the pick? They have their men, their husbands who support them, suffering some corajes, perhaps, but supported by their husbands. And me, what man do I have?"

"And you haven't felt a desire for a man since then?" I dare to ask.

"Ay!" Esperanza laughs wildly. "Look, no I haven't. I don't know why you're asking me, but it's been twelve years, my boy's age now. You know, they say to me, 'But there are some viejitas, sixty years old, who still go on with it.' Well, they're with their viejos, their husbands, or whatever. Whether they want to or not, they have to be at the mercy of their viejos, the way I was when I was with the viejo. Listen, I suffered and just prayed. And they say, 'So you'll be warm when you sleep . . .' Who needs to be warm like that? I just grab something to eat, and I warm up. So what do I need a viejo for?

"You're pulling words out of me. Look, it's just not worth the obligation of having to cook for a man, and what if he doesn't support me? And then having to be arguing all the time? I have my children, so I don't need to be stuck in any commitments right now with men."

"And what sort of a future do you desire for your daughters?"

"I can't answer that question with lots of fancy words, because I don't know how to read. But I'd say that if it were up to me, I don't think my daughters should get married. Look at the life I had. But then sometimes I think, I'll die and they'll be left to suffer alone. And people say to me, 'It's better for them to get married, because that way when you die at least you won't be left with any worries about your daughters. You'll know that they're being taken care of, whether for good or bad, however it goes for them, but at least they'll be taken care of. But all by themselves—.' And I say, 'Yes, but just knowing the life I went through.' And they say, 'But not all men are the same.' I say, 'Well, maybe so. Maybe so.' "

"So if you think it better that your daughters not marry, would you want them to have children anyhow?"

"No, not that either. No, as I say to them, 'Look, hijas, just because I had a man after I was left in the street, that doesn't mean you have to do the same thing. If you think you want to have children with a man, first think about who he is. You don't have a father at your side, but you have a mother. Think about it, say to him, "Go and arrange things with my mama. If you want me, it's to be your wife. Not just so you'll keep me busy, not just so you'll use me." Eh? Think about it hija,' I say to them.

"'For a woman, life is sad, eh? So, my daughter, tie up your skirts, and don't believe anything but what I tell you. I failed, *fracasé*, many times. And now look at the life I've had. To eat I've had to work. It's nice to have children, but you have to educate them, guide them on the right path. So, I'm telling you. How I wish my mama had talked to me like this when I was young.'

"That's how I talk to my daughters. 'First of all, you're not going to do what I did. There's a saying that the splinter resembles the stick it comes from. Just because I messed up, *fracasé* . . . But that was because I was abandoned, left on the street. Otherwise I'd still be there, I'd still be putting up with him.

"'Now I say to you, just because I did that doesn't mean you have to do it, too. No, my child, you have to think. I'm warning you not to fall into those ways. Take care of yourselves. Don't go around being crazy women. Look at so-and-so, look at the daughter of so-and-so—she has a father and a mother, and look at what she's doing. And you, just because you don't have a father at your side, don't you start doing that, too.

"'That's why I'm warning you and asking you to obey me. If tomorrow you end up having children, during my lifetime—no, hija, I'm very sorry, but it's going to be the street for you. And you'll have to support them however you can. That's why I'm warning you. If you don't want to understand . . . but you have to understand.'

"My older daughter gets angry. 'Ay, Mama, I'm not even thinking about the things you're telling me.'

"'Then why do you protest? If you want to have a boyfriend, think about who you're choosing. Don't just let any man trick you. Try to see if he's a good young man, even if he's poor, but see if he's going to meet his obligations to you, if he's going to marry you and be committed to you, even if in a poor way.'

"Me, I'm weighed down by church books. I drag the cross with me. That's why Doña Paula said to me, 'So you're getting married?' And I was embarrassed and didn't say anything. And she said, 'Just look where you ended up.' And I should have backed out then. I still had a chance then. And she said, 'Because there's a saying that a white dress is white, but it's very punishing. The cross is small, but heavy.' And yes, it's true, it's true.

"There's nothing like a daughter. God gave me daughters, thank God. Between a daughter and a son, a daughter is thousands of times better than a son. Of course, if a son is good and his mother is ill, whether he's embarrassed or not, if there's no one else to look after her, then he has to look after her. Give her a drink of water, at least. That is, if he's on his own, and so long as he's got a good head. But how often is a son going to look after his mother? A daughter, even if she's an angry sort, '*Orale*, hija, even if you're angry, you've got to look after your mama.'

"Sometimes my daughters talk back to me. Or the two of them get angry. 'No, hijas,' I say. Or, 'Do this for me. Bring this for me. *Andale*, do it.' That's how I guide them. I had the older daughter out working, and at first she had some very ugly ways of thinking, very ugly ways of thinking. She was answering back a lot. I said to myself, This isn't right. I said, 'Look. So you don't want to give me money? What do you think? Look, I raised you. I had you, I brought you up. You're big and strong. If I put you to work, it was because I couldn't do more to support you myself. And besides you're now a young woman and you're growing up, and I don't want you to hang around in the streets being a crazy woman. Look at those nieces of that Primitiva. Look at them. Is that what you want to be doing? They're going around with single men, with married men, with anyone.'

"And I said to her, 'Look, I can't be watching over you. I go to San Luis to earn a living. I don't mind supporting you, but why should I be supporting you now that you're grown up? You're women, you have to work. I go to San Luis to work. You're not just going to sit in the house. Well, look, before you go out acting crazy, I'd prefer that you went somewhere else where no one knows you. That's why I have you working. And you've also got to help me. What's yours is yours, and what's mine is mine, but you have to support me. Listen well.'

"'Ah, not me. Why should I give you money?'

"'Why should you give me money? Listen, hija, that's not the way it is. Has it never occurred to you that you might be punished? Look, you have to help me. I don't say that you have to support me from head to toe, but you have to help me. I could have you put in jail. What do you think? Why are your thoughts so ugly? That's not the way to think, hija.'

"She has quite a temper, the girl. And I said, 'Where do you think you'll go with that temper? There won't be any place for you. What's going to become of you? Your life will be impossible. Sad. Tomorrow or the next day, you'll let that craziness get into you, and you'll get involved with some man. Maybe he'll take you with him! And if not, he'll just play around with you and then dump you. How will you support yourself then?

"'Don't think I'll be your pimp. I won't do what that Juana does for her daughters. One of them got pregnant, *fracasó*, with a married man. "Yes, hija, bring me the baby." No, I'm not going to do that. I hope you're not thinking of doing what many have done here, who've gotten pregnant, *fracasado*, and their fathers and mothers have been their pimps. Not me. I may be mean—I don't doubt it—you can say I'm mean, but I won't do that. If you want to follow the good path, *órale*. But if you want to follow the wrong path, *órale*, take that path, and go. And if not, I'll have you put in jail. And let's see what you'll do.'

"The girl went right on not wanting to listen. Finally I grabbed the rope. And she answered me back, who knows what she said to me. And I grabbed the rope. I said to her, 'Look, maybe someday some man will take you and beat you, but I say I'm your mother and you're speaking wrongly to me.'"

› › ›

Esperanza pauses and says, "That's why I always say it's not having them that's hard, it's—"

I interrupt, "So you did hit her?"

"Yes, I gave her a few whippings," Esperanza replies, unabashed. "And she ran away crying and went to my mama. And I told my mama why I had hit her. I said, 'I'll say it in front of my mama. I hope God won't punish my mouth, but I won't be your pimp. I just won't. Behave properly, and you'll see.' I said to my mama, 'Look, Mama, what I didn't do to you, why should they be doing it to me?'

"And my mama said, 'Hija, you must be paying for having gone off with that viejo, for having had them.'

"'Yes, that's fine. I had them so they'd take care of me, not turn their claws on me.'

"I whipped her three times. I said, 'You go to work now, hija, and don't come back to my house.'

"She got angry and left. She didn't even say adiós. She was gone for eight, fifteen days. Then she returned.

"'Mama.'

"'Ah?'

"'I'm here.'

"'Has your coraje passed?'

"'Yes, Mama. Yes, Mama.'

"'You see, hija? You see how nice it is to be at peace? Why do you act in that ugly way?'

"'No, you're right, Mama. What you say is right.'

"'Behave properly, hija, and no one will say anything to you. You're too old to be hit by your mama. Tomorrow or the next day you'll have a viejo, right? And he's going to treat you badly. Because not all men are good. That's why, hija, I've already told you. One paycheck is for you, and the other is for me, so that you will support me and help me.'

"And that's how it was with the girl. She gave in. I said to her, 'I don't care if you make money, but I'm not going to let you pull out your claws. I want you to remember that I'm your mama.'

"With Norberta, my younger daughter, it's a different battle. But I talk to her. The thing is not to let her be idle. That's what the doctors told me, never to let her sit idle, because of her illness. The *aire* she got affected her thinking. That's why she needs to be busy all the time. What happened is that my mama overturned her crib when she was little and didn't cover her in time. And the girl got a kind of attack. She got hit in the back of the head and got an aire. I took her to be cured, but her head didn't recover.

"She didn't finish school. She got as far as the fourth grade. But by then she already had a woman's body. That was when some boys from the school molested her. There are so many abusive pelados. One of them grabbed her from the front, another one from behind. I complained to the teacher, but Norberta said, 'I'm not going back to school.' She was almost fifteen. I said, 'All right, hija, you didn't make the train. You didn't finish before your fifteenth birthday.' As a woman it was dangerous for her to keep going to school. 'If you were a man, even if you were twenty years old, you'd have to struggle till you got out of school. But you're a woman.'

"And they told me, 'Never let her sit idle, always give her work to do.' That's why I say to her, 'What are you doing just sitting there? You're not knitting? You're not washing those dishes? They're dirty. *Andale*, wash them. What are you waiting for?' They told me, 'Don't tell her anything is wrong with her because she won't be able to stop thinking about it and she'll be worse off.' '*Orale*, hija, to work.'"

› › ›

"No, comadre, I'm very rough with my children. But if I play around with them, if I joke around with them, then they won't respect me. I've seen it with my grandson, who calls his parents *tú*. And he says to them, '*Tú*. Crazy one. Be quiet, crazy one.' And I tell them, 'That child isn't turning out right.' And they say, 'Ay, he's still small.'

"Sometimes I think, Why should I use up my life worrying about my grandson? That's their problem. *Andale*, my grandson said to me, 'Well, *tú*.' I said, 'To me, hijo, don't say *tú*. You say *usted* to me whenever you like. You can talk to your father and your mother however you like, because they let you. But don't say *tú* to me.'

"'*Tú* this.'

"'No, hijo. Don't say *tú*. I'm your abuela. Don't say *tú* to me.'

"'Ah, *usted*, Abuela.'

"'Yes, that's me, hijo. Say *usted* to me.'

"And now the boy knows. 'Abuela, *usted*, where are you going, Abuela? What did you bring me?'

"With my children too. I want to be respected as *usted*. When they want to respect me, they should say *usted*, and if they don't want to do that, then nothing! I won't have them play around with me.

"They make me suffer corajes. They talk back sometimes. And I have my bitter hours. That Simeón is married to the woman. Well, they're married by civil law. And sometimes they get angry with each other, and the woman talks back to him. 'If I had used such words with your father,' I tell him, '*Híjole*, he would have knocked out all my teeth.'

"Simeón will say to her, 'Carmela, give me that.' Or, 'Where is that? Carmela?' And she with a serious face. 'Eh, woman! I'm talking to you.' Or he'll say, 'What is there to eat? Go on, give it to me, *ándale*.'

And she serious-faced. 'I'm talking to you, man! Why don't you pay attention to me?'

"And then sometimes I'll say to her, 'The man is talking to you. Give him his dinner.'

"'Man, Mama, she's a burra. She doesn't understand.'

"And I say to her, 'Listen, you should give the man his dinner when he comes home.' I say that when I get involved. And sometimes I don't say anything."

› › ›

The rain has been pouring as we have been talking. A clap of thunder cuts our conversation short, and we start to talk about the rain. Esperanza is worried about some frijoles she left outside to dry in her courtyard; they won't be good for planting if they get soaked.

Then she says, "So, you're leaving on the twenty-fourth?"

"Yes, on Friday," I reply.

"And you're taking all these kitchen things with you? Let's see what you'll leave me, comadre, as a keepsake."

"Comadre, and what would you think if I were to write a book about your life?"

"Well, as long as no one here knows about it."

"I'd change your name."

"So you've liked this?"

"Yes."

"Better than with the other women? It's that no one has suffered the way I have. And I don't know how to read, eh? I can write my name poorly, crookedly . . ." She pauses and with laughter in her voice says, "I've made a confession. Now you carry my sins, because it is as if I have been confessing with my comadre instead of with the priest! You will carry my sins now, because you carry them in your head."

She lowers her voice to a whisper. "If you're thinking about them, you're carrying them with you. It's the same way with priests. Priests confess people, right? And then, maybe not at that moment, but the following day, they confess their sins. But to whom? To the bishops. And the bishops, to whom? To the archbishops. And the archbishops, to whom? To God! Now you, comadre, who are you going to get rid of them with? You tell them somewhere ahead, so someone else can carry the burden."

PART TWO

*Esperanza /
Redemption*

*My anger has meant pain to me but it
has also meant survival, and before I give
it up I'm going to be sure that there is
something at least as powerful to replace
it on the road to clarity.*

> *—Audre Lorde, "The Uses of Anger,"
> from Sister Outsider*

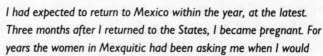

I had expected to return to Mexico within the year, at the latest. Three months after I returned to the States, I became pregnant. For years the women in Mexquitic had been asking me when I would have a child; one woman would exclaim every time she saw David and me, "Adam and Eve, Eve and Adam, just the two of you!" That I had myself begun to long for a child had been made clear to me in Mexquitic; a woman accused me of giving her baby granddaughter ojo (the evil eye) after I sat fondling the child for a long time too desiringly.

The day I returned home from the hospital with my son, Gabriel, there was an air mail letter, with the green and red striped edges, waiting for me. It was from Esperanza. She had dictated the letter to her son Mario, and he had made some of his own additions as well. They sent good wishes, but most of all they sent a strong message, repeated several times, that they hoped I would bring them a radio-cassette player when I returned to Mexico. This was maybe the third letter in which they had made the same request. I fully intended to bring them the radio-cassette player, as I had promised before leaving Mexquitic. Why the constant reminders?

Esperanza would not let me off the hook easily, not let me forget her just like that. There were things, real things, she desired from "the other side," and she was going to let me know what they were. My comadre had become part of my life, even when I was off duty as an anthropologist.

In becoming a mother I sympathized more emphatically with Esperanza's central tragedy, the loss of her children. How devastating it must have been for her to have lost six of her children, especially in a situation where motherhood was the only avenue by which she could gain a sense of self-worth. Not that she ever waxed romantic about motherhood, or anything else, for that matter. So I would be exaggerating if I were to claim that having Gabriel made me achieve instant rapport with my comadre. For my bourgeois body, my one labor had been more than I thought it was humanly possible to handle; when I asked my comadre about her labors, she shrugged and said

169

they had not been all that bad. More crucially, where I planned to have maybe just one child, my comadre had not envisioned the possibility of reproductive choice. For my comadre, the devil's imps that she always said popped out at midnight on the bridge in Mexquitic were the aborted children of La Llorona, the Weeping Woman of ancient Mexican lore.

Not only had I become a mother but a beginning assistant professor, who had constantly to be able to say what she was "working on." At first, it was colonial women's confessions to the Inquisition; but as time went on, it became clear to me that my comadre's confessions to me, the female-ethnographer-priest, were becoming my main source of "work" in the academy. Indeed, as she had foreseen, I was going to have to find a way of passing on her confessions to other listeners. With each return visit, Esperanza would take over my research just a little more, adding new chapters to the unfolding book of her life. Although she continued to tell me about family conflicts, in the years 1987 to 1989 she had more to say about her religious cosmology—though, as was her style, she would laugh at the earnest way I inquired about her beliefs and practices.

By elaborating upon cultural ideas of coraje, she had found a way both to express and overcome the pain of violence, of betrayal, of being a woman who had fracasado. Not that my comadre was ever going to let go of her anger. But in our later conversations, it became clear to me that she wanted to find redemption, too, but through a different system than that of the patriarchal Church. Mistreated by all the men in her life—father, husband, sons, and lover—my comadre, to my surprise, had gone seeking redemption in the veneration of the supermacho revolutionary hero Pancho Villa. Only years later, as I was struggling against so many fears to finish this book, did I finally begin to understand why a woman might need to steel herself in valor to find redemption in her own eyes.

SEVEN

The Pig in the Stream

I have never seen the demons, although to arrive where I should I pass through the dominions of death. I submerge myself and walk down below. I can search in the shadows and in the silence. Thus I arrive where the sicknesses are crouched. Very far down below. Below the roots and the water, the mud and the rocks.

—María Sabina: Her Life and Chants, *written by Alvaro Estrada*

September 8, 1987. David and I sit around the kitchen table with Esperanza, Norberta, and Mario. Everything is the same as two years ago, except that my little son, Gabriel, interrupts us every now and then with his one-year-old chatter, traces of which the tape recorder also catches. Esperanza is bringing me up to date on the events of her life. Just a year ago, she tells me, a bizarre and ugly pig turned up in the stream where her lilies grow.

"We went one morning to the milpa to fill in the hollows around the plants with fresh soil. When we got to the stream, the first thing I did was go look at the water pipe, because sometimes it gets tampered with. They've done wicked things to me there. And I looked and saw the pig! It was just lying there. It had huge nipples and smokey eyes.

"Mario threw a maguey stem at the pig and it didn't budge. I said, 'Who put this pig here? A pig doesn't just come and throw itself into the stream. So what's this pig doing here?'

"I clambered up the ridge, and then I turned the pig around to get a look at its feet, to see why it couldn't stand up. All its feet looked as though they had been chopped off, but I think it was just one foot that was actually missing. Its feet were very swollen.

"'Ay, look at how ugly that animal is. Someone must have come and dumped it here.'

"We didn't go back that day nor the next day. But Simeón went to have a look and came back to tell us what he had seen. 'The pig, where did you say the pig was?'

"'Not in the water, but by the edge of the water. Behind the elm tree. Its head was facing the river.'

"'Well, the pig is now lying dead in the water.'

"'Really?'

"'Yes, it's in the water, and it's dead.'

"'Ah.'

"Before we had even seen the pig, the owls had sung to us. They had sung early, at four in the afternoon, or four thirty. Early! With the sun out!

"They say that owls sing when they feel the cold, in October, November, or December, when they feel the cold coming. They sing at night, when the sun goes down. But it was not yet five o'clock that time, and the owls were singing. It gave me goose bumps down my whole body. I could feel my hair standing on end. And I said, 'What's up with these animals?' And those owls kept answering one another. I tried to talk back to them. 'What are you singing here for? What do you want?'

"I finally thought, It must be that Teodoro. He's the father-in-law of that Macario of mine, and he's the brother of that Primitiva. The man knows, he knows how to do things. Now that Teodoro is here on top of us, I thought. That man can't stand us since his daughter is with my Macario and we were in a court battle with them.

"And it would quiet down. They'd stop singing. And then we'd hear them screaming from somewhere else. But right there around the garden. We'd be about to leave. Then again, *Whooooooo! Whooooo! Whooooo!* That's what they sounded like, really ugly.

"I was very angry. 'Who are you singing to? You sons of— What do you want? Tell me what you want or what.'

"They were all shriveled up, with their beaks in their faces, and they sat there looking down at us.

"'Get a rock!'

"I tried to hit them with rocks. *Whooooo!* They'd fly away. You could see them heading straight toward the cemetery. Ay, those owls gave me goose bumps!

"Just at that moment, a son of my compadre Don Marcelo passed by. He says, 'What did you find, Doña Esperanza?'

"I said, 'An owl is up there singing at me. What does it want? Maybe it wants to kill me—I don't know. Why does it sing so much?'

"Then he says, 'Ah, yes, there it is. Knock it down.'

"'Let's see if I can.' And I tossed up more and more rocks. *Shuuuuu!* The owls flew off. And that was the last time they sang. And then, eight days after they stopped singing, we found the pig!

"It made me feel strange to see the pig lying there in the water. We'd pass by, and it made me feel I don't know what. Like fear. I don't know what I felt. I'd go into the garden. And I felt as though a dark shadow had fallen over me.

"'Now what are we going to do? It's going to smell, and the dogs will come and eat the carcass while it's lying in the water.'

"Ah, and then it was time for the town fiesta. Don Chito says, 'So-and-so lost a pig, but they say it's dark.'

"'No, this one is pink.'

"He says, 'Ah, well, who knows?'

"So that's as far as it went. The fiesta passed. And the pig was still there! Then Simeón says, 'Look, I grabbed a stick and pulled it out toward the edge, to see if the dogs will eat it. Because it's going to start smelling. Let's see if the dogs will eat it during the night.'

"The next day he went back. 'What do you think, Mama? Didn't I tell you I had pulled it out?'

"'Yes.'

"'Well, I left the stick there, and it seems like someone went and pushed the pig back into the water. I saw some footprints there in the mud by the edge of the river.'

"'Ah, so now that's on purpose. The pig is gone already, what with its intestines hanging loose in the water. How are the dogs going to eat it? It's smelling already.'

"So the days passed. I said, 'No, I can't stand this anymore.' There was such a smell there. I'd be working in the field and I could smell it. I felt such fear. It was ugly. 'Come on, children, let's go. The owls aren't singing anymore.' But I didn't say to them, 'I don't think this is good.'"

›››

"I went to talk to Chencha. She says, 'It's a curse. It's not good.'

"When Chencha worked, I spoke to the spirit of General Francisco Villa. I told him what was happening in my garden. He says, 'No, that's not good. That's an evil they've thrown there. But I'm going to take care of it. And I'm going to tell the medium to take care of this job of yours.' That's what he told me.

"After she finished working, I waited for her.

"'You know I spoke with Don Francisco,' I told her. 'He said you should take charge of this, that you should take care of this job for me.'

"She says, 'Yes, if you want me to, I'll do it, but it's going to cost you.'

"No, dear God! I said, 'Now where am I going to get that much from?'

"'That's what it's going to cost. Because what's happened is that they've thrown salt on your land so it will all dry up, so it will all go to waste. You will work and work, and it won't produce anything.' And she says, 'What they want is for all the plants you have in the stream to dry up. Who planted them?'

"I told her, 'Well, that boy Macario did. He planted some, and his father planted some. And I've planted some.'

"'Yes, of course,' she says.

"'But I want you to tell me who's responsible for this.'

"'I will tell you, but not yet,' Chencha says. 'Let me keep on working, so I can see where we stand.' Then she says, 'Come back tomorrow. And bring the small change, because I've got to buy some things to do the work for you. You need to pay me, so I can go buy the things I need.'

"It cost two hundred and forty thousand pesos. And it was all I had. I had the money in the bank, and I took it out. What was I to do? And now I'm broke. Now I don't have anything. It was a blow in the belly, as they say.

"The next day I went and Chencha says, 'So you're ready? Look, I'm going to go cure your field. But before I do anything, you have to remove what's in the water. Because that's the evil. How is the aid going to work if the rot is there? You have to clean it out before I can go do the cure.'

"'But how will I take it out?' I said.

"She says, 'Ask someone you trust to take it out for you.'

" 'But who?' I said. 'How am I going to say, "Here you, take this thing out of the stream for me?" '

" 'Well, you figure out how to do it. Tell them you don't know how that pig ended up there.' Then she says, 'No, you take it out yourself.'

" 'Me? Mother of the heavens, how can I do it? It's ugly. It's very ugly.'

"She says, 'Well, precisely. It will be much better if you take it out yourself than if someone else takes it out for you. If you take it out yourself, you have valor, you have spirit.'

"I went home and said, 'Who will come with me to the garden? I'm going to take out the animal that's there.' No one wanted to go. 'Well, I'm going. I'm going no matter what.'

"My mama says, 'I'll go with you, hija. Let's go.'

"We took a knife and a stick and made a hook out of wire to pull it out onto the edge of the riverbank, so as not to touch all that filth with our hands.

" 'Down there,' I said. 'You stay there, Mama. I'll go alone up to that part.' But my mama didn't hear me. She followed me to the stream. And I got there and covered myself with my rebozo, covered myself all up, but I was close to fainting. But God made it possible. I called upon all the saints and Tomasito and Francisco. I said, 'You're going to help me remove this filth. And with valor, not with fear. Let's go to it, whatever happens.'

"And I pulled it out. I got the hoe under it and pulled it up with all my strength. My mama was standing a short distance away. By then I could hardly breathe. My chest felt squeezed. And I felt sort of queasy. And there I was dragging it along. But I never turned back to look at the animal. I just kept pulling it, being careful not to lose it, just dragging it behind me. And then I threw it over by the edge of someone else's field, where there are a lot of weeds and where no one plants, off in a corner. And the dogs ate it, there where I left it.

"Ay, but I couldn't take it, that tiredness, that ill feeling. It was horrible what I felt. There were still a few pieces left, and I got them out with a stick and dropped them on top of a maguey and threw the rest in the weeds just beyond my field. I got all of it out. But I could hardly take it. Afterward we cut some branches of pirul, and we swept ourselves with them. I swept my mama and she swept me. Then we threw the branches in the water and left.

"We recited an Our Father. We don't know more than that. And a Credo, too. And then we left. 'Let's go. We got it out.'

"I was so out of breath, you can't imagine it. I went to the milpa and stood under another pirul tree and cleaned myself again with the branches of the tree. I cut some little buds from the tree. But my stomach felt horrible, as though I needed to vomit, and I took the little buds and put them on my stomach. With that I felt better. And in the afternoon we went home, very peacefully, thank God. And that was it.

"The next day Chencha came. I think it was a Sunday. Ah, I had beans, I had corn, I had fresh ears there in the garden. So Chencha arrives and says, 'Did you get it out?'

"I said, 'Yes.'

"'Good, let's go.' She took us in her car all the way to the milpa. Then she says, 'Please make a hole a meter long right there inside your garden. Make a hole. Go buy me a liter of alcohol.' She prayed and she prayed, from end to end of my field. And then, 'Let's see. Give me the alcohol.' She poured in the alcohol and lit a match and threw it in. Flames came rising up from the alcohol. 'There it goes,' she says. After the flames had died down, she says, 'Fill it with dirt. Pretend you're burying the dead.'

"So it blew out, as though nothing had ever been there. Then she made the sign of the cross over it. And that was all.

"From end to end of the milpa she had gone, saying, 'Ay, woman, no. They've ruined you. With your pardon, they've ruined your mother even! They just want to see you totally desperate. So you won't be worth anything.' And she went on, 'They want everything to dry up for you. Everything to go to waste for you. So you'll work and the land won't produce anything. You'll work and work and have nothing. But it's not going to happen.'

"She went to the four ends of the milpa. And she ended up at the stream. And that was it. Then afterward, when I'd go see her, she'd give me liter-size bottles full of who knows what. 'Here, take this and sprinkle it in your milpa. Sprinkle it in your milpa. Sprinkle the four ends of your milpa and your garden. And you'll see how next year I'll have to eat some very good ears of corn. You'll see.'

"And yes, she did eat them. No, thank God!"

›››

"You paid a lot of money for Chencha to cure your field," I say, trying to sound neutral. In truth, I'm astounded that she paid the equivalent of five hundred dollars, which for most working-class Mexicans amounts to four or five months' salary, to have her field "cured" by Chencha. "Were you really afraid the land would stop producing?"

"Yes, I was. How was I going to let it all dry up? All the plants, all the trees? It was a clear thing, comadre." She gives me a pitying look, astounded, in her turn, that I don't seem to understand the obvious. "Even a totally ignorant person can understand it. Owls, then the pig. How old am I, and I had never seen anything like that. The owls are gone. My field has been cured. It's been almost a year now.

"After she was done with her work, I put my question to Chencha. 'Now you're going to tell me who did this evil.'

"'All right, I'm going to tell you.'

"'Tell me with valor. Don't tell me with fear.'

"'It's your son, Macario.'

"'Him alone?'

"'No, he and someone else,' she says. 'What your son Macario wants is for it all to go to waste, for your land not to give you anything, for your land to get salted and not give anything. The other person—she was the one who put the pig there—she did it out of envy she feels for you. You've been in a feud with her.'

"'Yes, it's true,' I said.

"It was that Elvira. She was angry with me because I had filed a charge against them because her daughter and son and grandchildren threw stones at my girl, Norberta. I caught them doing it, and her girl yelled obscenities at me. I didn't like that and filed a charge against them. She even brought in a lawyer, but I just had my tongue to defend myself. If she didn't owe anything, why did she bring in a lawyer? So we don't get along.

"Chencha told me, 'She put in the pig, and he put in the remedy so the pig would hurt you, so you would die from one moment to the next and all of it would go to waste . . . Well, it didn't happen.'

"'Yes, fortunately.' And since then, they look at me with anger, because I didn't let them get away with it."

"Have you tried to talk to your son?" I ask, guessing what her answer will be.

"No! Hum! I'm here for him to come talk to me, not for me to go talk to him. I say that as a mother I'm not about to go begging to my son, licking up to my son. I raised him. He's big and strong. I'm here for him to look out for me, not for me to go begging to him. And then with those wicked ways of his, wanting to force himself on my girl."

"And don't you feel sad about what's happened?" I feel compelled to ask.

"Yes, of course. For my money, I feel sad. That's what I feel. Just that. I don't feel anything for my son."

"You don't feel bad about your son?" I persist.

"No. I suffered so much because of him, and then look at how he repaid me. No, comadre, why should I go beg my son to talk to me? After all he's done? After he took up with that woman and her father? No, we don't talk. They're in on it together.

"It's just that maybe they don't want to do me in, or they can't pull me down. But they could do it. Yes, they could. You don't think so? You saw what happened to Mama. How many have succumbed? They haven't killed me yet because God hasn't let them. And because a lot of people here know that I have Chencha, so they treat us as witches. If anyone tries to do me harm, they know it's going to be a battle."

EIGHT

The Stolen Eggs

It was a Sunday to be sure
The event that occurred
That young José Lizorio
Became angry with his mother.

Gentlemen, take heed
And pay close attention
This son arrived home drunk
And was disrespectful to his
     mother.

Gentlemen, most naturally
His mother was furious
She raised her eyes to heaven
And a strong curse did hurl.

May God will it, evil son,
And all the saints too,
That you fall down at the mine
And break into two thousand
     pieces.

Un domingo fue por cierto
el caso que sucedió
que el joven José Lizorio
con la madre se enojó.

Señores, tengan presente
y pongan mucho cuidado
que este hijo llegó borracho
y a su madre le ha faltado.

Señores, naturalmente
la madre se enfureció
alzó los ojos al cielo
y fuerte maldición le echó.

Quiera Dios, hijo malvado,
y también todos los santos,
que te caigas de la mina
y te hagas dos mil pedazos.

—"Corrido de José Lizorio," in María Herrera-Sobek,
The Mexican Corrido: A Feminist Analysis

July 13, 1988. At the kitchen table again after another year's ab-
sence. Same cast of characters. In a letter Esperanza had let me
know that Simeón and his wife Carmela were no longer living in her
house. There had been a quarrel; another son had proved ungrateful.
As is her manner of telling a story, Esperanza dove in by reconstruct-
ing all of the dialogues, showing how the feud grew into a Babel of
words that should never have been spoken.

"It all began with Simeón saying to Carmela, 'There's no water coming out of the faucet. Why didn't you fetch water?'

"And then Carmela said, 'The container has a hole in it.'

"'Couldn't you have covered it up with a rag and filled it up with water?'

"'No, I couldn't. I didn't have time.'

"'What do you mean, you didn't have time? What did you do all morning?'

"That's all they needed to get angry with each other. Then their little boy picked up the cat.

"'Put that cat down!' she yelled. She was very angry. I just sat there.

"Then he yelled, 'Leave that cat alone, you pig.' And then to her, 'What did you do all day? What other work did you have to do but to get water? Or do you have other things to do?'

"And she was in her room crying. Just because he was scolding her, she was crying. Then the little boy picked up the cat again, and Simeón kicked it. 'Hey, don't be kicking my cat,' I said to him." Esperanza laughs mischievously, and Norberta and Mario giggle.

"Then he uttered some curse. I said, 'Look, if you want water, Norberta got water. Take some from the bucket and tomorrow you can get more.' And he starts saying obscenities about Norberta, that why hadn't she filled up their buckets? That's when I got angry. I said, 'Listen, Norberta has no obligations with you. The obligation is your wife's.'

"Then he says, 'She says that you kept her busy all morning and that's why she got back late. She says you kept her busy working on your plants.'

"'My plants?' I said. 'Well, I'm sorry to have to tell you that I didn't work on any plants, nor did she.' I got really angry. 'Listen, woman, I don't usually care what you two do, but now I care, because you've brought my girl into it and now me, too. Well, you're lying. You know I left early and you stayed home. What plants did we work on? You're to blame that the man is angry. When a woman makes a commitment to a man, it means she's going to do her part, do things for the man. You should do what you need to do so the man won't be arguing with you. You should have everything done before he gets home. Yes, you're poor, but do the best you can with the little you have. Don't blame me!

If you want to live here like family, be like family. I won't allow you to pull me into your squabbles whenever you feel like it.'

"I stayed there in the courtyard, and Simeón went inside and shut the door to their room. I could hear him say, 'Why did my mama get so angry at you?'

"And she was crying and crying and crying. I had never said a bad word to her or gotten angry with her. But that day our feud began. I heard her say, 'I can take her on. You think I'm afraid of your mother? If I'm not to her liking, tell her to find someone else she likes better.'

"I was listening to her. I felt as though they had thrown fire at me! I stood up and opened the door. And I said, 'Listen. I heard what you said. Don't be saying that to me, because I didn't choose you for my son. If it were another woman and she did the same thing you're doing now, I'd be saying the same thing to her that I'm saying to you. Look, don't get me involved. If you don't feel comfortable here, you can leave with the boy. Take him wherever you want. I'm not stopping you. He's flour in your sack and you know it. You may be young and strong, but you're not going to tell me what to do.'

"That's how the argument got going. And then Carmela said a lot of things to Simeón. Then Simeón got furious and tried to get his hands on Norberta, but he wasn't able to hit her because she was with my mama. And my mama got into it, too. She was sick with the flu. And my mama got into it to defend the girl. And Simeón joined in with curses, mistreating my mama. If he had touched her, he'd be in jail right now."

› › ›

"The story goes like this. Norberta says that Simeón got back at midday, at two in the afternoon. We had already argued, and we were all angry with one another. I wasn't speaking to Carmela anymore, and she wasn't speaking to me. She'd stay shut up in her room. Their little boy would come to us, and she'd pull him away and push him back into their room.

"It was in January. I was getting over the flu, and my mama had just come down with it. I said to myself, I'm better, I'm going to sell. And I told the girl to stay with my mama, to give her water so she could at least swallow a pill and eat a tortilla.

"So the girl tells me that later that day, Carmela took her dishes out to wash. She put the dishes in a frying pan and poured soap on them. Then she took the greasy water from the dishes and threw it in the garden. Threw it into *my* garden! She didn't have any plants of her own anymore, because she had given them all to a comadre.

"Then Norberta says to her, 'Listen, why did you throw that dirty, soapy water into my mama's garden?' She asked because some of my carnations had dried up. Then the girl says, 'Ah, so you were the one who made my mama's plants dry up.'

"Then Carmela replied, 'Yes, I was the one. It was us, wasn't it?' That's what she said to the little boy. 'Right, son? Wasn't it us?'

"'Now you'll see how I'll tell my mama that you threw greasy water in the garden,' Norberta said to her.

"And she says, 'Go on, tell her. Don't think I'm afraid of you. I'm not afraid of you, nor of Mario nor of Gabriela. And I'm not afraid of your abuela nor of your mama.'

"Carmela went back into her room. And Norberta went with my mama. My mama had been listening from behind the *órgano* plant. And she asks Norberta, 'What were you talking about?'

"'No, Abuelita, what happened is that Carmela poured dirty water in my mama's garden.'

"And my mama says, 'Ah, you see? They think your mother is a fool. They do whatever they please with her.'

"Later that day, they were sitting there when they heard the cackling of a chicken. And since Carmela had chickens and I had chickens and my mama had chickens, my mama said to Norberta, 'Listen, hija, go see if the chickens are getting into your mama's plants. You know how she gets angry when the chickens get in there. Go see what the chickens are doing.'

"The girl went to have a look. The chicken was cackling up on the hill, so the girl ran up the hill after it. And the little boy was there 'going to the bathroom.' Then the boy says to her, 'Ah, so you're the one who's been robbing my mama's eggs. You'll see, I'm going to tell her!' It was one of Carmela's chickens that was cackling up there.

"And my girl says to him, 'Me robbing eggs? You liar! Do you see me with any?'

"'You'll see!' And the little boy ran off. 'Mama! Mama! That Norberta is the one who's robbing your eggs, Mama. That's why you never find any. She's robbing your eggs!'

"That's how the feud happened!

"It didn't take but a few minutes. Simeón got back in the pick-up truck and went straight to their room. Carmela told him what the girl had said to her, but she didn't say what she had said to the girl, what she had said against us.

"And then Norberta tells me that Simeón came out. He said so many obscenities to the girl. I wasn't there. I was in San Luis.

"Noooo! Then my mama says, 'Well, what are you arguing about? You have no shame. Here you are a mere lodger, and you still act like a wild beast. What is the girl doing to you? Are you supporting her? What eggs did she steal from you?' My mama was sick, and the coraje got into her. And then she says to him, 'And if she had brought me an egg, I think I would have deserved it! When you came here with your mama, after your abuela and your papa threw you out, that you don't remember, do you? Now you become a wild beast with me. Because you see me here like this, all shrunken and dying. What nice grandchildren I have! Remember how many years I supported you here, you and your brother and your mama? I supported you, and now what do I get? I even gave you a place to make your house so you could live here. And you behave very well, don't you? Sinvergüenza!'

"No, my mama said things to him. And he talked back to her. Curses that he said to her. And my mama, 'Go on, you've got nerve. Why don't you leave already? You're still clinging to your mama's ribs. And what are you doing for your mama? You're turning her into a dry stick of wood making her suffer corajes all the time. You don't appreciate anything. And here you are, stuck in here.'

"And Simeón, who knows what words he said to her.

"That night I got back from San Luis. I was just beginning to feel better, but my mama was practically dying already. Ay, no! Earth and heaven came together.

"That was on Friday. I got up the next day feeling worse. My throat hurt. I had a fever. I couldn't eat anything. And my mama lay in bed, too. We went to see the doctor. On Saturday the doctor wasn't there. He was out giving vaccinations. We were going to tell my sisters, but my mama didn't want us to say anything. And that night I didn't know if my mama would make it. She was trembling and trembling and trembling. She had a high fever, just from all the coraje.

"That Sunday she woke up still feeling trembly, but she got out of bed and made a meal for my brother. My mama didn't say anything to him.

" 'Why is Mama sick again? I left her well,' my brother says to me.

"And I say, 'No, Mama has the flu. Part of it is the flu, and the other part is the coraje she felt. That's what they tell me, because I wasn't here.'

"My brother left, and that Sunday my mama was very sick. But thanks to God we pulled her through. I used alcohol and more alcohol. My mama had already gone cold. All of her. Just her stomach stayed warm. And she was sweating and sweating and sweating, and shaking and shaking and shaking and shaking. No, she was going. And there was no doctor. On Sundays, there's no doctor. And she was saying, 'I'm going, I'm going, I'm going.' That's how she spent the night. I kept boiling pure orange juice for her and rubbing alcohol on her. She didn't want to eat. Nothing. She just made it to the next day, Monday. I said to her, 'Let's go, Mama. I'm taking you to San Luis.' And she says, 'No, I can't. I can't get up.'

"And they? They just strolled about, as though nothing were happening. What I felt was the coraje. With the little bit of strength I had left, I went to San Luis. I told my brother, and he came for her immediately. He found a taxi and had her attended to. She got two injections at once.

"And my brothers and sisters, three brothers and two sisters, turned against me because of my son. And my mama, they didn't bring her back the next Sunday nor the one after. About four Sundays later she came back. She was really going fast. If I hadn't moved on her . . .'"

› › ›

"When my mama was finally able to get up, she says, 'How is Don Simeón doing?'

"I said to her, 'There he is. He doesn't want to leave.'

"My sister-in-law and my brother said, 'So, he doesn't want to leave? He's making fun of you, you know.'

"Then my sister and brother spoke to the brother in Monterrey. They called him so he'd come the following Sunday. When my brother came, he said to Simeón, 'Tell me, why did you argue with my mama? Why did you mistreat her? I understand the argument began because of some eggs. My mama told the girl to watch over the chickens. If the girl robbed some of your eggs, it was to take them to my mama. How many of your eggs did my mama eat, so I can pay you back for them?'

"My brother said so many things to him, and Simeón just kept saying, 'I don't know what you're talking about.' Then my sister Hipólita spoke. She says, 'Look I don't care about you and your mama. I know how bad a life you give your mama. What I care about is *my* mama. So, I want you to leave the house right away.'

"Then Simeón says, 'Me? You want me to leave? I'll leave, but when I'm ready.'

"And she, 'No, you're leaving right now.'

"'Even if you kick me out, you won't get me to leave.'

"And my brother says, 'Ah, you think I can't kick you out? If you don't want to leave, *órale*, then you, sister, you can leave with your son.'" Esperanza snaps her fingers as she speaks. "'Your son is leaving and you can go, too.' That's what my brother said to me. And there he was snapping his fingers. 'You're going to leave. You're leaving with your son.'

"Then Simeón says, 'How nice! It's not just me who's being thrown out.'

"'So you got your wish? Your motive was to have me thrown out, too, right?' I said. 'Look, you've never wanted to behave properly, neither you nor your wife. What consoles me is that your wife gives you the very worst to eat. She gives you food mixed with pig shit to eat. I've seen her. How do those beans taste? Have you seen how the animals tip over the pot and come and get their beans? That's how she gives them to you to eat. That's what your wife does.'

"Then he says, 'That's none of your business. If she gives me food with shit or not, that's none of your business.'

"'Yes it is!' I said. 'So *órale*. Out, go on!'

"My brother spoke. 'Tomorrow I'll wait for you in court. I'll be waiting for you and your wife in court.' And Simeón with his arms folded. Then my brother says, 'I'll be waiting for you. And you, too, Esperanza, I'll be waiting for you in court.'"

› › ›

"No, no, no!

"And Simeón just stood there. He closed the door to his room, locked his wife up in there. And he stayed outside. Then I said to him, 'You see? Look at how you've behaved.'

"And he, 'What? What do you want?' He no longer respected me. He called me *tú*.

"In that moment to have nabbed him, stick in hand, and given him twenty beatings! No, he didn't respect me anymore as his mama. I said, 'Listen to me. I've already gone through this with one son, and now to have to repeat it again with you! So, you know what? You had a mama. Now you don't have a mama. So you'd better leave because I say you're leaving.'

"'Yes, I'll leave,' he says. 'But your rooms are going to fall.' He uttered an ugly curse. 'Your *pinche* rooms are going to fall!'

"'If you're such a man, knock them down right now!'

"'All right,' he says. And he perches himself on the door and starts swinging from it. And *zas*! He knocked down the door. It was already eleven at night. We took a walk around town, and when we came back there was such a noise in there! He was putting holes in the whole floor of the room! Pulling out the tiles he had put down! That day we didn't go to bed inside. Me, the girl, and the boy went to bed in another little hut we have, in the jacal.

"I thought to myself, The other son hit me and crucified me. And now I'm going to let this one get his way? The next day I decided to file a charge against him because of what he did. But when I got there at eleven the next morning, Don Jesús says to me, 'Doña! Come here. Simeoncito came early, very obedient the young man. He came early and told me the whole story. He says he got angry and said things, but it was out of anger. He's coming back at two. So you can go now and come back at two.'

"'Ah, that's fine. Of course.' So we left and went back at two. When I arrived, Simeón was already sitting there. But what happened was that Simeón gave Don Jesús a bribe! He gave Don Jesús a bribe so he wouldn't punish him!

"'You know, Simeón, your mama is accusing you because you've mistreated her. You've been disrespectful. So you tell me now how things stand.'

"'I'm saying that I'm leaving. And, no, I won't knock down the house. I'm already building my own house anyway. I don't have any argument with her.'

"Then Don Jesús says, 'Well, Doña Esperanza, how much time will you give your son before he has to leave? Until he finishes his house, or what?'

"Well, I felt sorry for him. I said, 'Let him finish his house. Let him finish and then he can leave.'

"So, what do you think, comadre? And afterward, it was no longer just me. It was my mama and my brothers and sisters who said they were going to bring a lawyer from Monterrey to put an embargo on all their possessions and throw the two of them into jail. They were very angry that Simeón had been disrespectful to my mama and that they had to spend money to get her cured.

"They'd bring my mama back on Sundays, and she'd say, 'Well, you know, I don't want your son here in my house again. Know it and understand it. And you're the one responsible. It's up to you to throw your son out, because I don't want him in my house. And I won't come back to my house until he's gone.'

"I would think to myself, Yes, I had him. It was my fault. I came to my mama's house when they were little. And then they grew up, and yes, it was my fault. So I tried to speak to Simeón.

"'Listen, Simeón. The truth is I want you to leave. It's true I said in court that you could stay until you finished your room. But I can't be suffering because of you. They're asking when you're going to leave.'

"'Why are they asking you about me? If they're so valiant, why don't they come to my house? You let them take advantage of you.'

"I said, 'Look, Simeón. It's my mama. I can't oppose my mama. I'm not like you. My mama may be difficult at times, but I have to respect her. I prefer that you leave because I don't want to be disrespectful of my mama.'

"'Ah, you want me to leave. Well, I won't.'

"'Look, don't be stubborn. It's better for you to go. You want the police to come and get you out by force?'

"'The police? Only if there were no justice for me to defend myself.'

"'*Andale*, then. But afterward, don't be asking why. That's what I'm telling you. Look, the truth is you've finished a room of your house, so why don't you leave? What's the point of you being here? You look at me with eyes full of coraje. I look at you that way, too. What sort of a life is this? Your child comes to my room, and his mama gives the poor creature a beating. Why should that poor creature have to suffer? Why don't you let him talk to us?'

"He didn't answer me. He and his woman sat there with grim faces. Then they went inside their room and shut the door."

› › ›

"Sunday. Then Monday I went to San Luis. Tuesday I didn't go. On Tuesday he came with the pick-up truck and took out everything he had without saying a word to me. He gathered up everything he had scattered around outside—bottles, sticks, containers, everything.

"Then Wednesday I went to San Luis. I said to the girl, 'Look, if Simeón comes at midday, just tell him he can leave the things I gave him when he got married. If I'm not good, then my things aren't good either. Just tell him to leave the things that belong to his mama.'

"He didn't come by that Wednesday. Thursday I didn't go to San Luis, and that night he came for more of his things. At seven, eight, he came with the pick-up truck. He took out the mattresses and the bed and the dresser and the stove. Then I spoke to him. 'Now that you're taking out your things, please leave me those curtains, that desk, that chair. Just leave them there. I gave them to you before you were married so you could use them. But seeing the way you've acted, I'm not giving them to you to take with you.'

"Then he says, 'I don't want to be arguing right now!'" Esperanza affects a staccato, gruff voice. Then she laughs. "'I don't want to be arguing right now!'

"I said to him, 'We're not arguing. I'm just telling you.'

"So they took out the mattresses. Then Carmela got to saying, 'Ha! Take the water pipe, too. After all, you put it in. After all, she doesn't show gratitude for that.'

"I said, 'Listen, who are you? You came here with your arms folded, and now you're a doña. Now you're giving orders. Now you're roaring.' I said to her, 'Take it out yourself. If you can, take it out yourself.'

"No, we had quite a feud. I say that I've struggled with my children. Now I'm older, more worn out. Coraje, corajes, that's for sure. Somehow I haven't died yet. But I haven't given in. You think I don't have enough corajes? No, listen to me, comadre, as though I were made of stone!"

NINE

Angelitos – Little Angels

The seedlings of my
　　　　　　soul　　　And the roots
have been ripped　　out　　tossed into　　a
　　　　　　　　　　　　　　　　grave.

—Carmen Tafolla, "Soulpain"

*July 13, 1988. Later the same evening, having told the story of her
continuing conflicts with her living children, Esperanza talked about
the children she has in the grave, her "angelitos," or "little angels."
And she told a story about another ungrateful son.*

"I have six angelitos and I put out six candles for them and
I light them. One learns these things from one's grandparents, because my mama does the same things. My mama learned
from her abuela. My mama has three angelitos. But Mama also has her
mama who died. And her papa who died. And her brothers. Not me, I
just have my angelitos.

"I put out flowers for them. I fill my table with flowers. I put all
their flowers on the table, in their vases. Then I put out their candles,
and in the middle I put out their bread. I give them their *pan de muertitos*, their bread for the little dead, sweets for the little dead. For your
mama, your papa, for everyone, you put things out. They say that for
the angelitos you put out a glass of water, because they're playing under the eyes of God and they get thirsty. Anyway, that's what I put out
for them. And their incense. And if you know how to pray, you say
an Our Father, and if you know more, you say a rosary; and whoever
doesn't know the whole rosary, then an Our Father, an Ave Maria, for
the angelitos. And the following year, it's the same thing. That's how it
is. That's why I believe in all of that. Because it's what I saw.

"I'd say to my abuela, because I grew up around my abuela—I was
with my abuela for two years. I'd see how she would put things out,

and I'd say, 'Why do you put that out? And why do you put that other thing out?'

"And she, 'What's this and what's that?'

"'But, Abuela, I'm asking because I want you to teach me. I don't know.'

"And she, 'Well, watch carefully.'

"And there it was. Every year. And she'd say, 'Look, when you have children, or your papa or your mama die, this is what you put out for the dead.'

"And I'd say, 'Don't tell me they eat that?'

"My abuela would get angry—she had a temper, my abuela. And she would reply, 'They don't eat. You're going to eat it, not them.'

"'So why are you putting it out?'

"'Go on, asking so many questions, you.' That's what she'd say when she was in a bad mood, but when she was in a good mood, she'd say, 'No, look, hija, you put these things out for the souls. You put out what they used to like, that's what you put out for them.'

"'And why, because they come for it?'

"'Yes, they're going to come for it. You'll see.' And we'd set things out. That's when she was in a good mood. When my abuela was angry, she'd say, '*Andale*, let's pray. Stop asking so many questions. Let's pray for the souls of the children.'

"'And where are they?'

"'They're going to come. They're going to come.'

"And there we were. Just my abuela and me. An uncle was there, but he slept outside. He didn't know about these things. It was just my abuela and me.

"'But, Abuela, where are they? There are no souls there.'

"And she, 'Hija, they're going to come. Let's pray. Praying they'll come.'

"And we'd be praying. She showed me how to pray. And then she'd say, 'Look, there they are already.'

"'But where?'

"I could hear some doves flying among the flowers.

"'Look, there they are already.'

"'But where are they?'

"'Look, there are the doves. That's them. Don't expect to see them anymore like you see yourself or me in the flesh. They're doves now.

Spirits are doves, and they come back. They don't eat what you put out
for them. They eat the aroma, that's what they eat. They take the
aroma back to God our Lord. Look, tomorrow, eventually, I'll die. If
you're with me, you'll remember me when I die. Look, what I like is
this and that. So you'll put out those things, and I'll come back. I'll fill
up just with the aroma. I'll fill up with that and go on. The image is
what I'll take back with me to God. Because when you die and come
back after a year—because God sends you back after a year—God asks,
"How did they receive you in your house? What did you bring back?"
And say you're there with your arms folded. "So they didn't want you
back at your house? They didn't receive you with anything?" Others come back—"What about you?" And they bring back
the appearance of the tables, how they put things out on the altar,
with lots of flowers, with sweets and all, and that's what they bring
back.'

"'Ay, that's not true,' I would say.

"'No, it's true. Well, don't believe it.'

"Then she'd say, 'Look, I'm going to tell you a story.' This is her
story: There was a señor whose señora died. And he had his mama. He
became a widower, but he still had his mama. And the man liked his
pulque. He was a drunk. He didn't have children, no. His señora died,
and he was left a widower, with his mama again. And his mama was
very close to the church. She was very devout. And the son was very
given to vice. And it happened that the time came for the day in November, for the Day of the Dead. And he was really drunk. And she
said, '*Andale*, hijo, it's soon going to be time for the blessed souls. Get
going, get some centavitos, so you can buy a candle for her, for the
one who was your wife. She'll come back to see you, and what will
you have for her? Nothing.' And he, 'Ay, Mama.' The man was really
drunk. 'Ay, Mama, that's not true. They don't ask for anything. They're
already dead.' 'Ay, you're ungrateful, hijo.'

"'All right, all right, if what you say is true, I'm going to go to the
hills and bring back a pile of firewood, and I'm going to set it down
here in the courtyard and throw gasoline on it and I'll throw a match to
it and I'll say, "All right, vieja, come here so you can warm yourself
up." She'll be coming all cold. "There's the fire."' And his mama said,
'Go on, ungrateful one.'

"They say that from twelve midnight on, the souls start to line up.

Then they go out. And they line up again at dawn, and they roam about until twelve noon.

"The day came. And that's what the man did. Those men, you know, given to vice. Determined men like that. So he went to bring firewood. And there was his mama looking on. She was setting up her altar with her candles, putting everything out for the souls.

"And at midnight, he got the fire going in the courtyard, spread out all that firewood and threw gasoline on it, and the flames rose up. Before daybreak, at four or five, he had his drinks, and then he said, 'I'm going to spy on them, Mama, to see if it's true.'

"And there he was, scrunched up at the edge of the main road, when all the souls come walking down the main road. They were about to pass, bearing everything that had been set out for them in their houses, on their tables, all nicely adorned. That's what they take with them, the appearance of things; the light is what they take.

"And that man was spying on them. And it dawns, and it doesn't dawn. And finally it dawns. He wanted to see the group pass by. No, he heard a murmur, a murmur that they were coming. The murmur came closer and closer and closer. And no, some lights appeared to him from far away. Ay, there they come already. There come the lights. And the man edged himself away from the road and hid behind a rock.

"And then my abuela said that he was waiting for the group of lights to pass by, to pass in front of him. He saw them coming, and he started to run, and he hid again, to one side. And when he looked again, there was nothing before him. And then he looked, and there before his eyes the whole group passed by.

"They came in their bulky shapes and with lots of lights. There they went. They made such noise. They were talking. They were talking, but no one could understand what they were saying. And then suddenly facing him was his señora. She said to him, 'This is what you put out for me. This is what I'll take with me.' That shape passed in front of him with the flames from the fire, what he had put out. When he looked up ahead, there she was bearing the flames from the fire.

"And the man got scared. And he went back to his house. It had already dawned. He got back to his house, but shaking.

"'So you're back?' And the man was practically crying. 'What happened?' No, the man couldn't talk. He was trembling. 'What happened, hijo? Why don't you answer me?'

"No, he was crying and crying. Finally he was able to repeat what his wife had said to him, that what he had put out was what she was taking back. 'You see, hijo? It's what I said to you. I told you, but you didn't want to understand. You don't want to believe.'

"He didn't last fifteen days. He died. The man died. Just from pure *susto*, pure fright."

Chuckling, Esperanza says, "That's why sometimes I believe." Then teasingly she looks me in the eye and says, "What do you think, comadre, are they lies?"

TEN

Una vieja orgullosa – A Proud Woman

The loss of the daughter to the mother, the mother to the daughter, is the essential female tragedy.

—**Adrienne Rich, Of Woman Born: Motherhood as Experience and Institution**

October 3, 1989. I was outside my front door just before noon. The sun was intense and blinding, and I had to cover my eyes to look down the street to see if the children were getting out of preschool. There were no mothers assembled yet by the gate to the school. I was about to shut the door behind me, figuring I still had a few minutes before going to pick up Gabriel, when I heard a hushed voice call out, "Comadre!" I stepped down to the curb again, and there was Esperanza walking toward me with great determination. She stopped before me and lowering her voice to a whisper said, "Guess what? My mama has thrown me out of the house! Tonight I'll tell you the whole story," she said, looking around nervously. We both knew there was not much time to stand around chatting. The mothers were starting to wander down toward the school. "I'm going to the milpa," she said, suddenly changing the tone of her voice to defuse any hint that she had just confided something important to me.

A few days before, Esperanza had told me that her half-brother Manolo was beginning to insinuate that she had overstepped the boundaries of the plot of land her mother had given her on which to build her two rooms and kitchen. Manolo, who was the best off of Esperanza's siblings and who "presumed to be so decent," was posing the most problems. Yet her other half-brother in Monterrey and half-sister in San Luis had also long been annoyed with Esperanza because their mother had given her some land on which to build her house within the maternal fold; however, they had done little more than give her angry looks on the few occasions when they came. Esperanza's sister, Hipólita, with whom she had worked in domestic service as a teenager, had just retired after years of working as a maid in San Luis; finding herself alone and unmarried, she had decided to come back to Mexquitic to live with her mother. Her younger brother, for his part, spent most of his time getting drunk. The latest phase of Esperanza's conflicts were now revolving around her arguments with Manolo about whether she had encroached upon land that her mother had not given her, and arguments with her sister Hipólita about whether Esperanza was bringing up her children properly. And, worst of all from Esperanza's perspective, the embers of her mother's anger about Simeón's disrespectful behavior toward her the year before had not yet cooled. Her mother ultimately blamed Esperanza herself; after all, it was she who had brought such a terrible son into the world!

That night Esperanza sat down at the kitchen table as though she had a mission. "They tell me that even my mama said I was a bruja." She was hurt and offended, even a little worried, I think, though she would never have admitted it.

 "Look, last night, I got back from San Luis at about half past seven."

"Almost eight," says Mario.

"Yes, at eight, and you kids were getting dinner ready. We ate at about half past eight, thanks to God who never fails to look after me. A woman in San Luis had said to me, 'Here, have this, marchanta. It's still good. If you don't want it, you can give it to your pig.' I had brought back that food, and I said to the girl, 'Here, *ándale*. Boil this.' So the food started to boil, and we went inside to eat. And then I thought of my mama. She goes to sleep early, but I said, '*Andale*, Norberta. I want you to take this taco to my mama.' I sent over a plate of broth with noodles and meat that the señora had given me.

"At the door Norberta called out, 'Abuela, Abuela, my mama sends you this taco.' They were inside, my mama and my sister Hipólita.

"And my mama says, 'I'm in bed. Just leave it on the table. The lights are out, so you'll have to find your way in the dark.'

"The girl left the food on the table and came back. When she re-turned I asked, 'What are they doing? Are they asleep?'

"'No, they're awake. They're in the room.'

"'What did they say to you?'

"'They told me to leave it there on the table. I left it there on the table in the dark.'

"So we ate and went to bed. The next day I woke up late, at half past eight. I got up and lit the fire. Another señora had given me some *chicharrones*. I cut them up and put them on to boil. They heated up quickly because they had a lot of lard in them. While I was doing that, I found a plate and served some cream and put out two tortillas and placed some pieces of meat on them and took the plate to my mama. It was almost ten when I took that food over to her.

"'What are you doing?' I said to them. My sister looked at me with a strange face. My mama just barely answered me.

"'Here, I've brought you a taco, let's see if you'll eat it. Are you still taking medicine?'

"'Yes, I'm still taking medicine.'

"I said, 'Well, I hope it won't make you ill. Those chicharrones have a lot of lard. A señora gave them to me.' My sister kept watching me.

"'I'm going now. I'm going to go eat.'

"'Ah,' my Mama says. 'Ah.'

"So I went home. We didn't sit down to eat right away because the girl was still preparing the tortillas. In the meantime, I saw my sister step out of my mama's house as though she were going to wash the dishes. And then the girl calls out, 'Come eat now.' The tortillas were warm. 'Come, *ándale*. Let's eat.'

"So we're about to sit down to eat. 'Come on, *ándale*.' I reached for a tortilla and poured some salt on it. At that moment, my mama comes to the door of the kitchen. I look up and there she is. I didn't see her come in. She had my plate in her hand.

"'Here's your plate.'

"'Yes, that's fine. I'm going to eat now.' I started eating the tortilla.

"*Ándale*, she went to the door and all she said from the courtyard was, 'Listen, Esperanza. I heard something in the street about your family.'

"Ay, in that moment I felt something stabbing me. She got me with the tortilla in my mouth, and I suddenly felt so sick.

"'Do you know that your family—I heard a story that your family

is going around speaking ill of my family. Around there, they told me,'
she says.

"'Who told you?'

"'No, someone told me. I hate to have to say it, but I have to say it.
I'd like you to vacate the house. I want the land back. I don't want
the house, I don't want the fruit trees, I don't want the nopales, I don't
want the plants. I want you to clear out, leave the land.'

"'But why, Mama?'

"'Because your family is going around speaking ill of my family. And
you're going around harming me.'

"'Who's harming you, Mama?' I said.

"She says, 'You're an arrogant vieja because you have a house, because you have a field. But you don't know how to handle your family.
I lent you the land for you to build your house. I didn't give it to you.
That's why I want you to vacate the land, to leave. I lent you the land
while your children were growing up. But your children are now grown
up. So now you can look for another place to live. You've got your field
there; that's where you should build your house.'

"Then I said to her, 'No, Mama, please tell me, who's speaking badly
about your family?'

"And she says, 'No, no, no. I can't tell you.'

"'What do you mean you can't?' I said to her. 'Who could it be?'

"'No, I was told that you're trying to harm me. That you want to
finish off my children. That you want to finish off my family. If they
die, who's going to support me? Who's going to look after me?'

"I said to her, 'But who's harming you, Mama? I don't know that
anyone is harming you.'

"She says, 'No, I found out by accident yesterday when I went for
tortillas. They've opened my eyes. And I want you to leave.'

"'But Mama,' I said to her, 'what's the reason?'

"'Look, I went for tortillas yesterday, and on the way back I met a
man who said to me, "Listen, señora. Wait, señora." I didn't want to
turn around to see him. Then he said, "Listen, señora, are you sick?"
And I said, "Me? Yes, I'm sick." And that man said to me, "Look, señora, I'm going to tell you something. Get smart, be alert. You have a
daughter, don't you? You have a daughter and she's very arrogant. You
gave your daughter a house." The man guessed at everything. "You
gave her a house and she's got a good field. She's very arrogant because

she's got things to lay her hands on. But don't trust your daughter, señora. Your daughter is harming your family. She wants to finish off
your family and you.'"'

"'No, Mama. Tell me who that person was. If it's that Simeón or
that Macario speaking badly of me, I'll slap them in the face. But why
would they do that?'

"'No, no, no. How can I tell you who it was? It was a man on the
street.'

"'Ay, Mama. There are no men who live in the street. Whoever it is
has a house somewhere. It can't just be a man from the street unless
it's one of those men who live in San Luis, those poor drunks who go
stumbling around on the streets, people who have no place to live. Ay,
Mama, it's got to be someone who's got a house somewhere.'

"'No, I don't even know the person. God knowş where he's from.
And he said all that to me.'"

As Esperanza pauses to take a sip of her soda, Norberta adds, "First
she said he was from the street. Then she said he was from a rancho."

"Yes, I know. I don't remember it all very well, what with my coraje.
It made me sad to hear her say that to me.

"'Well, I don't want any arguments,' Mama says. 'I want you to leave.
Look at how late it was last night when you brought me that food.'

"I said, 'Look, that's when I got home. We were just sitting down to
eat at eight. You know I get back late. But I always think of you, even
if I'm not with you during the day.'

"Then she says, 'Oh, what a coincidence. How do I know if you
haven't put the evil in that food?'

"I said, 'Listen to me. Listen, Mama. Are you saying I'm a bruja?'

"'Well, maybe so.'

"'No, Mama. Not that.'

"Then she says, 'So, I don't want you here. Leave me in peace. I don't
want arguments anymore, I don't want to be getting angry on account
of your family.'

"I said, 'Look, Mama, I'm going to tell you something. You should
have thought of this before. When you gave me the plot of land, I
wasn't asking you for it. You remember how when you came to give it
to me I was doing a levantada for the niño Dios. I was busy, and it was
Simeón who went with you and received the land for me. Mama, you
should have thrown me out then.'

" 'Ah, so you're in charge of everything because of what I've given you? You could have said, "No, I don't want it. I'm going off on my own." I wasn't forcing you to stay. Look, I'm telling you, that man opened my eyes.'

"I said, 'Look, Mama. And what about the papers I have? Aren't those any good anymore?'

" 'They're good for you. I lent you the land, I didn't give it to you. And here in my house, I don't want you bringing a notary or a lawyer or a juez or a presidente, nor any other person. You're leaving because I say you are. I'm the owner of my house. I don't want anyone coming to inspect things here. I'm the one who matters, because this is my house.' " Esperanza knocks on the kitchen table with her fist for emphasis. " 'Ah, and you're always getting together with that *vieja prieta*, that dark-skinned woman. You're in league with her.'

" 'Well, Mama, Chencha is the only *morena* I know. I'm not with her every day. Is that the morena you mean? Is it Chencha?'

" 'Yes,' she says. 'And that person who talked to me said not to trust you because you're in league with that morena.'

"Then I said, 'Ah, so it's Chencha. But you know her—she's the one who cured you.' And I said to her, 'Ay, Mama. Aren't you grateful to her, Mama? She's the señora who cured you.'

"And my mama says, 'Ah, because you wanted her to. Yes, she cured me, but I paid her for it.'

" 'Well, all right. So are you saying that now I'm doing you harm?'

" 'Well, maybe so. How do I know?'

"Imagine, she said all of that to me, that I'm a bruja, that I want to take over. And she went on, 'Your children aren't grateful. They came here with shit in their pants, and I gave them a house to live in. Look at how they've paid me for it—by trying to harm me!' And with that my mama started to cry.

"Look, it's clear, comadre. It all began in 1965, when I went back to my mama's house. That's what the law required, so the authorities sent me back to my mama. At first my family was angry with me when I got married. But afterward, with your pardon, comadre, when they saw me looking like a wet rat, their conscience was stirred up to see me so low down. That was when I got the land. My mama supported me and my sons for two years. And then after that I moved ahead on my own, and she didn't have to support me anymore.

"I was responsible for my mama until this past April when my sister Hipólita came back. Now it's her responsibility to look after my mama. My mama is older now and so she gets sick more easily. Now that my sister got the boot, she's with her. You see, my sister thought she was more in charge of things at the house where she worked than the señora of the house. She always said that she was the one who took care of the woman's husband. She sewed his clothes, replaced his lost buttons, washed for him, ironed for him. She did everything for the man. My sister even said to me once that the only thing left for her to do was to sleep with him!"

Grateful for a little comic relief, we all laugh. I take advantage of the pause to ask, "Weren't you moved when you saw your mama start to cry? Or did you just feel coraje?"

"Oh, no, I just felt coraje. We didn't even finish eating. She caught us with the food in our mouths, as I've told you, comadre. I fell ill. Ill that Sunday, what with the coraje I felt. Ill until the following Saturday when I went to get some medicine. And then on Sunday, I went to see Aurelia, who's a notary public.

" 'Do you have papers?' she says.

" 'Yes.'

" 'Did she sign them?'

" 'Yes, but she doesn't know how to sign her name. The two of us just made our thumb marks. The paper says she sold the land to me.'

" 'Then she can't do anything to you. She can't throw you out.'

"When I got home, a cousin from La Campana came to visit. I'm talking to my cousin, telling her the story, when my brother Manolo calls out, 'Esperanza! Esperanza! Let me see your papers.'

"I said, 'Ah, yes. Let me get them.'

"He just stood there, looking, looking, looking, looking, looking. He was there for a long time, a whole day it seemed, just to read a few letters. The sun was burning me. He's at it and at it, and my mama behind him. In one hand Manolo had my mama's papers and in the other hand my papers. We stood there for maybe fifteen minutes until he finally says, 'Ah, here's the problem. *¡Ay, Chihuahua!* Look, Esperanza, according to what it says in these papers, we have to take new measurements. But let me tell you something else. I want you to control your family, because they're affecting my family.'

" 'What? How?' I asked.

" 'Control your family, that's all I'm telling you. You're here as a neighbor. My mama gave the land to you, sold it to you, and now you're here as a neighbor. For my part, you can talk to me or not talk to me. But I'm asking you to control your family. Control these kids here, because I don't want them saying things to my family. Reprimand them.'

" 'But how do you want me to reprimand them? My kids have never said anything.'

" 'Look, I'm telling you.'

" 'If it's because of this girl, Gabriela, it's Hipólita who's upset with her.' You see, comadre, Hipólita says she can't bear the sight of the girl, even in a photograph."

The root of that animosity, my comadre explains, goes back to an incident that happened a year before, when Gabriela was working as a servant in San Luis and Hipólita saw her talking to a young man. Hipólita gave Gabriela a good scolding, but Gabriela, who's known to have a temper, answered back, saying she was not going to end up an embittered old maid like her.

"When I laugh, I really laugh. My sister tells me I laugh like a crazy woman. And Gabriela laughs just like me. The other day, when I went to give my mama a taco, Hipólita says to me, 'Listen, Esperanza, I'm going to tell you something. I don't care about your family, but I want you to tell that girl Gabriela not to go around laughing like that.'

"So, I'm telling you. What do you think, comadre?"

"I don't know, but I don't think they can throw you out if you have those papers," I reply, in as reassuring a tone as I can manage.

"But she wants us to leave."

"That's the worst part, that it's your mama."

"Now my mama has gotten turned around. I might have expected it from my brothers and sisters, but now it's even my mama. It's a pity I didn't go to school so I could read better. If I knew a little more, I could get myself out of this."

› › ›

How would this all end? I had no idea. Esperanza seemed to have told me the story not just to tell it to me, but in the hope that I, as an educated woman with some connections in the world, would have some advice, some notion of what to do. But I was at a loss. Esperanza, I sensed, was a little let down by the timidity of my reaction. Even so, she cheerfully made plans with me to go to Chencha's centro the next day, which would be October 4, the saint day of Saint Francis, San Francisco. We'd meet at the entrance to town, where the bus stops, at ten. Then we'd find our way past the market, past the busy avenues, to the knotted streets that would take us to the spiritism session and birthday party in honor of General Francisco Villa. If anyone could help Esperanza, it was Chencha and, speaking through her, the General himself.

ELEVEN

¡Viva General Francisco Villa!

Metallic and far ranging. His shouts, loud, clear, sometimes one after the other and vibrating. You could hear his voice from a great distance. His lungs seemed made of steel. . . . "The Villistas were one single man. Villa's voice could unite them all. One shout from him was enough to mount his cavalry." That's what Severo said, with the echo of the General's voice still ringing in his ears.

—Nellie Campobello, **Cartucho**

Eraclio Zepeda played the part of Pancho Villa in Insurgent Mexico, *the film by Paul Leduc, and he played it so well that ever since, some people think Eraclio Zepeda is the name Pancho Villa uses when he works in the movies.*

They were in the middle of making this film, in some little village, and the people were participating in everything in the most natural way without the director having to say a word. Pancho Villa had been dead for half a century, but it surprised no one that he should appear around there. One night after an intensive day's work, some women gathered before the house where Eraclio was sleeping and asked him to intercede on behalf of some locals in prison. The next morning, bright and early, he went to talk to the mayor.

"General Villa had to come for justice to be done," the people commented.

—Eduardo Galeano, **The Book of Embraces**

October 4, 1989. Saint day of San Francisco.

I put film in my camera and a cassette in my tape recorder and say goodbye to David.
The river is filled with rushing water and scrubbed clothes are

pinned all over the available nopal cactuses to dry. The dam is open, and several women are taking advantage of the flowing river to do their washing. I wave as I pass, imagining what the wagging tongues will say: Where is the gringa going alone so early in the morning with her camera bag? Didn't she leave her child at school? Shameless, isn't she? Leaving the poor señor gringo to do everything.

I climb up the steep path to the edge of the highway, hoping I won't run into any barking dogs at Don Albino's house. No, there are no dogs, *qué bueno*. I know the local technique for fending off a dog is to pick up a stone and throw it near the dog's feet, or just pretend to throw it, but somehow I am never fast enough. I walk along the edge of the highway, staying as close as I can to the edge, feeling the air being whacked by the cars and trucks racing past me.

At ten I am at the entrance to town. I find Esperanza squatting next to her bucket. Norberta is a few feet away. Then I see Gabriela coming toward us from a path behind the houses. "I told her to come after me," Esperanza explains. "I don't want people to see us all going together."

In San Luis we walk single file along the narrow streets leading to the market. As usual, Esperanza has me walk on the inside of the curb. She walks on the outside, occasionally stepping into the street to be next to me. "In Mexquitic they envy me, you know," Esperanza says as we follow behind Norberta and Gabriela. Then, loud enough for them to hear, she adds, "They envy me, because these two girls are already grown-up and they haven't *fracasado*. They haven't brought their babies to me yet."

It's true, I realize as Esperanza speaks, most girls of their social position and age are no longer virgins. The unavailability of her daughters increases their value but contradicts their lower-class status. That her daughters can resist the inevitable advances of men shows that they're tough; they're not going to give themselves away too cheaply. Having heard Esperanza's remarks the night before about how her mother and siblings think she's a *vieja orgullosa*, a proud woman, I can see how this pride in her daughters would be interpreted locally as yet more evidence of Esperanza's hubris. So, does she think her daughters are better than other girls of their class? Well, wait, they, too, will succumb; they, too, will fall.

We stop at the block near the market where one store after another sells nothing but candies and sweets. I buy several kilos of candies, and

Esperanza buys two packages of sugar wafers. She offers to carry my load of candy for me in her bucket. I politely try to refuse, but I soon give in without too much resistance. The camera bag is getting heavy, and the extra layer of clothing I put on for a cool Mexquitic morning is also weighing me down.

Around eleven, we find our way around the back streets of the city that lead to Chencha's centro. It is located in an obscure alleyway bordered on both sides with metal doors. In front of some of the doors there are the usual carts parked outside, from which, after dusk, the evening flow of people will buy things like hot, steaming corn. At the end of the alleyway is the iron door, white and glaring in the sun, with Chencha's name and hours of service painted on it in black letters. Unless you know, there is no way of telling that this is the "office" of a healer and spirit medium.

› › ›

As we approach Chencha's door, I feel a mixture of anxiety and excitement. On the first of October, at her monthly spiritism session, Chencha had surprised me by saying she was now going to give me "a green light"—that is, her permission to allow me to record and photograph whatever I liked of her centro. She had even said she would teach me how to cure. Chencha, like Esperanza, had been difficult to get to know; she, too, is assertive, no-nonsense, and exaggeratedly afraid of nothing. But after years of perseverance, I had won her acceptance, which was crucial to me since she and her spiritist centro had played such a key role in Esperanza's life. And like Esperanza, once Chencha decided to accept you, she accepted you wholeheartedly.

Just as it took years to win Chencha's acceptance, it took years for me to suspend my own unease at Chencha's "otherness." In all those years, I had been trying to decide what I thought of Chencha. I couldn't figure out whether she was a man cross-dressing as a woman or, indeed, as Esperanza and everyone else who knew her seemed to think, just a very "manly woman," *una mujer hombrona* or *macha*. No one described her as a lesbian, a transvestite, or a gay person, categories which seemed nonexistent among the participants of the cult. Since there seemed to be no doubt in anyone else's mind that she was, indeed, a woman, I finally gave up as irrelevant and simpleminded my desire to know whether she was "really" a female in biological terms. Esperanza told me that Chencha was married twice and that she had once seen her pregnant, though Chencha lost all her pregnancies because of having to take on so many "male" qualities to fight evil. Whatever Chencha's "true" gender identity, she clearly preferred the female world: she had adopted a little girl and lived in a house with several women servants and assistants.

Over the years, I had felt uncomfortable not only about Chencha's gender ambiguity but about the "work" she does. Her fees seemed to me to be exorbitant, though I knew such inflated prices were not uncommon for unwitchers and healers of her proven strength. Esperanza always said, "She charges a lot, but she's pure fire! She guarantees her work." The excessively high amounts Chencha charges, Esperanza seemed to think, had to do with the dangerous work Chencha does countering evil. Some healers die in the process of curing, Esperanza pointed out to me, such is the fierceness of the battle they must wage to free their clients from the evil spells of their enemies. After many years of skepticism, I have come to agree with Esperanza that her services are probably worth the price to her clients.

On my first meeting with Chencha in 1987, as I waited to speak with her, I sat on a torn-up couch in her dilapidated waiting room, watching as her secretary communicated with her in the next room through an intercom. The set-up was a cross between a doctor's and a car mechanic's waiting room. Signs on the wall read "All Work Guaranteed" and "Payment Required before Consultation."

When Chencha called me in and I found myself face to face with her, I discovered that she frightened me more than anyone I had ever met before. She was, indeed, hombrona, a manly woman, as Esperanza had described her, and that was partly what intimidated me. I kept thinking that at any moment this supposed woman, who clearly shaved her face, would pull off her dress and reveal a man's anatomy and maybe even attack me. Much as I tried to protect myself with my anthropological shield, asking questions, trying to elicit information about her life and work, Chencha kept asserting her greater power by answering me briskly, quickly, impatiently. All I managed to learn was that she came from Veracruz but that her family now lived in Mexico City, and that she had inherited her powers to cure from her grandmother, not from her mother, who had refused them. After five minutes I could barely stand to be in the tiny altar room with her, the candles at my

back red hot, lighting up images of Buddha, Pancho Villa, Niño Tomasito, and Christ. Could I photograph the altar, I asked her, as a last re-
sort. No, Chencha said, the altar could not be photographed, and I was
not the first to ask, either. Tired at having to do battle with her, I decided I should leave. My eyes darted to the door. The room, I noticed
with horror, was locked with a latch. Were those all the questions I
had, Chencha wanted to know. Yes, I told her, hoping she'd release me
fast. When I finally emerged into the courtyard again, I found it hard to
believe how scared I had been; my heart was racing and my hands were
moist with cold sweat. I breathed a sigh of relief at seeing David arrive
with toddling Gabriel. I was safe.

› › ›

As I enter Chencha's "office" with Esperanza, Norberta, and Gabriela, we find that the courtyard has already begun to fill up with
people. The table outside Chencha's altar room is filled with images of
Pancho Villa, including one of him on his horse, which I recognize as
the image that hangs in the center of Chencha's altar, an image that
will later be passed around for all to kiss. There are two images of
Amalia Díaz de Bonilla, who according to Esperanza was one of Pancho
Villa's wives, "because he had many of them." There are vases filled
with flowers all around the images and on the floor around the table.

Flowers and religious images always go together in Mexico, but here
in Chencha's centro they serve the additional purpose of lightening the
smells wafting up, now and then, from the exposed sewer pipe running
right in front of Chencha's altar room. Bottles of tequila and Faro ciga-
rettes—the cheap brands, because the General despised anything too
refined—are also scattered around the images and on the floor. People
keep arriving. A man and a woman, accompanied by their young son,
come in bearing a huge fancy cake and set it on the table; the sugar
letters, in perfect script, read *Felicidades Pancho Villa.*

Chencha shows up just before noon. Quickly she slips her white
robes over her floral polyester dress. The session has to start right
at noon.

Right at noon everyone begins singing *las mañanitas,* the traditional
Mexican birthday song, while one of Chencha's assistants rings the
bell above the doorway to Chencha's altar room. Coals of incense are
set out on the floor in a pot, and people take turns stepping over the

smoke in two long-legged movements, forming a cross. Then, with their hands, people brush themselves clean. On a chair a basin has been set out with water and floating flower petals, for everyone to rinse their hands.

After we all sit down again, Chencha almost immediately goes into a trance. Greeting us in a high-pitched voice, Amalia Díaz de Bonilla comes down first to let us know that our brother Francisco Villa is looking forward to his birthday party. Then Chencha starts trembling in her seat, and Amalia Díaz de Bonilla, one of Villa's many women, returns quietly to the spirit world.

› › ›

Heaving and roaring and croaking, Chencha, her eyes closed in trance, announces in a deep voice, "General Francisco Villa!" In the open courtyard with its roofing of sheet metal, a group of people composed primarily of women but also including a few men and children, break out singing the national anthem, followed by las mañanitas again, to welcome the spirit of Pancho Villa, who has come to preside over his birthday party. As the last words of the song are uttered, Chencha's assistant gets a cheer going: "*A la bim bom ba, Panchito, Panchito, Panchito, ra, ra, ra.*"

"At attention! In the name of God. With Christ's power. You know what you have to do," Pancho Villa announces gruffly.

Everyone starts marching in place.

"Together, now. Concentrating, now. Remember how you must work. That's too soft—I can't hear it!"

Everyone marches with more energy.

"There's a lot of force here."

We keep marching.

"Whose soldiers are you?"

Still marching, everyone responds in a loud chorus, "General Francisco Villa's."

"Whose?"

"General Francisco Villa's!"

The marching continues, louder than before.

"Who will take roll call?"

From different parts of the room, the participants yell out, one by one, their family names; each name is acknowledged by the General with the word *presente*, "present." This call and response, an odd rosary, continues for several minutes.

"I think I know my pueblo. I know who my soldiers are, and who are not my soldiers. The brother or sister who feels that he or she is Francisco Villa's soldier should stand up now. Now! Stand up!"

All of us rush to our feet.

A woman says, "We're all standing."

The General asks for testimonies from those people whose cures have been completed.

"How do you feel?" Villa asks.

"Much much better," replies a city woman.

"Much better or totally better?"

"Totally better. That's why it's a pleasure for me to come."

"Well, talk, tell. Tell the pueblo."

"I was very sick and now I'm feeling just fine. I've pulled through, thanks to God and the medium. And that's why it's a pleasure for me to come here again, and as many times as I can, to say what good they've done for me here. May it go on for many years."

"*Estás entregada*, you've been received. Go forward. You and your family. You won't die of hunger, neither you nor the little ones nor the old ones, because it is not my wish. Go and tell the person who harmed you, and say thank you. Because he doesn't know how to do things. You can go now. Be received. In the name of the Father, the Son, amen. Here you have your centro, for you and your family. I have spoken. This is my wish. My name is Francisco Villa. I receive you at this moment. And I give thanks to God, all powerful Father."

Others come forward with testimonies, and they, too, are entregados. A young city man speaks of a sudden paralysis that overtook him, making him unable to work. Since joining the centro, he's recovered again and wishes to thank the medium and Francisco Villa for restoring his health. After he finishes talking, people go up and hug him and say, "Felicidades for having been received."

There is a mix of people in the centro. The main assistant, a light-skinned woman, is clearly a city woman; she's well-dressed and works in an office. Both she and her daughter wear neatly pressed skirts and blouses. She and Chencha are comadres and address each other as such. There are also people from the ranchos, like Esperanza, like Eugenia (also from Mexquitic), who is startled to see me there, a man who sits in the back, with his cowboy hat and woven wool satchel, and a pair of women accompanying a young man in a wheelchair. After the testimonies are over, they tell their problems: the assistant is worried about losing her house to envious siblings; the man with the hat and wool satchel wants to know if his lost bull is still alive; Eugenia is concerned about an illness in her husband's family. Each is preoccupied with her or his own problems, yet some camaraderie in the quest for cures is established within this mix of people by the practice of having problems and testimonies uttered aloud for all to hear.

During a brief hiatus, Esperanza rushes into the altar room, offering two packages of chocolate wafers to the General, who asks her, in turn, to open one of the packages. The General pulls out a wafer and says to Esperanza, "How many spins do you want me to give this person?"

Esperanza, for once, finds herself at a loss for words. Then the General suggests she ask the question to everyone present. "How many times should a certain person be spun around?" she asks at the door of the altar room. A woman yells out, "Fifty." Another woman says, "A hundred." The General tops them both, "Three hundred and fifty! *Orale*. One, two, three, four."

People start counting.

"Faster!" Pancho Villa demands.

Everyone keeps counting. Wafer in hand, Villa turns it round and round in his hand with furious energy.

"That's too slow!"

The counting moves more quickly.

"Three hundred."

"That's too slow!"

The counting continues, frantic. "Three hundred and one, three hundred and two, three hundred and three . . . "

When it ends, Villa hands the wafer back to Esperanza and says, "Put it at the entrance of your house. *Andale*. With that your problem has been solved."

›››

The heavy scent of the flowers that has been disguising the thick odor from the exposed sewage pipe now begins to compete with the rich smell of mole, the dish of many chiles, spices, and chocolate by which celebration and festivity are defined in this part of Mexico. From the kitchen, women come one at a time bearing huge clay serving bowls of meat in mole sauce, plates of rice, kilos and kilos of tortillas, and crates of soda bottles. The large three-tiered birthday cake inscribed with the words *Felicidades Pancho Villa* has been perched on a stool next to the outside altar since the start of the session, and the man who brought this edifice of sugar now carries it into the room where Villa sits. Esperanza brings the rest of the wafers in, and I, the candies. Each item of food and drink is blessed in turn by Chencha in the role of Pancho Villa.

"In the name of God Almighty. If this work was done with black hands, may the evil one not plague you. I, General Francisco Villa, bless this chile. In the name of the Father, the Son. I bless the hands that made it. May you not become ill from this mole, because that is not my wish. Amen."

Plates heaped full of mole, tortillas to eat it with, and a bottle of soda are passed out to everyone in the courtyard. We all balance our plates, tortillas, and sodas as best we can on our laps. As we indulge in the feast, Pancho Villa yells out, "Who has died of hunger during this past month?"

"No one!" people respond.

"You will not die of hunger, for it is not my wish!"

I turn to the food on my plate, too. I have been taping and photographing and using all my powers of concentration to inscribe everything in my memory because I know I'll need to write about this later. I tune out and start eating. The mole is excellent, and I savor the chiles on my tongue. I'm not too sure about the meat, which seems to be mostly bone and gristle. I could try slipping it into a tortilla, as people do so gracefully, and nibble on it a bit, but I'd probably make even more of a mess of myself. You can always tell when people have been to a party; there's mole in the cracks of their mouths, mole under their fingernails, mole in orange-red spots and streaks on their clothes.

"Comadre," Esperanza says to me suddenly. "You're being called."

"What?" I ask. Then I hear Chencha/Villa calling out from the altar room, "Where is the one who wants to learn how to cure?" I realize she is referring to me. I hadn't expected to be included in the events to this extent, especially now that I'm running out of steam. I put down my plate of mole with some regret and go to the altar room.

"Do you want to learn how to cure?" Chencha/Villa asks me.

"Yes, I'd like to," I say, though it's not exactly what I feel. I was hoping to learn, in a less direct way, about the centro, who goes there and why, what the different spirits mean, and the reasons why Pancho Villa figures so centrally. But if this is what's called for, I'll give it a try; it won't be the first time an anthropologist has apprenticed herself to a medium.

"Go ask for three pesos there among the pueblo," Chencha/Villa says. "It has to be three pesos from three different change purses. Three pesos. They have to be pesos."

With the devaluations of the last few years, the one peso coin has become virtually obsolete. Heavy and grandiose one peso coins were still in circulation during our first stay in the early 1980s. The new coins now come in one hundred, five hundred, and one thousand peso denominations. So who's going to have a one peso coin, a coin that isn't even worth one thirtieth of a penny?

"I need three pesos, please," I say out loud to the assembled audience sitting in the courtyard. "Does anybody have a one peso coin?" I repeat, raising my voice hesitantly.

At the time, I only half understood how wickedly brilliant was Chencha's casting of me in this embarrassing role. There I was, a gringa, an icon of Americanness, and as such implicated in Mexico's debt and economic collapse, asking for the one peso coins that had been rendered worthless, in part, by the loan money that the United States had pumped into Mexico faster than it could pump out oil and other exports. Later I would learn of the *tres monedas de la Divina Providencia*, the three lowly coins that the devout Catholic offers to Divine Providence at the beginning of each month before reciting the prayer that one not lack *casa* (a place to live), *vestido* (clothing), and *sustento* (food). The idea of the three coins thus has roots in traditional religious practices, but I believe that Chencha drew on it to make a comment on my place in the scheme of things as a gringa.

After finishing their second and third helpings of mole, people begin to search their pockets and sift through their change purses. The man who brought the cake says, "No, I don't have a peso. Who has pesos anymore?" Someone else says, apologetically, "You don't see them anymore. I don't think you'll find one, doña."

And then, as though the scene has been rigged (has it?), three people in the room suddenly have one peso coins to give me. A very elderly woman, whose daughter had earlier cried in gratitude to Villa for saving her from death, is the last person to uncover, at the bottom of her change purse, a one peso coin.

I am delighted. I go back into Chencha's altar room and put the three pesos into her hand.

"Who said you wouldn't find three pesos?" Chencha/Villa demands to know in a loud, angry voice. Then she lowers her voice and whispers to me, "You're going to start from the bottom. Do you understand me? Charging very little. One peso will be for you, another for your family, and another for the pueblo." She places the three pesos in my hand and tells me always to keep them with me and not to lose them, otherwise I'll never learn to cure. I have those coins still.

More testimonies, more accounts of problems and sufferings come afterward, all of which Chencha, in the role of Villa, listens to intently, like a priest hearing confessions. Then all the little pictures of Pancho Villa that the assistant and other people have brought are taken inside the General's room to be blessed. These pictures are readily available in the market. They depict Pancho Villa's resistance as "the man who dared to invade the United States" and print prayers on the back praising Villa for having "triumphed over the powerful" and "made his enemies back down," while calling for his "spiritual protection to be spared from evil and find the necessary courage and sufficient valor to face the difficulties of life."

When the assistant emerges with the blessed pictures, she breaks out with, "Viva General Francisco Villa!" Everyone responds, "Qué viva! Qué viva! Qué viva!" Then, as if on cue, people begin singing the sad plaintive funeral song, "Adiós, adiós, mother of the sky, mother of the savior, adiós, my mother, adiós, adiós, adiós."

"General Francisco Villa, may God's peace stay with us. May she accompany you, my General," the assistant says.

"The mother of the Lord," responds Villa.

"Goodbye," a woman says. "May she be with you."

"May peace be with you, señor," a man says to the man at his side.

As though in mass—for this has been a kind of mass—we all turn to our neighbors and give each other "the peace," softly shaking hands.

Humming loudly, Chencha sends Pancho Villa back to the spirit world. Soon after, her gruff voice mellows and takes on the higher timbers and innocence of a child's voice as she summons the spirit of

Niño Tomasito, an angelito. So many women, like Esperanza, have children in the grave, that this could be anyone's angelito, returning, for a brief moment, to speak. Tomasito doesn't stay long. He asks for his candies and giggles when he receives them. People tease him and he giggles a little more. Then he says adiós, hurrying off to play again in the other world.

›››

After most of the participants leave, Chencha surprises me by getting another performance going. I'm already out of tape cassettes, out of film.

No longer Pancho Villa now, Chencha calls Esperanza's eldest daughter, Gabriela, into her altar room. When they come out, Gabriela is holding a rainbow-colored umbrella. She twirls the umbrella in one direction, then in another. Over and over she repeats the words, "Do you like my umbrella? Don't you like my umbrella?" We in the audience are instructed by Chencha to answer with a booming yes to her questions every time she asks them.

Then Chencha calls in Norberta. She gives her a cane and tells her to limp with it and say, "Don't you like my cane? Do you like my cane?" Norberta isn't limping energetically enough for Chencha, who snorts, "You're not doing your work," making the already embarrassed girl even more embarrassed. Chencha, it seems, has given each sister an object that metonymically represents key features of her identity as well as her point of least resistance—Gabriela, the vain and coquettish sister, gets a pretty umbrella; Norberta, the slow learner, the ill sister, gets a cane. Each has to act out the arousal of envy and desire for her claim on the world.

Soon Esperanza joins them; she is wearing the skirt part of Chencha's robe and walks around showing it off, like the *jarabe* dancers do, saying, "Don't you like my skirt?" People in the audience answer, "Yes. We like it." Or, "It's very nice." On the next round of question and answer, Chencha calls out in response, "What a presumptuous vieja you are!"

Then Eugenia, who is in an enviable position because her husband and sons have permanent work, gets into the act, Chencha having given her a Saint Martin image and some castanets. "Don't you like my Saint Martin? Don't you like my castanets?" she asks, walking

214

around the room. And people in the audience respond, "Yes, they're very nice." And, "Where did you buy them?"

The mother of the young man in the wheelchair goes around with a knife and scissors. "Don't you like my knife? Don't you like my scissors?" Later, when we are alone, the woman tells me that her son was shot at a party, but that he wouldn't have been paralyzed if it hadn't been for the evil that was worked on him. Before he became paralyzed, he had worked hard and supported the entire family. The knife and scissors speak metaphorically of how their lives have been torn to pieces. The young man himself, who Chencha says will walk again, is given a belt, and from his wheelchair he repeats, listlessly, "Do you like my belt? Do you like it?" All this hawking, all this evocation of envy, goes on simultaneously, in a cacophony of deliberately provocative display.

Just as the group performance starts to peter out, Esperanza, who has momentarily disappeared, emerges again from Chencha's altar room in her new costume. Around one of Esperanza's shoulders Chencha has draped a red kerchief, and on Esperanza's head she has placed a white cloth reminiscent of a rebozo. A metate, the traditional grinding stone, has been lying unused next to the outside altar throughout the party for Pancho Villa. Now Esperanza, following Chencha's script, kneels before it and starts pretending to grind corn. It is quite obvious to everyone present that Esperanza has been given the costume of her identity as a woman of an Indian and rural heritage. She has to keep grinding, saying "Do you like my grinding stone? Is my grinding stone nice?" As she asks her questions, all of us yell back in chorus, "Yes, yes." Then Chencha gives her a stick and tells her to beat the ground with one hand and to keep grinding with the other hand. Whenever she beats the ground with the stick Chencha tells Esperanza to say, "You dog, son of a bitch."

Esperanza gets so involved in her "work" that soon the sweat is pouring down her face. Whenever the grinding stone gets stuck, Chencha shakes her head and says, "They're working. It's evil."

Finally Chencha tells Esperanza to stop. Then she picks up a stick and starts beating the metate herself. "Stay in your place, metate!" she yells. Then she takes some black ribbon and ties the end of it to one of the feet of the metate. She keeps trying to circle the ribbon around the other three pegs, but the ribbon won't stay put. "Should I cripple him?" she asks Esperanza. Esperanza looks at her and just barely nods. Chencha speaks to the metate again. "Don't fight so much! I'm not doing it for money, I'm doing it for love!" She turns to us in the audience and says, "How he resists." After several efforts, she succeeds in tying up the feet of the metate. And then she turns it upsidedown.

After she's done, Chencha turns to me and asks, "So, what did you think?"

"It was tough," I say. "You really had to fight."

"Yes," she replies. "But he was no match for me."

› › ›

October 5, 1989. "My whole body aches," Esperanza says when she comes to visit me the next night. I'm not surprised. Her make-believe grinding had been furiously energetic. She seemed in those minutes to be reliving, at heightened poetic intensity, the years of real grinding she had done at her mother-in-law's house. We sit down at the kitchen table and, after the usual preliminaries of sodas and cookies, begin to talk about what transpired at Chencha's centro the day before. I hope between the two of us to work out an interpretation.

◎◎◎ "What did Chencha say? Didn't you ask her?" Esperanza says to me.

"Well, she said that the upper part of the grinding stone was your house, and that the lower part of it was someone's feet. That's what I understood."

"Yes, what I understood her to say, when you asked her, was that it was half body, half house. But what amazes me is that I didn't tell her anything! I went to greet her and say, 'Look, I brought you this. Today is our brother Pancho Villa's birthday, and I just brought you this.' And she says, 'Ah, put it over there, so it will get blessed.' I had brought her some *chayotitos*. 'Ay, I got a thorn!' she says, and then, 'Thank you.' I started to say to her, 'Ay, Chencha, listen, apart from this, I want to talk to you.' She says to me, 'I can't now.' They were putting out the incense already. 'When Pancho Villa comes down, *ándale*,' she says.

"And then when I went inside to her room, when she asked everyone to bring in the things they had brought for Pancho Villa's birthday so they could be blessed, and I brought my wafers and you, comadre, brought the candies, that was when I went inside and said, 'Brother Pancho Villa. Here are some wafers for you. That's all I have for you.'

"'Yes, yes, that's fine,' he said. 'But sister, you have a problem.'

"I said, 'Yes, you know it more than anyone.'

"Then he took the package of wafers in his hand and said, 'Take one out! Take one out of the package for me.' And I took one out, and he took it in his hand—and who knows what that was he did. Then he said, 'Here. Put this in your house. Put it in the doorway of your house.'"

"And did you really put the wafer in the doorway of your house?"

"Yes," Esperanza replies, laughing. "I put it there, and it was gone the next day. I hung it up between the aloe vera plants, at the doorway. And it was gone the next day. It had feet and walked away!"

Mario says, "Oh, she ate it."

"No, I didn't. It had feet and walked away! Maybe the dog ate it, or some rat." She laughs and goes on. "When it was all over yesterday, when Chencha was all done, she went back into the front room, and that was when she called me. She was giving out the cake. 'Here, *ándale*,' she said. 'Wait for me. I'm going to give you a little *chilito*.' She gave me lots of chile. Then, 'I'm going to give you some rice.' So she gave it to me, and then I said, 'Chencha, I think you're busy. So maybe you don't have time to sweep my girls, to give them a *barrida*. We'll come back another day.'

"And she says, 'Oh, no, no. This is a perfect time! This is the time to do it, just now.'

"I said to her, 'That's fine. It's just that you seem to be busy. And the thing is, I'm worried. I've come to tell you that I don't know what I'm going to do. It's my mama. Would you believe it? She threw me out of the house yesterday!'

"Then she says, 'Don't believe it. She won't do anything to you. Nothing.'

"'Now she's saying that I'm harming her and her family. She even called me a bruja.'

"And Chencha says, 'Listen, do you know how to work? *Andale*, get with it. I'll show you. You already have a reputation there in Mexquitic.'

"'For what? I wish it weren't for nothing.'

"'Look, if you like, I'll show you.'

"'No, no,' I said.

"That was all she said. And then she went inside and she started curing. She cured the girl, then had her come out with the umbrella. Then she spoke to my other girl and cured her. Then the señora went in. And then she called me in and said to me, 'I'm going to make you look even more attractive than the others.' And then what I had to do! She put those things on me and then said, '*Andale*, grind.' And now look at the shape I'm in."

"Your whole body aches, doesn't it, from all the grinding you did with the metate? You put so much energy into it."

"Well, it's that Chencha said, 'If you all work hard, that helps me. If you don't work hard, you don't help me.' And then, *hijole*, she had me do that. My back still hurts; it feels terrible. And I can barely move this hand." She shakes her hand as though it were a limp rag and looks mockingly at it. "Then Chencha says, 'Go in.' And I went in, and she says, 'And now you're going to put these things on and wear a different apron. This is to make them go crazy. To make all your enemies go insane.'

"Then Norberta went in. She had a bad headache, and Chencha sprinkled water from the crystal ball on her and prayed over her. She said to her, 'Come along.' And she took Norberta inside, and when she came out with that cane Chencha says, 'It's pure envy. You're all swimming in envy.'"

"And when you came out wearing that skirt—"

"That was to make our enemies go crazy. Didn't you hear her say, 'That's so they'll go crazy, like you see here.'"

"But wasn't it also to show the envy that people feel toward you, like when you kept saying, 'Do you like my skirt. Do you like my skirt?'"

"Yes, yes, *ándale*. Don't you see that Eugenia got Saint Martin?"

"Yes, Saint Martin and the castanets."

"Yes, that's because both her sons and husband work. And Saint Martin the knight was a rich man. When God our Lord appeared to him, he cut his cape in two with his sword to offer charity to God our Lord. So Eugenia got to do that, because her husband and sons are worth something, and people feel envy because of what they're worth."

"Has Chencha done this kind of curing before, or was this the first time?"

"I had never seen her do that before. She's more awake now, more studied. She knows more. She knew a lot to begin with, and then she started studying and studying and studying. She's still studying more.

"But compared to her, I think to myself, how many centros are there that have to work secretly? She doesn't hide from anyone. She even takes on the newspaper! She told me that when that other governor was in power, she helped him. She told me, 'I've done some work for him. That governor's crooked; he doesn't walk straight.' That's what she said to me. 'No, I don't hide from the government. I've got permission from the government.' That's why she put an ad in the newspaper. I've known so many centros that work secretly, on the outskirts, so no one will know about it. But not her. I've not seen anyone else say in the newspaper that there's a centro in such and such a place and this is the name of the señora or señor. And she does that. Some people find her through the newspaper, and others through people who know her. I think she knows even more now, because she guessed my problem without my saying anything to her."

›››

Later that night. Esperanza tells me of another accomplishment of Chencha's: her mother is no longer angry with her.

◎◎◎ "I took my mama a little pail of the small, red tunas, the prickly pears. She was just sitting there, and I said, 'Mama. Mama, what are you doing?'

"'I'm just sitting here.' She spoke to me in a soft voice.

"I said to her, 'Do you want some tunas? I brought you a few tunas. Don't you want them?' I went inside and got them. 'Look, we went and cut them this morning, and I remembered to bring you some. I didn't fill up the pail. My stomach isn't totally well yet.'

"'Ah, yes.'

"'I brought you these.'

"'Give me three, just three of them.'

"Then I said, 'Norberta, bring me the pail.' I said to her, 'Look, how few I have. I'm going to choose some good ones for you.' I filled up a little pail with them. They're still warm. Let's see if the yellow ones don't get you sick. I'm a little sick to my stomach and haven't felt like eating anything.'

"'Yes, that's too bad.'

"'But I'm going to try to eat some now. Here, give them a try.'

"'*Andale.*'

"She didn't speak badly to me anymore."

› › ›

October 15, 1989. When Esperanza returned to speak with me several days later, I learned that her father had died. She had said nothing to me about it until then. She told the story starting from the middle.

◎◎◎ "A cousin from La Campana said to me, 'He's already confessed; he's not dead yet. Go see him—maybe he'll leave you the house.'

"'No,' I said. 'If he had wanted to give us anything, he should have spoken to us when he was at his peak, not now that he's in his last throes. After the way he treated us. Anyway, he's got that daughter from the other woman.'

" 'I'm telling you to go see your papa.'

"He was very ill and had made his last confession. The daughter took him to the hospital, and he died there and was buried in El Saucito."

"And you didn't go to the funeral?" I ask.

"We didn't even know about it, nor did people from La Campana. I said, 'What happened to my papa? Did he die, or what?'

" 'She just took him away in a car and didn't return.' Now he's already in the ground. He died in June or July."

"How did your mother react?"

"No, my mama set off fireworks. She set off blessings. 'That son of this and that, let him be taken away, let him die!' Mama holds a lot of things against him."

"So she hasn't forgiven him?"

"Of course not. I don't remember what we were saying the other day. 'Well, Mama, you cursed him. You wanted him to die like a dog.'

" 'Now he's dead. After everything he did.'

"Mama had said that he ought to die like a dog, with no one to look after him. And she got her wish. There he was in his own filth, making everything on himself, and no one to look after him. Only that one daughter who would rush in for a minute to see him. In his filth, in his sty, just like a pig. Mama used to say, 'My only consolation is that when he dies, there will be no one to look after him and he'll die like a dog.' Mama got her wish. I said to her, 'You pay for everything in this life.'

"A comadre had gone and washed him, but the daughter came and took him away all naked, wrapped in nothing but a blanket. I said, 'It's happened. He died like a nobody.'

"I never denied he was my papa, but not my sister Hipólita—she hated him. 'I don't have a papa. I don't have anything,' my sister would say.

"That's how my papa came to his end. I'm orphaned now of a father. If I wanted to, I could ask Chencha to bring him down on the Day of the Dead. But I won't. Do you think you will go to Chencha's that day, comadre? Are you up to it? So you can see people cry. You're going to cry, too. Even Chencha cries. She's got her papa and her brother. She said she would bring them down. And everyone cries. You wait for

Chencha as Pancho Villa (1989)

them with a lit candle. And you go and kneel before them. Chencha cries, and all those who go to speak to the dead also cry.

"If it was my father, he'd say, 'Come, hija. I'm going to take you with me.' And then what if he took me?" She laughs nervously. "No, I won't do it. I have my angelitos. But mine were so small when they died. They couldn't speak yet. The oldest one was two years old. Those little things, what are they going to say?

"I could tell my papa that I'm sorry for not having gone to see him before he died; but no, I don't feel up to it. I'll just go and watch. I'll bring flowers for the altar. But I won't ask Chencha to bring back my papa."

PART THREE

Literary Wetback

Oscar Lewis, after being in India or Mexico, returns satisfied to his university. He has accomplished his work as an ethnographer. Ricardo Pozas doesn't return home satisfied after finishing his admirable biography of Juan Pérez Jolote. He will always feel the pain of the injustice with which we have treated the Chamulas. . . . The social sciences are a profession for erudite people, whose projects are doomed to never be put into practice. But even so, the ethnographer must accept her destiny, overcome her frustration, and go on researching. At the very least she can communicate her shame to others, for shame, as is well known, is a revolutionary sentiment.

—Fernando Benítez, Los indios de México

*But she had taken something with her
and later on, in the kitchen, she spread it
on the table. It was a road map so worn
that the creases and the torn edges had
been taped . . . She knew the distance,
in miles and kilometers, between gas stations and between places to spend the
night . . .*

—Harriet Doerr, **Stones for Ibarra**

*Esperanza peddling in the city of San
Luis Potosí (1988)*

Having made the drive to Mexico so many times, we have our own beliefs and practical knowledge, like Mexican migrant workers coming to this country, about how, when, and from where to make the border crossing to the Mexican side.¹ When David and I first crossed at Laredo as students in 1982, we were self-righteous and refused to tip the guards, so the contents of our car were examined from top to bottom. We're more mature now. We've also learned over the years that Sunday is a good day to cross because there aren't many guards around. It's easier not to have to explain why our car is loaded down with several cameras, a laptop computer, piles of books and papers, twelve gallons of Texan spring water (for Gabriel), and a roof rack holding sneakers, clothes, flashlights, and bars of Dove soap, all to give to friends in Mexquitic.

In spite of all we know, we're still uneasy. As we approach the border on a lazy Sunday afternoon in late summer of 1989, the two of us start to feel a wave of anxiety. There's something about being on the border that is unsettling. Something about having your belongings open for inspection. Something about having to declare who you are, what country you owe allegiance to. Something about having to pretend your identity is not already in question.

David has prepared a wad of dollar bills and holds them tightly in his hand as the guard motions us away from the Customs Office and asks him to open the trunk. I am sitting in the back seat with Gabriel and start to open the door, but the guard tells me I can stay in the car. This is something to be handled between the men. I sit with my fingers crossed and ask Gabriel to be very quiet. Why am I afraid? I feel as if anything can happen.

There is a hierarchy among the guards: the one in the red cap, an underling, calls over the other two. They all peer inside the trunk; the head guard tells the capped guards what to shuffle around and then asks a few questions about where we're going and what we're doing. "We're tourists," David tells them, pretending not to know Spanish. (David is tall, thin, and blond, so he's not supposed to know Spanish; even when he speaks it, people don't think he's speaking Spanish to them.) We've also learned through the years that it's best to reveal little about yourself at border crossings. David closes the trunk at their signal and hands the money to the guard giving the orders. Then the guard in the red cap bustles around to the front of the car to paste on the tourist sticker. "Ay, dame algo también," he says. David hands him a dollar, and we're off again, but now we're on the other side.[2]

If, from our perspective, the border begins in Laredo, from the perspective of people in Mexquitic, the border with the United States begins in the San Luis Potosí bus station. People's horizons face north. How could they not? Babies are fed Coca-Cola in their bottles, developing early a taste for the sweetness and power of el otro lado. There's hardly a family in Mexquitic that doesn't have some relatives in the United States. And there's hardly a man in Mexquitic who hasn't had an aventura doing back-breaking labor in the fields of Texas, California, and Iowa, only to return home with a story of how his manhood was diminished. "Allá, nos ven muy bajos, nos ven muy chiquitos" (Over there, they see us as very low, very small), a man from Mexquitic once said to us, bringing his hand down toward his knees.

All the people of Mexquitic, young and old, better-off and worse-off, negotiate constantly between the rural and the urban world, crossing the more mundane cultural and class borders between Mexquitic and San Luis Potosí almost daily. A bus runs back and forth from Mexquitic to the city every half hour. This easy connection to the city, which made it easy for border-crossers like us to find Mexquitic, has been a mixed blessing for the people of Mexquitic. It is in San Luis, which in the last few decades has become an expanding industrial city with a population of close to one million, that people get glimpses of the goods to be had—so few of which they can themselves hope to have—from el otro lado: the refrigerators, washing machines, televisions, tape recorders, the oval bars of pink Dove soap.

The most traditional form of livelihood in Mexquitic, described by Esperanza in her account and generally practiced by the poorest people, centers on the maguey, from which aguamiel is extracted to brew into pulque. A mildly alcoholic, yet nutritive drink, pulque is sold on Sundays in Mexquitic and on other days in the markets in San Luis. Although agricultural land in Mexquitic was won back from the hacendados after the Mexican Revolution, there are not enough government ejido fields for all. The smaller farmers grow white corn, pinto beans, and squash, but their modest harvest doesn't last for an entire year, so eventually they must buy their basic foods at the store; lo que más duele tener que comprar, what really hurts to have to buy, people say, is the ugly yellow corn that comes from el otro lado. The handful of better-off farmers, who often have access to private property, grow such cash crops as cauliflower, tomatoes, zucchini, and garlic; these are the big men of the town, whose pick-up trucks loaded with produce chug back and forth, every few days, from the fields of Mexquitic to San Luis.

Even those who work within agriculture tend to have other employment as well; men working as nightwatchmen, as masons, as mechanics, women running tienditas in the front rooms of their houses, where they sell Coke, beer, and bolillo rolls that are always a touch stale. Outside of agriculture, there is a large group of primary and secondary schoolteachers, many of whom are women from the better-off families who have battled for their education, often raising several children while teaching in posts distant from home. The many people who are landless must work for others in Mexquitic or for wages in the city; the men typically work at construction jobs, doing day labor as they find it, the women at cleaning houses, marketing, and selling gorditas grilled on charcoal stoves in the street.

And when times get rough, y el dinero no rinde, you work and work and your money just doesn't last, there's always el otro lado, beckoning dollars in every sip of Coke.

› › ›

Over the years, Esperanza and I often talked about the book I had promised to write based on our conversations. Inevitably these talks forced us to take stock of our different locations on the boundaries of power as a Mexicana and a gringa. We were continually aware that neither of us was exempt from the politics of our situations within the international division of labor created by neocolonial forms of capitalism. On the contrary, we felt caught in the shuffle, in the restless noisy movement back and forth across the borders of race, class, and nationality. As we talked to one another in the quiet of a kitchen with mint green walls, the truth of our interaction went beyond those walls and reached out into the fields worked by Mexican laborers in southern Texas, the California valley, and the Florida orange belt; reached out, too, into the maquiladora factories that have mushroomed in the last several years along the U.S.-Mexico border, using up the lives of so many young Mexican women.

Under these circumstances, our encounter could not simply be about the coproduction of knowledge and a final text called a life history.[3] It also had to be about the way transfers from our different border and class locations have been negotiated, for "the process of 'cultural translation' is inevitably enmeshed in conditions of power— professional, national, international."[4] These next few chapters take up these questions of the translation of power and the power of translation, as Esperanza and I have understood and acted upon them.

TWELVE

Literary Wetback

*Now there is another bridge to cross, one I have migrated far
away from home to find: the invisible bridge between the
marginal and the mainstream literary world. Like any frontera, this one requires the "right" credentials or the right
coyote to get me across. Without either one, all I am is a literary wetback, but that, too, has its own magic.*

—Alicia Gaspar de Alba, "Literary Wetback"

*July 23, 1988. Gabriel has gone to bed early tonight. David is at the
kitchen table with me and Esperanza, Norberta, and Mario. I have
asked Esperanza to repeat into the tape a sexual joke she told me
that my recorder didn't catch during our last conversation, and she
has broken out in wild laughter, with Norberta and Mario giggling
with her in between swigs of Coke. The joke is about an expression
used by market women that Esperanza heard soon after she became
a peddler. The market women say, "Revuelve la mercancía" (shake
up the merchandise), referring to the produce they sell, the zucchini,
string beans, peas; but the expression is also a coy invitation to
women to use their sexuality as a way for them and their children "to
move up in the world." As she tells the joke again, she teases David:
"Listen, compadre, do you allow me to talk about all this with my
comadre? Do you give her permission?" When David flusters, her
laughter becomes boisterous, and she turns to me and with a twinkle
in her eye she says, "Look, comadre, just shake up the merchandise.
There's no secret to it, comadre."*

"For my comadre this is very interesting," Esperanza suddenly exclaims. She wipes the laughter tears from her
eyes and gazes at me for a moment. "Does this seem very interesting
to you?"

"Yes," I answer.

"And you're going to write all this down and put it in a book?"

"Well, not all of it, some parts of it. Would you like to see how I'm writing it?"

"Let's see."

I turn to David and ask in English, "Can you bring what I have in the— It's in the study room. On my desk. The outline."

As we wait for David to return, Esperanza says, "Comadre, and this book you say you're writing, are you writing it over there, or are you writing it over here? And are you going to go around with all the women here in Mexquitic and talk? Because here they'll make fun of me."

"They wouldn't make fun. Why?"

"Yes they would. If you were to go around talking to them, and saying, 'Well, that woman who is my comadre, she said this, that, and the other.' Ay!"

"Well, no, I won't talk to them. If you don't want me to say anything to anyone, I won't say anything."

"No, nothing."

"Only over there, where it will be published, in English."

"Well that's up to all of you there. It's up to all of you, after all."

"Your story will be for the people on the other side, el otro lado."

Laughing, she replies, "El otro lado! The other side of what? The other side of river! Yes, the other side of the river, don't you see that there's a river there?"

"And what do you think of people on the other side reading your life story? Does that seem all right to you?"

"Well, I don't know. Over there I don't know them, and they don't know me. You will tell them so many things. And you think they'll like it? They won't, will they?"

"Why not?"

"I say that they won't. It's a life that isn't right— It's a life that's very, very— What do I want to say? Well, sad, very sad, yes—or very ridiculous!"

"No, comadre."

"I don't know. There's a saying, *ojos que no ven, corazón que no siente*, eyes that don't see, heart that doesn't feel." She pauses for a moment. "So are you going to give the book to people over there to read?"

"Well, first, when it's written, after it's published, we have to see if people over there want to read it. This is what I don't know. But I think they will."

"Ay, comadre, why are you using up your life on this?" She begins to laugh. Then she says, "Wracking your brain and struggling doing this? Well, if you think that this might be worth it for you over there, it's up to you, right? But I say that here, no. No. Here, no."

"Not here. And not in Mexico City, either, right? There, far away, in the city?"

"And then, what if they bring the books here? You know something, a señora who buys from me in San Luis showed me a book about a young man who ended up in prison. And he didn't come out until he was sixty, already a viejo as old as me, because I'm going to be sixty next year. And now the señora says that his historias are sold in San Luis. But they happened in Mexico City. That man tells his life story. And there are photographs of him, too, and he's very ugly. Very ugly! I said to the señora, 'And he wrote it himself?' And she says, 'Yes, he wrote it himself. It's about his life, what he's been through.' She showed me the book. The binding was falling apart. That's how thick it is. Is the book you're writing going to be something like that young man's book? Is that what you think it will be like?"

"Yes, but it will be in your words, based on what you've told me."

"Right, like that young man's book. The señora told me, 'It says everything here: what he did, how he spent his life. He wrote it all down. He wrote his historia.' I imagine it's going to be like that."

› › ›

That the life story of a former prison inmate could be turned into a book had evidently impressed Esperanza and also led her to wonder about the book I would produce about what she was telling me of her life. I realized that in this conversation we were negotiating both the terms by which I would be able to make use of her story and the terrain on which it could be made public: who should hear it, who should not, and where and why. Afraid of the ridicule she feels certain would ensue if people in Mexquitic knew she had indulged in a "confession"

233

with her gringa comadre, Esperanza has given me her story to smuggle across the border. Just as rural Mexican laborers export their bodies for labor on American soil, Esperanza has given me her story for export only. Her story, she realizes, is a kind of commodity that will have a value on the other side that it doesn't have at home—why else would I be "using up" my life to write about her life? She has chosen to be a literary wetback, and I am to act as her literary broker, the border-crosser who will take her story to the other side and make it be heard in translation. The question will be whether I can act as her literary broker without becoming the worst kind of coyote, getting her across, but only by exploiting her lack of power to make it to el otro lado any other way.

› › ›

Pointing to the stack of papers in my hand which David brought in, Esperanza asks, "And what's all that?"

I pull out an early version of my book proposal and go through the outline chapter by chapter, explaining that the book will start with an account of how we met, and then follow her story as she has told it to me, moving from the life her mama suffered to her experience of marriage and her relationships with her sons and daughters. Esperanza nods in approval as I retell her own story to her in condensed form; but when I tell her that I plan to discuss her idea that "you pay for everything in this life," she suddenly bursts out laughing. "Don't tell me they don't know that there!" she exclaims, making Norberta and Mario giggle. "They don't know that there," I say, trying to sound convincing. And she continues to be astounded, saying, "In this life, you pay for everything, and what isn't paid is charged to your account. . . . Even an angelito can't go directly to heaven, because at one, two, three, six months old, that child has already started to feel corajitos, little angers that they've felt when they've cried and gotten angry, right? They say that when angelitos die, they, too, have to dip a foot in hell. Even priests have to enter purgatory. So imagine one of us, already a sinner!"

She sighs and glances over at David, who is slumping down in his chair. "Compadre, are you tired?" David quickly straightens up, blinking the sleep out of his eyes; it's late and he's been up since dawn. "My compadre, you're tired! What fault is it of mine? My comadre here is asking me all these things." She glances back at me and in a scolding tone says, "What, don't you know anything about these things over there?" Not to irritate her, I nod, and Esperanza continues, "Of course, so that's how it is. For those who believe in God, right? Because I think there are people who don't believe in God. Not everyone believes."

Esperanza sighs again and sips politely from her Seven Up bottle. "Well, what do you think, comadre? Just lies I'm telling you, right?"

Unsure of how to respond, I answer with another question. "And what did you think of my outline, the plan I've got?"

"It's just fine."

"It is? What would you like to add to it? Do you want to add anything to those chapters? Is there something I'm leaving out?"

"No, it's going well."

Half-embarrassed, I ask a question that feels silly as I say it. "And what would you like people in the United States to think when they read your story?"

"They're not going to believe it."

"They're not going to believe it," I mimic.

And David, almost asleep in his seat, lethargically chimes, "I don't think so."

Esperanza breaks the nighttime stillness with a howl of laughter. "I don't think so!" she repeats. We all start laughing. "How is it possible? I say that they won't believe it."

› › ›

The view that her story will seem unbelievable to her potential American readers, and the intimation that she has been telling me lies, not the true story of her life in any sense, emphasizes the fictional or storied nature of the blended text we have been producing together over the years. There is no *true* version of a life, after all. There are only stories told about and around a life.

But beyond that, Esperanza doesn't seem to believe that absolution is really possible, that her clean comadre from clean America will truly be able to launder her story. Like the novelas about miracles that are so popular in working-class Mexico, and to which Esperanza is especially attached, there is an almost comic book miraculousness about the inducement that I, as redemptive ethnographer, have offered in promising to produce a book about the unfolding story of her life.

Do I believe her story? Will other gringos believe it, too? With my power and privilege as an academic woman who can write and publish a book, I can set things right—but will I? Is this all too good to be true?

To me, the sympathetic stranger, Esperanza could offer a different story about herself than she could townspeople in Mexquitic. Like any author, she has made a conscious decision about who should read her work, viewing me, and the gringos I will tell her story to, as a purer audience for her story. Yet this is a story that she firmly does not want townspeople to know. It is for export, intended for use far from its native land. Her narrative is not to be believed because it presents a private suffering and struggling self that clashes with the public self of the combative woman, the witch who doesn't know her place. Certainly no one would believe her version of her life story in Mexquitic. But will the gringos believe her? Or will they simply find her life ridiculously fictional? Across the border it's another world, another life. Maybe, over there, a rebirth is possible?

› › ›

Four days before my conversation with Esperanza, I made a small excursion with David and Gabriel to the Sanborns in the new shopping mall at the edge of the city near the massive fortressed homes of San Luis "high society." Just as in the banks, a guard stood firmly planted at the door. Sanborns, well-known to visitors of Mexico City, is a shiny bright luxury department store for tourists and local elites. There was a joke in the Mexican press after the storm produced by the publication of the Spanish edition of Oscar Lewis's *Children of Sánchez* about how Lewis was more dedicated than other American anthropologists because he would start off the day with a visit to the slums rather than stopping first at Sanborns for breakfast. I had gone in search of newspapers and magazines, of which Sanborns has an excellent collection, and with my corporate American Express card spent 90,000 pesos (about $45.00) on recently published books about Mexican history.

The next day, I went out peddling with Esperanza. She had been surprised by my request to go with her *de marchanta*. "Ay, comadre," she said to me the night before, "You're going to get tired. How are you going to go to all the places I go to?" At the time, I couldn't tell whether she was worried about what the women who buy from her would think (in other words, whether she thought I would be bad for her sales) or if the idea of her comadre, an educated woman from the United States, following her around her odyssey through the city simply seemed too absurd. Later I realized that she probably was truly concerned that I would get tired, and she probably suspected that I would slow her down—as, in fact, I did.

When I met her at the bus stop at the entrance to town, she seemed surprised that I had actually come. After waiting a few minutes we got on one of the old airless buses, its windows too rusted to open, that goes into the city every half hour. On the bus, Esperanza whispered to me that she saw her eldest son, Macario, that morning. He ignored her, and she ignored him. As we talked, the bus swelled up with people. It wobbled its way past the narrow curves sliced into the mountainside surrounding Mexquitic, burping out thick black clouds of diesel fumes. Once out of the curves, the bus driver sailed down the plateau lined with nopal and maguey cactuses on both sides. When we reached La Campana, several women got on carrying jugs of pulque to take to the market.

Esperanza told me she makes this trip to the city on Monday, Wednesday, and Friday, when she goes selling, and that on Thursdays she often goes in to clean houses. "You know, when someone is having a fiesta they invite me to come to clean up afterward." Her work as a marchanta is an extension of domestic service, I realized with belated insight. It is not just through the small amount of money she earns from selling that she makes her living, but through the charity of her clients, who give her used clothing and frequent gifts of leftover food and tortillas. Through her position as a marchanta, she secures the patronage of better-off women and thereby manages to survive in a deeply unequal society. There are women in Mexquitic who envy her. "*Me envidian,*" Esperanza says, because of her freedom to come and go, and her ability to do so well, so amazingly well, peddling on the margins, without being kept by a man or being locked into selling from a regular stall in the market. "They call me a beggar, a *limosnera*, a *mendiga*." But ever in control of such situations, she has a ready reply: "And what am I taking away from you? Am I taking away your husband?"

The bus makes its first stop in San Luis in an open plaza that people call *el mercadito*, which is just beyond the largest market of the city,

the Mercado República. As you walk past the plaza, you enter a maze
of stalls selling machine parts and hardware supplies. Then, just before
you hit the street, there is a niche with an image of the Virgin of Guadalupe framed with hundreds of milagros, tiny metal images of human
figures, body parts, houses, cows, and automobiles, any number of representations of sites where a miracle was, at some time, needed. Esperanza stops before the image and crosses herself. On her border crossings back and forth from the country to the city, there is a sense of
safety in passing under the caring eye of La Guadalupe.

At the market, we buy handfuls of produce: three lettuces, four cu-
cumbers, eight zucchinis, twenty carrots, and a bunch of chili peppers.
As she makes her purchases, Esperanza tells me that everything is so
expensive that she can no longer buy enough to fill up her buckets.
From her garden, Esperanza has brought more zucchini, garlic, chayotes, and peaches. She knows that the things from the rancho will sell
the best because they're just barely in season. "Afterward, when there's
a lot of something, they don't want it," Esperanza remarks. As we get
ready to go on our journey, she carefully balances a large plastic shopping bag on her head and a heavy pail in the crook of her arm. Even
though she's bought very few things, with the produce she had brought
from home she has quite a lot of weight to carry. "I'm starting to feel
tired," she says. "Before I used to walk through all of San Luis, carrying
my things. Now I just stop at the houses where I know people, where I
have my regular clients."

Going on foot down familiar streets that I usually drive past in my
car, we make our voyage through the city. I should walk on the inside
of the curb, Esperanza insists, not to slow her down. *"Así agarro más
vuelo,"* she tells me. I am reminded of a walk I took with a middle-
class Mexican man; he, too, continually stepped around me so he
could be on the street side. So there's a gender code to walking on the
street, I thought then; by walking on the street side, men protect
women from the rush of traffic and passers-by, or at least can feel that
they do. Esperanza, it seems to me, is transposing this gender code into
a class code.

At one door and another we stop, selling small amounts of her produce, often on credit, to her regular clients, middle-class women en-
closed in the house, cooking and cleaning; several of them answer the
door in their bathrobes. Whatever house we stop at, Esperanza ex-

plains: "Today I have company. She's a comadre from the United States. She wanted to come with me to see how I sell. She says it's good exercise for her." I nod and smile and try not to seem too weird. Some of the women seem surprised, others not terribly interested.

At our first stop, the woman who opens the door chats with us about her son, who lived for years in Chicago, where, she tells us, shaking her head, his legs would burn in the winter from the cold. After buying some zucchini from Esperanza, she goes inside and brings out a plate of leftover food. Esperanza empties the contents of the plate into a plastic bag and places it in her shopping bag. Another woman whose door we stop at afterward eyes me with suspicion and then instructs Esperanza to return later; on our return, she gives her a bag of day-old tortillas and some *masa*, cornflour dough she had not used. Though not lacking for food, Esperanza accepts these offerings of charity gracefully. What is edible she and her family will eat, she explains; what isn't will go to the chickens and pig.

After walking around from one end of the city to the other for an entire day, I figure that Esperanza has made about 5,000 pesos (just over $2.00). A few of the women who buy from her do not even pay, saying *después arreglamos cuentas*, promising to pay her back another day. To me this seems horrendous given the small amounts of money in which Esperanza deals, but she graciously agrees to offer credit several times. Esperanza says that if she sells everything she'll make 8,000 pesos, though the round-trip bus ride takes 1,000 pesos from these earnings. She is voyaging around the city to make a pittance, I say to myself, and there I've just spent a minor fortune on some books at Sanborns, a store that would certainly cast Esperanza out if she miraculously found her way there and even conceived of entering.

Even as I think my guilty gringa thoughts, I know that Esperanza is not one to accept pity from anyone. Walking down the arcade of the Ipiña building, Esperanza points to some men selling jewelry spread out on the floor. "How do they survive? That's what you ask yourself when you see people like that," Esperanza whispers to me. "And they see me, and they must say, and how does she survive? But thanks to God, I don't lack for anything. I've got enough to eat." Not only does she have that, I think to myself, but she also has the freedom to come and go, to wander at her pace around the entire city, with no man waiting at home to scold her.

Esperanza says that people are staring at us as we walk down the street side by side. We are indeed an odd couple: I, in sweatshirt, baggy pants, Ray-Ban sunglasses trimmed in cerulean blue, jogging pack clipped to my waist, and old Reeboks, a camera bag swinging from my shoulder, trudging along next to a nimble Esperanza, Indian-looking with her braids, apron, and plastic sandals, balancing her wares on her head and shoulder. "They see me as very *ranchera*, and you, comadre, a fair-skinned *güera* from the United States, following me." Rounding a corner, she says that some men delivering packages of "Bimbo" bread cannot take their eyes off us. "They're totally amazed," she says, chuckling in amusement.

Being seen—for the first time—as others see us is a moment of revelation for me, as though we've suddenly entered a hall of mirrors. It is one thing, I realize, to have Esperanza come secretly to my kitchen in Mexquitic and fill my waiting ears and voracious tape recorder with her stories. It is quite another to be in the street together as real people with real bodies, with real racial and class meanings attached to us. It's as though we've come out of the closet. There we are, two comadres walking side by side, transgressing a silent border simply by being together.

At one house where Esperanza has a comadre whose family is from the Mexquitic area, we make our longest stop. Arriving at the door, a young woman leads us into a narrow hallway and asks us to wait. "The señor is still here," she whispers. Apparently we can't go in until he comes out. Several minutes later, an elegant little man with Spanish features, all primped and clean, emerges from inside, passing by us with exaggerated formality. "*Con permisito*," he says, and goes out the door. Bonifacia, our host, then comes out. "My señor is very fussy," she says, and invites us in cheerfully.

Bonifacia comes from a rancho near Mexquitic, as she announces to me. "And you know what?" she says, teasingly looking me in the eye, "I always wanted to marry a gringo." I'm attracted immediately to her lively wit, and we're soon engaged in spirited conversation. Although I've never met her before, she knows all about David and me from her family in Mexquitic and from Esperanza. "What do you do with all the information you get?" she asks bluntly. "Do you sell it?"

I try to explain to her that David and I have been studying the history of Mexquitic in order to write a book. With this, we move, inevi-

tably, to a discussion of the Indian past of Mexquitic, which by definition is its history, as people from the town are quick to recognize. Her
sister, the young woman who greeted us at the door, says, "We're Indians. Our ancestors lived in caves." Bonifacia gives her a sharp look and
immediately snaps back, "You, maybe, but not me."

Revealing just how much she knows about us, Bonifacia remarks
that when she saw *Ni de aquí ni de allá*, the latest film sequel to the
India María series, she thought of me and Esperanza. The film is about
a gringo couple who bring the India María to the United States to serve
as their maid; the exploits of María in that setting make for hilarious
comedy. Serving us fresh gorditas stuffed with refried beans, Bonifacia
says, "Imagine you and your husband taking your comadre back, it was
like that."

Although the remark was made matter-of-factly, I am struck by the
irony of the remark and what it suggests for my work with Esperanza:
that her life story can cross the border with me, but that she herself
cannot make the crossing except as an undocumented domestic servant. She is making her crossing vicariously by allowing me to take
back her story. The border Esperanza and I had seemed to transgress
so effortlessly a moment before now stands between us again. Bonifacia's remark is a commentary on our class positions: while our personal relationship as comadres may mask our differences, I, a privileged woman, am in a position to employ Esperanza as my maid.

Later in the conversation, Esperanza remarks that people in Mexquitic like David and me. Bonifacia nods, unsurprised. "In Mexquitic they
don't say anything to you. You know, there are places where they don't
want you. But not Mexquitic. No one says to you, 'Why are you here?
What are you doing here?'"

"You see," says Esperanza, "Mexicans go to the other side. There
they throw them out, treat them badly. They don't let them cross.
They beat them or kill them. And all they want is to work."

"For you it's easy to cross, isn't it?" inquires Bonifacia rhetorically,
for she knows that it is. I am asked this question so often that I never
forget, in Mexico, the fact of that fundamental asymmetry—determin-
ing who can cross easily with a few dollars tip, as we do, and who has
to put their life on the line simply to find a little back-breaking work.

On our way home that afternoon, after stopping at several more
houses in other parts of the city, Esperanza tells me that she has one

more client left to see out by the stadium. But, she says, she'll go the
next day. She tells me that I must be tired from all the walking. I try to
assure her that I'm doing fine, but it's true, I don't walk with as brisk
a step as she does. Anyway, she says, she has to come back to do some
cleaning for someone and to pick up some clothing that a client wants
to give her. It occurs to me that I haven't noticed what she's wearing,
and I now see her tropical green skirt with its wide center seam. Did
she get it as a gift? Yes, she had, she says, but it hadn't been a skirt
when she got it; she had to rip open a pair of slacks to create a skirt for
herself. "We people from the rancho, we dress ourselves with whatever
we have at hand."

Esperanza tells me that all the clothing she ever has to buy for herself are aprons and knee socks, and even those things are getting expensive. At the Mercado República on our way home, I offer to buy her
an apron. "No, comadre, don't trouble yourself," she says. But, for a
change, I insist. Together we find an apron in a lilac plaid print with
frills down the sides that Esperanza says will be her apron for special
occasions. And then, as we wander through the market, I find an image
of Pancho Villa with the caption "The Man Who Dared to Invade the
U.S.A." As I stop to buy it, Esperanza says, "He had a lot of valor. And
so did you for coming with me."

Outside the market, we notice a group of people standing around in a
circle. As we get closer, I notice that they're listening to a man making pronouncements from the center of the circle. Esperanza tells me
that this man is always there when she goes to San Luis to sell. "I'm
not afraid of snakes," I hear him saying. "I'm afraid of those snakes
with two legs, those neighbors and compadres who want to hurt me!"
And with great flare, he pours himself a glass of water and says, "Your
comadre comes and offers you a taco. Don't eat it! Let it sit there for
three days, and you'll see the worms come out of that taco! The dirt
will come out of it! They envy you. They bear ill will toward you. Why
doesn't your daughter obey you? Why has your wife changed from one
day to the next? Why don't things go well for your son at his job? Why
are things going so badly for you? Amigo, it's the *cochinadas*, the pig
filth they throw your way. Over there at that market—what's it called?
República you say? In the Mercado República, they sell cochinadas of
every kind: black candles, containers filled with the crushed bones of
the dead, dirt from the cemetery, snake oil, cochinadas! Look, this is

water that God gives us to drink, and look at the cochinadas they've thrown into it!" Pouring the contents of a container into the glass of water in his hand, he looks at it with disgust and says, "Look, it's turned black! How many of you here believe in God? I'm with those who believe, not with those who come here and laugh."

Esperanza and I listen for a while. "He's right, you know," she says, as we head back to the mercadito to catch the bus to Mexquitic. "That Macario of mine, the woman got him a la mala, by means of evil." Arriving at the mercadito, Esperanza stops before the image of La Guadalupe and crosses herself again.

›››

In my country today, one doesn't have to be very wealthy in order to have the services of someone who doubles as washing machine, dryer, garbage disposal, salad mixer, vacuum cleaner, and bed-maker, who responds with a human voice, and who even says thank you when she gets her meager salary. When I was a child, the servants' lives and miracles fascinated me. . . . I discovered Mexico through them, and not even Bernal Díaz del Castillo had better guides.

—*Elena Poniatowska, "A Question Mark Engraved on My Eyelid"*

◎◎◎ In the space, then, of a couple of days in July of 1988, I spent, by rural Mexican standards, a fortune on books at a luxury store; accompanied Esperanza on her selling route through the city, where she sold handfuls of produce for pennies; and had, finally, a talk with her, which I inscribed on tape, negotiating the terms of the book I had yet to write about her life. I had crossed and recrossed borders, buying books, talking about books, entering and exiting different cultural-economic production zones at a speed that made things seem surreal.

How removed my fieldwork seemed from the fieldwork out of which modern anthropology was born, the sort of fieldwork where one retired to the most distant village one could find, or stranded oneself on an island, and took on the heroic role of the ethnographer, towering over all other outsiders and elites out of a sense of a higher calling. The dizzying pace at which I shifted roles, a pace that seemed especially confusing during those few days in July, left me at odds with myself. What was I doing, peddling with Esperanza one day and going to Sanborns another day, all somehow in the name of anthropology? How many masks could I wear without my face starting to stretch?

In Mexico, even the notion of fieldwork became ironic for me. Fieldwork, the sacred ritual of the tribe of anthropologists, was once even likened, in its importance for the discipline, to the blood of martyrs in Catholicism.[1] But it often seemed an almost absurd pursuit to me in the context of a social reality where I was made continually aware of my privileged position. How could I call what I was doing "fieldwork" when I was not allowed to forget about the existence of real workers crossing a real border to work real fields? Fieldwork in Mexico, for me, could only be about the way race and class intersected with, and intercepted, cultural understanding.

By calling attention to the race and class differences between Esperanza and me, Bonifacia put her finger on what a group of feminist researchers working on women's personal narratives have named the "Arthur Munby problem." A Victorian man of letters, Arthur Munby had a servant named Hannah Cullwick. Munby was fascinated by Cullwick's "dirty work," which he documented in elaborately posed photographs. Munby also convinced Cullwick to write down her life story in diaries, which were intended for his reading pleasure. For feminist researchers, the "Arthur Munby problem" is the problem of reconciling our quest for life stories with an awareness of the differences in power and knowledge that make other women serve as the subjects of our books in the first place. As women of greater privilege working on understanding the lives of women of lesser privilege in the highly unequal world of the late twentieth century, the "problem" before us is to avoid reproducing the Victorian experiential and textual power relations of Arthur Munby and Hannah Cullwick.[2]

I know that as I walked through the streets of San Luis photographing Esperanza with the bucket of vegetables on her head, I often felt as though we were playing the parts of Arthur Munby and Hannah Cullwick, I photographing the working-class woman at every turn, she willingly the subject of my gaze. I, too, like Arthur Munby, have turned myself into the "literary prince" for Esperanza, promising a Cinderella ending to her story by turning it into print. By telling her story to me, Esperanza agreed to have it inscribed in the doubly for-

eign world of the English language and the world of letters. There is an
irony to this agreement, as we are both aware.

What does it mean that Esperanza's *historia* can cross the border
with me, her middle-class educated gringa comadre (who can enter
Mexico anytime as a tourist), but that Esperanza herself cannot even
think of making the crossing except, at great risk, as an undocumented
domestic servant? Crossing the border evokes ambivalent images for
Esperanza. On the one hand, she sees el otro lado as a place where she
may achieve a new, more positive, identity, where people might view
her sympathetically in light of her suffering and quest for justice and
redemption. But on the other hand, her remarks during our visit to her
comadre in San Luis also showed that she thinks of "the other side" as
a site of political and psychological repression of Mexicans who seek
nothing more than honest work. Crossing the border by means of her
story offers a hope of liberation—the remaking of her self in her own
image—but that hope is embedded in the understanding that Mexicans
are treated harshly and cruelly in the same place she hopes her other
self will unfold. The terms of exchange are neither transparent nor
easy for Esperanza, and they are not for me, either.

I would be misrepresenting the terms of our exchange if I failed to
say that Esperanza's textual border crossing, like that of Mexican laborers, also carries with it the hope of obtaining more prosaic things
from "the other side." After our first conversations, she asked me for a
radio-cassette player, and her son Mario wrote several times to remind
me. When I gave it to her, she turned happily to Mario and said "We
got our wish!" (*¡Se nos concedió!*); I felt like a fairy godmother. She
wrapped up the gift in her shawl as though it were a baby and promised not to let anyone know she had gotten it from me, for if word got
around there would surely be bad feelings among our other friends in
the town. After our return to the United States, Mario wrote to say
that they would soon have electricity and that my comadre would like
a television. When I gave Esperanza the television, she reacted in the
same way she had before, "Hijo, we got our wish!"

During our visit in 1989, Esperanza surprised me with a gift of her
own. One night she sat down at the kitchen table, opened her rebozo,
and spilled out her collection of the *libritos* she had read over the years
about the life of Christ. These "little books," which she had carefully
saved in a box under her bed, turned out to be comic books that, in

weekly installments, tell gospel stories about Christ's curing of the lepers, the Last Supper, and Mary's ascent to heaven. Esperanza had told me she could no longer afford to buy these "little books," so I hesitated to accept her gift. But she insisted I take them. She already knew all the stories, she told me; they were in her head. Esperanza wanted me to have the only books she owned. She knows that, unlike her, I can only tell stories through books.

In the fall of 1990, the television I had given my comadre the year before sat on a small table in her bedroom next to her altar of religious images, protected from dust by a white crocheted cloth. In recent months, Mario has written to let us know my comadre needs a motor to irrigate her field and that it costs over a million pesos; could we bring it in our car, he wants to know, on our next visit? These, too, are part of the things being exchanged in our work and in my crossings back and forth from my academic production plant to the terrain of storytelling and wishing.

THIRTEEN

Gringa Sings the Blues

However "liberating" a narrative discourse we propose to write, it is one always intimate with power, and many of our "informants," "subjects," "consultants," "teachers," "friends" know it.

—*José Limón, "Carnes, Carnales, and the Carnivalesque"*

September 26, 1989

After days of driving we arrived in San Luis, quickly picked up the keys to our rented house from our compadre-landlords, and drove straight to Mexquitic. It was just after dusk when we arrived. Entranced, we drove into town, letting the car float down the narrow bridge, the one where Esperanza always says the imps come out at midnight. The Pérez kids were getting ready to return home after bedding their goats for the night in the empty lot that forms a pointed corner at the end of the bridge. The kids ran along next to the car, following us all the way to our house. They stood watching as we unpacked the car of all our mysterious belongings, and when we were done we politely said good night and closed the door.

The three of us were exhausted. I pulled the sheet of plastic off the bed. Then I found the bag of clean sheets and blankets. They were still tucked away in the wooden dresser, bought at the state folk arts store, that had cats carved into its two cabinet doors. I got Gabriel into his pajamas and David got into bed next to him. I was just pulling off my clothes when I heard an assertive knock on the door. Who could it be? I found the flashlight and went out to open the door. I should have recognized the knock after so many years.

"Comadre!" There was Esperanza. She was buoyantly happy to know we were back. Mario had passed by on his way home from their milpa and seen the car, she told me, and he had gone running home to tell her that not only were we back, but that we had a new car. Just before leaving Ann Arbor, we realized that the old Rabbit was no longer a safe car to take on the drive to Mexico. For the first time in my life, I went out and bought a spanking new car, using my fellowship money. I knew that this would reinforce people's view of us as rich gringos. I hated the way I now worried about any small scratch or dent on the car.

For the first time ever, I had to turn Esperanza away. I was so tired I could barely keep my eyes open. "But please come back another day," I said after a hug. I hoped she wouldn't be insulted.

"Of course we will, comadre," she said. "Now you get to sleep. You've come a long way and you must be tired."

Those were very tender words for Esperanza. I savored them for a moment. At the door, we said our goodbyes as usual, then we shook hands in the gentle and respectful way comadres should.

› › ›

October 5, 1989. Esperanza and I had been seeing each other frequently since our arrival in Mexquitic. There was more trust between us than ever before. At the same time, I realized that Esperanza was becoming increasingly worried about the impact of our friendship on her relations with townspeople. When we gave her a ride back from San Luis Potosí one day, she asked to be let off at the entrance to town, where the bus stops. "People are going to say I'm too attached to you, too acuache with you," she remarked. Later, around the kitchen table, she said, "Here people hate me even more when they see me with you. There are people who must say, 'Why does she go around with that señora?' It's as though it surprises them that you, such a decent person, go around with us. Because we're rancheros. And it makes them feel envy that we go around with you." Yet she continued to visit us at night, hiding in the bushes if she saw anyone near our house and sending her children ahead or behind her so no one would know they were all going to our house. When I would open the door, she would barge in, telling me in hushed tones that she was certain that all the young men hanging around the plaza knew where she was going.

While Esperanza worried about the envy and suspicion of her neighbors, I was developing a sense of unease about what exactly I owed to the community and to her and her family. Gabriel, well-fed and healthy, was bigger than all the other three-year-olds, and bigger than many of the four- and five-year-olds as well; the other mothers would say to me, "Over there they grow bigger, don't they?" Each day Gabriel went to the local preschool in fresh clothes; we took our wash to the city to be done for us at the laundromat because we knew the water in Mexquitic was contaminated with raw sewage. In contrast, I knew that my comadre Camila, with one outdoor faucet, struggled to send her little sons to school with clean faces. When the preschool offered the mothers the opportunity to buy a jogging suit uniform, "los pans," at the equivalent of thirty U.S. dollars, which I knew Camila could not afford, I wondered whether to buy them for her two sons. But then I held back: would that have seemed too patronizing; would I have put her in the position of having to tell all the other mothers that her rich comadre from the United States, not her proud husband who forbid her to sell gorditas in the street, had bought the uniforms?

I had similar qualms about whether to intervene in Esperanza's life and in her children's lives. After Mario finished junior high school, he had planned to go on to high school, but it turned out that the books— ironically, given my own book-making work with Esperanza—were too expensive. I was about to offer to pay for the books and his schooling when Esperanza remarked that she really did need his help in the field and that maybe it was better for him to learn how to work the land than to study for a less certain career.

Along with all this procrastination about my debts and account- ability, I was also feeling, by turns, ever more sad and resentful about how some people, especially those who knew us less well, would au- tomatically assume that we were in Mexico for the most crass mo- tives of exploitation and gain. Of course I understood very well that, no matter what we thought of ourselves, in rural Mexico we simply were the embodiment of U.S. power. But this intellectual understand- ing was not very comforting. I had a deep desire to somehow prove to people that, really and truly, I was a good gringa. I desperately wished everyone could peer into that part of me that exists apart from my location in relation to the border. An impossible—and in- deed foolish—hope. That night in my conversation with Esperanza, I gave myself permission to sing the gringa blues.

◉◉◉ "You trust me and believe what I tell you, don't you?" Esperanza says.

"Yes, I do. So if you tell me a lie, I'll believe it. I'll think it's true." We both laugh.

"So when are you coming back, comadre? Will you be back for the fiesta? Do you still feel like coming back?"

Hesitating, I reply, "Sometimes I say to myself, I guess we won't come back anymore. It's such a long trip. We start to feel lazy."

"So you don't think you'll come back?"

"I want to keep coming back. But sometimes I feel sad. Or I start to think that there are people who don't like us. I don't know. I say to myself, What do we come for? Maybe they're saying bad things about us. I don't know. Sometimes people say things to us."

› › ›

I am remembering the hurt I had felt several days before. While I was sitting in the half-open doorway reading, a boy had run past, gotten a peek at me, and yelled out with what to me sounded like venom in his voice, "Gringa!" But I don't want to tell Esperanza about this incident; it seemed very minor, even though it bothered me a great deal. So, instead, I decide to tell her about something I had noticed earlier that day.

◉◉◉ "For example, comadre, in the dust that's on the car someone wrote the words *Gringo Feo* (Ugly Gringo)." There were other words, too, but David, knowing how much these things bothered me, had erased them before I could see them. I had not been able to make out more than those two words.

"Really? On the car?" Esperanza says, perturbed.

"Yes, on the dust of the car," I repeat, already beginning to feel silly for having said anything.

"Ah, I see, on the dust of the car."

"Sometimes when things like that happen I feel sad," I say. "I start to wonder whether we should keep coming here when there are people who don't like us."

"With your pardon, comadre, but I think the ones doing that are the pack of young men in the town."

"*La raza,*" Mario adds.

"La raza," Esperanza goes on. "There's a lot of raza now that's grown up. It's the mob of young boys. The other time when we came over, they were hanging out around here, and when we left they were still here. They realize we're coming to see you."

"I guess it's just a few people," I say, reluctantly.

"Doesn't everybody talk to you in Mexquitic?" Esperanza persists.

"Oh, yes, everyone greets us," I admit.

"Comadre, it's been my good luck that nobody has ever said anything bad about you to me. Of course I don't get together with a lot of different women. Just, 'Good morning, good afternoon.' And, maybe sometimes I'll hear them say, 'How funny, the way they feel at home here.' But I've never heard anyone say anything bad about your persons. Why should they? Comadre, for my part, we even miss you! We always remember you. 'Ay, write to them. *Andale*, write to them. They haven't written back, maybe they've moved.'"

Then my comadre surprises me. She's remembered something I've told her about myself, a detail of my identity. "As I've told you, comadre, if God helps me, I'm going to plant a few rows, and when you come back next year I'll give you the ones you like the best, *los frijoles negros*, comadre, the black beans."

›››

Determined to be blue, I ask my comadre, "Tell me again about what your mama said about the photographs I took of her."

"She didn't like them. Norberta here says she tore them up." Esperanza looks at Norberta, who fidgets nervously in her chair.

"Was that because she didn't come out well in them?"

"It may be that. I don't remember very well. She came out, what did she say? All spotted."

"All dark," Norberta intervenes. "With that garbage of papers around her."

"She was standing in front of the images," I offer in explanation. As I remembered the photograph, Doña Nicolasa was in her room, posed before her wall of pictures of religious protectors; it had come out a little darker than I would have liked, because there was no light in the room, it was late in the day, and I had forgotten my flash.

Esperanza continues, "I just heard Norberta say, 'I'm going to tell my godmother you tore them up.'

"'They stuck me there and made me look all dark and ugly,' my mama said. 'How come yours came out so well? Why did they take my picture if they don't know how? If they don't know how to do it, why are they going around doing it? Why are they going around taking so many pictures?'

"I said to her, 'It's that they take them to bring them back to their tierra.'

"'Of course. Why do they go around taking pictures? They take them back, and they make money off of them. Here one's a ranchero, and they take our pictures and give them to those people who make calendars and they earn their money. And there your compadres go, too. Why do you think they're here taking photographs?'

"'Who knows?' I said.

"'Don't you remember that time when we were collecting taponas? And those viejos passed by in their car? And then they talked to us. Don't you remember? *Andale*, well those viejos wanted the pictures for those calendars. That's where they put the figurines they go around snapping up in the ranchos. Remember how they were going to photograph us that time, and we didn't let them?'

"That time they wanted to take some pictures of us collecting prickly pears. The men were on the highway, and there were a lot of taponas that year. My mama was still strong then. She had her pail of taponas and I had mine. There we were, peeling and peeling taponas. We were near the highway, and those two men must have noticed us, and they stopped their car at the edge of the highway.

"'Señoras, listen, excuse us.'

"My mama said to them, 'What did you need?'

"'No, look, señora, excuse us. Would you let us take some photos of you?'

"'What photos and what photos? *Andale*, don't let them,' she said to me.

"I moved away from the tapona and went behind a huizachito, and my mama did too.

"'Wait a minute. We're going to photograph you. Just stay there.'

"We sat down, and when we looked up they were coming toward us.

"'Listen, señoras, excuse us a moment. Please let us photograph you. We'll give you money, whatever you charge us. We just want to take your picture.'

" 'No, señor,' my mama said. 'Go somewhere else. Not me.' And my mama turned her back.

" 'No, look, señoras, we'll give you money.'

" 'No, señor, we are what we are, but we don't go around selling our-selves for money.' No, that's what my mama said.

"The men went up to the edge of the highway. Those men were stubborn. They took what they could from far away. And then they left.

" 'Mama, they were going to give us money.'

" 'What money, and what anything?' She just refused."

› › ›

These remarks are making me feel defensive. A few days before, dur-ing the town fiesta, a man carrying one of the huge marmota poles that are twirled around during the processions to the church came asking me to take his picture. He kept yelling out "Five hundred," and I, not understanding, kept saying that I didn't plan to charge him to take his picture. He twirled the marmota around, and though I had no particular interest in taking his photograph, to be polite I snapped a few shots. When he was done, he came to me demanding five hun-dred pesos. I tried to pay no attention to him, but he would not go away. Finally, I opened my purse and gave him the five one-hundred peso coins I happened to have. The total amounted to all of a quar-ter. The man was thrilled at his victory. Gloating over the money and laughing hysterically, he went back to the little group he was with. I heard him say to his companions, "She's going to sell them anyway."

This incident had irritated me terribly. I knew that my interaction with that man inscribed a certain history of Westerners photograph-ing others, in which those others were now seizing, if not the cam-eras, at least some of the power involved in snapping their pictures. Yet I had taken pictures that were useless to me against my will, just to be made the butt of a joke. Now, listening to Esperanza's story, I could feel the irritation crawling back into my skin. How could I ex-plain that I was innocent of such crass exploitation? Or was there any point in trying? Or was I so innocent? I had to admit, on the other hand, that I was impressed by Doña Nicolasa's knowledge of a mar-ket for photographs of exotic others and her resistance toward being a part of it, even if I resented being placed in the same category as the men who had stopped them on the highway. Her refusal to be objectified or commodified by men was admirable in every way—except when I felt implicated. And how could I doubt that I was implicated—hadn't my first encounter with Esperanza been a photographic one?

◉◉◉ "I've never sold a photo," I announce meekly.

Esperanza seems not to have heard. She goes on with her story. "So I tell you. And my mama said to me, 'Just look at the calendars—they're always showing what there is in other places.'

"'I don't know why they wanted to take photos of us, Mama.'

"'But at least we didn't let them.'

"That was when my mama used to be stronger. Yes, comadre, that's it. As for the picture you took, I didn't see, but she told me she had burned it. And before, when you gave me those two blouses, and she saw one of them on me, she said, 'Ay, what a nice blouse you have,' and I said, 'Ah, my comadre Ruth gave it to me.'

"'Ah,' she said. 'Your comadre Ruth gave it to you. Ah, that's hers. I saw her wearing it once.'

"'I didn't see her.'

"'That's hers. I saw her wearing it.'

"'Who knows,' I said. 'She gave it to me, and she gave these other things to Norberta.'

"'Ah, why does she just give *you* things?' my mama said to me."

Here I feel the need to make a confession. "You know, comadre," I announce, "your mama also asked me why I didn't give anything to her, so I gave her a blouse."

"Really? Who knows?" says Esperanza, shrugging her shoulders. "I haven't seen it on her. Maybe she burned it, too."

›››

October 11, 1989. Esperanza takes her seat at the kitchen table and suddenly asks me, "Comadre, have you heard about el panteón de los muertos vivientes?" I shake my head, translating to myself the expression I think I've just heard—the cemetery of the living dead? What can she be talking about? "You really don't know about it, comadre?" Esperanza says, honestly surprised. "No, I don't," I respond, passing out sodas to Norberta, Mario, and Esperanza. I take my seat at the kitchen table, not knowing what to expect. And my comadre goes on to tell me that this cemetery, located in a nearby rancho, has been around for seven years, as long as we've been coming to Mexquitic. And yet no one has ever told us about it.

◎◎◎ "Big trucks come with nothing but garbage, pure poison," Esperanza begins.

"It's waste from the factories," adds Mario, and finally the unsavoriness of this reality starts to become clear to me. Confirming my suspicions, David whispers, "Hazardous waste."

"They're making zinc or mercury there, too," Mario goes on.

"Eh?" Esperanza says. "My boy knows a little more. I just know what I've heard. This boy has gone by there on the bus, and he says it smells. I've seen it from the bus, when I've gone to Barrancas. You can see all that wire and some trees."

"But you were saying it was the living dead?" I'm still confused.

"That's what they say about them," Esperanza continues. In the newspaper, that's what they called the workers, 'The Living Dead.' Because those who work there, they say, have gotten consumed."

"Skeletons," adds Mario.

"They're skeletons already. But they're working there because they pay them good money— And what do they gain by earning good money? They're being consumed by it. That's why they tagged it the cemetery of the living dead. For my part, no matter how hungry we might be, I wouldn't send my boy there. Even if he could earn a million pesos in two or three hours. They say that the man who built the cemetery has intimidated the people of Rincón. He won't let them talk. That viejo must be a multimillionaire. They say he gave away millions to the people he bought the land from."

"Well, they shouldn't have given him permission," I say, with self-righteous anger.

"You see?" Esperanza replies.

"That's very dangerous for everyone's health," I continue in the same angry tone. But I am wondering about my own health, too, and feeling more than a little appalled that "our fieldsite," our destination in Mexico for so many years, this town with a fascinating colonial history, should turn out to be within a few miles of a toxic waste dump.

› › ›

October 26, 1989. A local television crew has come to interview David and me about our work in Mexquitic. Seated in the worm-eaten wicker chairs in the courtyard of the little house with the bougainvillea trellis, the two of us face the camera.

◎◎◎ First, the interviewer addresses her questions to David. He is able to speak in confident detail about his ethnohistorical research, about the Chichimecas, the Tlaxcalans, the eighteenth-century changes, the Revolution. After he is done, the overexcited interviewer, a bubbly city woman who finds everything about Mexquitic charming, turns to me. "Ruth, I know you have a lot to say, too. Now tell me, what work are *you* doing?"

Suddenly, with the camera aimed at me, I go blank. In horror I realize that there is very little I can say about my work to a local television network. Sure, I have done research on women's confessions to the colonial Inquisition, but I know that this material will not interest the interviewer, who wants to hear specifically about matters related to Mexquitic and San Luis Potosí. Sure, I have looked into the practice of spiritism in the region, but I don't think the participants in those cults will appreciate my talking about them on television. And sure, I am working seriously on the life story of one woman from Mexquitic. But how can I tell a television crew about that, especially when Esperanza has vehemently told me that she doesn't want me to tell anyone about the work we are doing together? It dawns on me that anything I can tell a Mexican audience will betray the confidences that have made my work possible in the first place. My only choice, it seems, is to remain mute.

I feel as though I am doing no work at all. Just as in the past, when anthropologists took along their wives to the field to serve as their helpers, I am simply a wife without a voice of her own. "Oh, yes, I'm working on women," I manage to say to the interviewer, adding a few obtuse lines about "folkloric practices" in Mexquitic, just to please her. This is a moment of profound embarrassment, but also of revelation. It shows me that I cannot easily use the work I am doing to gain authority, prestige, or glory—at least not in Mexico—no matter what Esperanza's mother thinks, no matter what the man with the marmota pole thinks. Only across the border will I be able to divulge the secret of my work with my comadre. Only as a translator will I find a voice.

FOURTEEN

*Ya sabe que estamos vendidos a sus personas**

The U.S.-Mexican border es una herida abierta where the Third World grates against the First and bleeds. And before a scab forms it hemorrhages again, the lifeblood of two worlds merging to form a third country—a border culture.

—**Gloria Anzaldúa, Borderlands/La Frontera**

October 27, 1989. What follows is the tail end of a long conversation in which I sought to elicit Esperanza's political views. The first association for her when I mention the word politics is hunger: the hunger she felt when she worked as a domestic servant in San Luis, and the hunger she felt when she was a married woman in her husband's house. When I ask her if she's voted in any election, such as the recent Mexican presidential election, she tells me that she only just voted for the first time for the local municipal presidente, and then only because she happened to be passing by as voters were being solicited. She voted for the PRI (Institutional Revolutionary Party) candidate because, as she explained, since her ejido field belongs to the government, and the government is all PRI, then she has to be for the PRI. After all my questions, Esperanza asks me if the PRI also exists on "the other side." After I tell her it doesn't, I make a remark about how the party that's been in power "over there" for the last few years has been giving so many privileges to the rich that the poor have gotten poorer.

---

* **"Now You Know That We've Been Sold to You"**

◎◎◎ "So there are poor people over there?" asks Mario in
amazement.

"Yes," I reply.

"And are you rich?" asks Esperanza, giving me a quizzical look.

"No, I'm not rich."

"No, comadre?" says Esperanza, clearly unconvinced.

"But everyone is rich over there," says Mario.

"They say that everyone is rich there. Is that true, comadre?" Esperanza asks earnestly. "For example, the clothing you've given me, right? They tell me that clothing like that gets thrown in the trash over there. It's thrown in the trash, and people from here go to get it. A woman who buys from me has told me that. She says, 'No, why do you think Mexicans from here try to go to the United States? People are really rich there. See these clothes? We got them out of trash cans.'

"'Really?'

"'Yes, what do you think? We do have to pay to bring them back. But the clothes are in the trash there. Clothes you can sell at a good price here. Over here, they'll sell you those clothes for five thousand, eight thousand pesos. We get back what we've paid to bring them across, because we don't buy the clothes, we get them straight out of the trash. All the rich people over there just dump their clothes in the trash.'

"'Really?'

"'Yes,' she says. 'Here the richest of the rich wear those clothes. And a poor person says that things went well for her if she gets to wear them. Over there, when rich people no longer want their old clothes, they don't just give them to a beggar the way we do here in San Luis. Do you think there's going to be a beggar asking for them in the United States? The rich people there wear the very best, and the clothes that are just so-so they throw away. They never give them away. I go with a friend and load up on those clothes, and here we sell them at a good price.'"

›››

Listening to Esperanza tell this story, I am reminded of a story I once read in a Mexican newspaper about slightly used American disposable diapers being sold in Mexico as new diapers. I imagine there must be a vast lore of such stories. But I hope Esperanza doesn't think the clothes I've given her came out of the trash!

◎◎◎ "Well there are places over there to bring old clothes," I try to explain, thinking of the Salvation Army. "Those clothes are given to people who need them. But it's true, a lot of things get thrown away over there."

"And people from here bring them back."

"But not everyone is rich over there, comadre. A lot of people are homeless."

"But that's not people from over there. Isn't it people from here?"

"No, people from over there."

"From there? Ah, who knows?"

"So you think everyone in the United States is rich?"

"Yes, everyone is very rich," replies Esperanza.

"That the United States is richer than Mexico, one hears that all the time," adds Mario.

"I've heard that the United States lent money to Mexico," continues Esperanza, "and that Mexico is now in debt to the United States. That's why everything we have here in Mexico is being handed over to the United States. When the governing rulers left office, they left Mexico sold to the United States. The last set of rulers that just got out hadn't finished paying the United States when the next government came in. I've heard people say in San Luis that a poor person here, a ranchero, whoever it may be, it's as if one is paying Mexico so that Mexico can pay back the United States. Because the United States has practically bought up Mexico. That's what you hear around here."

"And do you agree with it?"

"Well, that's what I've heard. They say that Mexico is sold to the United States. Because the United States lent who knows how much to Mexico for their oil."

"Millions," says Mario.

"Millions, not just thousands, and that's why everything the United States wants out of Mexico, there it goes."

"Then is your work as a marchanta for the United States, too?" I remark.

"Well, yes it is. That's why various people say, 'What help does the government give us? None. All the work you do and everything you earn is taken away by the government, and there goes your money, and we still haven't finished paying. Mexico still isn't finished paying the United States. So it's as if we've been sold to the United States.' And I

259

ask myself, but how? 'Just think about it.' That's what the husband of one of the women who buys from me in San Luis said. 'Think about how you sell. Do they pay you well?'

"'No, they don't.'

"'Well, there's the proof. Why? Because the government of Mexico is sold to the United States. Each presidente leaves the ruler's seat a little bit more sold. We never finish paying. Another one comes in, takes a *mordida*, and makes something for himself. What's he going to pay back to the United States? That's why everything the United States wants with regard to oil, it just needs to send orders to Mexico: Send This Much. Whether Mexico wants to send it or not, it's got to go there. And what about the vegetables? You people from the ranchos bring truckloads of vegetables to the city. And where does it all go? Far away. Of course it goes far away. And what does San Luis get? The leftovers.'

"God only knows. Whoever knows how to read can understand, and whoever doesn't just listens to what's being said. Someone like me who can barely read, they tell you one thing and another thing and soon you've forgotten it all."

"What do you feel when you hear that your country has been sold?"

"In part, I'm just content that I'm already old. At any moment now I'll die. Just my children will be left, right?" She starts to laugh and stops herself. "So it's as though they've already been sold. Only God knows what will become of them tomorrow and later on. Whatever I've done, I've done. Now that I'm getting older, what am I going to do? If I die of hunger now, so what? So Mexico is sold!

"What I've heard is that with the new presidente in power, there may come a time when we will become his slaves. I don't know exactly how. But that man said, 'We're going to become slaves. Year by year, as he goes on, we're on the verge of becoming slaves to him.'

"Well, comadre, so is this what you wanted me to talk to you about?"

"Yes."

"So you see, now you know that we've been sold to you, to your persons." She laughs, this time, with real abandon.

"Sold to their government," corrects Mario.

"Yes, not to us, to the government," I say, a touch too glad for the correction.

›››

November 1, 1989. Day of the Dead. Six years ago I met Esperanza on this very day, trying to photograph her in the cemetery. We are packing up to get ready to leave in two days. Esperanza has come to say adiós. She tells me that she talked to Chencha again, who said to her that she shouldn't worry about losing her house. "Your brother and his family were trying to hurt you, but now they won't be able to. They can't do anything to you anymore," Chencha declared confidently to her. Esperanza continued to marvel at Chencha's powers, saying, "On the third of the month, my mama threw me out, but by the end of October it was all straightened out. Things were hot, fast. I didn't let the time slip by, and I ended up in good hands, on a day where there was fierce healing going on. Look at that, in less than a month." After we've been talking for a while, David walks in, exhausted from packing. The conversation is in midstream.

◎◎◎ "So, comadre, what title would you like me to give the book?" I am asking.

"Ay, my compadre is falling asleep!" Esperanza says laughing, as David collapses into one of the wicker chairs. And then she says, "What do you mean, comadre? I don't understand you. No, comadre, this comadre of yours can't do anything with her head. I think it's up to you. You're the one writing the book."

"But don't you have any preferences?" I persist. "Every book has a title, comadre. Isn't there a title you'd like?"

Seeing David slump farther down in his chair, Esperanza exclaims, "*Pobrecito*, compadre, you're falling over you're so tired!" Apologizing profusely for keeping us up late, she rises from her chair, but not without saying, "Well, look, comadre, you give it whatever title you find easiest. I once heard a cook ask the woman she was working for, her patrona, the question, 'Señora, what should I cook for today?' And the patrona said, 'Oh, you make whatever makes you feel the most coraje. Cook whatever makes you angriest.' So, my comadre, you do with this book whatever makes you really angry."

› › ›

November 4, 1989. At the American border, crossing back into Laredo. Back on this side, we tell the guards we went to Mexico as tourists. We've learned through the years that, not to be hassled, it's always wise to bring back a bottle of tequila or Kahlua, so we'll have "something to declare." I declare my tequila bottle and we're waved along, told only to stop and pay our Texas state liquor tax at the booth by the exit. Not quite a bribe—more like an offering to the border spirits.

Working-class Mexican men joke about going north as tourists. "*Me voy de turista*," they say. Theirs is the tourism of the poor, the kind of being somewhere else that can only be bought with the cheap sale of their own labor.

Crossing so easily into the land of air-conditioning, I start to feel like an "academic tourist," just back from my professional vacation somewhere between *el México profundo* and *el México imaginario*. In my bags, together with more tapes of conversations with Esperanza, which I will use to write "the life history of a Mexican woman street peddler," I bring back some pottery and weavings purchased at the state folk arts store, a bottle of tequila, Esperanza's comic books, and new history books from Sanborns.

› › ›

November 7, 1989. On the road. Driving home. Everything always seems unreal when I cross back to this side. Passing the familiar sites again: Burger King, Exxon, Best Western . . .

› › ›

November 12, 1989. At home in Ann Arbor. A quiet Sunday reading the New York Times. Home again, I am finding that border crossings are much in the news with the crumbling of the Berlin Wall and the East German exodus to the West, which our media depicts as a journey to freedom and a triumph of capitalist democracy. What a marked contrast, I think, to the way South/North crossings, especially from Mexico to the United States, tend to be depicted; these crossings are illegal, and they are made by alien hordes of dark people for the single purpose of earning dollars.

It is my birthday, so I take a closer look at the front page of the *Times* than I usually do, looking for hidden meanings, something special, something memorable. I am stunned by what I see.

Side by side, with apparent nonchalance, there are clear representations of East/West and South/North crossings: on one side, the headline, "Vast Fraud by Migrants Found in Amnesty Plan," and on the other side the headline, "East Germans Flood the West," underneath which is an article, "Family Says of the West, 'It's a Dream.'"

On the lefthand side of the paper, we learn of "one of the most extensive immigration frauds ever perpetrated against the United States Government," when all the U.S. wanted out of the amnesty plan was "a cheap, reliable and legal supply of farm workers." While the article does not mention Mexican migrants at all, it is clear that the implicit reference is to them. The expendability of unnamed Mexican bodies is presented with utter naturalness.

Turning to the righthand side, we follow the Schmalfeld family on their storybook visit around West Berlin as they "eye the cars, stores and apartments like children at a candy counter." Their visit is romanticized, their desire for the goods of the world sanctioned in a way that never happens with Mexican migrants.

That day I promise myself that this life history of one Mexican woman must speak against such representations—and, somehow, that it must make a difference. I promise myself to write angry—just as Esperanza said I should.

›››

September-October 1990. Return trip to Mexquitic. No book yet, I have to tell Esperanza. By then I know all too well how exhausting it is to transcribe tapes, so I stop feeding the tape recorder. I can't bear to translate any more of our talk onto paper.

Just as we're getting ready to leave for "the other side" again, I visit my schoolteacher-compadres in San Luis to tell them I'd like to rent their house in Mexquitic for another year. Suddenly they announce that they've decided they no longer want to rent their house to us. Our visits have been getting shorter each year and, they say, since they hardly go back to Mexquitic anymore, it's too much trouble to continue to be responsible for our belongings while we're away. In any case, they want to fix up the house from top to bottom. Then maybe they'll sell it. Or at least rent it for a lot more money.

After all those things that have traveled with us for years are put away in boxes, after the slightly wobbly table, the once-crowded shelf, the dented Austin refrigerator, the gas stove with the one good burner, and the worm-eaten chairs have been taken out (the sink beyond clean-ing is not ours, so it stays), I go inside the kitchen for the last time. If walls have ears, how much these walls must know.

›››

May-August 1991. At my desk in Ann Arbor. I tell myself that until I finish this book, I cannot return to visit my comadre. In the heat of summer I stay home and revise and write, revise and write. Some-times, around midnight, with the computer still buzzing, I seem to re-turn to that kitchen with the mint green walls. Disguised as a *bruja gusana*, I burrow my way back into the kitchen, where neither my comadre nor I will return, and gather the crumbs left from our words, our laughter, and the questions neither of us could answer, or even knew how to ask.

›››

September 1991. Computing Center, University of Michigan

> down in the bowels of the brick building
> Esperanza's words come out
> clean, neat, pretty
> permanent-pressed on new white paper
> folded into fresh plastic bags
> with zip-lock tops.

›››

November 28, 1991. A letter from my comadre: Por lo que respecta a la historia comadre, si le doy el permiso de que su traduccion sea a cu-alquier idioma yo le deseo que el libro de la historia le salga bien y como dice usted ojala y se venda y gane dinero para que su trabajo de venir asta Mexico no aya sido en vano o sea que no aya perdido su tiempo.

(With regards to the historia, comadre, I do give you permission to translate it into any language. My wish is that the book of the historia come out well for you; and as you say, hopefully it will sell and make money so that your work of coming to Mexico will not have been in vain and you will not have wasted your time.)

PART FOUR

Reflejos / Reflections

Writing ethnography offers the author the opportunity to reencounter the other "safely," to find meaning in the chaos of lived experience through retrospectively ordering the past. It is a kind of Proustian quest in which the ethnographer seeks meaning in events whose significance was elusive while they were being lived.

—Dorinne Kondo, "Dissolution and Reconstitution of Self: Implications for Anthropological Epistemology"

De debajo de la capucha de Torquemada sale, ensangrentado y acero en mano, el continente redimido! Libres se declaran los pueblos todos de América a la vez. (Out from under Torquemada's hooded cloak, the continent, bloodied, sword in hand, comes forth redeemed! All the peoples of the Americas, together, declare themselves free.)

—José Martí, "Madre América" (1889)

Looking for evidence of women's resistance only in articulated protests . . . I ignored the possibility that their resistance was to be found precisely in their self-constructions.

—Lynne Phillips, "Rural Women in Latin America"

The television I bought for Esperanza amid the images of her home altar (1990)

Initially, I felt uncertain of how to render Esperanza's voice, and what the purpose of my doing so would be. What would the gringos, and especially the gringas, make of her tales of violence, loss, and suffering, of her quest for redemption through a spiritist cult where Pancho Villa is worshiped? But leaving the gringas and gringos aside, I had to come to terms with something even more basic: what did I think of what she was telling me? After so many years of generously funded border crossings, was one woman's life story "enough" to bring back? The reflections that follow are an extended reply to these questions.

I found that I couldn't easily place Esperanza's life story in the economy, in politics, and in history, which I felt duty-bound to do as an anthropologist. At first, as I listened to Esperanza, I was troubled by the thought that maybe her *historias* were not "historical enough," at least not in the sense that I had been taught to think about what constituted history in the Anglo-American academy. I couldn't see a way to locate Esperanza's history in History in the way that, say, Sidney Mintz had been able to do for Taso Zayas, or that Paul Friedrich had been able to do for Primo Tapia.[1] Esperanza had participated only indirectly in the key political struggles of her time, and she spoke of politics in the conventional sense (the Mexican Revolution, *agrarismo*, political feuds, the national elections) only at my urging, but without much enthusiasm. I noticed that male anthropologists working with Latin American male subjects provided neat chronologies in their life history texts, showing the intersection of individual, local, and national events. But such a chronology would have been absurd in the case of Esperanza, with her defiant location between the worlds of women and men, past and present, this life and the afterlife.

Turning to feminist models for structuring the life history narratives of Latin American women, I found—at first to my disappointment—that Esperanza didn't fit the part of the exemplary feminist heroine for whom Western women are always searching among "native women."[2] Her story seemed to offer neither a moral nor a mirror to the gringas who would be its most likely readers. I couldn't turn her into a "secular saint" speaking about gender, ethnic, and class struggle and the call to action through her metonymic personal voice.[3]

269

Esperanza's story led elsewhere, defying at every turn any of the heroic feminist or political interpretations I might have wished to subject it to, defying at every turn any possibility of my gaining glory from her struggles. As Elena Poniatowska said with regard to Jesusa Palancares, a working-class Mexican woman whom Esperanza resembles in many ways, "If I were to transform her into a neighborhood Zapata, I would betray all those hours we had together."[4] Not to betray the hours Esperanza and I spent together, I have sought to think about her *historia* as she speaks of it, as a history and a story about rage, suffering, and redemption. Having an *historia* of her life to tell, that is the heart of her ability to rename and remake the world into which she was born. As a Chicana character in a story by Sandra Cisneros remarks, "Making the world look at you from my eyes. And if that's not power, what is?"[5]

Most social science writing on rural women in Latin America has emphasized the political and economic aspects of women's experience. Surprisingly few researchers, themselves women, have focused on the way the women subjects of their studies narrate their understandings of their world; and hardly any have sought to make these understandings central to the recasting of theoretical frameworks.[6] Anthropologist Lynne Phillips suggests that if we are to produce histories that empower our subjects, it is time that we allowed for other women's "misbehavior," what she describes as "their different ways of making sense," to "take over" our research projects.[7]

Staying close to Esperanza's own conceptual categories and producing a book with her voice centrally located in the text, I hope I've allowed for enough creative "misbehavior." The reward of this approach is that Esperanza's story suggests that there are other possibilities for seeing Latin American women as actors that expand upon their roles as daughters, wives, and mothers, as workers and political activists. Her story suggests that a woman from the margins of the other America can also be a thinker, a cosmologist, a storyteller, or even a novelist working within that embedded literary tradition which, in the absence of schooling and access to the means of production, consists of the living stories that she and her mother have lived and told, and the stories that her daughters have yet to live and tell.

›››

If what Esperanza had to tell defied some narrative models for thinking about life history, in other ways I could see how she might be readily stereotyped. Before I could begin to understand Esperanza, I had to acknowledge that the figure of such a woman already exists in academic as well as mainstream reporting as a pretheorized reality, an already-fixed representation. Didn't I first gaze upon Esperanza through the eyes of Diego Rivera's representation of Mexican Indian womanhood?

One female folklorist traveling through Mexico writes of the single scene that encumbered her vision wherever she went: that of a young woman carrying "a tiny baby tightly wrapped in a rebozo, and always her belly was big with child. . . . I spoke to many women about their situation, and always their sadness disturbed me. They were not joyful in their motherhood, they were resigned."[8] Similarly, Octavio Paz's image of the Mexican woman is "an image of immobility, secretive, passive, an idol, a victim who is hardened and rendered insensitive by her suffering."[9] So ingrained is this image of the long-suffering Mexican woman that it has been suggested by a North American female researcher that the counterpart to "machismo" in Mexico is "marianismo, the cult of feminine spiritual superiority," a superiority which "engenders abnegation, that is, an infinite capacity for humility and sacrifice."[10]

Looking beyond Mexico, critiques of Western feminism by women of color make painfully obvious the ways in which even the most well-meaning first world women have unselfconsciously created a cultural other in their images of women of color, upon whose backs they have built analyses that establish their authority and right to speak about what is a meaningful female life.[11] According to Chandra Talpade Mohanty, the texts of non-Western women's lives written by feminists in the West tend to present portraits of the third world woman as leading "a truncated life based on her 'feminine gender' (read: sexually constrained) and being 'third world' (read: ignorant, poor, uneducated, tradition-bound, domestic, family-oriented, victimized, etc.)" while subliminally portraying themselves as "educated, modern, as having control over their bodies and sexualities, and the freedom to make their own decisions."[12] Not surprisingly, as Mohanty notes with irony, "fertility is the most studied aspect of women's lives in the third world. This particular fact speaks volumes about the predominant representations of third world women in social-scientific knowledge-production."[13] Inverting this tendency to view the women they study as passive victims, and perhaps overcompensating, some feminist anthropologists have lately stressed the existence of female cultures of resistance, thereby extending the Western feminist self-representation of what constitutes agency to their subjects.[14]

Clearly, any ethnographic representation—and I count my own, of course—inevitably includes a self-representation. Even more subtly, the act of representing "almost always involves violence of some sort to the subject of the representation," using as it must some degree of reduction, decontextualization, and miniaturization. "This is one of the unresolvable problems of anthropology," as Edward Said tells us.[15] Yet I think there is hope insofar as we realize that ethnographic work is inherently paradoxical, being "a process by which each of us confronts our respective inability to comprehend the experience of others even as we recognize the absolute necessity of continuing the effort to do so."[16]

While Esperanza would seem to suit the image of the "abnegated mother" and "long-suffering Mexican woman" of conventional Mexican gender representations, she does so only in an ironic fashion. For always, in her version of her story, she was awake, alive, and thinking; always she was a critical subject, even when she would have seemed—in the eyes of a gringa—to be leading the worst kind of "truncated life." Suffering alchemized into rage provided the clear and fiery light of consciousness for her to plot the story of her life as her-story rather than his-story.

If we are to go beyond first world representations of third world women as passive, subservient, and lacking in creativity, then clearly one important task for feminist ethnographers alert to and respectful of the differences between women is to listen well to the stories that other women have to tell, capturing the key images and offering interpretations that mirror the narrative forms they themselves use to tell their life stories. At this juncture in the politics of feminism, it is gratuitous to think that an ethnographer "gets" a less-privileged woman's "experience" by taking down her life story; and it is even more gratuitous to think that her work is done when she has framed the other woman's "own words" with a few comfortable generalizations that make no connections to her own position as the one who brings the story back across the border. Privileged feminist ethnographers are now in the ironic position of being able to mime the role of the doctor-husband portrayed in Charlotte Perkins Gilman's parabolic "The Yellow Wallpaper" (1892). Knowing what was best for his wife, he confined her to a room with yellow wallpaper where she was not to tire herself by doing any kind of thinking or writing.[17] Above all, the stories that we bring back in other women's words for translation on our side of the border need interpretive homes that will not turn out to be prisonhouses with yellow wallpaper.

› › ›

As a genre, the life history is a hybrid form that inscribes the doubled voices of a native speaker and a translator. One problem with the genre has always been its use of the Western form of the autobiography to encase the self-narrative of a person marginalized by the West, a person usually lacking access to the means of production and often even the ideological constructs necessary to turn talk into an autobiography in the first place, let alone into pages in a book.

"Most anthropologists have assumed," writes Renato Rosaldo, "that the life history is a natural and universal form. If crudely unmasked it might not be too much of a parody to say that the prevailing anthropological view is as follows: place a tape-recorder in front of Mr. Non-literate Everyman and he will tell the 'real truth' about his life." Rosaldo writes of his disappointment after trying to elicit the life history of an Ilongot man named Tukbaw, from whom he was unable to draw out "a revelation of the dark and hidden depths of his intimate and private being" such as we have come to expect in Western autobiographies. Only later did he come to realize that his expectations had been "at once a-historical and anti-anthropological," and that conceptions of what it means to be a person, live a life, and tell a life story are social constructs with profound cultural and class implications.[18]

Similarly, in my work with Esperanza, I often sought, to little avail, to get her to speak to the emotional and intimate aspects of her life, especially those having to do with love and sexual desire. From this talking past one another, I realized how different a conception she had of the language of sentiments from my own.[19] Her life story, as she told it to me, was not a revelation of the "real truth" of her inner life but an account of those emotional states (which were also often bodily and religious states) that she construed as worth talking about—physical suffering, martyrdom, rage, salvation.

The American idea of "letting it all hang out" struck her as vulgar, as it does most rural Mexicans. Her notion of a life story had nothing to do, then, with the revelation of dark secrets (despite the fact that she viewed it as a confession), but with the telling of thickly dialogued stories in which she was at times the victim, at times the heroine, and at times the keen listener, bearing witness. And very simply, there were things that she just refused to talk about. Sexuality, for example, a key subject that we have come to expect to find discussed in autobiographical work by women, was a matter she would only speak about allusively, almost in code.[20] I could insist as much as I wished, but she held firm to what she thought was worth telling in a life. I controlled the tape recorder and did the writing, but I respected those silences of Esperanza's as though they were her fiercest words.

It has long seemed to me that most life histories stop short of their goal of decentering Western notions of whose life deserves a place in the world of (our) letters. We ask for revelations from others, but we reveal little or nothing of ourselves; we make others vulnerable, but we ourselves remain invulnerable. I've tried to do something a little different here. I stand revealed throughout the book as a character in the narrative, asking not always very cogent or useful questions of Esperanza.[21] Here, in this last section of reflections, I hold up a number of mirrors to my comadre's story, mirrors large and small, that are as revealing of me as they are of her. And at the end of the book, I emerge from the shadow of the biography to make a fuller connection back to my own life story from Esperanza's story, translating myself to dig down into the tangled roots of how I attained the authority to be the one inscribing my comadre's *historia* in this book.

FIFTEEN

Translated Woman

In the Indian or the Bengali context . . . when there are wed-dings in the family, I discovered, after my marriages broke up, and I became of a certain age, that when the bride or the groom was blessed, I have to step out of the room, because I'm the mark of bad luck, as a married woman without a husband; . . . it's no use actually taking an adversative posi-tion in that context because, on the other side, it's also true that in the so-called 'developed,' feminist countries like the United States, my credit in the heterosexist commodified mar-ketplace is very low because I'm an intellectual woman, past her first youth, so one has somehow to work the dialectic be-tween these two things, and for me these roles are much more immediately politically problematic than the ones you have mentioned.

—Gayatri Chakravorty Spivak, commenting in an inter-view on her position as "a Third World woman [and] high-ranking U.S. academic," **The Post-Colonial Critic**

As Gayatri Spivak suggests, there is no pure feminist realm outside patriarchy, either on our side or across the border. Spivak anticipates the possibility that her role as "the mark of bad luck" in the Bengali context, which is her home location, will be viewed as "other" by feminists on this side of the border. Almost in the same breath, Spivak translates her Bengali positioning into a lan-guage that feminists (like her interviewer) on this side will understand, noting her "low credit" in a different market, that of the postfeminist West, where successful intellectual women not properly harbored in a heterosexual relationship are still a source of suspicion and anxiety. It is in the dialectic between such positionings, not in any absolute defi-nition, that, Spivak suggests, women find their place in patriarchy. Or, to put it in the terms of this book, it is in translation that women find out who they are.

That Bengali and Western inscriptions of transgressive women are mirror images of each other is not the only point suggested by Spivak's reply to her interviewer. Having made clear her own position as a transgressive woman, Spivak does something quite subtle: she transgresses the very terms of the question by refusing to place herself in the domain that her interviewer finds politically problematic. To be a third world woman and an internationally successful academic figure is, after all, a contradiction in terms. Instead, Spivak relocates herself in the kinship and sexual domain, where, as she says, she finds what she feels are the much more immediately problematic roles to negotiate.

The question of whether feminism translates across borders has lately begun to preoccupy feminist ethnographers who want to learn how to listen and respond to the words of women from other cultural, racial, and class backgrounds. Spivak's act of translation suggests some of the contradictions of such a feminist project. In this chapter, I want to enter the debate by reflecting upon the issue of feminist translations. I will attempt a reading of Esperanza's story in terms of the question of where to locate the transgressive woman in patriarchy and in feminism—and, particularly in the case of Esperanza, the transgressive woman whose social position does not make it possible for her to own the words "patriarchy" and "feminism." It is significant that Esperanza locates her story in the kinship and sexual domain, and I want to understand how that positioning is politically problematic for her—even as I keep before me the memory of Esperanza's laughter breaking the evening stillness whenever I would get too serious about trying to analyze what she was telling me. My aim is to work the dialectic between Esperanza's no-name feminism and my feminism of too many names, to go beyond the search for heroines on either side of the border.

› › ›

In making Esperanza's story the subject of a book, one of my major worries has been that her story, if misread, could project an exaggerated view of the role of violence and anger in Mexican life. I was haunted by the resentment that surfaced in the Mexican press when the Spanish translation of Oscar Lewis's *The Children of Sánchez* first appeared, which many Mexican commentators felt stereotyped working-class Mexicans as violent, abusive, and mired in a damning misery they were powerless to surmount. This stereotyping was especially irritating in light of the fact that Lewis himself remained fundamentally unaware of his racial and class position as an American researcher, acting as though he were offering a clinical diagnosis rather than a social analysis.[1]

There was a time when Euro-American researchers comfortably attributed Mexican domestic violence to a series of cultural or psychological failings that included machismo, marianismo, amoral familism, and the culture of poverty, among other pathologies. I didn't want Esperanza's story to be read as another stereotypical view of Mexican men as brutal beasts and Mexican women as passive victims. I thought about the strong reservations that some black male (and a few female) critics have expressed about Alice Walker's *The Color Purple* and its portrayal of black masculinity and domestic violence in African-American families. This criticism has been directed, not so much at the accuracy of such representations, as at the way these images become grist for the racist white imagination. As bell hooks comments, "When black women suggest that the most exploitative and oppressive force in the lives of black females is black men, white society is free from the burden of responsibility; they can easily ignore the painful and brutal impact of racism."[2] It continues to concern me that Esperanza's story might be appropriated in a similar way on this side of the border.[3]

Esperanza's distrust of marriage and her difficult battle to be at the head of her family are aspects of her story that are amenable to being read in ways reminiscent of the damaging images propagated by white observers about the black female-headed household.[4] In classical sociological and ethnographic accounts of the Mexican and Mexican-American family, stereotypes similar to those surrounding the black family perpetuated images of the authoritarian, oversexed, and macho husband and the meek and submissive wife surrounded by children who adore their good and suffering mother. These stereotypes have come under strong critique in the last few years, particularly by Chicana critics, who have sought to go beyond the various "deficiency theories" that continue to mark the discussion of African-American and Latina/Latino family life.[5]

It is no longer possible, unless one's ears and eyes are shut, to suggest that domestic violence is a problem only for a few select minori-
ties of the underclass. In the United States, domestic violence has become one of the major social problems of our time, and it is currently
being addressed in the battered women's movement and in education
offering nonviolent alternatives to relationships based on power and
control.[6] At the same time, the backlash against American women
has never been more virulent.[7] In the aftermath of the appointment of
Clarence Thomas to the Supreme Court despite Anita Hill's charges of
sexual harassment, it will take extraordinary courage for American
women to continue to break the silence about the repressive gender
system in which they are caught.

When I began my work with Esperanza in 1985, I could not foresee
how sharply her story would reflect upon, and mirror, the situation of
women on this side of the border. My comadre is a woman who has
refused to keep quiet about the violence that was enacted upon her
body in the name of patriarchal law. Like any woman who speaks her
mind, she has paid a price for not cutting out her own tongue. And
that price (which Anita Hill also had to pay) is having people call her,
"Witch! Witch!"

›››

"A woman's life," it has been said, "can never be written taking
gender for granted."[8] The historia Esperanza told me is, above and beyond anything else, a long meditation on her own engendering. Esperanza begins her narrative by telling the story of her mother's life as
she witnessed it during the early years of her childhood. This mother-
daughter mirroring is a key theme in her account; often it seems as
though she is collapsing time and through her life giving birth to her
mother's life, while foreseeing the life her daughters have yet to live. In
childhood, by witnessing her father's brutal treatment of her mother,
Esperanza gains a vivid sense of the violence of patriarchal domination. The violence is not only physical but psychological, and it is
intended to engender in the girl-child a profound consciousness of
the fallen woman that lies in wait for her in her own small body. Her
father's continual taunting of Esperanza and her sister as being "pimps"
for their mother, covering up affairs that he is certain she must be having, is an example of the kind of violence that left its mark on Espe-

ranza. The scar left by her father's words is reopened later in the story when Esperanza marries Julio and he levels the same kind of accusations at her that her father used to direct at her mother, even while keeping her virtually locked up in the house.

And yet her mother's words, while not violent in the same way as her father's and her husband's, do not offer consolation. The words her mother utters after she decides to leave Esperanza's father are hard: "I didn't bring any children with me, and I'm not taking any children with me." She initially refuses to take Esperanza and her two other children with her, thus disengaging her womanhood from motherhood. Despite the mother-daughter mirroring and sense of continuity that Esperanza emphasizes in her account, she never celebrates motherhood or maternal thinking as do some North American feminist thinkers. Her sense of mothering is always darkened by an awareness of the class limitations that make mothering for rural working women a bittersweet wager at best, entered into with reluctance and ambivalence.

Her mother's escape from the dark, violent, closed, male-dominated world of the marriage bed is followed by the escape of Esperanza and her siblings, who as small children steal off at dusk with a few blankets to rejoin their mother. Esperanza, too, when her time comes, escapes from what in her account is the incarceration of marriage, refusing to bear the cross of the white wedding dress any longer (though she attenuates her sense of agency at various times in her narrative by saying that if her husband hadn't thrown her out of the house because of his mistress, she would still be there suffering with him). In this part of rural Mexico, when women commit themselves to live with a man, they must leave their houses and become part of the houses of their husbands. Even when a woman is not married by church or civil law to her husband, the pattern of patrilocal residence and patriarchal authority still applies, though being married by neither law or only by civil law does make a woman feel freer to break out of the arrangement when it becomes too oppressive. Esperanza's mother was married only by civil law to her husband, and it was the realization that she was not bound by "church books" to tolerate her husband's cruelty that made it thinkable for her to leave him. Yet her mother is acutely aware that the law is patriarchal, that it is the law of the fathers, and she says that even if no law protects her, she will leave.

But even before Esperanza's mother leaves her father, she resists being under his control by holding back food from him while making sure that her children are fed by her own efforts. Esperanza's father tries to prevent her mother from working at other people's houses, accusing her of crying about her problems to her neighbors, but quite probably ashamed that he cannot properly support her and his children. She secretly grinds corn and makes beautifully formed tortillas that Esperanza, the young daughter, marvels at. This childhood story reveals the way in which Esperanza, like other children of the working class, learns about the contradictions of the power of patriarchal law when it is embodied in fathers who are themselves at the bottom of the social heap. The "master of the house," it turns out, is not much of a master anywhere else. When children witness the disjuncture between social and domestic power, they gain critical tools for taking apart the very terms of gender hierarchies that are inextricably embedded in class hierarchies; and so they learn, as did Esperanza, about "men making circumstances and women remaking them, about men earning more money than women, about men being meant to keep their children, but women doing it, in fact, about how a social world is set up."[9]

After leaving her husband, Esperanza's mother works for her comadre in Mexquitic. This pattern of local patronage and class relationships, now much less frequent, is interpreted by Esperanza in terms of the greater kindness and largess of people in the past. Her mother not only worked for others, however; she also raised sheep and goats, which she brought with her to her husband's house, and she had a garden. These things are the products of her labor and rightfully belong to her, as she states in court. And when she leaves her husband, she also demands and gets back those ancient kitchen tools so intimately associated with rural women's domain in Mexico, her *metate*, her grinding stone, and her *molcajete*, her mortar and pestle, both of which she had inherited from her own mother.

Work outside the home is presented as an important source of personal strength for women. Esperanza views her adolescent years in San Luis Potosí from 1940 to 1948 as a time of immense personal freedom from male domination, a moment of independence and self-sufficiency. While I had expected her to focus in greater detail upon social exploitation, Esperanza instead highlights the way in which she freely moved

from job to job, always seeking the best possible pay and working conditions. For her, working hard as a domestic servant and cafeteria attendant did not even come close to matching the brutal exploitation
and violence she experienced as a married woman.

›››

The construction of female sexuality as being in need of vigilant
control appears early in the narrative in the father's taunting of his
daughters for being "pimps" for their mother. Later, after Esperanza's
mother leaves her father, her grandmother tells her that her mother
left him because she likes pleasure and wants to be a woman of the
street. Ethnographers have often noted the contrast between house and
street in rural Mexican towns. For a woman to be of the street rather
than of the house signifies that she is out of the bounds of patriarchal
control, and she ceases to be a *mujer de respeto*, a respectable woman.
The respectable woman is construed as the opposite of *la mujer del
gusto*, a woman who likes pleasure, that is, sex. It is not only men
who level at women the accusation that they are mujeres del gusto,
but women level the same accusation at other women. The accusation
is one of the best put-downs in a society where church teachings and
the dominant gender ideology make women feel that they are not supposed to admit they get any pleasure from sex. In fact, many women
do have relationships with more than one man, often in a serial pattern, and it is not unusual for older women to have relationships with
younger men. It seems clear that many women are not content to leave
their sexuality safely confined to the house. But those women who become publicly known as mujeres del gusto pay a price: they lose status
and respectability and become associated with the lower working class
in the local social hierarchy. Such women are viewed as *locas*; they
are "crazy women" because they flaunt their bodies and their desire
openly.

In Esperanza's account, it is possible to see the ways in which as a
young girl she was socialized to accept certain gender and sexual ideologies. An important sexual story is the account of how Esperanza's
father hung her, exposing her buttocks, an act which she describes as
shameful and indecent, almost a kind of rape. Once she is at her mother's house, Esperanza, still a young girl, is told, "Don't be falling now."

The reminder to the young girl that there is a sexual woman inside her, who must hold back her desire, is made explicitly, in an angry voice by the father, in the cautious warning by the mother.

Abduction does away with the pretense (for Julio) of seduction or courtship. In telling the story of how Julio "bothered" her so much that she finally had to agree to stay with him, Esperanza also reminds herself, over and over, that she could have run off, that there were possibilities for resistance which she ultimately did not pursue. And yet she really didn't have a choice. Esperanza was concerned, for good reason, with her reputation, which she knew would be compromised if word got around that she had spent a night with Julio. She refused to say exactly what transpired between them, despite my vulgar efforts to elicit such detail; but it seems that she came very close to having sex with Julio, close enough that she felt there was no longer any turning back. But the point is that it didn't matter whether anything had happened; just the fact that she was out with Julio at an indecent hour was a powerful symbolic statement.

Julio promised to do his "duty by her," that is, to marry her, so she could maintain her status as a respectable woman. However, the respect she thereby earned was partial. In the eyes of the priest who lived in Mexquitic at the time, she was *robada*, "robbed," rather than *pedida*, "asked for," because Julio did not go through the formal process of discussing the marriage with her mother before approaching Esperanza. Such concepts continue to be important; the respectable girls are always pedida, while those who become pregnant out of wedlock are said to *fracasar*, literally "to fail," or "mess up," conveying the social failure of a woman whose sexuality is out of the bounds of patriarchal control.

When her mother found Esperanza in the courtyard of Julio's house, she refused to say anything more to her than, "Get away! Shameless!" Her mother took both Esperanza and Julio to the town court, which is a common course of action when a woman has left the parental house without consent. By filing a charge, Esperanza's mother was publicly proclaiming that her daughter's virginity had been tampered with and that it was Julio's responsibility to offer some kind of compensation to her. Patriarchal law exists within a framework of ownership and possession, in which women are objects of exchange. But what has not always been seen is that women are also subjects who are conscious of themselves as the things being exchanged; insofar as they are subjects, they also own something, "even if it is only their labor, and the babies they produce."[10] Esperanza was, however, a relatively helpless subject in her early years as a young (virgin) girl, and her agency and oppositionality within patriarchy were so limited as to be almost nonexistent. By taunting Julio to be a "real man" and marry her daughter immediately, Esperanza's mother sought to redress the disgrace of her daughter's loss of honor, so as not to give her daughter away too cheaply, not give her away for nothing. Her mother, in representing the interests of patriarchy, defined herself as a subject at the cost of objectifying her daughter, of putting a price on her.

Seeking to confer on Esperanza the kind of respectability that she herself had lost leaving her own husband, Esperanza's mother, ironically, pushed her daughter into a marriage that Esperanza had grave doubts about. In the weeks of preparation for the wedding, a townswoman fitted Esperanza for her white wedding dress. Later Esperanza was to recall the seamstress's prophetic words: "'So you're getting married, young woman?' 'Yes.' 'Good, but be careful,' she says. 'A white wedding dress is very beautiful but also very punishing.'" These words about the wedding dress become the frame from which Esperanza looks back at her marriage. They are powerful words that suggest the critical distance with which mature rural women approach a key sacrament of patriarchal church law.

In her narrative, Esperanza plays on this image of marriage as incarceration, as a cross to be borne, and as a darkness from which she was not able to see the light of day until her emergence into freedom sixteen years later. Her story is built on the contrast between her cloistered life during marriage (a constricting female space) and her later life as a working woman and fully public person (who, as in her adolescent years, is again self-sufficient and independent). A week after her wedding, the reality of her bondage, of being cut off from the world of her mother, her family, and her woman friends, is brought home to her by her mother-in-law. Just as her own mother upheld a social-religious order based on patriarchal domination that had exerted its violence against her, so, too, her mother-in-law turned out to be as brutal as, or more brutal than, Julio in her reinforcement of the idea that women should be subordinate to their husbands in marriage. Even to peek out the door, Esperanza learned early on, was a transgression.

›››

In 1950, a year after marrying, Esperanza had her first child, a daughter, who lived for only nine months. The child died, Esperanza said, because she had suffered a *coraje*, a very deep anger or rage, after finding Julio with another woman by the riverbanks. Julio had also begun, by this time, to beat her often, terrorizing her and thereby preventing the questioning of his dominance and authority. Esperanza became a battered woman, isolated, afraid, intimidated. While he was continually unfaithful—ending up in jail six times for dishonoring different young women—he accused her, constantly, of having lovers. After her first child died, she learned from a healer that the child had sucked her anger in with the milk; the anger pent up within her had poisoned her milk, causing her child's death.

The death of one child after another, six in total, while she was Julio's wife undermined her sense of herself as a mother. As Esperanza put it, she was never without corajes, she suffered from one continual coraje, a deep welling up of rage that killed the children she gave life to. This coraje was not simply an emotional state but an illness state that forms part of Mexican women's realm of suffering and healing.[11] Esperanza enters this realm in the course of talking about the loss of her children with the local midwife and curandera. But in her narrative, coraje is more than an illness state; it becomes a central metaphor for reflecting upon her condition as a woman under patriarchy. Coraje expresses Esperanza's sense of the wrongness of the violence inscribed on her body in the name of patriarchal law. It is her own body that has been history to her, and it is this body that must be healed by being rehistoricized in the magical space of the Pancho Villa cult.

›››

The years of her marriage—with its violence, its rage, its toil—are described in great detail in Esperanza's narrative. Clearly, however, a key turning-point in Esperanza's life story is the moment when she finds Julio in San Luis with the woman he would eventually bring to his mother's house as his wife, usurping her place in his household. Here, as earlier in the story, Esperanza is in the position of voyeur,

watching her husband flirting or interacting with another woman, as
he acts out the sexual freedom that is denied her.

A subtle linguistic shift takes place in her story when she finds Julio
with his mistress, which is impossible to render in the English translation. In Spanish, however, she ceases to refer to Julio as *usted*, the
formal you, and now begins to call him *tú*, the informal you, used to
speak to equals, children, and people of inferior rank.[12] The formal you
is always used by rural Mexicans in relationships of respect and deference; that is the way children should address their parents, younger
siblings their older siblings, wives their husbands (particularly of Esperanza's generation), and comadres their comadres. It is significant
that Esperanza recalls saying to Julio at this point in her story that she
had until then respected him more than her own father. Her realization that he no longer merits this kind of verbal respect begins the process of her questioning of patriarchal domination and her effort to release herself from the names written on her back by the violent hands
of the fathers.

Esperanza had already begun to see the tables turning before this incident, when a village man threatened to have Julio sent to a stricter
jail in San Luis for molesting his daughter. But she had not expressed
her welled-up rage until she inflicted pain on the unmarried urban
woman of pearls and permed hair (symbols of her non-Indianness), the
woman who had won Julio's affection. This was the conversion experience that in her narrative turns her into a fighting woman, a myth of a
woman, powerful enough to be viewed as a witch who blinds the man
who betrayed and humiliated her. And yet, sadly but not surprisingly,
she rebels by beating up another woman as she herself was beaten by
Julio—as though it is ultimately the woman, rather than Julio, who
is to blame for his adultery. Here, in her account, another chapter of
her life begins in which, forced to work and earn money to support
her family, she recovers the independence and autonomy of her
adolescence.

Naturally, this is Esperanza's story, told from her perspective, and it
is our sympathy toward her plight that she seeks to garner through the
telling of her story. Yet because Esperanza is so skilled at constructing
her story in terms of dialogue, one also learns as much about Julio's
plight as about hers. Clearly, we are not expected to feel any sympathy
for him, but Esperanza's recollection of how his own mother taunted

him continually about being a kept man—"*atenido, mantenido*"—because she supported him and his family, suggests how difficult Julio's
position must have been as well. These constant affronts to his masculinity, with their implication that he was not "man enough" to be an
adequate provider, suggest that Julio's womanizing needs to be seen
not as a stereotypical form of machismo, but in social and economic
terms as a desperate effort to "own women" because he could own
nothing else. While his womanizing is a source of pain to Esperanza,
that alone is not the basis of his inadequacy as a father and husband;
after all, as she well knows, many men have been unfaithful to their
wives. It is his inability to provide for his family that is his key failing as a father. And his key failing as a husband is not simply that he
beat Esperanza, but that he beat her in cruel and exaggerated ways that
were an abuse of patriarchal power. Both Esperanza and Julio, then, can
be seen to be trapped by the roles of the dominant gender ideology. But
since this is Esperanza's story, it is only she who we see subjectively
challenging this ideology in the moments when it is most harshly op-
pressing her.

After catching Julio with his mistress, Esperanza briefly returns to
her mother-in-law's house to wait for her last child by Julio to die from
the coraje that she knows will afflict him. Here Esperanza is explicit,
not only about the pain inflicted on her by her former husband, but
by her mother-in-law as well. With irony, she recalls the lies that her
mother-in-law told about her, covering up for her son by telling townspeople that Esperanza's last pregnancy was "baggage" she had brought
back from her selling trips to the city.

One gets a sense of a women's world of talk and secrets in this part
of her narrative, as Esperanza reconstructs both the gossip that her
mother-in-law circulated about her and the way in which she herself
found out about the gossip and finally turned it to her advantage. Esperanza shows herself gaining the power to talk back to her mother-in-
law, just as she gained the power to talk back, and talk down, to Julio.
She is able to use the connections made with city people like Rosita
the lawyer while she was employed as a domestic servant to further
her aims, even as her mother-in-law tries to undermine these connections by reducing them to a sexual outing. In her narrative, Esperanza
masterfully inverts her initial position as the powerless young married
woman peeking out the door, telling how the last time she stood at the

same door, as she prepared to leave the house forever, she did not move out of the way for her mother-in-law.

Shortly before their child died, Julio returned with the new woman and sent a message to his mother that she should get rid of Esperanza. But his mother never got a chance to do that. A week after her child's death, Esperanza went to court in Mexquitic demanding that she be given her husband's plot of ejido land. This was land that had been expropriated from a nearby hacienda after the Mexican Revolution and redistributed to the people of Mexquitic. The fields in the ejido are worked by individual families as their own, but ultimate title to the land resides in the state, which has the authority to take plots away from those who do not work them. Esperanza had legitimate rights to the field because Julio had been away from the town for two years. As his wife, Esperanza could lay claim to it; when patriarchal law is at its kindest, a wife is worth whatever her husband is worth. But few women in her position would have gotten up the nerve and the resources to fight to take the land away. Esperanza, however, had her mother as a role model, here as in other earlier cases of defense of her interests before the law. It is striking how often mother and daughter used the law to their advantage even while feeling that "no law" could help them.

Esperanza viewed the land as owing to her for her years of labor and suffering in her husband's house. Having worked and earned money as a young woman and begun to work again after leaving Julio, she had a keen sense of the value of things. The land was the price of her rage. Having taken away this major source of livelihood from her husband and mother-in-law, Esperanza returned to her mother's house with her two young sons, returning to the maternal domain just as her mother before her had done.

The mirroring of mother and daughter receives another elaboration in this part of her narrative. Esperanza remarks: "Because we took the plot away from my mother-in-law, that was when she placed the illness, the evil way, on my mother." It was Esperanza's mother who helped Esperanza to raise herself up, paying to have her field cleared and then sown with corn. Out of spite and envy, Esperanza thinks, her mother-in-law ensorcelled her mother, causing her to be ill for seven years. With the pain of her own body, her mother paid for her daughter's actions. Yet it was through this long illness, and the unrelenting quest for a cure, that Esperanza became acquainted with Chencha, then a young girl of fourteen, who would become Esperanza's guide and oracle in her struggle with evil.

During the long period of her mother's illness, Esperanza began to work as a peddler. She considered it embarrassing to sell in the town where people knew her and decided to sell in San Luis instead. Eventually she found her path: to be a *marchanta*, peddling flowers and vegetables door to door. In the city, where no one knew her past, she could become another person, a friendly and engaging "India María" figure catering to middle-class housewives. Her ability to sell and earn her own money gave her confidence, and Esperanza now makes a decent living as a self-employed marketing woman on the margins of the capitalist economy, surviving independently of a husband.

› › ›

Three years after leaving Julio's house, Esperanza began a relationship with a man ten years younger than she. Consciously, it seems to me, she decided she would no longer be anybody's woman nor anyone's wife. Selecting as her lover a much younger man was already a strong statement of her growing freedom to let desire come before duty. She chose not to live with her lover, the guard Jorge, but she did have three children with him. As she puts it, "I wasn't washing his clothes," and so she neither expected her lover to be loyal to her nor to support her. Nor, in turn, did she feel she had to mourn at his grave.

In telling her story of her relationship with Jorge, a story which remains half-told, Esperanza suggests that she might have saved face and stayed with her husband. Part of the price of being respectable is that you cover up for your husband and swallow your pride, something that Esperanza clearly refused to do. She is a proud woman, an arrogant woman, *una vieja orgullosa*, and it is precisely that pride and that arrogance that many of her women neighbors find unpardonable, a pride and an arrogance that, for a time, even alienated her own mother.

Esperanza's pride flies in the face of the low status to which she descends after ceasing to be under the control of a husband. As soon as the word got out that Esperanza was pregnant out of wedlock, her mother-in-law began to go out with Julio's new woman, introducing her to everyone as a godchild. Then Julio's children with the new woman began to be seen in the street. The eldest child, while out buying beans one day, announced that his father never went out anymore because he was blind. Esperanza's mother-in-law spread the rumor that Esperanza and her mother had bewitched him. Subsequent events seemed to prove the rumor true. Soon after her mother-in-law's death, Julio's new woman took all of her children and packed everything in the house into her brother's pick-up truck, leaving Julio. Thus, in the spiritual economy of Esperanza's narrative, which is based on the idea that "one pays for everything in this world" (*todo se paga en este mundo*), Julio pays for his arrogant abuse of patriarchal power by turning into a weak, pathetic, castrated figure.[13] Esperanza awakens to an intensified seeing, while he retreats into further darkness and dependence.

Aware of the rumor that she bewitched Julio and made him blind, Esperanza shrugs her shoulders and says that only God has such powers, and that Julio's blindness was a payment exacted by the divine for the sufferings he caused her. She certainly feels no remorse or pity for him, which further fuels the rumor that she must be a witch. Or at least a woman with a heart of stone.

›››

When Esperanza's customers—to whom Esperanza was also in the habit of telling a compressed version of her life story—would ask her why she didn't find another man and marry again, she would reply, "'No, what do I want men for now? I just beg God to give me a daughter. Because what will I do alone with two sons? They will grow up. Sons grow up. I distrust my sons. Because men are men. What will I do alone with them?'" Then turning to me, she added, "With your pardon, comadre, as the saying goes, doesn't the devil have horns?" Esperanza never does explain outright what this expression means, but in stating the obvious—that, of course, the devil has horns—she seemed to be alluding to another fact that is equally obvious to her: that you cannot trust men sexually, not even your own sons once they're grown up. Thus she was happy, she says, when God gave her two daughters.

Within Esperanza's gender ideology, all men, including one's own sons once they come of age, are subject to animal desires for sex. The main story Esperanza tells in support of this gender ideology concerns her eldest son, Macario, who tried to molest her eldest daughter, his half-sister, while Esperanza was away from the house selling. Again she experiences a welling up of rage as she comes to realize that her son, like his father, belongs to the male realm and therefore is beyond her control; as a woman, she was no less vulnerable than her daughter to being raped by her son. It is significant that Simeón warns his mother that to report Macario's crime would only endanger Gabriela's reputation, not Macario's; in the end, within a system of patriarchal law, women are always responsible for being abducted or raped.

If women's sexuality needs to be controlled because women cannot control it themselves, men's need for sex is insatiable and so they are "like animals in that they seek their own satisfaction and are not concerned with the needs of others." [14] Esperanza's narrative shows how women frequently take the male perspective on their own and other women's sexuality when blaming themselves or trying to slander another woman. Restraint and self-righteousness is exercised by women about their own sexuality. It's the women who fall, *fracasar*, but they fall from a pedestal of self-control that is always, in part, of their own construction. A keen example is the way Esperanza suspects that her daughter may not have been totally innocent in the attack by her half-brother. To be sure that her daughter knows that ultimately *she* is going to be at fault if she "falls," Esperanza beats her for good measure.

In Esperanza's narrative, Macario comes to seem more and more like his father: cruel, deceptive, obsessed with sex. As if chasing his half-sister had not been ugly enough, he then moved on to a relationship with his own uncle's former mistress, Esperanza's sister-in-law. For Esperanza this was a disgusting act of incest, but she could not convince Macario to leave the woman. Esperanza later learned from Chencha that the woman got control of Macario by force, the force of evil, putting magic powders in some guavas she gave him to eat. Since Macario's actions, from Esperanza's perspective, represent an irrational decline into animality, they only make sense to her if they are viewed within a context of witchcraft. The story about the pig in the stream, which culminates in Chencha's curing Esperanza's field of the spell that had been placed on it, is a story, ultimately, about Macario, the rejected son. There is something unfinished in her relation with Macario, and she must continue to wage a cosmological battle, with her life and her money, to push it closer to some sort of resolution.

After leaving his mother's house, Macario rejoined his father, taking up with the prohibited woman in spite of Esperanza's rage. Feeling betrayed as a mother, Esperanza disowned Macario, refusing in her usual way to submit to patriarchal notions of the all-forgiving martyred mother. She speaks to neither the evil son nor the evil father, though all live in the same small town. She says she feels rage against them both and will forgive neither.

In 1988 Esperanza told the story of her recent conflict with her second son, Simeón, and her daughter-in-law, Carmela, who had lived in her house for seven years. Esperanza ends up throwing Simeón out of the house just as several years before she had thrown Macario out, and she does so because both sons, in different ways, have insulted and mistreated the women of the house. Both sons, indeed, grow up to be men, betraying their mother by not respecting her authority as head of the family. Esperanza's alliance with her mother rather than with Simeón again reveals a mother/daughter mirroring. Yet Simeón's impolite treatment of his grandmother fuels a family conflict that ultimately has negative consequences for Esperanza, whose own position as a hanger-on in her mother's house has long been a source of tension with her siblings.

This conflict shows Esperanza in her role as mother-in-law to Carmela. When it is Esperanza's turn to be in the authoritative role, she, like her mother-in-law before her, takes the male perspective and advises Simeón to do a better job of disciplining his wife. After Simeón and Carmela left her house, Esperanza did not speak to them for several months, but then Simeón began to visit her again and she accepted him back. Carmela, however, has not set foot in Esperanza's house again, nor has she invited Esperanza to her house. Given her sense of hierarchy and respect, Esperanza feels it is her daughter-in-law who must apologize to her, and so she has not made any effort to seek a reconciliation with Carmela.

When Carmela and Simeón were married in a collective church ceremony in the fall of 1990, Esperanza had hoped that Carmela would make peace with her during the mass. However, Carmela did not do so, and after the mass was over she did not personally invite Esperanza to her wedding party. Although Esperanza did not admit it, she clearly hoped to be invited to the party. Moreover, she hoped to form part, with the godparents, of *la primera mesa*, that is, the first table to be served, the table of honor. She had dressed up for the mass, donning a silk blouse I had given her and black patent leather high-heeled shoes.

Only in the evening, after most of the guests had left, did Simeón go by her house to invite her to eat mole; she refused to go, saying she was not about to go help him scrape the pot.

There is also continuing enmity between the two brothers, Macario and Simeón, because of the way in which Macario took advantage of Simeón's labor and money to build his house. The two brothers now live next to each other as neighbors on the upper and lower part of the same hill, but they have nothing to do with one another and have not exchanged a word in years.

›››

Understanding that her sons would become men, Esperanza longed for daughters. All her daughters by Julio had died young, and entering into a relationship with Jorge was a conscious move on her part to try to conceive the daughters she wanted. Yet with her daughters, Esperanza has a sense of profound inner struggle, and feels an intense need to keep them to the straight and narrow. Her advice resonates with the tradition of the advice Nahuatl fathers gave to their daughters, but it springs from her own hard experience. She doesn't want her daughters to go through what she has—and that is why she relentlessly pounds into their hearts and minds the story of her life—but she knows that they will. As she puts it, again in the language of a spiritual economy, "One as a mother has to pay for what one did with one's own children. Since I had my failures with another man, one of them will have to do the same." Esperanza knows that she is a fallen woman, a woman who has *fracasado en la vida*, and though she realizes that one of her daughters will very likely reproduce her life as she reproduced her mother's life (her mother, too, had children out of wedlock), she still struggles to beat sense—and an awareness of being tied to her, of the matrilineal bond—into her daughters.

When her eldest daughter, Gabriela, then working as a domestic servant in San Luis, refused to support her, saying "Why should I give you money?" Esperanza decided it was necessary to teach her a lesson. There is a contradictory quality to the words that Esperanza chooses to accompany the beating she gives Gabriela. I have tried to understand these actions in the light of Esperanza's notions of a sexual economy. She scolds her daughter because part of the bargain between them is that her daughter must retain her value by not putting herself into circulation sexually. While Esperanza knows that she must "pay" for her sexual "failing" by seeing one of her daughters repeat her experience, she still wants to prevent this fate from unfolding by keeping her daughter within her control. Having been the provider, Esperanza also wants an economic return from her daughter. This system of exchange is part of a matrilineal economy, in which money flows through the uterine rather than the paternal line. Money has a metaphysical value as a way of showing that there is a bond between women from one generation to the next, a bond that exists outside, and in spite of, paternal control. When her daughter threatened to break this bond, Esperanza felt she had to beat Gabriela so she wouldn't forget that she, like Esperanza herself, was born of the inscription of pain on her mother's body.

› › ›

Esperanza's beating of her daughter also encodes her effort to carry into practice her own complex and contradictory gender identity. Esperanza has a keen sense of her gender blending, of how she has had to be father and mother, economic provider and nurturer, upholder of the social-religious order, and a mirror in which her daughters can read a past that threatens to become their future. "All those years, I have been both man and woman to them, supporting them, helping them grow up. . . . How many women are there in Mexquitic who use the hoe, the pick? They have their men, their husbands who support them, suffering some corajes, perhaps, but supported by their husbands. And me, what man do I have?"

One sees both Esperanza's pride in pulling off each role and her ambivalence about being a woman who has taken on male roles. I read in Esperanza's narrative a desire to be a macha—a woman who won't be beaten, won't forgive, won't give up her rage. A macha, too, in the sense of wanting to harness a certain male fearlessness to meet evil and danger head on. It is this macha quality that fascinates her about Chencha, who flaunts her manliness as the supermacho revolutionary hero Pancho Villa in the theater of spiritism. Feeling that she, too, is not fully a woman in the socially conventional ways, Esperanza found in Chencha a powerful interlocutor with whom she could identify, and she found in Chencha's spiritism sessions a safe place to act out her ambiguous gender identity.

It may be that Esperanza chose me to hear her story because I, too, by being in command of the tape recorder and the writing, with all the power that signified, was something other than "just a woman." Her half-joking questions to David about whether he gave his permission for me to talk to her, especially when we got onto raunchy subjects, suggest that she saw me as being in command of my relationship with David. She was continually amazed at the way David did so much of the child care, but secretly glad, I think, that I had the freedom to come and go with her on peddling trips and visits to Chencha's spiritist centro. While my relationship with David certainly seemed to her to be an odd gringoesque reversal of male and female roles, Esperanza nevertheless seemed pleased that I, like her, was not at the mercy of a husband and not ashamed to act independently of him.

Esperanza's sense of having been betrayed and mistreated by all the men with whom she has been on intimate terms—her father, her husband, her sons, and, to an extent, her lover—has led her to create and reinforce ties to other women—her mother, her daughters, her clients, Chencha, and even me, her gringa comadre. Although her relationships with men form a major part of her narrative, her points of reference are always women-centered. She begins her narrative by comparing herself with her sister, who started out, like her, as a maid, but who, unlike her, never married, never had children, becoming a sour woman who dislikes Esperanza's wild laugh, who envies the way she refuses to be embittered despite the hard times she has been through. The narrative progressively asserts a triangular structure, creating a plot between mother, daughter, and the daughter's daughters, in which Esperanza speaks with two voices, that of mother and daughter.[15] The male world increasingly retreats into the background of Esperanza's narrative. As Esperanza repeats several times so I am sure to hear it, the plot of heterosexual romance is not a part of her story. She sees "romance" for what it is—a construction. When I tactlessly ask point blank, Esperanza says it loud and clear: sex is not anything she misses; she doesn't need a man to keep her warm in bed.

And yet there are ironies in the way Esperanza has tried to establish and reinforce solidarity among the women of her family while construing the relationships between them in terms of the lurking danger of becoming fallen women, of succumbing to the maternal curse of *el fracasó*. She has developed a critique of compulsory heterosexuality and, at the same time, expects the norm to be reproduced by her daughters. Outside the circle of her family, Esperanza is highly suspicious of her women neighbors—it is the other women in town, the serpents with their wagging tongues, whose criticism of her work with me she most fears. Esperanza may be a refugee from the male bosom, but she doesn't feel totally nurtured by the female bosom, either.

›››

In *The Woman Warrior*, Maxine Hong Kingston writes that her mother told her she would grow up to be a wife and a slave, "but she taught me the song of the warrior woman, Fa Mu Lan. I would have to grow up a warrior woman."[16] The mother passes on to the daughter the rules of patriarchy, rules she must obey; but the mother also passes on, concealed behind the mask of fantasy, the tools for resisting that patriarchy, tools the daughter may use, but at her own risk. The daughter eventually realizes that, despite what her mother says, there's more glory in being the woman who jumbles up the rules of patriarchy than in being the woman who quietly submits. But there's a hitch: the fantasy of being a woman warrior does not translate very well into "real life."

From the first time I heard Esperanza tell her story, I thought of her as a woman warrior. I was attracted to the image of the tough woman who had struggled to define herself in opposition to the way society would define her. But I was also repelled by, and more than a little afraid of, the woman who had tried to advance her female cause by appropriating characteristics culturally ascribed to men, even to the point of beating her own daughter and women rivals. Although I could render her attitudes and actions intelligible, how far could I go in celebrating them as models of feminist resistance and agency?

Images of such valiant fighting women as the Amazons, the Warrior Queens, Cihuacóatl (the Aztec Snake Woman), the Mexican *soldaderas*, and Nicaraguan female revolutionaries exert their hold on feminist imaginations.[17] Images of battle, warfare, minefields, can(n)ons—the revision of the various canons of knowledge, in which feminists have been actively involved—suffuse the feminist effort to restore active agency to women in the past and the present and across cultures. But does the Warrior Woman exist at the expense of the Peace Woman?[18] Shouldn't feminists cease perpetuating the warmongering of patriarchal discourse? Or is it hopelessly naive to try engaging with the language and role of the Peace Woman when oppressive gender systems continue to limit and distort what women and men might be?

I could try to reimagine Esperanza as the Peace Woman. But what to make, then, of her search for redemption through a spiritist practice that centers upon the resolutely male warrior figure of Pancho Villa? Rage poisoned her breastmilk and turned her into a woman so fierce she is feared for her witchcraft powers. Witches have been celebrated in radical feminist thought for "resisting patriarchy and the rationality through which it exercises its power."[19] But what kind of heroine is Esperanza, this woman who both values and denigrates relationships with other women? No, I don't see any way of turning her into a Peace Woman or, for that matter, a Nice Witch; she will be a Woman Warrior to the end. I picture Esperanza hearing all this and laughing hysterically. *Comadre, por favor, no se ría! Es para que entiendan las gringas, comadre* (Comadre, please don't laugh! It's so the gringas will understand, comadre).

Ultimately, Esperanza's transgressions against patriarchal ideology are tied up in paradoxes. That she appropriates culturally male values that oppress her as well as other women in order to liberate and redeem herself is contradictory. Her violence toward other women, and ultimately toward herself, is problematic. Her fascination with Pancho Villa, in light of her experience with male domination, is ironic. Of course, the question remains: From whose perspective, whose absolute scale of feminist perfection, are her attitudes and actions being measured?

Her critique of, and struggle against, the dominant gender ideology, like any such critique, any such struggle, is necessarily ambiguous. To paraphrase a Billie Holiday song, "She's no hero out of books."[20] But Esperanza's struggle to define herself, through gender and in spite of gender, ambiguously gendered rather than passively gendered, points the way to the possibility of true gender transformation. So does her struggle to make herself whole, to be self and other, "woman" and "man," in the face of the metonymic misrepresentation that would reduce her to the insignificant partness of being only a subjugated female.[21] Finally, her willingness to try to define herself for my sake, a woman from across the border, enacts something fundamental about feminism as a commitment among women to speak to each other about their differences as women, if for nothing else than to find themselves in translation.

› › ›

One of the limitations of North American feminism has been its narrow definition of the kind of knowledge and practice that can be counted as feminist. Can I not speak of Esperanza as engaging in feminist thinking and practice in the way I have? As Lynne Phillips would reply, to move toward an acceptance of many feminisms "means giving up our power to define what feminism is."[22] And that, it turns out, has been far from easy for North American feminists to do. Commenting on the way in which the creative and critical writing by women of color collected in *This Bridge Called My Back* has been superficially cited by white feminists but not seriously engaged with, Norma Alarcón wryly notes, "Difference is handed over with one hand and taken away with the other."[23]

These issues become more heated when considering the many uncertainties that now hang over the entire project of feminist ethnography and life history studies. No one is quite sure anymore of how to reconcile feminist politics of social transformation and international sisterhood with a research practice in which relatively privileged academic women seek out, record, and publish the edited voices of relatively underprivileged women from somewhere else in the name of a feminism to be borne across the border. Working to put feminist principles that challenge neutrality and objectivity into practice, feminist ethnographers have found themselves caught inside webs of betrayal they themselves have spun; with stark clarity, they realize that they are seeking out intimacy and friendship with subjects on whose backs, ultimately, the books will be written upon which their productivity as scholars in the academic marketplace will be assessed.[24]

The feminist ethnographer is a dual citizen, who shuttles between the country of the academy and the country of feminism. She's an odd kind of bilingual woman. To her subjects she speaks in a tongue bristling with seductive promises that she will not be able to keep. To her colleagues, she must speak in a way that will persuade them that "working on" another woman is a contribution to the discipline she has vowed to serve; they will ultimately judge her work on the basis of how well she can translate the other woman's tongue into a language

they can understand. While the academy makes her work possible, it
also thrusts her into the contradiction of having to use the discourse of
feminism against herself and her subjects. Under these circumstances,
how do you remain in the academy without becoming a sell-out, a
Malinche to feminism? [25]

› › ›

It was that very sense of dissonance at being a bilingual woman
having to negotiate the languages of feminist solidarity and academic
affiliation, among other languages, that led me to seek a fiercer connection between Esperanza's engendering of herself and who I am, or
rather, who I have become in the years since my certification as an anthropologist. And one of the things I have become is a professor, more
exactly, a Woman professor, which is not exactly the same thing as a
Professor. One reason the feminist ethnographer cannot caress the
hand of the academy too lovingly is because, no matter how decon-
structive her feminism may be, within the profession of anthropology
she is, and remains, a woman.

There is a subtle slip, which feminist critics seem to have missed, in
the now infamous introduction James Clifford wrote for the volume
Writing Culture that I find very revealing of how women's writings
occupy an ambiguous place in the history of anthropology. In the very
first paragraph of his introduction, where Clifford discusses the cover
photograph of the book showing a male ethnographer and contribu-
tor to the volume at work on his writing, he comments: "It is not the
usual portrait of anthropological fieldwork. We are more accustomed
to pictures of Margaret Mead exuberantly playing with children in Ma-
nus or questioning villagers in Bali." [26] As I say, this is a slip. Anyone
who knows the work of Margaret Mead knows that she was an incred-
ibly prolific writer who outwrote her male colleagues and used her pen
to explore genres ranging from ethnography to social criticism to autobiography. But the slip attests to the fact that it is the image of the
woman ethnographer as the one who plays with the children and questions the villagers, not the one who writes the texts, that lives on, despite the conception of anthropology as a profession that is especially
receptive to the contributions of women. Having spent several years
thinking about the meaning of male dominance in a Mexican woman's

life, I find it sobering to consider the ways in which the profession that has made it possible for me to study this question is itself entrenched in a quiet pattern of male dominance that speaks with its silences.

It is, of course, easy to scapegoat Clifford and his colleagues for their oversights and to cast the blame on them for what is really a much larger epistemological failing within the discipline itself. When you train as an anthropologist, you are not encouraged to think about the genderedness of the texts you read or the texts you will write, nor are you encouraged to see their embeddedness in racial and class contexts. You take "core courses," which teach you how to recognize and produce a compelling theoretical argument, in which you primarily read Euro-American male thinkers.[27] You mainly read women anthropologists for their critiques of androcentrism, and you mainly read anthropology or cultural criticism by people of color for their particular accounts of local places, or at best, as grist for your already grinding theoretical mill. You don't read either for "high theory," the sort of understandings that are supposed to be of such translocal importance that they can serve as grids for work anywhere. The more neutralizing the translation of local accents, the better. Ironic, isn't it? Can this be the discipline whose legitimacy is so wrapped up in foreign languages and worlds?

In reality, anthropology has been a discipline wrapped up in calling a spade by any other name than a spade, especially in regard to "customs" affecting, and often abusing, women. As Rosario Morales says, writing of her experience studying anthropology at Harvard, "We studied concepts of pollution and marriage customs and puberty rites, and no one mentioned rape: the fact of it or the pain of it, of what it means to be a little girl of eight and be married and be raped."[28]

Part of the project of feminist ethnography should be, I think, to question the studiously distant translations of women's lives across borders that have been such standard fare in anthropology. Susan Sontag noted years ago, in an essay about Lévi-Strauss, that "the anthropologist, as a man, is engaged in saving his own soul."[29] The anthropologist, as a woman, can forget about her soul. For me, as a Woman professor engaged in the project of "writing culture" with another woman less privileged than myself, I feel it crucial to challenge how, as a woman, I am scripted into the discipline that gives me permission to script my comadre's translated tongue.[30] To do any less than this, it seems to me, is to become a talking serpent making a revelation that, in the end, does not make any difference.

› › ›

Ay, comadre, so what does all this have to do with those conversations we had in the kitchen with the mint green walls? I imagine you laughing now, gazing at me in amusement, and saying, "Well, if this is what you need to do so they'll understand en el otro lado—well, *ni modo*, it's up to you, but keep me out of it."

When the fiction writer Jamaica Kincaid, a West Indian New Yorker, was asked to talk about her writing process in an interview, she replied that she needed "a great deal of domestic activity to write." And she went on to say, "I know a woman and she comes to see me in the morning and we sit at the kitchen table. We just sit and talk. That's not how I write, but in a way it is. I sit with this woman and we sort of arrange the world. We talk about Bush. We talk about the Russians. We talk about Nicaragua. We talk about the homeless. We sort of settle the day—the world. Then, at about eleven o'clock, I say, 'Well, goodbye,' and I go off to my office—a room at home. And I do whatever I do. . . . If I actually ran the world, I'd do it from the kitchen."[31]

My grandmother, after a long conversation, especially one in which we've argued about politics, as we frequently do, always says, "*Bueno, ya arreglamos el mundo*" (Good, we've solved all the world's problems). So it's a pleasant surprise to hear Jamaica Kincaid say that she settles the day and the world in her kitchen conversations with her woman friend, and then feels ready to do the work called writing. Likewise, this text based on the talk of two comadres in a Mexican kitchen, the talk of two comadres who are as different as night and day, has everything to do with where anthropology and feminism stand in relation to each other right now.

› › ›

In the metatheories of early feminist anthropology, the domestic and public domains were seen as separate female and male domains, and it was assumed that the denial of legitimate authority to women in the public domain as well as their too intimate association with the domestic domain accounted for their lower status and greater power-lessness relative to men.[32] Working within the project of grand social theory that their training had taught them to value, feminist anthropologists in the 1970s sought to offer universally valid explanations for sexism. But by the 1980s, the criticisms made by women of color and lesbian feminists suggested that these metanarratives were mirror reflections of the white, middle-class, heterosexual, professional women who had proposed them. In making claims to universality, these metanarratives unwittingly erased differences among women and made ethnocentric assumptions about what constitutes female fulfillment.[33] So when Jamaica Kincaid says she *needs* domestic activity to *be able* to write, she revalorizes the kitchen as a site of power, where the politics of the public world are discussed, criticized, and, momentarily, settled. She revalorizes it in the face of a North American feminism that would blame the kitchen for women's subjugation and label women who write from the kitchen as not feminist enough to be entitled to the name.

The younger generation of women now working in the 1990s as academic anthropologists have found themselves needing to respond, on the one hand, to the misplaced male criticism of feminist anthropology as not showing enough awareness of the way ethnographic texts get written and, on the other hand, to the displacing criticism women of color and lesbian critics of "the third wave" have directed at all totalizing feminist projects. Feminist *ethnography* has begun to emerge as distinct from feminist *anthropology* in its reflexiveness about the politics of practicing feminism and experimental cultural writing, and in taking as its focus women's relationships to other women.[34]

This feminist ethnography is located on the border between the opposite tendencies to see women as not at all different from one another or as all too different, for to go too far in either direction is to end up *indifferent* to the lives of other women.[35] Against the "increasingly paralyzing anxiety over falling (from what grace?) into ethnocentrism or 'essentialism,'" these newly emerging feminist ethnographers accept the fact that they're already fallen women.[36] They've *fracasado* at the holism of feminism in their desire to defamiliarize Western feminist consciousness of gender, femaleness, oppression.[37] And they've *fracasado* at the holism of anthropology in their desire to keep feminist issues in the books at a time of antifeminist backlash at home.

The ground of feminist ethnography is its blurring of self/other or subject/object divisions that have been the legacy of anthropology as male soul-saving. The sense of dissonance of being a woman "doing" research on another woman is brought to the forefront of the ethnographic process.[38] Indeed, it is vitally necessary for the field of anthropology as a whole to embrace this sense of dissonance. To get beyond the self/other division that has marked Western thinking is the best hope we have for liberating anthropology from the legacy of its links to colonizing domination.[39]

› › ›

Esperanza challenged me continually to articulate the connections between who she is as a visibly invisible Indian street peddler and who I am as an academic woman with a certain measure of power and privilege. Inevitably, if you sit facing another woman at the table for long enough, you start to feel like mirrors for one another. To be sure, Esperanza and I were in many ways exaggerated, distorted mirrors of each other. Yet I think we both came to appreciate, in our own manner and in our own voices, something of our mutual multistrandedness as women, as one translated woman encountering another.

When I began this project, I had no name yet for what I was doing. When I began, I was, like Esperanza, a no-name feminist. That I can now call myself a feminist ethnographer and this book a work of feminist ethnography does not mean, however, that I am "more" of a feminist than Esperanza. If anything I am "less" of a feminist, I who have sought to see the patriarchy in Esperanza's life through the lens of a patriarchal discipline, I who have crossed the border as an employee of a patriarchal academic corporation, I who have been so generously patronized by the inheritances of men who in their lifetimes made enough money to create foundations in their names.

No, there's not a chance of my being a heroine on this side either, comadre.

SIXTEEN

In the Labyrinth of the General and His History

I am a fighter, not a statesman. I am not educated enough to be President. I only learned to read and write two years ago. How could I, who never went to school, hope to be able to talk with the foreign ambassadors and the cultivated gentlemen of the Congress? It would be bad for Mexico if an uneducated man were to be President. . . . The next correspondent that asks me I will have him spanked and sent to the border.

—Pancho Villa, *speaking to John Reed,* Insurgent Mexico

She pervades poetry from cover to cover; she is all but absent from history.

—Virginia Woolf, A Room of One's Own

Condemn me. I don't mind. History will absolve me.

—Fidel Castro, La historia me absolverá

*I come from a long line of eloquent illiterates
whose history reveals what words don't say.*

—Lorna Dee Cervantes, *"Visions of Mexico while at a
Writing Symposium in Port Townsend, Washington,"*
from Emplumada

In the huge shadows cast by all the *caudillos, jefes, generales,* and *coroneles* that have populated the historical reality and literary imagination of Latin America—that was where you had to look to find the women, forgotten and voiceless. But now, at long last, in the new imaginative work of Latina and Latin American feminist writers, the women have begun to emerge from the shadows

303

of those men who seemed bigger than life, and to speak their own truths about those men who lay beside them in their beds.

It is in bed, precisely, that Sandra Cisneros begins her story, "Eyes of Zapata," in which speaks Inés, one mistress among many of the revolutionary hero Emiliano Zapata. Unable to sleep anywhere, "always waiting for the assassin's bullet," *el gran general* Zapata sleeps soundly in the bed of his lover Inés as she watches over him, putting her nose to his eyelashes, which reminds her of the soft skin of his sex (not the phallus of power), and running her eyes over his extravagant general's costume, gun belt, and silver spurs. As she watches Zapata sleep, snoring in her bed, Inés asks herself, "Are you my general? Or only that boy I met at the country fair in San Lazaro?" Night flying through the shadows of time and memory, Inés reflects on the story of her relationship to Zapata and on the nature of war and love. She recalls the stench of the dead and how the bodies hung in the trees, "curling and drying into leather in the sun day after day, dangling like earrings, so that they no longer terrify, they no longer mean anything. Perhaps that is worst of all." And she interrogates the sleeping general with a profoundly feminist question: "Ay, Miliano, don't you see? The wars begin here, in our hearts and in our beds. You have a daughter. How do you want her treated? Like you treated me?"[1]

In *Arráncame la vida*, the Mexican novelist Angeles Mastretta gives voice to Catalina, the wife of a general fifteen years her senior who becomes governor of the state of Puebla but, despite his ambitions, never the president of Mexico. It is Catalina who tells the story of the general's rise and decline, from his early days as a lively-eyed teller of historias, in which he won every battle and destroyed every traitor to the Revolution, to his final bitter days, betrayed by everyone around him, including Catalina, who he knows no longer loves him but another man, *her* lover, who he had a hand in killing. As Catalina takes a final look at the general in his coffin, she tries to find some sweetness in his face, but instead finds "that stiff look he had when he got angry and spent days without talking to me . . . and when even saying good-night would have slowed down the thoughts spinning in his head." She tells herself that, indeed, she's going to be much better off without him, and that now that he's dead she's going to find a smaller house that suits her better, a house by the sea, "where I will rule, and nobody will ask me for anything, nor order me, nor criticize me." Throwing a fistful of dirt into his coffin already in its grave, she suddenly realizes that she can't remember her general's face. "I wanted to feel sadness at not being able to see him again. I couldn't. I felt free. I was afraid."[2]

These powerful evocations of the voices of women speaking from the labyrinth of the general and his history offer a way to think about what women, when allowed to speak, might say about that history, so as to reinsert themselves into his-story and thereby rewrite it as her-story. The generales have never doubted that history would remember them, that history would absolve them. And the women? They have been sitting at the bedside or standing at the gravesite of the general and speaking their truth about his history into his silent ears.

›››

Do I go too far if I suggest that something akin to what Sandra Cisneros and Angeles Mastretta are doing in their written fiction is taking place in the theatrical fiction that Chencha, and followers like Esperanza, enact about Pancho Villa and the Mexican Revolution in the back alley "office" in San Luis Potosí? Actually, I want to go further and suggest that a powerful commentary on women's place—which is the absence of a place—in official Mexican history is embedded in the spectacle of the spiritist representation of Pancho Villa. And then I want to go just a little further yet and suggest that in that extraordinary spectacle where Chencha, the manly woman, acts out the role of the supermacho revolutionary hero, Pancho Villa, both church and nation are turned upsidedown. Gender, history, and healing become the trinity in the mass enacted in Chencha's "office." What is being appropriated, acted upon, and put into question in the spiritism sessions led by Chencha is nothing less than Mexico's revolutionary past and its unfulfilled promise of redemption for those who are still suffering—as represented in the ambiguous hero/antihero figure of Pancho Villa. All this is accomplished, not by means of written texts, which few among Chencha's spiritist followers have access to, but through improvisational and interactive theater.

Immediately I anticipate questions. So why, then, has a group primarily made up of women, led by a woman ambiguously gendered, appropriated the figure of Pancho Villa and made him a key intercessor for them in the spirit world? Where is the history, and more crucially, where is the women's view in all of this? And where, indeed, is the healing here?

The effort to find answers to these questions has inspired the reflections in this chapter. I could not have predicted when I began thinking about this book that to tell the historias of a Mexican street peddler I would ultimately have to find a way of telling the historias of Pancho Villa.

›››

To understand the recovery of the past as spectacle in Chencha's spiritism sessions, I have turned to a recent analysis of the redemptive power of history. In an essay about images of the witch, Sylvia Bovenschen tells us that "the experiential appropriation of the past differs qualitatively from that of the scholar in the archive." Her point of departure is the appropriation of the image of the witch by contemporary women in a demonstration against Italian abortion laws in Rome, in which a hundred thousand women shouted "Tremble, tremble, the witches have returned!" Bovenschen suggests that the appropriation of the witch image for its symbolic potential plays a redemptive role for women, who must continue to engage themselves in the unfinished struggle for liberation from oppressive and anachronistic female roles. Such an experiential appropriation of the past, unlike the historian's appropriation, incorporates "elements of historical and social fantasy which are sensitive to the underground existence of forbidden images; it is anarchical and rebellious in its rejection of chronology and historical accuracy." Yet, paradoxically, it is this sensitivity to forbidden images and this rebelliousness in making a claim on history that opens up the possibility of seizing the past and seeing it fully in its relation to the present and the future. Sylvia Bovenschen goes on to say, adding irony to the cauldron: "The past can still seem so close only because the structures of gender-specific suppression appear to have remained so constant—even if for the moment we are relatively safe from being burned at the stake."[3]

To assume the witch role deliberately, appropriating a negative feminine myth from history's reservoir in the name of resistance and struggle, Bovenschen argues, is a way for women collectively to take over the myth and, by autonomously redefining it, be freed from it. At such a moment, when the past is made relevant to the present and the future, the redemptive power of history for women is unleashed. What is recovered and set free is the underground history, the unincorporated history, or in the words of Michael Taussig, "the magic of history and its healing power."[4]

For Chencha and her followers, the magic of history and its healing power is recovered via the religious imagination rather than through outright demonstrations or militancy in the streets.[5] Yet this religious imagination, sparked by an unconscious at once political and feminist, recognizes and plays upon the construction of official history by the ruling powers as a triumphantly masculine national epic history. The appropriation of Pancho Villa as a protector offers a highly charged reading of history by a feminist unconscious that is able to envision the past, where slumbering male generals lie dead, as still so close because the hero cults of the Mexican state continue to leave women on the margins of the nation. And, from the perspective of a political unconscious, what can be more charged than to venerate, together with God the Father, the Son, and the Virgin Mary, the only revolutionary hero whom the Mexican state has found resolutely difficult to incorporate into its myth of the Revolution?

Resurrecting the image of Pancho Villa evokes, among many other contradictory meanings, the promise of social reform symbolized by the Mexican Revolution begun in 1910, in which one million people lost their lives. This is a promise which, at the end of the twentieth century, has yet to be fulfilled for the rural and working poor in a society where the propertied classes and ruling elite have championed the popular Indian and mestizo classes, but have embraced, in practice, a glaringly uneven capitalist development. A "secret agreement" between past generations and the present one is forged in the refusal to let Pancho Villa be silenced, even in death.[6] To keep him speaking to the living, who are still suffering, is to keep alive the grievances that threaten to unmask, at any time, the duplicity of the Mexican state's institutional appropriation of the Revolution for itself.

› › ›

Yet from both a political and a feminist standpoint, Pancho Villa is an extremely ambiguous figure, and a slippery figure to pin down to any specific set of meanings. From my desk in Ann Arbor, I can locate through my computer the many sources on Pancho Villa available at the University of Michigan library, but whose history do I recover through this process? Of the history I need to recover for my own understanding, how much is implicit as social knowledge and how much is knowledge irrelevant to Chencha, Esperanza, and other participants in the cult? These are difficult questions that are not wholly answered by Bovenschen's analysis.[7] The brief history of Villa that follows is not fully known to all the participants in the cult. Esperanza, for example, knows little more about Villa than that he was a general of great valor during the Revolution. And yet an experiential history of Villa is embedded within the cult, and it is what makes its magic and its healing effective.

Among the ways Villa is remembered, it is his multivocality as a symbol that most stands out. Every Mexican is familiar with the multivocality of the Virgin of Guadalupe, who has served as both a mother figure and a warrior woman—it was around her banner that the early Independence fighters rallied. Like other spirits and saint figures, the meanings attached to Villa are diverse and often contradictory, yet immensely potent. As two American historians recently put it, "When it comes to understanding Pancho Villa, you may have one partial truth, perhaps another; his aura, then and now, exercises the imagination."[8]

Villa, a man associated with the northern frontier of Chihuahua, a region conquered from the Apaches by the expansion of ranching, was the epitome of a crosser of boundaries. His life and deeds placed him on the borderline between Mexico and the United States, and the elusiveness of Villa stems from his place on that boundary edge. Crossing between life and death, image and reality, in Chencha's cult, Pancho Villa lives on as a figure of the border.

As is true of most legendary figures, little is know about Villa's past. At the age of seventeen, according to one popular legend, he left home and went into hiding for having murdered his sister's rapist, a young landowner. In his early manhood, he lived in the wild as a cattle rustler and bandit, and abandoned his name Doroteo Arango for that of Pancho Villa, a bandit of lore.

By the start of the Mexican Revolution in 1910, he shone as a daring officer in the army of Francisco Madero, who overthrew the thirty-four-year dictatorship of Porfirio Díaz and became the first revolutionary president. After the assassination of Madero in 1913 by an opposing faction, Villa became governor of the state of Chihuahua and general of the powerful División del Norte. The División was the northern division of the revolutionary forces that was initially supplied by arms from the United States, which traded with Villa and supported his currency.[9] Yet Villa was not a strategist who watched from a distance while his soldiers shot at the enemy from the trenches; he was an equestrian warrior, who fought at the side of his horsemen, dramatically leading "massive cavalry charges across awesome expanses of desert."[10] By his own admission, he was said to have himself killed in battle 43,000 men—an accounting intended to inspire fear and horror of his power to exact vengeance.[11]

His invincibility in battle was part of Villa's aura. So was his reputation for being a womanizer of great virility. So, too, was his whimsical Robin Hood generosity. While huge sums of money passed through his hands, he was not greedy. Yet his efforts to redistribute wealth were notoriously flamboyant, as when he confiscated a Spanish department store to give presents to the poor and sweets to the children one Christmas morning. Even with his flair for drama, he had an organized program of agrarian and urban reform. When he became governor of Chihuahua, he confiscated the property of the wealthiest hacendados in the state and declared that after the Revolution he would distribute their lands to his soldiers and to those peasants from whom the land had been taken. In his speeches, Villa spoke in defense of "the cause of liberty and justice, so long denied us and so much hoped for by my long-suffering countrymen, . . . the fifteen million Mexicans who have been enslaved, living in the most abject poverty, oppressed and buffeted by their old and wealthy exploiters."[12] Although Villa's name became associated with the cause of the rural and working classes from which he himself had emerged, his politics were sufficiently vague and his charisma so compelling that his popularity and aura cut across class interests, making him a legend in his time.

That Villa became a legend had everything to do with his location within crossing distance of the border, which made him an object of the American gaze and of American "media hype." Reporters, photographers, and moviemakers all wanted the "scoop" on the bandit revolutionary.[13] And, crucially, there were the onlookers in the United States government. Villa, for his part, courted the favor of American leaders, and the Americans, in turn, initially gave him their support as a potential strongman who could unite and control a nation split apart by civil war while guarding American business interests.

Villa's willingness to be gazed at coincided with the peak of the picture postcard craze in the United States. Thousands of American soldiers and guardsmen were stationed along the recently conquered and still smoldering border regions of the Mexicano southwest, creating a demand for postcards of the Mexican Revolution. Villa, one of the key symbols of the Revolution, was pictured regularly on these postcards. The many pictures that survive of Villa, including those used in Chencha's spiritist cult, probably have their origins in the picture postcard. "He loved to have his picture taken, and the producers of postcards eagerly obliged. When he directed his army toward the important federal stronghold of Torreón, he invited motion picture cameramen along to record the action. He even staged some battle sequences at their request. Villa posed before Torreón and then captured the city."[14]

As long as American support was on his side, Villa was represented as the colorful, swashbuckling revolutionary leader, a figure of nostalgia for the American Wild West as well as of the utopian winds of change sweeping over Mexico. But when that support turned against him, he returned the gaze of the Americans in a way that made them close the door forever to his easy border crossings.

In 1915 the United States chose to recognize as president of Mexico the more conservative and "stable" Venustiano Carranza who, together with Alvaro Obregón, had gained the upper hand in consolidating national power. Adding injury to insult, the American government then allowed five thousand Carrancista troops to cross American territory, breaking with their previous commitment to neutrality and making it possible for Carranza to vanquish Villa at Agua Prieta in Sonora. By this time, Villa's penchant for the old-style cavalry charges that were the stuff of legend were leading to disastrous defeats at key battles. Villa was quickly being reduced to a regional figure. Incensed by the American betrayal of him, and with his power on the decline, Villa took action in a way that would forever complicate his role in Mexican history.

Villa had good reason to believe that in return for American support Carranza had agreed to a secret pact that would have virtually turned Mexico into an American protectorate. He could believe this because he himself had earlier been approached about such a pact, which he had rejected.[15] Convinced that Carranza might have sold out to the United States, in March of 1916 Villa led several hundred horsemen on a raid of Columbus, New Mexico, in which seventeen American soldiers and civilians were killed.

Six days later, several thousand United States soldiers invaded Mexico under the command of General John Pershing to carry out a "punitive expedition" to get Villa "dead or alive," as Woodrow Wilson ordered. By the fall, there were 200,000 guardsmen and army regulars from around the country guarding the border regions from Texas to California. They engaged in "watchful waiting" against another attack by the Villistas (hundreds of whom were killed in retribution by American forces after the raid), while waging literal and social warfare against Mexican-Americans.[16] The border became a staging ground for the United States military's experiments with modern equipment and forms of training, which would later be deployed in World War I. "America had Pancho Villa to thank for bringing the U.S. Army up to par with the nation's ambitions as a world power."[17]

Yet "the man who dared to invade the U.S.A." and "the cause of it all," as the picture postcards put it, was never caught by Pershing's soldiers during their ten-month invasion. According to a folk tale, Villa had the ability to "transform himself into a little black dog barking at the heels of befuddled pursuers."[18] This is a suggestive image given that the black dog is a favorite disguise of the devil.[19] Esperanza, as well as other participants in Chencha's spiritist cult, recognize that Villa's power is a little bit por la mala, a touch on the side of evil, not satanic perhaps, but not saintly either. In folk legends, his magical power was strengthened by his attack on the United States and the inability of an army of 10,000 shamefaced American soldiers to catch him.

But in reality his political and military power diminished rapidly as he lost territorial control to the forces of Carranza. The Mexican government cast him as an "enemy of the Revolution," while the American forces reconstrued Villa as a wild Apache and his movement as banditry.[20] Although weakened militarily, Villa fought on until 1920. Then, "tired of fighting, he went off to grow cotton," as a corrido puts it. Villa, el gran general, surrendered to the new government and received, in exchange, a northern hacienda, where he lived, as a discredited revolutionary, until his assassination in 1923.

Villa's Mexicanness was celebrated by the Mexican press when he died; the middle classes, who were at once attracted and repelled by the rustic manners and lack of bourgeois courtesies of the "centaur of the north," hailed him "as a diamond in the rough who could have been president or as great as Napoleon, if only he had been educated."[21] Yet there were no official memorial events for Villa in subsequent years as there were for the other canonized revolutionary heroes, Madero, Carranza, and the peasant leader Zapata from the region of Morelos, all of whom became part of the cast of the "institutional" Revolution.

Official Mexican history consigned Villa to oblivion because he was an ambiguous figure, an antihero more than a hero. As one Mexican historian concluded, Villa's attack on the town of Columbus invalidated him as a national hero, because his rash actions had provoked the invasion of Pershing, which had been extremely humiliating to Mexicans.[22] Perhaps because the government initially disqualified Villa as a hero, he became, in song, legend, and popular memory, "the outlaw with uncanny power over men."[23]

Not until the 1960s did the central Mexican government choose to recognize Villa as a national hero, doing so for quite pragmatic reasons. Villa's incorporation into official history came in the years of increasing national tension, which culminated in the 1968 student massacre at Tlatelolco. This was a moment when the government badly needed both to bolster its revolutionary image and to solidify its weakening patriarchal control—what better spirit to invoke at such a time than the spirit of Villa? His remains (minus his head, which was stolen, according to a corrido, from his grave by the Americans, who were annoyed at not having caught him) were transferred to the Monument of the Revolution in Mexico City and an equestrian statue of him was placed on the avenue named for the División del Norte.[24]

Villa, possibly the most famous Mexican in the world, has become a key symbol of the "revolutionary/macho," with his huge sombrero and his large mustache, his chest decorated with cartridge belts, and his pistol in his hand.[25] The middle-class male intellectuals of his time, who recognized that the only fighting strength they had brought to the revolutionary cause was "the feeble experience of [their] books and . . . early ideals" felt that in Pancho Villa they had found a true man: "'Now we'll win all right. We've got a man.' A man! A man!"[26]

Villa himself never doubted his manhood. He effused virility, conquering men in battle and women in love; he was said to have had many wives, all of whom he provided for, fulfilling his patriarchal obligations. He had no patience for elegant politicians, like those who surrounded Madero after his victory, calling them the *perfumados*, the "perfumed ones."[27]

Indeed, one strategy the postrevolutionary government used to accomplish the contradictory aim of bolstering its revolutionary image while solidifying patriarchal control was to make manhood itself a virtue. In the twin forms of the macho figure (Zapata, Villa) and the father figure (Madero, Carranza), manliness became institutionalized as the defining feature of the revolutionary heroes. Villa, perhaps more so than any other figure of the Revolution, "fused and confused sexual and political rebellion."[28] He seemed the very embodiment of the power of manhood.

As the macho hero, Villa could be incorporated into the state party's rhetoric and emptied of meaning as a political figure. But as a revolutionary hero, his image would always contain the seeds of discontent for the institutionalized Revolution. The efforts to whitewash Villa could not erase his class background, which kept him beyond the bounds of official power and on the side of the many Mexicans schooled in suffering rather than in privilege. When Carranza, born and raised an hacendado, criticized Villa, born and raised a sharecropper, for his lack of education, Villa responded by saying that "the school of suffering alone has enabled me to go further than some men who have had the benefit of long study." Yet Villa also recognized (perhaps with false modesty), when asked whether he wanted to be president of Mexico, that he was a fighter, not a statesman, and said, "I am not educated enough to be President. . . . How could I, who never went to school, hope to be able to talk with the foreign ambassadors and the cultivated gentlemen of the Congress?"[29]

› › ›

Neither Villa the macho nor Villa the revolutionary are images that can be internalized by women in any simple or direct way. The Mexican woman who wants to see herself as a warrior hero can turn her gaze to the soldaderas, the women soldiers who fought in the Revolution. While some soldaderas offered little more than models of recklessness in war and love, or the conventional models of domestic help behind the scenes, many took up the male ideal of valor.[30] They dressed as men to be able to fight, and a few even led troops in battle as generals and colonels. Such women, as Gustavo Casasola observed, "needed to masculinize themselves completely; both inwardly and outwardly: dress like a man and act like a man; go on horseback, like the rest, be able to endure long marches and, at the hour of combat, prove with weapon in hand that she was no longer a *soldadera*, but a soldier." The choice was to fight like a man or stay put in the traditional female roles. As Adelita, one such heroic, if short-lived, fighting woman was supposed to have said, "*Orale*, everyone in, and whoever is afraid can stay behind and cook beans!"[31]

Villa, more than any other revolutionary leader, was opposed to soldaderas following his troops, since he felt they weakened the mobility of his cavalry forces. Female soldiers were prohibited from joining his elite cavalry unit, the Dorados (Golden Boys), and its members could not, under any circumstances, be joined by a soldadera in battle. Villa also showed his brutality toward women on more than one occasion. In December of 1916, he had ninety Carrancista soldaderas and their children massacred in the town of Camargo and then rode his horse over the dead bodies in a scene that one observer said seemed to come out of Dante's inferno.[32] In early 1917, wanting "to take revenge upon those peasants in the town of Namiquipa who had cooperated with the Americans and formed a home guard against him, he allowed his men to rape all their wives."[33] While Villa also honored women for their courage and married several of the women he had affairs with, thus extending status and protection to them, his attitude toward women was on the whole more negative than that of most other revolutionaries. Yet when questioned directly by journalist John Reed about whether the stories that he had violated women were true, Villa gave a characteristically elusive answer, saying, "I never take the trouble to deny such stories. They say I am a bandit, too. Well, you know my history. But tell me; have you ever met a husband, father or brother of any woman that I have violated? Or even a witness?"[34]

No matter whose truth we accept, women's veneration of Villa in contemporary spiritism still has a way of seeming hopelessly contradictory and crazy. But his exaggerated masculine values were ultimately those of the larger society. The soldaderas, like other heroic women of the revolutionary period, were not given a place in the official history of the revolutionary state. Their story was cast out of official memory, left to be remembered mainly in folk ballads, or in a spiritist cult like Chencha's that reinscribes women into revolutionary history.

If its revolutionary heroes were by definition masculine, then the Mexican nation that was born of their heroism was also by definition masculine. "The problem of national identity," writes Jean Franco, "was presented primarily as a problem of *male* identity and it was male authors who debated its defects and psychoanalyzed the nation."[35] The theories of machismo put forth by Samuel Ramos and Octavio Paz treated the macho as the quintessential Mexican, who deployed an excessive masculinity to compensate for the inferiority complex he felt as a peon in a colonized society that honored the manhood of its heroes as a means of defending class privilege; within this scheme, the Mexican woman figured most strongly in the archetypal image of the "treacherous woman," La Malinche, who, as both lover and translator to Cortés, betrayed her people to the Spaniards.[36]

If national identity, in its heroic mode, was figured as male, how then could Mexican women "plot themselves into a narrative without becoming masculine or attempting to speak from the devalued position?"[37] Under these circumstances, is there a place for women in the narrative of national history, or is the only narrative open to them that of a romance outside history and the nation?

›››

Esperanza, like Chencha herself, seems to me to be seeking an answer to this question by turning to Pancho Villa as a "metaphor of historical imagination."[38] Plotting herself, with a vengeance, into a national narrative of male heroism, dominance, violence, and coercion, she is writing herself out of the masochistic marianismo narratives of the suffering Virgin and the treacherous woman archetype. And she is writing herself back into national epic history by reenacting that history and appropriating that history as performance and as healing. Refusing to be seduced into femininity, she is cutting out a new window from which to view, and enter, a male narrative that seems to be sealed off to her gaze.[39] But the window, once cut out, turns out to be a looking glass: the image of Villa within spiritism is a representation of a

representation, of Villa's own acting out of the role of Pancho Villa in
photographs, movies, and legends, a theater of healing propped on a
theater of history.

In the course of the spiritist performance, a key transformation takes
place: gender is released from its fixity. Femininity and masculinity become masks, not essential identities. It may well be that the stereotyped gender casting of "real life" left Chencha with little choice but
to play a male lead in the theater of spiritism; yet her performances,
both in real life and in spiritism, seem to turn both womanliness and
manliness into masquerades, in which there truly is no difference between the genuinely gendered identity and the mask.[40] As Chencha,
playing the part of Pancho Villa, takes roll call, has everyone march in
place, and checks to see if those present are truly General Pancho
Villa's soldiers, the Mexican Revolution is replayed, not as farce, but
as ambiguously gendered history.

The participants accept as their guide in this journey into the magic
of history an ambiguously gendered woman, who likes to meet evil
head on, but who cannot do her work unless paid handsomely in
money—which is the keenest form of blood sacrifice to those scratch-
ing out a living on capitalism's fringes. The woman they accept as
their guide is also politically ambiguous, claiming to be, like the Villa
she impersonates, on the side of the pueblo but boasting nevertheless
that she is beyond the law because even the top men in the state government (including the governor) come to her when they need to have
some "work" done. And yet this very same woman acts as a confessor,
listening carefully to the moral, domestic, and financial problems of
her supporting cast and attempting to offer solutions. As she sits inside
her altar room, robed in white, her eyes closed in trance, with people
kneeling before her and whispering their confessions, she resembles a
priest; and female priest she becomes, dispensing male redemptive
power.

For a woman like Esperanza, whose own gender blending has led her
to confront the limits of her feminine identity, Chencha is indeed an
ideal interlocutor.[41] Esperanza turns to Chencha, too, because she is
not fully content with the idea of turning the other cheek. While she
knows that God eventually punishes all sinners, there is always, as she
once told me, the fear that if one just takes insults and threats from
others passively, like a log, one might just be turned into firewood. Ac-

tion must be taken, vengeance sought, before that happens. Chencha's links to strong spirits like Pancho Villa open up a more direct channel of communication with the court of divine justice, where lies the ultimate power to balance the spiritual economy, right wrongs, punish evil, and safeguard precarious livelihoods.

When Chencha and her participating audience, made up primarily of women, act out relations of domination and submission and of gender transformation, they are forging a secret agreement with Villa, the macho revolutionary, that they will venerate him if he will impart to them some of his male valor and fighting strength for use in their own unfinished female and class struggles. The identification with this male hero takes place in full awareness of male domination. Esperanza accepts Villa's machismo, brutality toward women, and legacy of violence consciously, with a vengeance, and taps into it for her own purposes. As Chencha's theater of cruelty and healing takes account of the terror and submission of revolutionary history, patriarchy is reproduced ironically, making Pancho Villa a twentieth-century Saint Michael, a key defender of women in their daily battles against the dragon of male domination.

› › ›

There is also the dragon of capitalist domination to contend with, and Villa's battle strength and reputation for executing justice, combined with his Robin Hood qualities, gives him a place in the spiritual economy as well as in the political economy. The current historical moment in Mexico resonates with the historical moment in which Pancho Villa lived in a way that, once more, opens a clearing for a multivocal symbol of resistance to the established order.[42] Between a widespread loss of faith in the government as the emblem of the institutionalized Revolution, a collapsing economy, and growing cleavages between rich and poor, Mexico is again in a moment of severe crisis.

In the period between 1982 and 1990, the period of our fieldwork, the same size coin shifted from one peso to two hundred pesos, and most recently to one thousand pesos. As Mexican money has grown more worthless, its display in the showcase windows of city exchange houses seems to have grown more elaborate. These *casas de cambio*, with their big signs advertising that they "buy dollars," are dream sites

for the poor, who stop to stare at their money displays from all different periods of Mexican history and from different Latin American
countries. At any time of day, one is likely to find families from the
countryside gazing rhapsodically at the displays, which use cornucopia
images and hugely enlarged dollars as measuring rods.

In the time of the Revolution, every general had his own money
printed up, which was good for as long as he controlled a region; there
were nearly two hundred kinds of worthless paper money in circulation. "Life had to be used today, like paper money."[43] As in revolutionary times, life again must be used today, like paper money—except
that this worthless money has become at once so unattainable and so
necessary. It is significant that Chencha, in her role as Pancho Villa,
assures her congregation, "You will not die of hunger, for it is not my
wish!" This affirmation gives voice to a historical memory of hunger,
the severe hunger that accompanied the shortage of food and the
worthlessness of money during the Revolution. But it also carries profound meaning for Esperanza, who knows from her mother that the
Revolution was a time of hunger, and that while at the moment she is
not yet hungry, hunger is a real possibility when surviving as a woman
on the margins. If she has been willing to pay exorbitant amounts of
money to Chencha for her spiritual aid, she has always done so in the
belief that the very survival of her personal and familial domain was at
stake, a survival on which there is simply no price.

Esperanza has told me about how, on her selling trips through the
city, she marvels at those showcase windows with their displays of
money. For her ever to come into so much money, she would have to
find it as buried treasure, she says, but she would rather not find it
ever, for such money is the devil's money, death's money. For her part,
she is content so long as she can work and not lack for beans and tortillas. But, ay, how the envy of others even for her small claim on the
world beats her down and makes her keep fighting!

›››

One other dragon that all Mexicans must contend with, of course, is
the dragon on the other side of the border, a dragon that is likely to
respond with "punitive expeditions" such as Pershing's ten-month invasion in search of Villa.[44] As the man who even 10,000 American soldiers could not catch, Villa represents the possibility of a challenge to

the dragon to the North, a dragon impossible to slay perhaps, but one that every now and then needs to have its toes stepped on. Esperanza's keen awareness that Mexicans have been sold to the United States by their government suggests that she is awake to her status as a colonized person. Who but Pancho Villa can offer the hope of one day overcoming her colonial status? Could it be that the desire to keep alive the spirit of Villa is also a way of turning the mirror back at us on this side of the border?

SEVENTEEN

The Biography in the Shadow

The life history may be thought of as a process that blends together the consciousness of the investigator and the subject, perhaps to the point where it is not possible to disentangle them. . . . If the investigator relies in a primary way on personal resources in understanding the subject of the life history as another person, then in some sense the life history may represent a personal portrait of the investigator as well. The portrait would take the form of a shadow biography, a negative image.

—*Gelya Frank, "Finding the Common Denominator:
A Phenomenological Critique of Life History Method"*

Okay, so technically speaking, I'm not a gringa. I'm Cubana, born in Cuba, raised in a series of noisy apartments in the sad borough of Queens, New York, that smelled of my mother's sofrito. I spoke Spanish at home, learned English in school, where I was in the "dumb class" for a while until I could speak, the first in the family and El Grupo to become a profesora. I was crossing borders without knowing it long before I met Esperanza—but through knowing her, I've reflected on how I've had to cross a lot of borders to get to a position where I could cross the Mexican border to bring back her story to put into a book. We cross borders, but we don't erase them; we take our borders with us.

I have supposedly been privileged from the beginning, a Cubanita, another "model minority," a success story, the welcome mat of the American government spread at my feet, in grateful exile from the shackles of communism in the land of freedom, always grateful, never asking for too much, thank you, thank you very much, *gracias por todo*, and sorry for any trouble. "What sa matta?"—as Abuelo, my grandfather, my father's father used to say, just about the only words I ever heard him speak in English. As a young girl I was told constantly that it was impolite, even immoral, to criticize the United States. "What sa matta? *¿De qué te quejas? ¿Dime, qué te falta?*" Always those refrains: What don't you have? You think you could have worn that dress, those shoes, if we had stayed in Cuba? You think you would have been able to read all those books? You think you'd be so free to talk the way you do? You should say thank you to this country.

I'm a Cubana, but in Mexico I'm a gringa because I go to Mexico with gringa privileges, gringa money, gringa credentials, not to mention a gringo husband and a gringo car. After all, I cross the border with an American passport. In her poem, "Legal Alien," the Chicana poet Pat Mora describes the shift of identity that takes place depending on what side of the border you are standing on:

> an American to Mexicans
> a Mexican to Americans
> a handy token
> sliding back and forth
> between the fringes of both worlds
> by smiling
> by masking the discomfort
> of being pre-judged
> Bi-laterally.[1]

The kindest compliment about my identity I ever received in Mexquitic came from the local thief and juvenile delinquent as we stood around in Don Juan's general store having a beer with a few men just returned from a stint working in the States. This young man, just out of jail again, took a sip of his beer and said to me, "People like you here. We think of you as a *norte mexicana*." He was trying to tell me that while I'm not quite Mexican, I'm not quite American either, because I speak Spanish so well and interact easily with Mexicans; I'm something in between, a cross between a North American and a Mexican, a "North Mexican."

I like this mestiza identity. I can indulge in the thought that I am something other than a gringa, I who have sought, like the Puerto Rican writer Rosario Morales, always to be "the reasonable one," the easy-to-get-along-with-Latina, the Latina who makes no waves and

claims no difference for herself, the Latina who is "white like you, en-
glish-speaking like you, right-thinking like you, middle-class-living
like you, no matter what I say."² But being "the reasonable one" in
Mexico meant that I also had to grin and bear it when they took me for
a gringa. How could I explain that I was not a gringa, not totally a
gringa, anyway? Trying to figure out where I stood on the border between the United States and Mexico, I felt as though the fault lines of
the divided America were quaking within me. Which America was my
America? To which of the Americas did I owe allegiance? How well I
remember the pain in a compadre's voice when I refused his request
that I claim him as next of kin to help him get across the border. "But
didn't you tell me that you and your family aren't from there, that you
also had to struggle to get in?" he asked, deeply hurt.

In our little Cuban circle of El Grupo, we were well aware of our
privilege relative to other Spanish-speaking emigrants, especially
Puerto Ricans and Mexicans, who did not get as warm a welcome as
we had from the American government. We had the privilege of our
color, our aspiration to be middle class, our symbolic capital as wormy
resisters of Fidel Castro's impudent challenge to the United States.
The yanquis had been nice to us, *bien chéveres*, so why should we be
difficult? No one seemed to notice that we had ended up with the yanquis because of the long history of United States intervention in Cuba.
We were content to be able to go to La Rumba Restaurant every week-
end for *frijoles negros* and *bistec de palomilla*, and to Miami Beach for
two weeks vacation in July, during the off-season, the only time we
could afford to go, when the yanquis thought it was crazy to be there,
burning enough layers of skin to last us until the following year.

So I have been privileged, to be sure, from the beginning. And among
those privileges I, too, must include, as does Sandra Cisneros, that "I
grew up with a mother who prepared me for a life in literature instead
of a life in the kitchen."³ It is a strange privilege this, of having a
mother who even today comes to put order in my house, clearing out
my closets and filling up my freezer with *frijoles negros*, chicken cut-
lets, blintzes, and *tamales*, a mother who every year before I go to
Mexico buys costume jewelry, sneakers, flannel nightgowns, *vestidi-
tos*, and *pantaloncitos* for me to take to all my comadres and godchil-
dren, a mother who does all this so that I can keep working, writing,

doing what I need to do to survive. So the native woman in my life, the woman who was first "other" to me, has in some sense always been my mother, the woman who has done my woman's work so I could read and write books. My mother prepared me for a life reading books instead of a life in the kitchen, and yet, without my knowing it, that life beyond the kitchen led me back to a kitchen, the kitchen in Mexico, the kitchen in this book.

It is not just my mother who has done my "woman's work" so I could read and write books. My gringo husband has also spared me from a life in the kitchen. He cooks, cleans, washes the clothes, does the grocery shopping, picks up my mail at the office; he spares me from the everydayness of things, so I can shut myself up at home and do my work. He even puts in all the missing accent marks on my Spanish words. He's a saint of a gringuito, really. From the beginning I let him know that I'm mean and hard to live with, and never grateful enough. I have accused him of taking away my culture when he won't let the *plátanos fritos* burn in the oil till they're totally oozing and charred. My mother sometimes tells me to cool it, that *los hombres se cansan*, you know. Don't think he'll put up with it forever, she warns me. And in Mexquitic, the women also told me, "*Es de los buenos, así que cuídelo.*" Finding a good man, a man who doesn't need a mother, doesn't beat you, doesn't put you down, is a privilege, it seems. So, yes, my gringo husband is another one of my "privileges."

Yet how often haven't I asked myself, What is a Cubanita like you doing with all these ambitions of reading and writing books? Having explored here the many ironies of turning Esperanza's *historias* into a book, I realize that what I haven't said yet is just how wrenching has been my own relationship to books and the world of book-learning. Unless I find the words to tell the story of how I came to be able to write the story of another, less-privileged woman's life, I feel that this book will not be complete. I need to tell the story of how I came to the privilege of my pen. That is the biography in the shadow.

› › ›

Ruth's spoken and written Spanish is excellent, almost flawless, and is not limited to the quotidian "kitchen Spanish" of so many native speakers residing in the U.S. Ruth's Spanish is a tool worthy of her sophisticated and knowledgeable approach to literature.

 —Undergraduate teacher's narrative evaluation,
  spring 1975

I found Ruth's sense of poetic drama particularly compelling. She is at her best when her imagination can get full rein. It's a pity when the facts sometimes get in the way! But I would hate for her to be any more pedestrian. Occasional weirdness is well worth having when there are moments of such insight and even poetry.

 —Undergraduate teacher's narrative evaluation,
  spring 1975

I do not think that Philosophy is an activity for which Ruth is by mental nature exactly suited (that is certainly not meant as a derrogatory [sic] statement, god knows, she may be blessed in this regard); she is an associator rather than an arguer, her imagination seems to be more plastic than abstract. She did very well with very difficult material in a situation for which she was not by training prepared or by natural affinity disposed.

 —Undergraduate teacher's narrative evaluation,
  spring 1976

◎◎◎ As a young girl, I ate books, especially novels, poetry, and philosophy books. The more books I consumed, the more shame I felt about who I was and where I had come from. I was already plotting to leave Queens, and books were to be my passport to the other worlds I wanted to enter, the worlds of thinking, writing, soft voices, quiet study. How I used to irritate the hell out of my father, who liked to sing cha-cha songs out loud at the top of his voice, with my need for long silences; he'd accuse me of having turned the house into a funeral parlor.

And yet my father wanted me to go to Queens College, so I would continue to live at home until I got married, as had been the custom for young girls in Cuba. But I knew we would all have gone crazy if I had stayed home. My brother was a budding musician, and he liked loud rock at the time, not the Mozart that I had tried, in vain, to introduce into the family. The only place where I could read in relative peace was at the bottom of the stairs leading up to our apartment. My mother knew I dreamed of attending an elite private university away from home, and she snuck money out of the checkbook for me to pay the application fees. When the acceptances came in, my father was furious at the little betrayal concocted by my mother and me, but he finally relented; and in the fall of 1974 I left home for one of the little ivy colleges, hoping to become a writer. Once there, I decided to major in the College of Letters, an expanded "Great Books of the Western World Program," under the assumption that if I could read the "great books" I would gain the tools to think great thoughts and write great books.

I felt insecure, wondering whether I had been admitted solely as a "Hispanic," but I intended to prove that I was not a minority student who required special privileges or accommodations. I turned down a room in the Latino House. I knew that I could pass. My Spanish, as my Anglo-American Spanish professor put it in his narrative evaluation, was not "kitchen Spanish" (thankfully!) but some properly literary Spanish that had been wiped clean of the dirt from its roots. And I spoke English, unlike my parents, without a "Latin" accent; in fact, I spoke with an affected British accent that I had taught myself after trying it out first in a high school play (that affectation soon wore off, and I started speaking with what my brother called a "college accent"). I passed so well that I used to irritate a boyfriend when I spoke of how foreign I sometimes felt in the United States. "Come on, you didn't just get off the boat," he'd say.

Maybe I hadn't just gotten off the boat, but the world of the academy, where people seemed invested not in loving books but in being able to talk about them impressively, was a world for which my immigrant milieu had not prepared me. No one in our Grupo of sales clerks, accountants, and engineers turned owners of shoestores and envelope factories could understand what this College of Letters, this *colegio de letras*, was about, and they all thought I was wasting my time. I was continually reminded by my mother that my studies, even with the financial aid I received, were a *sacrificio*, and that I had to be grateful for the education I was getting. My mother had begun to work outside the house at a clerical job, and I knew very well that the development of my mind was being financed by the labor of her body. My father, meanwhile, was still fuming that I had left home. The guilty daughter, I worked summers as a typist in New York City to earn my keep, and after my first semester at college I arranged to graduate a year early by doing independent coursework. I didn't dare tell my parents I was miserable at college; I didn't dare tell myself, either.

And then "it" happened, or rather two events took place that are intimately associated in my memory. In the new year of 1976, I came back from a semester abroad in Madrid, where I had gone to "perfect" my Cuban Spanish. I was home for a few days before returning to college and was trying desperately to read Plato, a stack of Greek tragedies, and Thucydides, which I had promised my teachers I would read and study on my own as part of the plan to allow me to graduate a year early. I remember I took Plato with me to the kitchen, the narrow kitchen in the Forest Hills apartment with the pale yellow formica counter and the matching wallpaper of massive sun-drenched marigolds that matched the sheets on my parents' bed, those sheets which years later I would take with me to Mexquitic. I was drinking orange juice and holding down a page of Plato with my mother's browning copy of *Cocina Criolla*, the cookbook she had brought with her from Cuba, when my father appeared in the kitchen. I had been away for six months, but somehow I had already managed to make my father angry.

"*Ni buenos días, ni* Hi Papi, *ni nada.*"

"Sorry, I was reading," I mumbled.

He sat down on the other bar stool by the counter and looked straight at me. My mother must not have been home. Fear began to gnaw at my throat when I noticed he had some airmail letters in his hand. Pulling out one of the letters from the pile, he began to read aloud in the tone of a prosecutor, "I miss you so much. Mami y Papi, *no saben cuanto les quiero. Mucho cariño, su hija, Ruty.*" I realized with dread that he was reading aloud from one of my letters, a letter I had written home from Spain.

He put the letter back in the envelope, folding it exactly where it was already creased. Then he tore it up, slowly, methodically. I was so stunned I couldn't say a word. He took up the next letter and tore it, and the next and the next. How many letters were there? I can only remember a pile of little pieces of paper, colorful as confetti, with my writing on them, embers lying on the yellow formica counter. He tore the letters with the cool precision he used to shave his face or wipe his mouth after dinner.

"*¡Son mentiras!* Lies!" And then in a singsong imitation, "I miss you so much, Mami y Papi."

I cannot find my tongue.

"*¡Mentiras!* You love your mother and your father, then you show it! *¿Un beso para tú padre? ¡Nada!* You can't kiss your father hello? You can't kiss your mother hello? *Tanto qué ella hace por ti. Nada* . . . Those letters, *sabes lo qué son? ¡Caca! ¡Mierda!* Shit! *¡Pa la basura, todo!*"

He edged the neat little pile of torn up letters into his palm and squashed them. With his other hand, he opened the cabinet door under the sink. He opened his palm and the mush of words landed in the garbage heap piled high with chicken bones and burnt yellow rice from the previous night's dinner. I simply sat there, and when he left I turned back to Plato.

A few days later I was back at college. Although at the end of the semester I would be taking my comprehensive examinations in the College of Letters, I decided not to devote my time to studying. Instead, I chose to direct a García Lorca passion play, *The House of Bernarda Alba*, about a mother's struggle to maintain control over her daughters and their virginity, a play that required an all-female cast. No grades were given for coursework done in the College of Letters, just narrative statements, so the "comps" counted a great deal, and both students and professors took them very seriously. I remember everybody around me studying like mad, and I, lost inside the house of Bernarda Alba.

Although the García Lorca play was a success, my comps were disastrous. No, I didn't fail them; that, at least, would have been dramatic. Instead, I received a "creditable," an ugly, borderline grade that only I and the worst goofball in the class received in a group of honors, high honors, and highest honors. I was crying by my mailbox in the College of Letters when the teacher I most venerated then, an immeasurably articulate professor of philosophy, the one who wrote in her narrative evaluation that I was not mentally suited to pursue Philosophy with a capital P, saw me and led me into a colleague's office. After a few brief words of consolation, she proceeded to ignore me and tell her colleague how useful it was to have an objective scale by which to rate the students in the class.

In the months that followed, I was treated as a reject of the intellectual assembly line. That, not the grade, was what really hurt. I was left out of a Heidegger tutorial with the philosopher I had venerated. I could find no one to supervise my senior thesis. And then a professor who had taken pity on me began to put his arms around me whenever I'd go to his office, and he'd ask if I wouldn't go to a motel with him; I hadn't yet learned to say the words "sexual harassment." All I knew was that the keepers of the "great books" no longer thought me worthy. Despite my grand hopes, where I really belonged was either in the College of Remedial Reading or in a motel bed being nice to my male professors. So now I knew the truth: I was in college because I was "Hispanic." I had never left the "dumb class."

Out of a sense of shame, I had left behind all the things associated with home in order to cross the border into the world of Letters, only to discover that this world didn't want me and that there was no returning home, either. Like the trail of bread left by Hansel and Gretel, the path home was strewn with the pieces of my letters my father had torn up, and I no longer knew my way back.

› › ›

Over the years these two events, my father's tearing up of my letters home, and my being cast into the margins of the great Letters, have come to occupy the larger space in my memory of primal scenes. They are primal scenes of my tongue gone dry, scenes of terror, when both my heart and my mind were broken in pieces. I reveal them for the first time here because they offer a parallel from my life to the kind of annihilating violence Esperanza describes in her account, violence that ravaged the emerging self of the young woman. The violence directed at me was psychic, not inscribed on my body, as it was for Esperanza, and, given my class position, I was properly fed in the midst of my sufferings. But the pain was nonetheless profound; its thick ink still clogs my pen.

Between my father's tearing up of my letters for not being true and the doubts of my teachers about whether I was fit to join the great tradition of Letters, I received the message that I was both an emotional and an intellectual failure. Only now, fifteen years later, can I begin to imagine other readings of those events. I wonder now whether my father's act of violence toward me, what I perceived as his rape of my letters, was his way of challenging the frighteningly cold, distant American person I seemed to be turning into, the daughter who had no hugs or kisses for her mother and father, the daughter who was moving farther and farther away from home. In that light my refusal to study for the comps may, in turn, have been my way of returning his act of violence by undercutting the family sacrifice to educate me. By treating the great books, my passport into those other worlds I so desperately wanted to enter, as unimportant to me, I expressed my defiance. No longer would I be the good schoolgirl, through whom he and my mother could vicariously claim that the yanquis had been good to us. But neither would I be able to rise above the bottom of the stairs in the Queens apartment, for I had clipped my own wings.

My calling in life, I had begun to think, was to be a typist, forever typing other people's words because I did not deserve to inscribe any of my own. I was then, and am still now, an ace typist, having learned to type at the age of nine. It was my father who had the idea that I should learn to type. He brought home a step-by-step typing manual with an orange cover and told me that I was to do a lesson a day and learn to type without looking at the keys. A car accident that he had been unable to avert late one night on the Belt Parkway had left me immobile for a year with a broken femur. The typing was meant to teach me a useful feminine working-class skill while I recovered. At the age of nine, I could be thrilled at my typing skills; but at the age of nineteen those same skills felt like a life sentence, an ironic comment on my destiny. And much later, as I approached my thirty-fifth birthday while working to turn my comadre's words into paper, I would again be consumed with worry about whether the fearful prophecy of my being a typist, forever transcribing someone else's words, had in some quite fiendish way actually come true.

››››

> Let me show you my wounds: my stumbling mind, my
> "excuse me" tongue . . .
>
> —Lorna Dee Cervantes, "Poem for the Young White
> Man Who Asked Me How I, an Intelligent, Well-Read

Person, Could Believe in the War between Races,"
from Emplumada

◎◎◎ Not long after those events, as I licked my wounds, I
started, ever so hesitantly, to think that, maybe, just
maybe, there was a problem with the view that what was most worth
knowing about culture and thought could be contained in a single
shelf of books. I started to wonder about the exclusions in that shelf,
and the sense of entitlement of its keepers.[4] At the same time, not
claiming too much consciousness in retrospect, I also know that I felt
horribly, hopelessly stupid. Some part of me did believe that the comps
had, indeed, been an objective measure of my place in the scheme of
things, as the venerated teacher had thought, too. Like the teenage
girls about whom Carol Gilligan has recently written, I experienced an
acute sense of not knowing what I knew.[5]

As those not-knowing-what-I-knew thoughts began to take form in
my head during my final year in college, I decided to take my first
course in anthropology. It was a course in theories of society and culture taught by a defrocked priest turned philosopher turned anthropologist. I was in the wilderness then, so the insight that all products
of culture, great books included, were social constructions, not timeless monuments that spoke in a universal language, fell upon me like
manna. Maybe, just maybe, it was not a lack of "natural affinity" or a
deficient "mental nature" that kept me from doing better in Philosophy with a capital P, but a sense of alienation at its cultural and linguistic otherness.[6] In anthropology I felt I had found an intellectual
home. Here, the little shelf of great books was seen for what it was:
just one little shelf.

My first teacher of anthropology pushed me to go to graduate school.
With his unrelenting insistence, I applied to two schools and got into
one of them. I decided that this time I was going to discipline myself
better. I would not resist being taught. I would take my exams seriously. If I could get through graduate school I would prove to myself I
was not so stupid after all—maybe, blessed as I was in my philosophy
teacher's estimation, I'd never be mentally suited for Philosophy, the
Queen of all the disciplines, but I would earn a place in Her court.

In graduate school, I forced myself to learn to write cold-blooded
logical essays with a beginning, middle, and end; and I forced myself to

keep my flights of imagination in check, to learn to muzzle them to facts. I worked very hard and the work paid off; I became a star pupil. When it came time to write my dissertation about the way of life and history of a small peasant village in northern Spain, I wrote an elegant exposition about the relationship between family inheritance and communal land tenure. There was no link between this topic and my life; it was a pure intellectual exercise.[7] My teachers liked my dissertation enough to recommend it for immediate publication, so that at a fairly young age and at an early point in my career, I already had a book to show for myself.

But when the dissertation was done, I felt as did Michelle Cliff: "My dissertation . . . was responsible for giving me an intellectual belief in myself that I had not had before, while at the same time distancing me from who I am, almost rendering me speechless about who I am. At least I believed in the young woman who wrote the dissertation—still, I wondered who she was and where she had come from."[8]

Graduate school had given me back the confidence in my intellect that had been knocked out of me in college. But I realized that this confidence had been won at a price: in my years of graduate school and dissertation writing, I had been forced to put aside all the burning questions of my own identity and the painful memory of the torn personal and literary letters that had propelled me into anthropology in the first place. I had come to feel that my personal identity was neither relevant nor important. There was nothing special about me. Society, culture, history: didn't those collective forms have everything to do with what we are? My life I had put on hold; I'd eventually get to reply to it, I thought, when I found some time. As an anthropologist, I had an obligation to give voice to others. To give myself voice was narcissistic, indulgent; even now, I still feel the weight of this view.[9]

The dissertation writing, and the writing I initially did about colonial Mexican women's confessions to the Inquisition, established me, in ways I do not fully understand, as a member of the professional managerial class. I believed in the young woman who, not quite thirty yet in 1986, saw her first book published by a prestigious university press, gave birth to her first baby, and took her first almost-real-job as a postdoctoral fellow at the University of Michigan. I was still speechless about who I was and I still had an "excuse me" tongue, but my credentials told me that at least I had an intellect.

As I began to work seriously on Esperanza's life story while making myself believe I was a professor at Michigan, I wanted this project to start pointing me home after the years of academic exile. I had no clear idea at first of how the life history of a Mexican woman street peddler was going to say anything about the Cubanita who had gone away to college against her father's wishes planning to become a fiction writer but turning into an anthropologist instead. I was reading and teaching all the personal narratives I could get my hands on, and especially those written by American women with knotted borderland identities, but I had begun to think that whatever personal statement I was going to make would have to be done in a different context. I couldn't see a way to mix Esperanza's narrative and my narrative in the same pot.

And then some unexpected things happened. It was 1988. I had one year left of my three-year position at Michigan, when I was offered a job at an idyllic university in California. For me, that campus on the hill with the ocean on the horizon became the imaginary Cuba I had longed to find; what could be better, a Cuban friend joked, than a Cuba without Cubans? Just as I was trying to decide whether I ought to accept the job in my imaginary Cuba, I was asked whether I might be interested in a job at Michigan. There was no regular job available at the moment, I was told, but there were funds available for positions designated "target of opportunity," to be filled by minority people. Would I consent to being considered for a position as a Latina? I said I would. A colleague in my department confessed that as far as she was concerned I was just like her, that she didn't see me as a Latina, but that the minority route was a way to get me in.

A few weeks later the request for a minority position for me was turned down by the administration. Apparently I was not an authentic enough Latina because my four grandparents had been European Jewish immigrants to Cuba. An extensive genealogy was put together, not unlike the *limpieza de sangre* writs of the Inquisition that sought to determine "purity of blood," and it was decided that "my race" wasn't pure Cuban because I had European blood in my veins.[10] Anyway, quite apart from that, it wasn't Cubans the administration needed to fill the target of opportunity slots; they already had at least two Cubans on the faculty. The best the administration could do was offer me a three-year visiting position, which might eventually be turned into a regular position. I was told that a visiting position at a major university was

worth a lot more than a tenure-track position at the smaller college I
wanted to go to in California. Unconvinced, I turned Michigan down
to go to my imaginary Cuba.

That took place in May. And then in July, while I was in Mexico
working with my comadre on this book, I was awarded a MacArthur
fellowship, a fellowship with tremendous mystique in the academic
world. It is impossible to apply for a "Big Mac." The award comes from
heaven like the Archangel Gabriel, and it's yours for five years without
any strings attached. Immediately a telegram arrived for me in Mexico:
overnight, it seemed, a real position had become available for me at
Michigan, not just a visiting position. It was difficult not to be cynical;
being told first that I was not a legitimate Latina, then being told that I
ought to be happy to stay on at the university with a temporary job,
and suddenly, because I had won an important prize, being offered a
tenure-track position. No, I thought to myself, let me just go to my
imaginary Cuba. But in my new state of grace, Michigan would not let
me get away so easily. I was asked what it would take to get me to stay.
"Tenure," I replied, feeling as if I'd asked for the moon. And, to my
surprise, a few months later I was offered tenure. Tenure for me, the
Cubanita that had once been turned back at the border?

Then I was really stuck. Should I stay at Michigan with the job written in stone and the financial security, or take a risk and go to my
imaginary Cuba, where I now had the lesser offer of a position with no
definite promise of tenure? Staying seemed safe and easy and smart;
leaving seemed difficult and brave and romantic. How I agonized over
this decision.

I have a huge need for financial security; the immigrant in me has a
fear of ending up homeless and in the gutter. Over the years, I had also
taken on the role of breadwinner within the little threesome of our nu-
clear family exiled in the Midwest. David had put his career on hold in
order to care for Gabriel and had not yet finished his dissertation. In
between teaching, writing, and conferences, I had given Gabriel my
breast full of *leche nerviosa*, as my father called it, the "nervous milk"
of work and worry. And now I had to decide not only what was best for
me but for the three of us.

I made the mistake of sharing some of my uncertainty with my parents. For them the answer was obvious: stay at Michigan. "Oh, wow,
you have a daughter at Michigan? *No, Ruty, la gente se impresiona*

mucho cuando uno dice Michigan." I'd be silly to give up a job at such an important university. Angered, I answered back, "You just use me to gain prestige!" That was a cheap shot, I knew, and I was ready for the scolding. "That's not nice, Ruty," my father said. "We're proud of you, *pero si quieres que no hablemos de ti, no vamos a decir nada!*" And again I was the evil daughter, who deserved to have her letters torn up.

Reluctantly, I told the people at California that I needed tenure if I was to go there. Never in my wildest fantasies had I imagined I would be in a position to make such demands. I know that to outsiders it seemed as though I was ratcheting up the offers with supreme chutzpah, but I felt miserable about the whole process. Meanwhile, back at Michigan, people were becoming upset because I had not immediately grabbed the offer of tenure. What else did I want, after all? To stall for time I began negotiating: for time off from teaching, for salary, for a late deadline for my decision. It all felt out of character to me. The only thing that was in character was my indecisiveness.

While I was in Miami Beach in late February of 1989 visiting my grandmother, I got a call from Michigan. Somehow they had managed to track me down. They were very sorry but they could not give me any more time to decide about the job offer; by the following week, I had to take it or leave it. I politely listened to this ultimatum and didn't get angry, didn't protest. I was "nice." I said "please excuse me" and "thank you," just as I was taught by my parents. Then I called California. So, were they going to give me tenure? I needed to know right away. Well, they'd see what they could do, but they weren't sure they could work anything out that quickly.

On the day I had to make my decision, I got a call from the "sheriff" of my imaginary Cuba. Clearly, she was annoyed at all the trouble I was causing. "You've jumped over too many hoops," she said to me in her staccato voice, "and now you want me to let you jump over another hoop. I don't know why you're so worried about tenure. If you've gotten all those awards, then you shouldn't have to worry—if you deserved them, that is . . ." The Cubanita was being put in her place, at last. I wanted to be angry, but I felt I deserved that scolding, too. I was asking for too much. I had to be grateful for what I had been given; don't ask for too much, and always be grateful, say thank you, thank you very much, *gracias por todo.*

I had just hung up with the sheriff when the phone rang again. It was my mother, wanting to know what I had decided. She was calling from her basement office at New York University, where she works as a typist. *"¿Qué vas a hacer, Ruty?"* she asked, tender, concerned, anxious. She had already told me quite clearly that she would be sorry if I moved so far away to California. But I didn't want to hear about her desires; I wanted to be American, free to go wherever I pleased. I could feel the rage I had been withholding gathering force. Any minute I would yell, scream, be ugly. "I don't want to talk to you! Leave me alone!" And I hung up. Several minutes later I got my composure back and called the chair of anthropology at Michigan. "I'll be happy to take the job," I said. "Sorry for all the trouble I've caused. I really want to thank you. Thank you. Thank you for being so patient. Thank you."

The misery that followed is still so inchoate to me that I can't fully describe it. I cried every night of that March, that April, that May, maybe that June, of 1989. David and Gabriel would already have fallen asleep and the Mickey Mouse song tape that Gabriel insisted on listening to night after night would be playing in my ear, and I would be crying and crying in the dark. I had no idea why I was crying. I was supposed to be happy. I had a job, a job at a "good" university. "What sa matta? *¿De qué te quejas? ¡Dime, qué te falta!"* The tears would start and there was no stopping them. After a while, they were like old friends. "Hello, heartache, sit down."

I was now lost in a different wilderness, the wilderness of success in the university system, success I myself had striven for. After being the woman who couldn't translate herself, I had suddenly become the woman who translated herself too well. And in the midst of it all, I was planning to turn the tales of a Mexican street peddler into a book that would be read within the very same academy that had toyed with my most intimate sense of identity and then, with even less compunction, bought me out. Fresh from the horror of being a translated woman, I would now turn around and translate another woman for consumption on this side of the border.

For, you see, once I took the job at Michigan, I was immediately tabulated into the list of new minority hirings. Whenever there is a minority faculty event, I'm invited. At women's studies gatherings I am sometimes introduced as a woman of color. There are still so few minority faculty on campus that even a gringa Latina, an impure Cubanita like me, counts for something.

›››

Will I lose my job for saying all this? The Cubanita inside me, impure though she may be, is still afraid to speak up. Will her letters be torn up? Will they take the fellowship away? Be grateful, be grateful, say thank you. Sorry, Michigan. You're not angry with me?

›››

Telling this story of how I came to my place of privilege in academics, I feel as though I have put out a search warrant for that woman who thought it worthwhile to sit listening year after year to another woman's story in the kitchen of a little cement house in a Mexican town. I have a clearer picture now of this woman who has been hiding behind the story of another woman's life. I recognize her. I understand that part of her interest in creating this text of a Mexican woman's life story has to do with her own painful, and unresolved, confrontation with the great books, as well as with her father's mutilation of her writing; and that her desire to recognize Esperanza as a writer whose words are written in the sand of storytelling and conversation has to do with her own lack of language, "the language to clarify [her] resistance to the literate" as well as her adulation of the literate.[11] The biography in the shadow of the biography.

›››

In September of 1990, when I was in Mexquitic again, I had a few minutes to myself and was trying to sit down and read a book (what else?) when I heard a knock at the door. I swung open the narrow wooden door not knowing who to expect at that late morning hour and saw an elderly man standing there expectantly. Children's clothes hung from his outstretched arms as though they were two rails specially made for the purpose. Ah, a peddler, I thought. *"¿Gusta ver el surtido que traigo de ropa de niños?"* he said to me, politely zestful. I thought to myself, Well, I could be nice and look at what he has to offer and maybe buy something if it's not too expensive, but that's going to take time and I haven't been able to read a single book since I got to Mexquitic. *"No, ahorita no, gracias,"* I said, and closed the door.

336

And then, when I went inside, I began to think I had done something terrible, something terribly self-denying. Both my Russian and Turkish grandfathers were peddlers in Cuba; my maternal grandfather eventually came to own a little lace store, but my paternal grandfather, *el turco*, remained a peddler. It's only recently that my father has begun to talk openly about how Abuelo went from door to door selling blankets that he carried on his back and men's suits that he draped on his arms. For my father, who was dragged along on peddling trips to the outskirts of Havana, this truth about his past and his origins has been a source of shame, long hidden, and he spoke with irony about how his father wanted him to learn the "family business." Now my father is the Latin American sales representative for a large textile firm in New York, but in moments of self-deprecating humor he has called himself a peddler of *basura*, of junk; it is his job to sell the fabric no one wants to buy on this side of the border to clients in Panama, in the Dominican Republic, and, yes, in Mexico. He's a translated man himself.

Because of my father's shame, it didn't occur to me at first that my work with Esperanza, the Mexican street peddler, was also a bridge to my own past and the journey my family has made to shift their class identity. How many cultural and class borders I, too, have crossed to end up in the position of being able to turn away the peddler that came to my door, while in all good conscience devoting years to writing up hundreds of pages of another peddler's life story.

I may cringe when I am at a party hosted by a colleague deeply committed to working-class and postcolonial struggles who just happens to have Persian rugs with just the right patina in every room of the house, but I also know that it is for life in this world and this social class that I have been preparing myself since finishing graduate school. During the years I lived in Mexico after my doctorate, without any definite sense of my final destination, didn't I start to collect hand-knotted linens, an inlaid wood hope chest, bark paintings, ceramic tiles, lacquered trays from Olinalá? I didn't have a home yet of my own—I wasn't sure where home would be—but one day I dreamed of a house filled with the things I had brought back from my travels, and maybe even a Persian rug or two.

"Tell me more about what Abuelo sold in Cuba," I ask my father. And he tells me that for a long time my grandfather sold blankets from the United States, because blankets that said "Made in U.S.A." were highly valued. And, he adds, with a sudden flash of memory, the brand name of the blankets was Beacon. Who could have known that two generations later, across another border, his granddaughter in the United States would compose a book about a peddler, and that this book would be borne into print by a publishing house bearing the same name as the blankets her grandfather once sold on the streets of Havana?

› › ›

I have mixed feelings about everything.
Soy un ajiaco de contradicciones.
Vexed, hexed, complexed,
hyphenated, oxygenated, illegally alienated . . .

> —*Gustavo Pérez Firmat, "Bilingual Blues," from*
> **Carolina Cuban**

◎◎◎ With all the discussion of ethnographic writing going on at the moment, so little is said about how each of us comes to the pen and the computer and the authority to speak and author texts. When Clifford Geertz writes about "the burden of authorship" or James Clifford writes about "ethnographic authority," they don't say authorship is a privilege to which many of us are not born, but arrive at, often clumsily, often painfully, often through a process of self-betrayal and denial; they don't say that authorship is a privilege constituted by the gender, sociohistorical background, and class origins, or lately, class diasporas, of the anthropologist doing the writing.[12]

As anthropologists we often deny, or leave behind in our closets, our class-embeddedness and travel far away to work with peasants, construction workers, miners, hunter-gatherers, peddlers, and factory workers. But when we come home, we tend to live out our lives in "good" middle-class neighborhoods where we rarely encounter the working people we become so close to in the course of doing our projects. Those whose nationality, racial, ethnic, or class position make them uneasy insiders in the academic world often feel as if they are donning and removing masks in trying to form a bridge between the homes they have left and the new locations of privileged class identity they now occupy.[13] How far can one go in shuttling back and forth across these borders without losing everything in the translation? José Piedra, a Cuban-American literary critic, says that a friend character-izes him as someone who describes Spanish America to the gringos, "of whom you are almost one." As Piedra notes, gringos have a long history of crossing into Spanish America, "to seduce and borrow our land, people, and texts," and now, ironically, some of us on this side of the border are "moving into their homes and academic settings, as if we were ourselves pretending to be second-rate *gringos*."[14]

For a long time I tried to be a second-rate gringa. Having been put through a personal crisis of representation, I now claim the right to speak from somewhere else, as another new mestiza who has infil-trated the academy.[15] If I'm going to be counted as a minority, if I'm going to be on the margin, then I'm going to claim that space and speak from it, but in the interests of a politics that challenges the lan-guage of authenticity and racial purity. I will no longer apologize and say, "I'm a Latina, but don't worry, I'm not a 'real Latina,' I don't need special privileges," constantly feeling that I haven't passed "the ethnic legitimacy test."[16] I will take my place with other "halfie" ethnogra-phers, who know what it is like to be placed in situations of being "other," of being the represented rather than the representer, and who therefore are unable "to comfortably assume the self of anthropology . . . the self is split, caught at the intersection of systems of difference."[17] Under these circumstances, you become an ethnogra-pher but refuse to speak from a position of unsituated authority; in-stead, you try to speak from that very *ajiaco de contradicciones* that makes you a halfie, a mestiza, a Norte Mexicana, almost a gringa, but not quite. Yet I realize that I will continue to slip in and out of shadow, as I become non-Latina for purposes of inclusion and Latina for pur-poses of exclusion, just the way my comadre is visibly Indian and yet invisibly Indian in Mexican society.[18] And the dilemma will remain: the mestiza still speaks, in large part, to the gringos and gringas, whose homes and academic settings she has moved into. She is illegally alien-ated. Translator, traitor.

"We grow up repudiating the local and the personal in favor of what will get us ahead and away," writes Mary John in a suggestive essay about her own place in the Western academy as a feminist student from India who has come to the United States in pursuit of a "good" education. Noting how the increasingly ritualistic litany of naming

one's race, class, and gender intersection has become unsatisfying, she
calls for a more profound questioning of how identities are shaped in
the process of attaining a university education. "Education is more obviously a process," she writes, "by which we learn to avow and remember certain knowledges and devalue and forget others." What we
cannot tell ourselves we know, what we have to repress of ourselves in
the process of becoming educated, become the "sanctioned ignorances" of our knowledge.[19] It is the sanctioned ignorances of my own
ethnographic authority that I have tried to interrogate here.

We all bring different burdens of memory, different sanctioned ignorances, to the task of writing ethnography, to be sure. And there is a
special burden that authorship carries if you have ever occupied a borderland place in the dominant culture, especially if you were told at
some point in your life that you didn't have what it takes to be an authority on, an author of, anything. It means writing without entitlement, without permission. It means writing as a "literary wetback,"
as the Chicana poet Alicia Gaspar de Alba puts it, without "the 'right'
credentials . . . to get across."[20]

It is not just Esperanza, then, who is a literary wetback. Even though
I have borne her story across to this side of the border, I recognize that
I, too, in a quite different way, am a literary wetback in the world of
academic letters, a wetback despite the papers that tell me I'm okay,
I'm in, I'm a legal alien.

› › ›

Now that I am on the other side, I must confront the challenge of playing the role of *la profesora* in ways that go against the grain of education's power to not let students know what they know. But I tend to be
demasiado nice and have felt like an intellectual maid when students
come to me for help cleaning up their proposals and papers before they
show them to their more aloof and intimidating professors.

During the summer of 1991, as I struggled to finish this book, I let
myself be interrupted by the visit of a young woman who came with
her parents and sister to tell me that she had decided against attending
graduate school at Michigan. She had expressed her desire to be at
Michigan under any condition, and so I had taken time to work at obtaining a teaching assistantship for her. But as the summer drew to a
close, she began to have second thoughts, and when it turned out she

could still go to another top university with a full fellowship, she decided to back out. Her mother intensified the pressure by saying that she didn't understand why you would want to have to work to study when you could go to a university where they would pay you to study. But this student, who had heard me speak at a conference and begun to view me as a role model, wanted very much to work with me. Herself the daughter of a father who is a professor, she had called me at home several times to let me know of her interest and her indecision. I had given her as much time as she seemed to need, identifying fully with her predicament. The woman professor, the impure Cubanita come up from the bottom, feels she has to give of herself; she's still paying her debt, still showing her gratitude.

August 5, 1991. It is late morning, the day after Gabriel's birthday party, and my hair is still slightly wet. I've quickly pulled it up under a thick braided headband. The student and her family sit with me in the living room. I try to act the professor, steady, calm, offering kind words of sympathy, but as the confident, youthful-looking mother with the tennis figure looks me over, I imagine her thinking: for this husky Latina woman come up from peddlers, this woman who works on life histories and god knows what other marginal things, my precious daughter is going to give up a fellowship at a good university where grey-haired men in grey suits will give her a good education? I'm conscious of the tomato-red band squeezing my temples, the ringlets wet on my neck, and as the mother continues to watch me, I start to feel like Carmen Miranda, tropical fruit ripening, rotting, on my head. I start to think I can imagine how Esperanza must have felt when I kept pointing my camera at her as she walked down the streets of San Luis Potosí with the bucket of produce on her head.

›››

When I left Mexquitic in 1990 at the end of October, I felt sad that I would have to miss the Day of the Dead that year. And then, just after I returned to Ann Arbor, I heard that Sandra Cisneros and her students were going to put up an altar in the main office of the American Culture Program. When I saw the altar, with the candles lit, the offerings of sweet pan de muertos, and all the santitos, I felt such joy. Here, in the humdrum florescent space where learning is supposed to take place, there was grace, beauty, light; there was the "living border," a

new world of possibilities made "out of the experience of displace-
ment," a closing of the gap between "our America" and "the other
America, which is not ours."[21] At the center of her altar, Sandra had
hung up Ester Hernández's *La Ofrenda*, a silk screen print of a short-
haired Chicana in profile, with the image of the Virgin of Guadalupe
radiating from her naked back.

I came full circle—or better, the circle widened, stretched, opened,
for me that day. I met Sandra Cisneros for the first time on the Day of
the Dead, the same day I met my comadre Esperanza Hernández. On
that day, in a class discussion in which I took part, Sandra Cisneros
spoke of the newfound delight that she and other Chicanas have discovered in the spiritual practices of Mexican women. Chicanas like
herself, who have made it into the academy or the literary world, are
reclaiming these practices, she said, because their families were often
afraid that claiming them reduced you to being a backward Mexican.
Now they light candles for each other before a decision on tenure or
the publication of a new essay, poem, or book. And every year, for the
muertitos, they make their altares.[22] On this side of the border, it has
now become possible for Sandra Cisneros to say, *"Nos estamos haciendo muy brujitas"* (We're becoming very witchy), and laugh.

› › ›

*July–August 1993. By December of 1992 I had the book. I held it in
my hands. Smiled along with the picture of my comadre and I giggling on the back cover. Opened the book. Closed it. Taught it. Ped-
dled it. And all the time I was wondering: what will my comadre think
when she sees the book? Finally, I placed it in her hands. She kept
it for a few days. Showed it to her customers in San Luis. Listened as
I read passages to her from it. Then she gave the book back to me. "I
already know my historia," she said. "And besides, this is in English.
My children can't read it." I insisted she keep the book as a souvenir.
"No, comadre, you take it back. Sell it. So it won't be sitting there." If
I returned next time with the book in Spanish, would she accept it
then? Yes, she would. . . . It pained me to pack the book away again.
But I understood that not accepting *Translated Woman* was my
comadre's way of refusing to say goodbye, of refusing to be translated, of refusing to end this book.*

Notes

Chronology

Notes

Introduction

1. Ruth Behar, "Sexual Witchcraft, Colonialism, and Women's Powers: Views from the Mexican Inquisition," in Asunción Lavrin, ed., *Sexuality and Marriage in Colonial Latin America* (Lincoln: University of Nebraska Press, 1989), p. 193; and "Sex and Sin, Witchcraft and the Devil in Late-Colonial Mexico," *American Ethnologist* 14 (1987): 35–55. In contemporary Mexico, there is a strong belief that abandoned or wronged women can punish their husbands or lovers through witchcraft. See Lola Romanucci-Ross, *Conflict, Violence, and Morality in a Mexican Village* (Chicago: University of Chicago Press, 1986), pp. 108–10.

2. On these links, see Renato Rosaldo, "From the Door of His Tent: The Fieldworker and the Inquisitor," in James Clifford and George E. Marcus, eds., *Writing Culture: The Poetics and Politics of Ethnography* (Berkeley: University of California Press, 1986).

3. Sidney Mintz, "The Sensation of Moving, While Standing Still," *American Ethnologist* 16 (1989): 786–96.

4. See, for example, Jean Briggs, *Never in Anger: Portrait of an Eskimo Family* (Cambridge: Harvard University Press, 1970); Lila Abu-Lughod, "Fieldwork of a Dutiful Daughter," in Soraya Altorki and Camillia Fawzi El-Solh, eds., *Arab Women in the Field: Studying Your Own Society* (New York: Syracuse University Press, 1988); Dorinne Kondo, "Dissolution and Reconstitution of Self: Implications for Anthropological Epistemology," *Cultural Anthropology* 1 (1986): 74–88.

5. Here I am drawing on Judith Friedlander, *Being Indian in Hueyapan: A Study of Forced Identity in Contemporary Mexico* (New York: St. Martin's Press, 1975), p. 72. For a detailed discussion of the history and politics of ethnic identity in Mexquitic, see David Frye, *Indians into Mexicans: The Politics of Identity in a Mexican Town* (Austin: University of Texas Press, forthcoming).

6. Lourdes Arizpe, *Indígenas en la ciudad de México: El caso de las "Marías"* (Mexico City: Sep/Setentas, 1975), and "Women in the Informal Labor Sector: The Case of Mexico City," *Signs* 3, no. 1 (1977): 25–37. For recent feminist work by Mexican women that deals with women's work as part of a web of power and gender relations, see Orlandina de Oliveira, ed., *Trabajo, poder y sexualidad* (Mexico City: Colegio de México, 1989). The "India María" is an

archetypal image of the working Indian woman; in Mexico, there is a comedy film series about "la India María," and in Peru there is a comic book as well as a famous telenovela, "Simplemente María," that has been shown in several Latin American countries, including Mexico.

7. On women's marketing in Mexico, see Beverly L. Chiñas, *The Isthmus Zapotecs: Women's Roles in Cultural Context* (New York: Holt, Rinehart, and Winston, 1973). Extensive work on market women has been done in Peru by Ximena Bunster and Elsa M. Chaney, *Sellers and Servants: Working Women in Lima, Peru* (New York: Praeger, 1985), and Florence E. Babb, *Between Field and Cooking Pot: The Political Economy of Marketwomen in Peru* (Austin: University of Texas Press, 1989). Also see Linda J. Seligmann, "To Be In Between: The *Cholas* as Market Women," *Comparative Studies in Society and History* 31 (1989): 694–721.

8. Guillermo Bonfil Batalla, *México profundo: Una civilización negada* (Mexico City: Secretaría de Educación Pública, 1987). For an excellent historical account of different perspectives toward indigenismo in Mexico, see Cynthia Hewitt de Alcántara, *Anthropological Perspectives on Rural Mexico* (Boston: Routledge and Kegan Paul, 1984).

9. Gloria Anzaldúa, *Borderlands/La Frontera: The New Mestiza* (San Francisco: Spinsters/Aunt Lute, 1987).

10. As Carolyn Steedman notes in her account of her mother's life as a woman from the English working classes, her mother told her life story to her to teach her lessons, not to entertain, and the main lesson was about "all the strong, brave women who gave me life . . . and all of them, all the good women dissolved into the figure of my mother, who was, as she told us, a good mother." See Carolyn Kay Steedman, *Landscape for a Good Woman: A Story of Two Lives* (New Brunswick: Rutgers University Press, 1987), p. 3.

11. In the words of Laurel Kendall, writing about the story of Youngsu Mother in *The Life and Hard Times of a Korean Shaman: Of Tales and the Telling of Tales* (Honolulu: University of Hawaii Press, 1988), p. 13.

12. Daphne Patai, *Brazilian Women Speak: Contemporary Life Stories* (New Brunswick: Rutgers University Press, 1988), p. 7.

13. James Clifford, "On Ethnographic Allegory," in Clifford and Marcus, *Writing Culture*, pp. 113–19.

14. Walter Benjamin, "The Storyteller," in *Illuminations* (New York: Shocken Books, 1978), pp. 89, 91.

15. The quote about testimonial novels is from the Cuban writer and pioneer of the genre, Miguel Barnet, *La fuente viva* (La Havana, Cuba: Editorial Letras Cubanas, 1983), p. 30. The *testimonio*, or documentary novel, has been recognized as a literary genre in Latin America since the Cuban writers' organization, Casa de Las Américas, began offering a prize category for works in that genre in 1971. This seems to have been a contestatory move on the part of the Cubans to challenge the "boom" canon then being established of liberal Latin

American literary works, a point forcefully made by George Yúdice, *"Testi-monio* and Postmodernism," *Latin American Perspectives* 18 (1991): 26, spe-cial issue: *Voices of the Voiceless in Testimonial Literature.* For a fuller discus-sion of an approach in many ways opposed to the testimonial literary style, where the dialogic ground of verbal performances shows through in written ac-counts, see Dennis Tedlock, *The Spoken Word and the Work of Interpretation* (Philadelphia: University of Pennsylvania Press, 1983), and "Questions Concern-ing Dialogical Anthropology," *Journal of Anthropological Research* 43 (1987): 325–37, which is followed by an interchange of letters with Stephen Tyler.

16. The critical literature on life histories, women's autobiographies, and oral histories is quite large, and growing constantly. I offer a more extensive account of these developments in my essay "Rage and Redemption: Reading the Life Story of a Mexican Marketing Woman," *Feminist Studies* 16 (1990): 223–58. For a synthesis of the problems and methods of life history research, see L. L. Langness and Gelya Frank, *Lives: An Anthropological Approach to Biography* (Novato, Cal.: Chandler and Sharp, 1981), and Lawrence C. Watson and Maria-Barbara Watson-Franke, *Interpreting Life Histories: An Anthropo-logical Inquiry* (New Brunswick: Rutgers University Press, 1985). The genre of life history in anthropology was first explored in the context of Native Ameri-can lives, and this tradition has been analyzed in several excellent recent works, for example, H. David Brumble III, *American Indian Autobiography* (Berkeley: University of California Press, 1988), and Arnold Krupat, *For Those Who Come After: A Study of Native American Autobiography* (Berkeley: Uni-versity of California Press, 1985). In the last few years there has been a veri-table boom in feminist writing about women's life stories. Among key works, see Susan N. G. Geiger, "Women's Life Histories: Method and Content," *Signs* 11 (1986): 334–51; Bella Brodzki and Celeste Schenck, eds., *Life/Lines: Theo-rizing Women's Autobiography* (Ithaca: Cornell University Press, 1988); Per-sonal Narratives Group, eds., *Interpreting Women's Lives: Feminist Theory and Personal Narratives* (Bloomington: Indiana University Press, 1989); Joanne Braxton, *Black Women Writing Autobiography: A Tradition within a Tradi-tion* (Philadelphia: Temple University Press, 1989); Sherna Berger Gluck and Daphne Patai, eds., *Women's Words: The Feminist Practice of Oral History* (New York: Routledge, 1991).

17. Angie Chabram, "Chicana/o Studies as Oppositional Ethnography," *Cul-tural Studies* 4 (1990): 242, special issue: *Chicana/o Cultural Representations: Reframing Alternative Critical Discourses.* For a succinct overview of the Chicano critique of anthropology, see Renato Rosaldo, "Chicano studies, 1970–1984," *Annual Review of Anthropology* 14 (1985): 405–27. For a sampling of recent Chicana/o criticism, see Héctor Calderón and José David Saldívar, eds., *Criticism in the Borderlands: Studies in Chicano Literature, Culture, and Ideology* (Durham: Duke University Press, 1991).

18. See the perceptive essay by Norma Alarcón, "What Kind of Lover Have

You Made Me, Mother? Toward a Theory of Chicanas' Feminism and Cultural
Identity through Poetry," in Audrey T. McCluskey, ed., *Women of Color: Perspectives on Feminism and Identity*, Women's Studies Monograph Series, no. 1
(Bloomington: Indiana University, 1985), pp. 85–110. For examples of poetry,
essays, and fiction by Chicanas and other Latinas, see Alma Gómez, Cherríe
Moraga, and Mariana Romo-Carmona, eds., *Cuentos: Stories by Latinas* (La-
tham, N.Y.: Kitchen Table, Women of Color Press, 1983); María Herrera-Sobek,
ed., *Beyond Stereotypes: The Critical Analysis of Chicana Literature* (Binghamton, N.Y.: Bilingual Review Press/Editorial Bilingue, 1985); María del Carmen Boza, Beverly Silva, and Carmen Valle, eds., *Nosotras: Latina Literature
Today* (Binghamton, N.Y.: Bilingual Review Press/Editorial Bilingue, 1986);
Evangelina Vigil, ed., *Woman of Her Word: Hispanic Women Write* (Houston:
Arte Publico Press, 1987); Alicia Gaspar de Alba, María Herrera-Sobek, and De-
metria Martínez, *Three Times a Woman: Chicana Poetry* (Tempe, Ariz.: Bilingual Review Press, 1989).

19. See the comments on this issue in Renato Rosaldo, *Culture and Truth:
The Remaking of Social Analysis* (Boston: Beacon Press, 1989), pp. 49–51.

20. See, especially, José Limón, "Agringado Joking in Texas-Mexican Society:
Folklore and Differential Identity," in Ricardo Romo and Raymund Paredes,
eds., *New Directions in Chicano Scholarship*, Chicano Studies Monograph Series (San Diego: University of California, 1979); "*Carne, Carnales*, and the
Carnivalesque: Bakhtinian *Batos*, Disorder, and Narrative Discourses," *American Ethnologist* 16 (1989): 471–86; "Dancing with the Devil: Society, Gender,
and the Political Unconscious in Mexican-American South Texas," in Calderón
and Saldívar, *Criticism in the Borderlands*. In his review of Anglo-American
anthropological representations of Chicanos and Mexicans, Américo Paredes
showed how misunderstandings and mistranslations of their verbal art, which
is full of jokes, insinuations, and double and triple meanings, made possible the
elaboration of theories that stereotyped Chicanos and Mexicans as passive, fa-
talistic, and afraid of change. In the expert hands of Paredes, these theories dissolve like so many clouds of smoke, but it is crucial to remember that knowledge, however falsifying, is indeed power, and that such views have held sway
in ethnographic discourse for far too long, creating barriers to other ways of
telling Mexican and Mexican-American lives. See Paredes, "On Ethnographic
Work among Minority Groups," in Romo and Paredes, *New Directions in Chicano Scholarship*.

21. Yet it is no accident that so many Chicanas ended up in English literature departments. Gloria Anzaldúa writes, "I, for one, became adept at and ma-
jored in English to spite, to show up, the arrogant racist teachers who thought
all Chicano children were dumb and dirty. And Spanish was not taught in grade
school. And Spanish was not required in High School. And though now I write
my poems in Spanish as well as English I feel the rip-off of my native tongue."

See Gloria Anzaldúa, "Speaking in Tongues: A Letter to Third World Women Writers," in Cherríe Moraga and Gloria Anzaldúa, *This Bridge Called My Back: Writings by Radical Women of Color* (New York: Kitchen Table, Women of Color Press, 1981), pp. 165–66. Anzaldúa's collage of history, poetry, and self-reflection in her book, *Borderlands/La Frontera* is an effort to recover all the languages taught *and* untaught her, which include at least eight different forms of Spanish and English combinations. From a quite different perspective as a fiction writer, Sandra Cisneros has devised innovative ways to mold the language that her Chicana/o and Mexicana/o characters speak so that their English resonates with expressive *mexicanismos*. Her texts are *enchilados* with literal translations from Mexican Spanish, and she gives her characters, such as the Mexicana narrator in "Eyes of Zapata," a translated language in which to speak experiences lived in Spanish. See Sandra Cisneros, *The House on Mango Street* (New York: Random House, 1991), pp. 14, 16. The story "Eyes of Zapata" is included in *Woman Hollering Creek and Other Stories* (New York: Random House, 1991).

22. On the transformations taking place in notions of subjectivity, community, and nation as a result of the border crossings of transnational capitalism and of Mexican laborers, see Roger Rouse, "Mexican Migration and the Social Space of Postmodernism," *Diaspora* 1 (1991): 8–23. A lucid argument for a concept of the borderlands in ethnographic inquiry is made by Renato Rosaldo, "Border Crossings," in *Culture and Truth*, pp. 196–217. Such a concept would seem to offer a way to move beyond the idea of the "native" in anthropological discourse, challenging, as well, the ethnographic practice of zeroing in on one feature of a group and treating it as representing the ethos of an entire place; see, on these issues, Arjun Appadurai, "Putting Hierarchy in Its Place," *Cultural Anthropology* 3 (1988): 36–49.

23. Hayden White, "The Fictions of Factual Representation," in *Tropics of Discourse: Essays in Cultural Criticism* (Baltimore: Johns Hopkins University Press, 1978); E. L. Doctorow, "False Documents," in *E. L. Doctorow: Essays and Conversations*, ed. Richard Trenner (Princeton: Ontario Review Press, 1983), p. 19.

24. Clifford Geertz, "Blurred Genres: The Refiguration of Social Thought," in *Local Knowledge: Further Essays in Interpretive Anthropology* (New York: Basic Books, 1983); Michael M. J. Fischer, "Ethnicity and the Post-Modern Arts of Memory," in Clifford and Marcus, *Writing Culture*. That the message of the elusiveness of historical truth has reached the level of mainstream consciousness is shown in the recent piece by James Atlas, "Stranger Than Fiction," *New York Times Magazine*, June 23, 1991, pp. 22, 41–43, to which one person earnestly replied by saying that even the Bible is full of presumably exact quotes from God that could not possibly have been remembered verbatim "before the days of printing" (Letters to the Editor, July 21, 1991, p. 6).

25. I borrow this example from Rouse, "Mexican Migration and the Social Space of Postmodernism," p. 8.

26. Doris Sommer, "Irresistible Romance: The Foundational Fictions of Latin America," in Homi K. Bahabha, ed., *Nation and Narration* (New York: Routledge, 1990).

27. Gabriel García Márquez, cited in Lois Zamora, "Novels and Newspapers in the Americas," *Novel* 23 (1989): 44–62. Also see, by the same author, "The Usable Past: The Idea of History in Modern U.S. and Latin American Fiction," in Gustavo Pérez Firmat, ed., *Do the Americas Have a Common Literature?* (Durham: Duke University Press, 1990).

28. Smadar Lavie, *The Poetics of Military Occupation: Mzeina Allegories of Bedouin Identity under Israeli and Egyptian Rule* (Berkeley: University of California Press, 1990), p. 318. I am indebted to Lavie's work for the ideas of allegory and paradox I try to develop here. James Clifford has forcefully articulated the position that all ethnographies enact allegories in his essay, "On Ethnographic Allegory," in Clifford and Marcus, *Writing Culture*.

29. Inez Cardozo-Freeman, "Serpent Fears and Religious Motifs among Mexican Women," *Frontiers* 3 (1978): 10–13. Also see Harold Schechter, *The Bosom Serpent: Folklore and Popular Art* (Iowa City: University of Iowa Press, 1988). Gloria Anzaldúa, like Esperanza, describes herself as having an embattled relationship with serpents. However, her engagement with the serpent lore she learned growing up in South Texas is different in that she builds from that lore to turn around the negative Christian associations of women with serpents and create a new positive identification with Coatlicue, the Snake Woman of Mesoamerican religion. See Anzaldúa, *Borderlands*, pp. 25–51.

30. Although I am beginning to feel more and more that it is not a lie to call myself a Latina, in recognition of my color and, especially, my location on this side of the border, I have kept in mind the strong words of Gloria Anzaldúa: "She attempts to talk *for* us—what a presumption! This act is a rape of our tongue and our acquiescence is a complicity to that rape. We women of color have to stop being modern medusas—throats cut, silenced into a mere hissing." See Gloria Anzaldúa, "La Prieta," in Moraga and Anzaldúa, *This Bridge Called My Back*, p. 206.

31. In thinking about the issue of translating a Mexican working-class vernacular into the privileged form of an English language literary text, I have been inspired by the eloquence with which Henry Louis Gates writes about how African-Americans dealt with the paradox of representing the spoken voice within the written text of their autobiographical slave narratives. Gates notes that "the trope of the Talking Book is not a trope of the presence of voice at all, but of its absence." See Henry Louis Gates, Jr., *The Signifying Monkey: A Theory of African-American Literary Criticism* (New York: Oxford University Press, 1988), p. 167.

32. This discussion of translation as a historical metaphor in Mexican and Chicana consciousness is based entirely on the brilliant essay by Norma Alarcón, "Traddutora, Traditora: A Paradigmatic Figure of Chicana Feminism," *Cultural Critique* 13 (1990): 57–87. The view of translation as betrayal, "but a necessary betrayal, and a productive one," has been a key feature of French feminist discourse, as discussed in Nicole Ward Jouve, *White Woman Speaks with Forked Tongue: Criticism as Autobiography* (London: Routledge, 1991), p. 92.

Part Three Introduction

1. See Ted Conover, *Coyotes: A Journey through the Secret World of America's Illegal Aliens* (New York: Vintage Books, 1987).
2. For all we've learned about border crossings, there are always surprises. When we crossed again in 1990, also on a Sunday, the guard on duty that day ignored the dollar bills sticking out of David's shirt pocket. All he said was *buen viaje,* and waved us on. This more relaxed approach to the American tourist appears to be the result of the anticorruption campaign of Salinas de Gortari and the prospect of a free trade agreement with the United States.
3. As Claudia Salazar notes, "Life-history texts are, after all, the product of an encounter between the ethnographer (a real Self) and real "others"—who cannot and must not be reduced to a discursive construction of our language." See Claudia Salazar, "A Third World Woman's Text: Between the Politics of Criticism and Cultural Politics," in Gluck and Patai, *Women's Words*, p. 102. Also see Jacob Pandian, *Anthropology and the Western Tradition: Toward an Authentic Anthropology* (Prospect Heights, Ill.: Waveland Press, 1985), on the issue of power in ethnographic relationships, and Vincent Crapanzano, "Life Histories," *American Anthropologist* 86 (1984): 953–60, on the issue of power in life history research.
4. Talal Asad, "The Concept of Cultural Translation," in Clifford and Marcus, *Writing Culture*, p. 163. For further discussion of the complexities of cultural translation in anthropology, see Clifford Geertz, "Found in Translation: On the Social History of the Moral Imagination," in *Local Knowledge;* on the links between translation and domination in the colonial context, see Vicente L. Rafael, *Contracting Colonialism: Translation and Christian Conversion in Tagalog Society under Early Spanish Rule* (Ithaca: Cornell University Press, 1988).

12. Literary Wetback

1. George W. Stocking, Jr., "The Ethnographer's Magic: Fieldwork in British Anthropology from Tylor to Malinowski," in Stocking, ed., *Observers Observed: Essays on Ethnographic Fieldwork* (Madison: University of Wisconsin Press, 1983), p. 84.

2. The "Arthur Munby problem" is discussed in Personal Narratives Group, *Interpreting Women's Lives*, p. 11. For an excellent account of the production of *The Diaries of Hannah Cullwick*, see the essay by Julia Swindells in the above anthology. Further discussion of the issues of privilege can be found in Daphne Patai's introduction to *Brazilian Women Speak*.

Part Four Introduction

1. Sidney W. Mintz, *Worker in the Cane: A Puerto Rican Life History* (New York: Norton, 1960); Paul Friedrich, *Agrarian Revolt in a Mexican Village* (Chicago: University of Chicago Press, 1970).

2. For a sharp discussion of the "native women better off" argument often used by feminist anthropologists, see Micaela di Leonardo, introduction to *Gender at the Crossroads: Feminist Anthropology in the Postmodern Era* (Berkeley: University of California Press, 1991), pp. 10–17.

3. See Doris Sommer, "'Not Just a Personal Story': Women's *Testimonios* and the Plural Self," in Brodzki and Schenck, *Life/Lines*; Laurel Bossen, "Secular Saints: The Making of Women Heroes in Latin America," in Silvia Arrom, Mary Ellen Brown, and Darlene J. Sadlier, eds., *New Research: Latin American Women's Studies*, Women's Studies Program, Occasional Series 5 (Bloomington: Indiana University, 1991). Also see the ironic poem by Jo Carrillo, "And When You Leave, Take Your Pictures With You," in Moraga and Anzaldúa, *This Bridge Called My Back*, pp. 63–64. Recent examples of testimonial literature by Latin American women include Domitila Barrios de Chungara, *Let Me Speak: Testimony of Domitila, a Woman of the Bolivian Mines* (New York: Monthly Review Press, 1978); Elisabeth Burgos-Debray, *Rigoberta Menchu: An Indian Woman in Guatemala* (New York: Shocken Books, 1984); Medea Benjamin, *Don't Be Afraid Gringo, a Honduran Woman Speaks from the Heart: The Story of Elvia Alvarado* (San Francisco: Institute for Food and Development Policy, 1987). These recent life stories follow the trajectories by which these three intelligent and articulate women—who already had gained a reputation for their activism—awoke to a heightened political consciousness of gender, racial, and class domination. Esperanza's narrative falls outside of this emerging testimonial tradition; from a Marxist perspective, she still has the wool over her eyes. Yet for her, too, telling her story, as in the case of more politicized Latin American women, is part of her struggle.

4. Elena Poniatowska, "And Here's to You, Jesusa," in Doris Meyer, ed., *Lives on the Line: The Testimony of Contemporary Latin American Authors* (Berkeley: University of California Press, 1989), p. 155. This essay is an account of Poniatowska's work on *Hasta no verte Jesús mío* (Mexico City: Ediciones Era, 1969). Norma Alarcón suggests that, as an upper-class white Mexican woman writing about a working-class Mexican woman, Poniatowska found she had to come to terms, consciously or unconsciously, with "the complex-

ity of the relationship between a woman of color (or native one) and Anglo-European patriarchal history and thought." See Alarcón, "Traddutora, traditora," p. 84.

5. Sandra Cisneros, "Never Marry a Mexican," in *Woman Hollering Creek*, p. 75.

6. A key exception is Daphne Patai, *Brazilian Women Speak*, who comes to her research on Brazilian women from a background in literature. Works that seek to integrate accounts of political economy with women's personal stories include Susan Bourque and Kay Warren's *Women of the Andes* (Ann Arbor: University of Michigan Press, 1981) and Patricia Fernandez-Kelly's *For We Are Sold, I and My People: Women and Industry in Mexico's Frontier* (Albany: State University of New York Press, 1983). For work that connects social change and life history research, see Rina Benmayor, "Testimony, Action Research, and Empowerment: Puerto Rican Women and Popular Education," in Gluck and Patai, *Women's Words*. For a fuller bibliography, see the article by Lynne Phillips cited in the next note.

7. Lynne Phillips, "Rural Women in Latin America: Directions for Future Research," *Latin American Research Review* 25 (1990): 101.

8. Inez Cardozo-Freeman, "Games Mexican Girls Play," *Journal of American Folklore* 88 (1975): 14.

9. Octavio Paz, *El laberinto de la soledad* (1950; Mexico City: Fondo de Cultura Económica, 1981). This passage is also cited in Cardozo-Freeman, "Games Mexican Girls Play," 13.

10. Evelyn P. Stevens, "Marianismo: The Other Face of Machismo in Latin America," in Ann Pescatello, ed., *Female and Male in Latin America* (Pittsburgh: University of Pittsburgh Press, 1973), p. 94. For accounts of similar stereotypes about Chicana women, see Alfredo Mirandé and Evangelina Enríquez, *La Chicana: The Mexican-American Woman* (Chicago: University of Chicago Press, 1979), and Carmen Tafolla, *To Split a Human: Mitos machos y la mujer chicana* (San Antonio: Mexican American Cultural Center, 1985).

11. Let us remember that a key critique by radical women of color was called, precisely, *This Bridge Called My Back*. For a sequel, see Gloria Anzaldúa, ed., *Making Face, Making Soul: Haciendo Caras, Creative and Critical Perspectives by Women of Color* (San Francisco: Aunt Lute, 1990).

12. Chandra Mohanty, "Under Western Eyes: Feminist Scholarship and Colonial Discourses," in Chandra Mohanty, Ann Russo, and Lourdes Torres, eds., *Third World Women and the Politics of Feminism* (Bloomington: Indiana University Press, 1991), p. 56. A related critique can be found in Marnia Lazreg, "Feminism and Difference: The Perils of Writing as a Woman on Women in Algeria," *Feminist Studies* 14 (1988): 81–107. The lack of coevalness in ethnographic texts is often reproduced in feminist texts which represent third world women as mired in the past or arriving at modernity, as Aihwa Ong puts it,

"when Western feminists are already adrift in postmodernism." See Johannes Fabian, *Time and the Other: How Anthropology Makes Its Object* (New York: Columbia University Press, 1983); Aihwa Ong, "Colonialism and Modernity: Feminist Re-Presentations of Women in Non-Western Societies," *Inscriptions*, nos. 3/4 (1988): 87, special issue: *Feminism and the Critique of Colonial Discourse*.

13. Chandra Mohanty, "Cartographies of Struggle: Third World Women and the Politics of Feminism," Introduction to *Third World Women and the Politics of Feminism*, p. 6.

14. See, for example, Irene Silverblatt, *Moon, Sun, and Witches: Gender Ideologies and Class in Inca and Colonial Peru* (Princeton: Princeton University Press, 1987), and Emily Martin, *The Woman in the Body: A Cultural Analysis of Reproduction* (Boston: Beacon Press, 1987). For a critique of the recent academic obsession with finding resisting subjects, see Lila Abu-Lughod, "The Romance of Resistance: Tracing Transformations of Power through Bedouin Women," *American Ethnologist* 17 (1990): 41–55.

15. Edward Said, "In the Shadow of the West," *Wedge*, nos. 7/8 (1985): 4–5, special issue: *The Imperialism of Representation, the Representation of Imperialism*.

16. Linda Brodkey, "Writing Critical Ethnographic Narratives." *Anthropology and Education Quarterly* 18 (1987): 74.

17. Charlotte Perkins Gilman, *The Yellow Wallpaper and Other Stories* (New York: Bantam Books, 1989).

18. Renato Rosaldo, "The Story of Tukbaw: 'They Listen as He Orates,'" in Frank Reynolds and Donald Capps, eds., *The Biographical Process: Studies in the History and Psychology of Religion* (The Hague: Mouton, 1976), pp. 145, 147–48. For further critiques, see Gelya Frank, "Finding the Common Denominator: A Phenomenological Critique of Life History Method," *Ethos* 7 (1979): 68–94; Michael W. Young, "'Our Name Is Women; We Are Bought with Limesticks and Limepots': An Analysis of the Autobiographical Narrative of a Kalauna Woman," *Man* 18 (1983): 480.

19. For suggestive new anthropological work on the rhetoric of the emotions, see the essays in Catherine A. Lutz and Lila Abu-Lughod, eds., *Language and the Politics of Emotion* (New York: Cambridge University Press, 1990).

20. An important parallel here was the effort to produce a special issue on the sexuality of Latinas for *Third Woman*, a project which was slow in its realization because of the social taboos about discussing sexual desire openly in many of the communities in which Latinas have grown up. See Norma Alarcón, Ana Castillo, and Cherríe Moraga, eds., *Third Woman: The Sexuality of Latinas*, vol. 4 (Berkeley: Third Woman Press, 1989).

21. The recent shift in ethnographic writing toward presenting the ethnographer as one more participant in the interaction is insightfully analyzed by Bar-

bara Tedlock, "From Participant Observation to the Observation of Participation: The Emergence of Narrative Ethnography, *Journal of Anthropological Research* 47 (1991): 69–94.

15. Translated Woman

1. The variety of responses to Oscar Lewis's book in the Mexican press have been collected in John Paddock, "*The Children of Sánchez* in the Headlines," in *Mesoamerican Notes*, vol. 6 (Mexico City: University of the Americas, 1965), pp. 69–135.

2. bell hooks, "Representations: Feminism and Black Masculinity," in *Yearning: Race, Gender, and Cultural Politics* (Boston: South End Press, 1990), p. 72.

3. Yet I take heart knowing that Chicanas, many of them lesbians, have spoken out against sexism in their communities both bravely and sensitively. In the words of Gloria Anzaldúa, "Though we 'understand' the root causes of male hatred and fear, and the subsequent wounding of women, we do not excuse, we do not condone, and we will no longer put up with it. . . . As long as to be a *vieja* is a thing of derision, there can be no real healing of our psyches." See Anzaldúa, *Borderlands*, pp. 83–84.

4. See, for example, *The Nation*, July 24/31, 1991, special issue: *Scapegoating the Black Family, Black Women Speak*. For a wide-ranging theoretical perspective, see Patricia Hill Collins, *Black Feminist Thought: Knowledge, Consciousness, and the Politics of Empowerment* (Boston: Unwin Hyman, 1990).

5. See Maxine Baca Zinn, "Family, Race, and Poverty in the Eighties," *Signs* 14 (1989): 856–74, special issue: *Common Grounds and Crossroads: Race, Ethnicity, and Class in Women's Lives*.

6. On family violence as historically and politically constructed, see Linda Gordon, *Heroes of Their Own Lives: The Politics and History of Family Violence, Boston 1880–1960* (New York: Viking Press, 1988). For an account of recent social movements seeking to end violence against women, see Susan Schechter, *Women and Male Violence: The Visions and Struggles of the Battered Women's Movement* (Boston: South End Press, 1982). Also see *Women's Studies Quarterly* 13 (1985), special feature, "Teaching about Women and Violence"; Jaina Hanmer and Mary Maynard, eds., *Women, Violence, and Social Control* (Atlantic Highlands, N.J.: Humanities Press International, 1987). The most lucid writing I have found on male violence is by bell hooks, "Violence in Intimate Relationships: A Feminist Perspective," in her collection *Talking Back: Thinking Feminist, Thinking Black* (Boston: South End Press, 1989).

7. Susan Faludi, *Backlash: The Undeclared War against American Women* (New York: Crown Publishers, 1991).

8. Personal Narratives Group, *Interpreting Women's Lives*, p. 5.

9. Steedman, *Landscape for a Good Woman*, p. 81.

10. Ibid., p. 69.

11. For further discussion of emotional states as illness states in women, see Kaja Finkler, *Spiritualist Healers in Mexico: Successes and Failures of Alternative Therapeutics* (New York: Praeger, 1985), 65; Paul Farmer, "Bad Blood, Spoiled Milk: Bodily Fluids as Moral Barometers in Rural Haiti," *American Ethnologist* 15 (1988): 62–83. Coraje also bears a close resemblance to the rage that Ilongots experience at the death of close kin, moving them to want to expel grief by headhunting, a subject dealt with in Renato Rosaldo, "Grief and a Headhunter's Rage: On the Cultural Force of Emotions," in *Culture and Truth*. Even more broadly, rage is a culturally forceful state of consciousness, whether it refers to feminist rage or the diffuse anger that oppressed people feel in colonial settings. See, for example, Emily Martin's discussion of the suppressed anger that women feel as second-class citizens in American society in *The Woman in the Body*, pp. 135–36.

12. For a discussion of the significance of pronouns, see Paul Friedrich, "Structural Implications of Russian Pronominal Usage" in *Language, Context, and the Imagination: Essays by Paul Friedrich*, ed. Anwar S. Dil (Stanford: Stanford University Press, 1979).

13. The idea of spiritual accounting is a constant theme in Mexican women's popular discourse. Guadalupe, whose death is the subject of a multinarrative by Oscar Lewis, used almost the same terms of expression as Esperanza, saying, "Yes, we pay for everything we do in life. God is slow but he doesn't forget." See Oscar Lewis, *A Death in the Sánchez Family* (New York: Random House, 1970), p. xxi.

14. Holly F. Mathews, "Intracultural Variation in Beliefs about Gender in a Mexican Community," *American Behavioral Sciences* 31 (1987): 228.

15. My analysis is informed by Marianne Hirsch, *The Mother/Daughter Plot: Narrative, Psychoanalysis, Feminism* (Bloomington: Indiana University Press, 1989).

16. Maxine Hong Kingston, *The Woman Warrior: Memoirs of a Girlhood among Ghosts* (New York: Random House, 1975), p. 24. Similarly, Elsa Barkley Brown, an African-American historian, writes lucidly about the seeming contradictions of her mother's advice to her. Although her mother told her that raising a family should be a woman's sole aim in life, she still gave her daughter a check covering tuition for graduate school that represented the pooled funds of mothers, sisters, aunts. See Elsa Barkley Brown, "Mothers of Mind," in Patricia Bell-Scott et al., eds., *Double Stitch: Black Women Write about Mothers and Daughters* (Boston: Beacon Press, 1991), pp. 81–85.

17. Among the recent studies that consider heroic fighting women, see Sharon MacDonald, Pat Holden, and Shirley Ardener, eds., *Images of Women in Peace and War: Cross-Cultural and Historical Perspectives* (Madison: University of Wisconsin Press, 1987); Antonia Fraser, *The Warrior Queens: The Legends and the Lives of the Women Who Have Led Their Nations in War*

(New York: Random House, 1990); Elizabeth Salas, *Soldaderas in the Mexican Military: Myth and History* (Austin: University of Texas Press, 1990); Margaret Randall, *Sandino's Daughters: Testimonies of Nicaraguan Women in Struggle* (Vancouver: New Star Books, 1981).

18. Even as she questions the idea that mothers, or for that matter women generally, are intrinsically peaceful, Sara Ruddick has suggested that "maternal practice" can lay the groundwork for peace politics and antimilitarist resistance to the ubiquity of war. Her argument is problematic in many ways, not the least of which is her inattention to the violence that Adrienne Rich characterized as being at "the heart of maternal darkness." In Jean Bethke Elshtain's work on women and war, she has cautioned against dichotomizing women as automatic pacifists and men as warmongering destroyers. Similarly, Ruth Roach Pierson suggests that women's potential for opposition to war is rooted in their historical exclusion from power and wealth, not in their maternal practices. See Sara Ruddick, *Maternal Thinking: Toward a Politics of Peace* (New York: Ballantine Books, 1989); Adrienne Rich, *Of Woman Born: Motherhood as Experience and Institution* (New York: Norton, 1986); Jean Bethke Elshtain, *Women and War* (New York: Basic Books, 1987); Ruth Roach Pierson, "'Did Your Mother Wear Army Boots?' Feminist Theory and Women's Relation to War, Peace, and Revolution," in MacDonald et al., *Images of Women in Peace and War*, pp. 205–27.

19. Chris Weedon, *Feminist Practice and Poststructuralist Theory* (New York: Basil Blackwell, 1987), p. 9.

20. I've changed the gender of this line from "My Man" on *The Billie Holiday Songbook* (Polygram Records, 1985).

21. I am indebted to James W. Fernandez for this keen insight. For a fuller discussion than I offer here of the ways in which wholeness is enacted in ritual and social action, see by Fernandez, *Bwiti: An Ethnography of the Religious Imagination* (Princeton: Princeton University Press, 1982) and *Persuasions and Performances: The Play of Tropes in Culture* (Bloomington: Indiana University Press, 1986).

22. Lynne Phillips, "Difference, Indifference, and Making a Difference: Reflexivity in the Time of Cholera" (paper read at the Canadian Sociology and Anthropology Association Conference, Kingston, Ontario, June 3, 1991), pp. 4, 20.

23. Norma Alarcón, "The Theoretical Subject(s) of *This Bridge Called My Back* and Anglo-American Feminism," in Calderón and Saldívar, *Criticism in the Borderlands*, p. 37. For a different perspective on the turn toward attending to the differences among women, see Susan Bordo, "Feminism, Postmodernism, and Gender-Scepticism," in Linda J. Nicholson, ed., *Feminism/Postmodernism* (New York: Routledge, 1990).

24. See Judith Stacey, "Can There Be a Feminist Ethnography?" in Gluck and Patai, *Women's Words*; Kamala Visweswaran, "Betrayal: An Analysis in Three Acts," in I. Grewal and C. Kaplan, eds., *Scattered Hegemonies: Postmodernity*

and Transnational Feminist Practices (Minneapolis: University of Minnesota Press, 1993); Phillips, "Difference, Indifference, and Making a Difference."

25. As Daphne Patai puts it, "most of us do not want to bite the hand that feeds us; but neither do we want to caress it too lovingly." See her essay "U.S. Academics and Third World Women: Is Ethical Research Possible?" in Gluck and Patai, *Women's Words*, p. 139.

26. Clifford, "Introduction: Partial Truths," p. 1. For feminist critiques of Clifford's work, see Deborah Gordon, "Writing Culture, Writing Feminism: The Poetics and Politics of Experimental Ethnography," and Kamala Visweswaran, "Defining Feminist Ethnography," *Inscriptions*, nos. 3/4 (1988): 7–44, special issue: *Feminism and the Critique of Colonial Discourse*. The colonialist and racist resonances of the book's cover are sharply analyzed by bell hooks, "Culture to Culture: Ethnography and Cultural Studies as Critical Intervention," in *Yearning*.

27. For example, every core reading list includes the work of Marx, Durkheim, and Weber; the more recent canon includes Gramsci, Raymond Williams, and Bourdieu (for theories of society) and Geertz, Clifford, and Marcus and Fischer (for theories of how the anthropologist is an author and critic). Have women not produced theoretical work of equal significance, or have they written theory differently? We need to seek answers to this question. Obviously, I am not saying works by male thinkers are not important or should not be read. What I am calling for is greater balance in the official reading lists of the discipline, so that they can take account of the work of both women and men and the differently situated ways in which they have written theory. I also think more attention needs to be given to the ways the canonical texts we do read reproduce certain gendered relations of power within the profession.

28. Rosario Morales, "Concepts of Pollution," in Aurora Levins Morales and Rosario Morales, *Getting Home Alive* (Ithaca: Firebrand Books, 1986), p. 62.

29. Susan Sontag, "The Anthropologist as Hero," in *Against Interpretation and Other Essays* (1966; New York: Doubleday, 1990), p. 77.

30. I am currently preparing an anthology with Deborah Gordon, tentatively titled *Women Writing Culture: A Reader in Feminist Ethnography*, that will take up these issues in more detail. For a brilliant feminist history of anthropology since the sixties, see also Deborah Gordon's dissertation, "Engendering the Ethnographic Imagination: Feminist Readings, Anthropological Texts" (University of California, Santa Cruz, 1991).

31. Donna Perry, "An Interview with Jamaica Kincaid," in Henry Louis Gates, Jr., ed., *Reading Black, Reading Feminist: A Critical Anthology* (New York: Penguin Books, 1990), p. 503.

32. A classic example is Michelle Zimbalist Rosaldo, "Woman, Culture, and Society: A Theoretical Overview," in Michelle Zimbalist Rosaldo and Louise Lamphere, eds., *Woman, Culture, and Society* (Stanford: Stanford University Press, 1974), pp. 17–42.

33. For further discussion, see Nancy Fraser and Linda J. Nicholson, "Social Criticism without Philosophy: An Encounter between Feminism and Postmodernism," in Nicholson, *Feminism/Postmodernism*, p. 33.

34. One of the earliest and most cogent agendas for this emerging feminist ethnography can be found in Kamala Visweswaran's essay, "Defining Feminist Ethnography."

35. In the words of Lynne Phillips, "If feminism becomes by definition exclusionary and/or hegemonic (because we can never "know" the other, we can only be reflexive about that which we think we know) . . . this kind of relativity ultimately leads to political paralysis and even *indifference* to the experiences of other women." See "Difference, Indifference, and Making a Difference," p. 2.

36. Bordo, "Feminism, Postmodernism, and Gender-Scepticism," p. 142.

37. Deborah Gordon, "The Unhappy Relationship of Feminism and Postmodernism in Anthropology," *Anthropological Quarterly* (Spring 1993).

38. Stacey, "Can There Be a Feminist Ethnography?"; Lila Abu-Lughod, "Can There Be a Feminist Ethnography?" *Women and Performance* 5 (1990): 7–27; Ann Oakley, "Interviewing Women: A Contradiction in Terms," in Helen Roberts, ed., *Doing Feminist Research* (London: Routledge and Kegan Paul, 1981). "What feminist ethnography can contribute to anthropology," writes Lila Abu-Lughod, "is an unsettling of the boundaries that have been central to its identity as a discipline of the self studying the other" (p. 26). Or, as Sally Cole puts it, "The creation of a self through opposition to an other is blocked, and therefore both the multiplicity of the self and the multiple overlapping and interacting qualities of the other cannot be ignored . . . offer[ing] the promise of finally undermining the assumption of anthropology that we stand outside." See Sally Cole, "Is Feminist Ethnography 'New' Ethnography?: The Taming of the Shrew in Anthropology" (working paper for discussion by the South Central Women's Research Colloquium, McMaster University, March 15, 1991), p. 25.

39. As black feminist scholar Patricia Hill Collins has pointed out, "Either/ or dualistic thinking, or . . . the construct of dichotomous oppositional difference, may be a philosophical lynchpin in systems of race, class, and gender oppression." See "Learning from the Outsider Within: The Sociological Significance of Black Feminist Thought," in Mary Margaret Fonow and Judith A. Cook, eds., *Beyond Methodology: Feminist Scholarship as Lived Research* (Bloomington: Indiana University Press, 1991), p. 42.

16. In the Labyrinth of the General and His History

1. Cisneros, "Eyes of Zapata," pp. 85, 95, 105.

2. Angeles Mastretta, *Arráncame la vida* (Mexico City: Cal y Arena, 1990), pp. 221, 222, 226. Translations from the Spanish are my own. The book has

been translated into English as *Mexican Bolero* (New York: Viking Penguin, 1990).

3. Sylvia Bovenschen, "The Contemporary Witch, the Historical Witch, and the Witch Myth: The Witch, Subject of the Appropriation of Nature and Object of the Domination of Nature," *New German Critique* 15 (1978): 84–85, 90.

4. Michael Taussig, *Shamanism, Colonialism, and the Wild Man: A Study in Terror and Healing* (Chicago: University of Chicago Press, 1987), p. xiv. I learned of Bovenschen's work through Taussig's work, which uses her analysis as a point of departure for understanding Putumayo shamanism. I, in turn, have tried to combine the ideas of Bovenschen and Taussig to understand both the gendered and healing aspects of Pancho Villa spiritism. For my understanding of the religious imagination, I am indebted to James W. Fernandez's *Bwiti*.

5. For a similar use of the Catholic religious imagination for the resurrection of revolutionary heroes, see Albert Soboul, "Religious Feeling and Popular Cults during the French Revolution: 'Patriot Saints' and Martyrs for Liberty," in Stephen Wilson, ed., *Saints and Their Cults: Studies in Religious Sociology, Folklore, and History* (Cambridge: Cambridge University Press, 1983).

6. As Walter Benjamin put it, "The past carries with it a temporal index by which it is referred to redemption. There is a secret agreement between past generations and the present one." Silvia Bovenschen responds, "It is as if the empirical witches perceived this secret agreement Benjamin describes; as if those directly affected by the present are closer to the past than historical reflection." See "The Contemporary Witch," pp. 84–85.

7. In much the same way, it has to be said that many of the bridges between the stories of terror in the past and the stories of healing in the present, which form the two parts of Michael Taussig's *Shamanism, Colonialism, and the Wild Man*, are suspended by leaps of faith rather than by fully made connections. I am not sure that I can do any better here.

8. Paul J. Vanderwood and Frank N. Samponaro, *Border Fury: A Picture Postcard Record of Mexico's Revolution and U.S. War Preparedness, 1910–1917* (Albuquerque: University of New Mexico Press, 1988), p. 182.

9. Friedrich Katz, "From Alliance to Dependency: The Formation and Deformation of an Alliance between Francisco Villa and the United States," in Daniel Nugent, ed., *Rural Revolt in Mexico and U.S. Intervention* (San Diego: Center for U.S.-Mexican Studies, 1988), p. 244.

10. Ilene V. O'Malley, *The Myth of the Revolution: Hero Cults and the Institutionalization of the Mexican State, 1920–1940* (Westport, Conn.: Greenwood Press, 1986), p. 88.

11. Haldeen Braddy, *The Paradox of Pancho Villa* (El Paso: Texas Western Press, 1978), p. 58. This book presents the negative American perspective on Pancho Villa and is useful both as a sample of that particular representation and for its supply of legendary stories about Villa. For a general model of the

social and economic meanings of banditry, with Villa analyzed as one example among many cruelly violent yet heroically-remembered Robin Hoods, see Eric Hobsbawm, *Bandits* (1969; New York: Pantheon Books, 1982).

12. Friedrich Katz, *The Secret War in Mexico: Europe, the United States, and the Mexican Revolution* (Chicago: University of Chicago Press, 1981), p. 144; "Pancho Villa, Peasant Movements, and Agrarian Reform in Northern Mexico," in D. A. Brading, ed., *Caudillo and Peasant in the Mexican Revolution* (Cambridge: Cambridge University Press, 1980), p. 71; Rubén Osorio, "*Villismo*: Nationalism and Popular Mobilization in Northern Mexico," in Nugent, *Rural Revolt in Mexico and U.S. Intervention*, p. 163.

13. O'Malley, *The Myth of the Revolution*, pp. 88–89.

14. Vanderwood and Samponaro, *Border Fury*, p. 117.

15. Friedrich Katz, "Pancho Villa and the Attack on Columbus, New Mexico," *American Historical Review* 83 (1978): 112–14. Although I have accepted Katz's reading of Pancho Villa's motives for the attack on Columbus, there are dissenting views, which see in Villa's attack only the actions of a prototypical bandit and *guerrillero*. See the exchange of letters between James A. Sandos and Friedrich Katz, "Communications," *American Historical Review* 84 (1979): 304–7.

16. Vanderwood and Samponaro, *Border Fury*, p. 12. On the literal and social warfare directed against Mexicanos in South Texas during this period and afterward, see David Montejano, *Anglos and Mexicans in the Making of Texas, 1836–1986* (Austin: University of Texas Press, 1987); José Limón, "Dancing with the Devil: Society and Cultural Poetics in Mexican-American South Texas" (manuscript).

17. Vanderwood and Samponaro, *Border Fury*, p. ix.

18. Braddy, *The Paradox of Pancho Villa*, p. 16.

19. I discuss a Mexican Inquisition case focusing on a woman's interaction with the devil in the form of a little black dog in my essay "Sex and Sin, Witchcraft and the Devil in Late-Colonial Mexico."

20. O'Malley, *The Myth of the Revolution*, p. 91; Ana María Alonso, "U.S. Military Intervention, Revolutionary Mobilization, and Popular Ideology in the Chihuahuan Sierra, 1916–1917," in Nugent, *Rural Revolt in Mexico and U.S. Intervention*, p. 222. As Alonso's research indicates, sectors of the Chihuahuan peasantry who had been supporters of Villa accepted the protection of the American soldiers and displayed little anti-American feeling, suggesting that legends about Villa as a hero probably had greater impact in regions that were farther away from the orbit of his direct influence.

21. O'Malley, *The Myth of the Revolution*, p. 94. "Partly because of his rude upbringing and partly because of his disposition, he never observed the forms of courtesy with anybody," wrote Martín Luis Guzmán, *The Eagle and the Serpent* (1928; New York: Doubleday, 1965), pp. 299–300.

22. Luis Garfias, *Truth and Legend on Pancho Villa: Life and Deeds of the Famous Leader of the Mexican Revolution* (Mexico City: Panorama Editorial, 1981), p. 348.

23. O'Malley, *The Myth of the Revolution*, pp. 98, 111. On Villa as presented in revolutionary ballads, see Merle E. Simmons, *The Mexican Corrido as a Source for Interpretive Study of Modern Mexico, 1870–1950* (Bloomington: Indiana University Press, 1957).

24. O'Malley, *The Myth of the Revolution*, p. 144.

25. Ibid., p. 3. See Américo Paredes, *"With His Pistol in His Hand": A Border Ballad and Its Hero* (1958; Austin: University of Texas Press, 1988), for an account of the life and lore surrounding Gregorio Cortez (1875–1915), a border hero who in many ways was a predecessor of Pancho Villa. The ballads about Gregorio Cortez never fail to describe him as having "his pistol in his hand," evoking the Mexican-American right of self-defense at a moment of intense political violence in southern Texas. Cortez's masculine heroism, like Villa's, was put to the test when he stood up, as a man alone—"the way real men fight" (p. 51)—to many and more heavily armed gringos. In the words of the ballad: "Then said Gregorio Cortez,/With his pistol in his hand,/'Ah, so many mounted Rangers/Just to take one Mexican!'" For an analysis of the literary and political implications of the work of Paredes, see José Limón, "Américo Paredes and the Mexican Ballad: The Creative Anthropological Text as Social Critique," in Smadar Lavie, Kirin Narayan, and Renato Rosaldo, eds., in *Creativity: Self and Society* (Ithaca: Cornell University Press, forthcoming).

26. Guzmán, *The Eagle and the Serpent*, p. 44.

27. Osorio, *"Villismo,"* p. 152.

28. O'Malley, *The Myth of the Revolution*, pp. 143–44.

29. Martín Luis Guzmán, *Memoirs of Pancho Villa* (Austin: University of Texas Press, 1965), p. 348; John Reed, *Insurgent Mexico* (New York: D. Appleton, 1914), p. 138.

30. The meaning of the struggle of the soldaderas is currently being recuperated in all the richness of its mythic and historical implications by Chicana scholars. See Elizabeth Salas, *Soldaderas in the Mexican Military*; María Herrera-Sobek, *The Mexican Corrido: A Feminist Analysis* (Bloomington: Indiana University Press, 1990).

31. Casasola is cited in Anna Macías, *Against All Odds: The Feminist Movement in Mexico to 1940* (Westport, Conn.: Greenwood Press, 1982), p. 42. Adelita's words are cited in Julia Tuñón Pablos, *Mujeres en México: Una historia olvidada* (Mexico City: Planeta, 1987), pp. 134–40. For a life story of a soldadera, see Elena Poniatowska, *Hasta no verte Jesús mío*. Soldaderas tended to be women from the rural and working classes who accompanied their men to battle. Middle-class educated women played different roles in the Revolution. María Arias Bernal, nicknamed "María Pistolas," a normal school graduate, held demonstrations at Madero's grave to protest Huerta's takeover of the

government, for which she was jailed. María Hernández Zarco, a typesetter, printed a speech denouncing Huerta as a tyrant after her employer refused to do so, a speech that was read in the Senate by a male senator who announced that it had been printed by a woman. Beatriz González Ortega, the director of a normal school in Zacatecas, turned the school into a hospital after Pancho Villa's attack on the city, treating the wounded of both sides, whether federal troops or Villistas, for which policy she was whipped and almost killed by Villa. "Here I tend only wounded Mexicans," she was reported to have said when Villa demanded to know who among the wounded were federal troops, so they could be executed. Villa relented after friends intervened on her behalf, and he treated her respectfully thereafter. On these women, see Macías, *Against All Odds*, pp. 38–39 and the bibliography on pp. 169–72.

32. Salas, *Soldaderas in the Mexican Military*, p. 46.

33. Friedrich Katz, personal communication, letter of August 30, 1990.

34. Reed, *Insurgent Mexico*, p. 131.

35. Jean Franco, *Plotting Women: Gender and Representation in Mexico* (New York: Columbia University Press, 1989), p. 131. As Elena Poniatowska points out, the Mexican Revolution was not only institutionalized but novelized from a male perspective, so that a brilliant writer like Nellie Campobello, who wrote about the Revolution from the perspective of a little girl, was barely recognized in her own time. See Poniatowska's introduction to the recent translation of Nellie Campobello's *Cartucho* and *My Mother's Hands* (Austin: University of Texas Press, 1988).

36. O'Malley, *The Myth of the Revolution*, p. 8; Samuel Ramos, *El perfil del hombre y la cultura en México* (1934; Mexico City: Espasa-Calpe, 1986); Paz, *El laberinto de la soledad*; María Herrera-Sobek, "The Treacherous Woman Archetype: A Structuring Agent in the Corrido," *Aztlan* 13 (1980): 135–48. For a new reading of Ramos and Paz, set within an account of Mexican-American male working-class speech and body play, see Limón, "*Carne, Carnales*, and the Carnivalesque." For an account of the many important Chicana feminist revisions of the story of La Malinche, see Alarcón, "Traddutora, Traditora."

37. Franco, *Plotting Women*, pp. 131–32.

38. The phrase is from William B. Taylor, "Between Global Process and Local Knowledge: An Inquiry into Early Latin American Social History, 1500–1900," in Olivier Zunz, ed., *Reliving the Past: The Worlds of Social History* (Chapel Hill: University of North Carolina Press), p. 173.

39. On the issue of female spectatorship in narrative cinema and other domains, and the feminist appropriation "with a vengeance" of male narrativity, see Teresa de Lauretis, *Alice Doesn't: Feminism, Semiotics, Cinema* (Bloomington: Indiana University Press, 1984), pp. 103–57, especially pp. 137, 157.

40. I have condensed ideas from various sources here, including Joan Riviere, "Womanliness as a Masquerade," *International Journal of Psycho-Analysis* 10 (1929): 303–13; Sue-Ellen Case, "Toward a Butch-Femme Aesthetic," and Yo-

landa Broyles González, "Toward a Re-Vision of Chicano Theatre History: The Women of El Teatro Campesino," in Lynda Hart, ed., *Making a Spectacle: Feminist Essays on Contemporary Women's Theatre* (Ann Arbor: University of Michigan Press, 1989). In light of Chencha's "acting," I found it enlightening to read, in the essay by Yolando Broyles González, about the problems that actress Socorro Valdez has had with the Teatro Campesino. Because she does not look stereotypically feminine, Valdez has never been allowed to play a lead female part, like that of the Virgin of Guadalupe, but she has played numerous male leads and sexless characters like *La Muerte.*

41. Holly Devor, *Gender Blending: Confronting the Limits of Duality* (Bloomington: Indiana University Press, 1989). Also see Joseph A. Boone and Michael Cadden, eds., *Engendering Men: The Question of Male Feminist Criticism* (New York: Routledge, 1990). In this analysis of Pancho Villa spiritism, my aim has been not to do a general study of the cult, but to focus on the meaning of the cult for Esperanza and other women. I realize this leaves much unanswered about the cult. One unexplored issue here is the meaning the cult has for the handful of men who also participate, though in a more low-key manner than the women. The men whose participation I have followed seem to respect Chencha for many of the same reasons the women do: for her strength, bravado, and effectiveness as a healer. It may be that some of these men, for example, the young man in the wheelchair, also find Chencha a good interlocutor when confronting the limits of their masculine identity. Gender blending, together with shared class positions on the margins of Mexican society, are among the key features that bring together women and men in the cult.

42. See, for example, Larry Rohter, "Bandit Wears Halo in Unsaintly City," *New York Times*, May 11, 1989, for a news story about the regional hero Jesus Malverde. Hung as a bandit in 1909, Malverde continues to be popularly regarded as a Robin Hood figure, and he has become a folk saint in the state of Sinaloa. The veneration of Malverde as a folk saint suggests that, as with Pancho Villa spiritism, the national domain is displaced onto the religious domain in contemporary discourses of popular critique and resistance. I would like to thank Benjamin Orlove for his kindness in sending me the news clipping about Malverde.

43. Anita Brenner, *The Wind that Swept Mexico: The History of the Mexican Revolution of 1910–1942* (1943; Austin: University of Texas Press, 1971), p. 51. Stories abound of the real money—gold and silver—that was buried in the ground during that period of worthless money. Pancho Villa, it is said, left some of his treasures hidden in a series of caves. (Braddy, *The Paradox of Pancho Villa*, p. 28.)

44. Here it is useful to recall the point Américo Paredes has made about machismo being as much an American as it is a Mexican construct, which is amply revealed in the bravado of both Pershing and Villa. Machismo as a concept dates to the revolutionary period and as a term only to the 1940s. See

Américo Paredes, "The United States, Mexico, and *Machismo*," *Journal of Folklore Institute* 1 (1971): 17–37. Similar displays of machismo on the part of the American government were apparent in the recent punitive expeditions against Manuel Noriega of Panama and Saddam Hussein of Iraq.

17. The Biography in the Shadow

1. Pat Mora, "Legal Alien," in Gloria Anzaldúa, ed., *Making Face, Making Soul*, p. 376.

2. Rosario Morales, "I Am the Reasonable One," in Morales and Morales, *Getting Home Alive*, p. 148.

3. Sandra Cisneros, "Living as a Writer: Choice and Circumstance," *Feminist Writers Guild* 10 (1987): 8.

4. Thinking about Renato Rosaldo's account of the "Western Culture Controversy" at Stanford University has helped me to find the words for retelling the College of Letters story. For years I thought this was a story about my personal failure; now I've come to see it as a story about a youthful and undefined but nevertheless true confrontation with the idea of authority implied in a core list of the "great books" of Western civilization that every cultivated person should know. See Rosaldo, *Culture and Truth*, pp. 218–24, and "Feeling History: Reflections on the Western Culture Controversy" (paper prepared for the conference "The Historical Turn in the Human Sciences," Ann Arbor, Michigan, October 4–6, 1990). For a historical analysis of the controversy at Stanford, see Mary Louise Pratt, "Humanities for the Future: Reflections on the Western Culture Debate at Stanford," *South Atlantic Quarterly* 89 (1990): 7–25. Also see Eric Alterman, "Not So Great," *The Nation*, November 19, 1990, pp. 584–85, for an account of the recent celebration of Encyclopaedia Britannica's publication of the sixty "Great Books of the Western World," whose editor-in-chief told Alterman that no African-Americans were included "because no black American was necessary. No black American has written a great book." The pain of such distinctions was articulated movingly by Renato Rosaldo when, in speaking of his own education, he said, "I thought that if I could read the shelf of books, I would be an intellectual. But then I had to speak to the exclusions of that shelf of books" (talk given at the conference "Writing the Social Text," University of Maryland at College Park, November 18–19, 1989). I am grateful to Renato Rosaldo for his vivid image of the shelf of books, which has been a spark for my own thinking.

5. Carol Gilligan, "Joining the Resistance: Psychology, Politics, Girls, and Women," *Michigan Quarterly Review* 20 (1990): 501–36. Reprinted in Lawrence Goldstein, ed., *The Female Body: Figures, Styles, Speculations* (Ann Arbor: University of Michigan Press, 1991).

6. Even so, I did feel some lingering disappointment that I had not successfully grappled with what I had been indoctrinated to think was the most prestigious and fundamental of intellectual discourses. Explaining why the French

feminist theorist and psychoanalyst Luce Irigaray chose to present herself for the French doctorate in philosophy, Toril Moi notes that "the choice was an obvious one: in our culture, philosophy has enjoyed the status of 'master discourse.'" In the words of Irigaray herself, "it constitutes the discourse of discourses." See Toril Moi, *Sexual/Textual Politics: Feminist Literary Theory* (New York: Methuen, 1985), p. 129.

7. More recently, I have been able to see that there were links between the dissertation work and my life, but those links were deeply submerged beneath the intellectual project. See my self-reflexive essay, "Death and Memory: From Santa María del Monte to Miami Beach," *Cultural Anthropology* 6 (1991): 346–84.

8. Michelle Cliff, "A Journey into Speech," in *The Land of Look Behind* (Ithaca: Firebrand Books, 1985), p. 11. Cliff's realization led her to write in ways that would touch the rage she was not supposed to feel as a light-skinned Jamaican.

9. Even with the current literary and self-reflexive turn in anthropology, the caution remains that the writing not be "too confessional." See, for example, Marcus and Fischer, *Anthropology as Cultural Critique*, p. 30.

10. American Jewish colleagues who have read this chapter react in much the same racially prescribed way as the university administration did to my claim to Cubanahood. They cannot believe that I can think of myself as being Cuban; and yet that is, for me, a primary ethnic identification. After all, I did grow up speaking Spanish and watching my parents being discriminated against as Latinos. The American Jewish rejection of any claims to European ethnic identity, with its roots in the Holocaust and anti-Semitism, makes it difficult, I think, for North American Jews to understand the different sensibility of Latin American Jews, for whom nationality is not conflicted in the same way by anger and legacies of exclusion and hatred.

11. Cherríe Moraga, "It's the Poverty," in *Loving in the War Years*, p. 62.

12. Clifford Geertz, *Works and Lives: The Anthropologist as Author* (Stanford: Stanford University Press, 1988), pp. 129–49; James Clifford, "On Ethnographic Authority," in *The Predicament of Culture: Twentieth-Century Ethnography, Literature, and Art* (Cambridge: Harvard University Press, 1988). For a nuanced, self-reflexive approach to the burden of authorship, emphasizing the role of the ethnographer as a positioned subject, see Rosaldo, *Culture and Truth.*

13. For Chicano/a intellectuals working within the institutional framework of Chicano studies, "the evocation of the community as a central subject of Chicano studies operates as a litany which guides our daily academic practices and absolves us of the guilt stemming out of our distance from our nonacademic constituency—a distance which is a consequence of our own diaspora as intellectuals from the working-class populations in the factories, fields, and barrios." See Rosa Linda Fregoso and Angie Chabram, "Introduction: Chicana/o

Cultural Representations: Reframing Alternative Critical Discourses," *Cultural Studies* 4 (1990): 203. The border that Chicana/o intellectuals have to cross to enter the academy is not only a racial, ethnic, and cultural border, but also a class border. Taking on "the full trappings of the life of the college professor" after growing up working class forces each scholar who has made the crossing to the other side to internalize, and seek somehow to resolve, the conflicts within the hierarchy of the American class system. See Jake Ryan and Charles Sackrey, *Strangers in Paradise: Academics from the Working Class* (Boston: South End Press, 1984), p. 5. In most academic settings it is still considered "bad taste" to talk about these diasporas and the uneasiness that such border-crossers experience, even when they succeed. But I think we need to start asking, as does Paul Rabinow, the fundamental question: "Who established and who enforces these civilities?" See Paul Rabinow, "Representations Are Social Facts: Modernity and Post-Modernity in Anthropology," in Clifford and Marcus, *Writing Culture*, pp. 253–54. It is the civilities that are especially difficult to challenge for those who enter academic settings as refugees, migrants, illegals, and exiles.

14. José Piedra, "The Game of Critical Arrival," *Diacritics* 18 (1989): 34–61.

15. For inspiration in coming to terms with my mestiza consciousness, I am indebted to Gloria Anzaldúa, both for her work, *Borderlands*, and for supportive conversations with her. Coco Fusco, a Cuban-American art critic, remarks that during the last five years she has been asked to speak as a Cuban, a Latina, a black person, and a person of color. "What category," she asks, "do Americans have for someone composed of Taino, Yoruba, Catalan, Sephardic, and Neapolitan blood?" See Coco Fusco, "Managing the Other," *Lusitania* 1 (1990): 80. I am grateful to Kristin Koptiuch for kindly bringing this essay to my attention.

16. The phrase is from Gloria Anzaldúa, "En rapport, In Opposition: Cobrando cuentas a las nuestras," in *Making Face, Making Soul*, p. 143. As Anzaldúa writes, "They have us doing to those within our ranks what they have done and continue to do to us—*Othering* people. That is, isolating them, pushing them out of the herd, ostracizing them. We shun the white-looking Indian, the 'high yellow' Black woman, the Asian with the white lover, the Native woman who brings her white girl friend to the Pow Wow, the Chicana who doesn't speak Spanish, the academic, the uneducated. Her difference makes her a person we can't trust. *Para que sea 'legal,'* she must pass the ethnic legitimacy test we have devised." Similarly, Audre Lorde has written, "We are Black women, defined as never-good-enough . . . If I am myself, then you cannot accept me. But if you can accept me, that means I am what you like to be, and then I'm not the real thing. But then neither are you. WILL THE REAL BLACK WOMAN PLEASE STAND UP?" See Audre Lorde, "Eye to Eye: Black Women, Hatred, and Anger," in *Sister Outsider* (Trumansburg, N.Y.: Crossing Press, 1984), p. 170. Or, as the artist Guillermo Gómez-Peña says, "I am Mexican but I am

also Chicano and Latin American. At the border they call me *chilango* or *mexi-quillo*; in Mexico City it's *pocho* or *norteño*; and in Europe it's *sudaca*." See Guillermo Gómez-Peña, "Documented/Undocumented," in Rick Simonson and Scott Walker, eds., *The Graywolf Annual Five: Multicultural Literacy* (Saint Paul: Gray Wolf Press, 1988), p. 128.

17. The term "halfie" comes from Kirin Narayan, who has explored the ironies of partial insiderhood in a lucid unpublished manuscript, "Beyond Dichotomies: How Native Is a 'Native' Anthropologist?" that she kindly shared with me. Ideas about "halfie ethnographers" have been perceptively developed by Lila Abu-Lughod in her essay, "Writing against Culture," in Richard Fox, ed., *Recapturing Anthropology*, School of American Research Seminar Series (Seattle: University of Washington Press, 1991). Halfie women anthropologists who have reflected on their identity within their texts include Kirin Narayan, *Storytellers, Saints, and Scoundrels: Folk Narrative in Hindu Religious Teaching* (Philadelphia: University of Pennsylvania Press, 1989); Smadar Lavie, *The Poetics of Military Occupation*; Dorinne Kondo, "Dissolution and Reconstitution of Self" and *Crafting Selves: Power, Gender, and Discourses of Identity in a Japanese Workplace* (Chicago: University of Chicago Press, 1990); Kamala Visweswaran, "Betrayal." The quotation in the text is from Abu-Lughod, "Writing against Culture," p. 140.

18. My image of the shadow identity comes from the work of Patricia Williams, a black law professor. She recalls how a man with whom she used to work accused her once of making "too much" of her race; he bluntly told her that he didn't even think of her as black. "Yet sometime later," she adds, "when another black woman became engaged in an ultimately unsuccessful tenure battle, he confided to me that he wished the school could find more blacks like me. I felt myself slip in and out of shadow, as I became nonblack for purposes of inclusion and black for purposes of exclusion." See Patricia Williams, *The Alchemy of Race and Rights* (Cambridge: Harvard University Press, 1991), pp. 9–10.

19. Mary John borrows the term "sanctioned ignorances" from Gayatri Spivak, who originally used it to refer to the limits of Foucault's perspective as a self-contained Western intellectual, expanding it to include the disavowals not just of Western but of postcolonial, particularly feminist, intellectuals. See Mary John, "Postcolonial Feminists in the Western Intellectual Field: Anthropologists *and* Native Informants?" *Inscriptions* 5 (1989): 49–73, special issue: *Traveling Theories, Traveling Theorists*.

20. Alicia Gaspar de Alba, "Literary Wetback," *Massachusetts Review* 29 (1988): 242–46. In plotting myself into this account of my intellectual autobiography as a "literary wetback," I'm not trying to heroicize or exaggerate my marginality, but rather to speak to the difficulties that outsiders encounter in attempting to work through their cultural adaptation to the exotic world of academia. Certainly, the idea of including an intellectual autobiography within

a biographical account is not original with me. As the first epigraph to the chapter shows, the idea was suggested some time back by Gelya Frank. Recently, Paul Friedrich has included a detailed intellectual autobiography in his *The Princes of Naranja: An Essay in Anthrohistorical Method* (Austin: University of Texas Press, 1986), an account of the intricacies of local Mexican politics that is based in seven political life studies of men. In reading Friedrich's sensitive account of his early involvement in the world of ideas through his relationship with his own professor father, I realized how different my own entrance into that world had been; and I realized that it would be impossible for me to write my "intellectual autobiography" with the degree of confidence, and sense of belonging, that he could assume for himself.

21. The first quote is from Juan Flores and George Yudice, "Living Borders/ Buscando America: Languages of Latino Self-Formation," *Social Text* 24 (1990): 57–84; the second quote, from Caren Kaplan, "Deterritorializations: The Rewriting of Home and Exile in Western Feminist Discourse," *Cultural Critique* 6 (1987): 198; and the third quote, from José David Saldívar, "The Dialectics of Our America," in Pérez Firmat, *Do the Americas Have a Common Literature?* p. 67.

22. This year, 1991–1992, I am serving as codirector of Latina/Latino Studies (irony of ironies), and remembering the tradition started by Sandra Cisneros, David and I put up an altar in the program office in memory of another comadre, Pancha Hernández, who was killed early one morning in 1990 while running across the highway to catch the bus from Mexquitic to San Luis Potosí.

Chronology

1930   Esperanza is born in La Campana, a rancho in the municipality of Mexquitic.

1938   Her parents separate. Esperanza and her siblings follow their mother to Mexquitic.

1939   Esperanza goes back to La Campana, living with her grandmother for six months, and then returns to Mexquitic.

1940   Esperanza is taken by her mother to San Luis Potosí, at age ten, to work in domestic service. Over the course of the next nine years, she works at about five different jobs, including working as a cook for the family that will eventually help her to obtain her husband's field in the ejido.

1949   Marriage.

1950   Birth of first child, a girl, who lives nine months.

1951   Birth of second child, a boy, who dies after a year.

1952   Birth of third child, a girl, who lives for almost two years.

1953   Birth of Macario, who survives.

1954   Julio beats Esperanza with a machete when Macario is nine months old. She runs away from her husband to live and work in San Luis Potosí. She returns when Macario is about two years old, gets caught, and is convinced by Julio to return to the domestic fold with him.

1956   Birth of Simeón, who survives.
           Birth of comadre, Ruth, in Havana, Cuba.

1958   Birth of sixth child, a girl, who dies. Julio has escaped from jail and is living in hiding in his mother's house. He is hidden while the wake for his daughter takes place.

1962   *Arrival of Ruth and her family in the United States.*

1963   Esperanza and Julio move to San Luis Potosí.

1964   In January, Esperanza returns to Mexquitic to send her sons to school and to maintain Julio's rights to his field in the ejido. In

May, she finds Julio in San Luis with the new woman. Shortly afterward they leave for Tampico and on June 24, Esperanza's last son by Julio, named Juan, is born.

1965   In May, Julio returns from Tampico with the woman, but goes to live with his sister in the rancho of Paso Blanco. In June, just days before his first birthday, Juan dies. Esperanza leaves her husband's house and goes to live with her mother. She fights for the field in the ejido and is successful. Her mother is bewitched immediately after Esperanza obtains the land.

1968   Birth of Gabriela, eldest daughter of Esperanza.

1970   Birth of Norberta, second daughter of Esperanza. Noberta begins to suffer from epileptic seizures as a child and shows learning disabilities, which Esperanza attributes to a fall from her crib that her mother was unable to stop in time.

1971   Esperanza's mother is finally unwitched and fully cured by Chencha, then a young girl of fourteen, who several years later becomes the leader of a spiritist cult surrounding the figure of Pancho Villa.

1973   Birth of Mario, youngest son of Esperanza.

1980   Conflicts with Macario about his incestuous attempts to molest Gabriela, his half-sister.

1981   Simeón brings his wife by civil law, Carmela, to live in Esperanza's house. Macario leaves Esperanza's house.

1982   Birth of the first son of Simeón and Carmela.

1985   **The comadres begin to work together on this book.**

1987   Esperanza's field in the ejido is ensorcelled, and it turns out that Macario, the son she has rejected, is responsible. Her field is cleansed of evil by Chencha.

1988   Simeón and Carmela leave Esperanza's house. Birth of their second son.

1989   Esperanza herself is briefly thrown out of the house by her mother, but with the help of Chencha/Villa good relations are quickly restored.

          Ruth becomes a tenured professor.

1990   Simeón and Carmela marry in a collective church wedding, but do not invite Esperanza to the wedding party.

1991   **This book takes shape.**